IRELAND

A Traveller's
Handbook

IRELAND

A Traveller's Handbook

PASSPORT BOOKS

NTC/Contemporary Publishing Group

This edition first published in 2001
by Passport Books, a division of
NTC/Contemporary Publishing Group, Inc.
4255 West Touhy Avenue
Lincolnwood (Chicago), Illinois 60712-1975
U.S.A.

Copyright © Appletree Press Ltd 2001

This book is compiled from the following publications:

The Irish Landscape First published in 1989 by Appletree Press Ltd
Text by James Brindley

Irish Museums and Heritage Centres First published in 1996
by Appletree Press Ltd Text by Hugh Oram

The Animals of Ireland First published in 1988 by Appletree Press Ltd
Text by Gordon D'Arcy

Birds of Ireland First published in 1986 by Appletree Press Ltd
Text by Gordon D'Arcy

Irish Trees and Shrubs First published in 1994 by Appletree Press Ltd
Text by Peter Wyse Jackson Illustrations by Janice Dean

Irish Wild Flowers First published in 1987 by Appletree Press Ltd
Text by Ruth Isabel Ross Illustrations by Greg Moore

ISBN 0-658-01225-8

Library of Congress Catalog Card Number: 00-136228

Published in conjunction with Appletree Press Ltd.
www.appletree.ie

CONTENTS

CHAPTER ONE
LANDSCAPES

The Irish landscape is a complex of many factors, and a knowledge of how they operate will add to the enjoyment of many a familiar scene. Ireland's regional characteristics are very distinctive: Kerry and Antrim, Clare and Dublin, Donegal and Wexford; each has its own pleasant type of scenery. More impressive than anything else, however, are the striking contrasts on a local scale: the little lakes tucked away among Cavan's drumlins, the broad plains and rugged mountains of the west, the crowded islands and sweeping hills around Clew Bay.

An island exposed on the Atlantic seaboard, its coastline is rugged to an unusual degree. The land itself is rich and green, moistened by the prevailing south-westerlies and mellowed by the Gulf Stream which warms its shores. The land is old. Its most ancient rock formations date back a thousand million years.

FOUNDATIONS OF THE LANDSCAPE

Connemara, Mayo, the Ox Mountains, Donegal and Tyrone: these are the oldest parts of Ireland whose rocks initially accumulated as muds, sands and limestones. Subsequently depressed deep into the earth's crust, recrystallised (metamorphic), they are now glittering schists, sparkling quartzites and marbles. In extreme circumstances such rocks form streaky, contorted gneisse, whose surfaces, smoothed by the passage of ice sheets over them in much later times, crop out plentifully beneath the peat which is such a constant aspect of the west Ireland scene.

Quartzites produce the impressive pyramidal peaks and jagged knife-edge ridges so prominent in Errigal and Muckish, in the Twelve Pins and Nephin. Other quartzites of rather younger age in the west form Croagh Patrick and in the east the Sugarloafs of Wicklow. They appear among the Irish slate formations. Slate has a distinctive fissility and slate country is characterised by pleasant rolling uplands. It occurs in a great belt reaching from Down to Cavan, again in east Leinster, and in the cores of the smaller hill ranges of central and southern Ireland: Slieve Bloom, Slievenamon, the Knockmealdowns, the hills of Clare and others.

The igneous rock granite, a coarse-grained rock with the individual minerals readily distinguishable to the eye, is a product of the deep earth's crust. Its intrusive domes and cauldrons formed some miles below surface are now revealed by long denudation of their cover. The big veins of white pegmatite which traverse it sometimes carry enormous crystals: creamy feldspars a foot or more long, big silvery "books" of mica, and less common black tourmalines, green beryls and pink garnets.

The most wide-ranging structures in all these rocks are sets of joints, more or less regularly arranged fractures which control their breakdown into boulders. Granite is a tough rock which forms some of Ireland's finest mountain land in the Wicklows, Blackstairs, Mournes and Bluestacks. In the warmer, moister climate of Tertiary times which preceded the Ice Age, it was very susceptible to chemical rotting and there are other granite areas – Galway, Ardara and the Rosses in Donegal, the Tullow region south of the Wicklows – where it has been reduced to subdued lowland as a result.

The most widespread and most familiar of Irish rock formations are the sedimentary Old Red Sandstone and the Carboniferous Limestone which, at four hundred million years and younger in age, have been spared the metamorphic events of the older rocks. In the south of Ireland these two great series, some miles thickness *in toto*, were involved in powerful earth movements, so that they are now disposed in the series of enormous fold arches and troughs which has produced the east–west morphological grain of Munster. Broad backs to the Old Red Sandstone folds develop our country's southern mountain ranges, warm-tinted though barren highlands, which include some of Ireland's highest and wildest peaks. The younger Carboniferous Limestone which overlays them has been removed by erosion, but it remains in the narrow troughs which lie in between, the rich lowland valleys of Munster.

The layered nature of these rocks (bedding or stratification) is clearly evident on the ground. Deep red tints to the sandstones, which give the formation its common name, mark the "Old Red" as the accumulation of an ancient desert region. In contrast, the succeeding limestone formed on a warm, shallow sea floor, as is revealed by its multitudes of beautifully preserved fossil creatures: long-extinct sea lilies, sea mats, corals, lampshells and others. They crowd the bedding surfaces in the coastal cliffs of Hook Head and Bundoran, presenting a vivid and little-disturbed picture of that ancient sea floor two hundred and fifty million years ago. Passing northwards from Munster the fold structures gradually die out and flat limestone underlies the monotonous Central Lowlands – ill-drained and hidden under a blanket of young glacial deposits and peats. In the west this formation rises in the high region of the Burren where the special features of limestone topography are strikingly developed. Limestone, almost uniquely, is water-soluble to a significant degree. The amount of calcareous crust which deposits inside kettles in limestone districts is clear evidence of how much lime can be taken into solution. As the rainwater soaks down and enlarges joint cracks to leave grotesquely etched limestone pavement above, the loose soil dries out and disappears, producing a rock desert where vegetation is confined to crevices and protected pockets.

Solution activity proceeds and enlarges joints to gaping grykes so that the subsurface formations are gradually honeycombed with great cavernous passages through which the water flows in underground rivers down to as far as percolation can reach. Here and there wholesale removal of the rock has produced extensive open depressions in the landscape, some of which hold permanent water-solution lakes such as Loughs Corrib and Mask, and Lough Leane in Killarney. In other cases these are most of the time dry, grassy flats ("turloughs", from *tuarloch*, "a dried-up lake") which in wet weather suddenly become inundated as broad expanses of water are formed. Where they are not too far removed from the coastline, some of these land-locked lakes have a tidal rise and fall as eloquent testimony to the cavernous nature of the limestone in which they lie.

Limestone country has a wonderful range of curious landscape features. Abandoned underground river channels are represented by caves with their spectacular growths of tufa, a limestone deposited from the hard waters in the form of drooping stalactites from the roofs and matching, upward-reaching stalagmite growths. The Mitchelstown caves in Tipperary and the Dunmore caves in Kilkenny are notable examples. Some of them were hyaena dens in the remote past, into which these wild scavengers brought a variety of their food remains: deer, wolves, brown bears, with baby mammoths a conspicuous delicacy. Their larger parents were too big to be shifted, it seems, for they are absent from the masses of chewed bones buried in the cave floors.

Where parts of the cave roofs have fallen there are collapsed gorges in which the rivers, once concealed, now flow in daylight. Swallow holes into which the surface streams suddenly disappear are numerous, as are resurgences where, conversely, underground rivers well out at the surface. Armed with the relevant Ordnance Survey Sheet one may enjoy a quiet walk in the vicinity of Yeats's famed Thoor Ballylee amid a whole succession of these features. The Devil's Punchbowl is a fine swallow hole in this district; another is the Shannon Pot in County Cavan from which Ireland's largest river first emerges into the open.

In the north of the country sandstone and shale horizons are also present in the Carboniferous formations which rise high in the topography to produce the spectacular table mountains of Sligo and Leitrim: Ben Bulbin and the Bricklieve Mountains in the limestone, Cuilcagh and others in the sandstone. Here, and in the less striking Castlecomer and Slieveardagh plateaux in the south, coal seams and ironstone bands are present also (hence Slieve Anierin, "the iron mountain") though not in quantities sufficient to support a heavy industry today. Paradoxically though, because of their unusual geological situation, Ireland's coal mines, such as they are, operate not from the earth's deep recesses but from high up in the hills. Where similar structural conditions occur at the coastline they give rise to striking cliff scenery. South Clare has, in the Cliffs of Moher, the greatest range of sheer rock faces in western Europe; Fair Head in County Antrim is similarly impressive.

North-east Ireland (County Antrim and the Lagan and Bann Valleys) is a quite distinctive part of the country. Protected under a great pile of basalt lava flows, and largely hidden by them, is a series of younger sedimentary formations: Chalk, Lias Clays, and the desert-formed New Red Sandstone, which are familiar elements in south England's landscape but are restricted to the north-east of this country. Antrim's chalk cliffs are a replica of those which guard St George's Channel. The flint nodules within the white limestone, present solely in this part of Ireland, were the raw materials for the flint knappers in the early years of the human era, and the products of their factories along the coast at Larne, Whitepark Bay and elsewhere travelled widely over Ireland.

Everywhere in this region the dominant surface rock is dark, oily-coloured basalt lava: in buildings, in quarries, in coastal cliffs. Its succession of flows, individually a score or so of feet thick, build up to a pile totalling thousands of feet, and about sixty million years ago this represented a style of volcanism akin to that which is active in Hawaii today. Gases frothed from the hot lava surfaces to give vesicles which soon filled with lovely crystals of zeolites as well as chalcedony and opal. When the cooling was regular, individual flows often shrank into a honeycomb pattern of cracks perpendicular to their surfaces. These peculiar surfaces have made the Giant's Causeway an object of world fame.

Basalt lavas form the surfaces of the high plateau but at its south-west extremity crustal rifting has dropped them down in a deep fault trough, its floor more than a thousand feet below sea level, to form the site of Ireland's biggest lake, Lough Neagh. It has filled up with sediment long since, so that the 153-square-mile expanse is now shallow water and shows little evidence of its structural origin. On the other side of the plateau conditions along the coastal cliffs make for large-scale instability at many places and it is a typical landslide area. The soft clays of the Lias formation often occur at the base of the cliffs and surface water percolating down into these causes them to slide and flow under the big load of chalk and basalt on top. As a result, dislocated blocks of the plateau, some of them many acres in area, have in the past slipped down seawards. The Larne promontory is a major example and at Garron Tower others are very prominent, while on a lesser scale the cascading slips of clay even today pose a threat to the Antrim coast road in wet weather so that it requires constant surveillance.

SURFACE AND MORPHOLOGY

The topography of the land has been shaped by quite different factors than those which formed its rocks – the processes of weathering and erosion. Rivers are responsible for the latter as they deepen their channels – just as the run-off from a rain shower carves little gullies in any exposed soil surface, in the long term the landscape is removed piecemeal until the ultimate result is a featureless, low-lying peneplain.

This sequence of events is slow indeed to run to completion and a new uplift of the land may intervene to re-elevate the topography so that the whole erosion cycle is started anew. There may in fact be repeated uplifts. Calary plateau is a familiar example of an uplifted erosion surface and, above it, the rolling uplands which top much of the Wicklows (the Featherbed, for example) are the fragmentary remains of older, higher levels. Great flat expanses at 100–200 feet covered with blanket bog dominate much of western Ireland, and in Ulster the rolling uplands of south Armagh at an even level around 400 feet are equally emphatic surfaces. As regards the rate at which they work we must think in terms of millions of years instead of the hundreds of millions represented by the more ancient rock formations.

For the latest elements in Ireland's landscape the time perspective shortens still further, to the last 100,000 years or so. The lowlands are dominated by the effects of great ice sheets, thousands of feet thick perhaps, while in the mountains there were more restricted valley glaciers fed from higher-level ice caps. The former left an undulating cover of their ground moraine, namely boulder clay, thick over central Ireland and fertile from its content of limestone pebbles, if not generally free-draining. Sometimes patches of this ill-sorted material stagnated beneath the moving ice and were moulded into oval mounds by the sheet passing over them. These are the drumlins which form a great belt across the north Midlands from Donegal to Downpatrick. There are no easy passages for outgoing drainage through this jumbled mass of small hills, the so-called "basket of eggs" topography, and many swampy lakes fill the depressions between them, producing the typical landscape of counties Cavan and Monaghan, and the Irish Lakelands.

In the declining stages of the glacial epoch great quantities of meltwater flooded the low ground. Wherever this was held up gravels, sands and muds, washed out of the boulder clay, settled in temporary lakes the abandoned sites of which are seen today as flat-bottomed old lake basins. Such is "Glacial Lake Blessington", the area which now holds the modern reservoir, and the gravel-filled basin of the old "Glacial Lake Enniskerry" on the opposite side of the northern end of the Wicklow mountains. These floods, too, spread a gravel and sand wash out from the receding ice front which, at the local points of discharge, often developed into long, ribbon-like ridges running for miles across country: the eskers strikingly seen around Tullamore and in many other parts of central Ireland.

Glacial activity was generally in the nature of erosion of the surfaces over which the ice sheets passed. Even the very toughest materials such as the granite crags at Killiney Hill on the outskirts of Dublin, or the red sandstones of West Cork and Kerry, have been smoothed off, scratched and deeply scored by the great mass of overriding ice as their outcrop forms today so well reflect. Geographers apply the quaint French term roche moutonné, literally "sheep rocks", to such round-backed outlines.

Mountain valleys such as Glendalough and others in the east Wicklows, Anascaul, Caragh and many in Kerry, as well as those of the hill regions of Mayo, Donegal and the Mournes, have a characteristic U-shaped profile where they were greatly enlarged by the passage of massive ice streams along their channels. Side tributaries now spill into them over the high lip which exists at each side, in picturesque waterfalls, and here and there basins in their broad floors hold pretty lakes: Caragh Lake, Glendalough, Lough Dan and many others.

Mountain areas had their individual ice caps from which valley glaciers were fed and where, after the lowland ice had gone, local snow patches remained long enough to rot their way down into sunken pockets whose forms remain as bowl-shaped amphitheatres or coombes, sometimes very large and deep, remote, and often filled with lonely corrie lakes. Greatest of the latter is the spectacular Coomshingaun in the Waterford Comeraghs. Mangerton Lake in Kerry and the twin Loughs Bray in Wicklow are also well known.

The last 1,000 years (post-glacial times) saw the formation of the youngest features in the landscape. In the upper reaches of Ireland's rivers torrents flow in deep, narrow valleys via a succession of cataracts. Their lower courses are older, smoother, and with gentler gradients. Here the valley floor has opened out over a flat spread of gravel and sand – a flood plain across which the channel courses to and fro in a series of meanders. A recent uplift would, of course, increase the stream gradient and hence eroding power, and a similar effect might result from a change in volume of the flow. In such cases channels in the flood plain are deepened to leave conspicuous terraces high on each side. This may lead to rivers incising their courses so as to form series of rock-cut gorges as, for instance, in the picturesque middle reaches of the Barrow and the Nore, the Boyne Valley lower down its course, the Dargle Glen and many others.

In Ice Age times the amount of water taken up in the continental ice sheets was such that sea levels the world over were lower by hundreds of feet than they are today. Europe's Atlantic coastline then reached unbroken from Portugal to points off the west coast of Ireland which, with England, was part of the continental mainland. When the ice melted, continental shelf islands became isolated as levels rose, and gradually the waters spread up the large river mouths in extensive tidal estuaries. This produced a characteristic aspect in the swollen lower reaches of south-east Ireland's major rivers such as the Suir, Nore, Barrow and Slaney.

The island's boundary is a drowned coastline of this sort and in regions of varied topography the effects on its scenery are both diverse and spectacular. The hilly coasts around Cork city enclose a whole complex of deep and far-reaching inlets. More striking is the region further west of this where the mountain lands of southern Ireland head straight out to sea at the extremities of Cork and Kerry. Here the highland ridges are a succession of rugged salients which tail off in rocky islets after ranging thirty miles and more into the Atlantic: Bantry, Kenmare, Dingle and the others. Between them are broad, deep-going inlets ending in fertile sheltered farmland where the low limestone basins channel the main rivers seawards.

In the crystalline terrain of the north and west of the country jagged quartzite ranges meet the Atlantic in some of the wildest cliff scenery to be found anywhere: Croaghaun (Achill) and Slieve League (Donegal) both have faces dropping 2,000 feet straight into the ocean. In a less emphatic manner this scenic pattern is repeated elsewhere on Ireland's coastline. The low, rocky headlands of north Dublin, for example, alternate with broader, sand-barred inlets at Baldoyle, Malahide and Portraine. Deep inlets of a different sort, more akin to the spectacular Norwegian fjords, are the few examples further north where highlands with former glaciated valleys reach the sea, namely the fjord-like glaciated valleys of Carlingford on the east and Killary on the west.

The ten millennia, or about four hundred generations, which have elapsed since ice sheets finally left Ireland must seem an enormous span in terms of human life, but it is a trifle compared with the aeons of time involved in our country's evolution. Nonetheless, the interplay of climatic change, vegetation and landscape development, and human activities which took place during this short period make it the most significant and most interesting part of Ireland's story. When rising sea levels finally broke the continental links around 8,000 years ago Ireland and England achieved their modern outlines. Their flora and fauna, however, evolved somewhat differently. Ireland has some surprising plants and animals: southern or Mediterranean forms, which are relics of the time when the Irish coastline was one with that of the Iberian peninsula. The strawberry tree (Arbutus) so distinctive in the Killarney woods, is otherwise found no nearer than Spain and this is the case too with the Spotted slug (Geomalacus). Our location as an island more remote than Britain from mainland Europe has made its recolonisation even less complete than that of our sister island which, in turn, is notably poorer than that of Europe. Several familiar creatures such as moles and dormice failed to reach this land, as did all of the snakes for, whatever tradition may say about the role of our patron saint, they were in fact too slow-moving to complete the voyage ahead of the rising sea.

Most widespread of these recent events has been the growth of peats. Peat studies, and those of the foetid muds at lake bottoms, are crucial in elucidating the evolution of post-glacial vegetation and, with it, climatic change. These deposits preserve the pollen which is discharged in great amounts by flowering plants and, since different pollens are readily identified, the peat succession in a bog holds evidence of the vegetation and climatic changes as it accumulated. They show that conditions have varied much since the ice left Ireland. At first it was an unattractive place: a cold barren tundra with mosses and Arctic shrubs such as we see today in the Scandinavian highlands. It could, however, support the giant Irish deer (*Megaloceras*) in considerable numbers, for at the base of many bogs are muds with the remains of Arctic plants and it is these that often contain the "Irish Elk" skeletons. A few species with Arctic affinities such as the Irish hare are with us still. But climate improved steadily and after a thousand years was capable of supporting the first modern forests of pine and spruce, a taiga such as we see in Finland today. The remains of these oldest forests are to be seen here and there in our bogs as a multitude of pine stumps (bog deal) still rooted *in situ* in the sands at the base of the peat.

The climate was rather better in those days than it is now and these remains often appear where no trees grow today, such as high up on the Featherbed Mountain in Wicklow or out on the bleak windswept lands of Mayo. In fact, Ireland's modern conifers are recent reintroductions since the native Irish pine had disappeared already in prehistoric times. As the climate steadily improved the conifers were replaced by deciduous hardwoods: mixed oak, ash, elm forests; they would be the natural vegetation of the Irish lowlands today. About 6,000 years ago the climate reached its optimum, considerably warmer and moister than it is now, and it has oscillated quite a bit since then. The bulk of peat growth took place during the moister phases of the past, between 4,000–6,000 years ago, and again around the turn of the Christian era. Ireland's climate is now somewhat drier and colder; little peat grows and, in fact, on exposed hillsides it is often seen to be eroding.

Ireland's bogs are either raised "red" bog or blanket bog. Raised bog occurs extensively in the waterlogged terrain of the Central Lowlands with its impeded drainage. There the bog mosses act as a gigantic sponge and so build up in the centre to a level well above that of the surrounding countryside. Blanket bog develops as a continuous layer of peat wherever rainfall exceeds about 50 inches annually and so it ranges down to sea level on the west coast, rising higher on the mountains in the east of the country. The great barren wastes of north Mayo typify blanket bog, while a view from Croghan Hill, almost dead centre geographically in Ireland, yields an impressive vista of raised bog, in this case the great Bog of Allen.

THE GREEN MANTLE

For a visitor the most memorable aspect of the Irish landscape is likely to be the luxuriance and variety of its plant life. Tree growth is almost entirely inhibited over a broad belt along the Atlantic seaboard: blasted hawthorn trees seem to lean uniformly inland, the salt winds trimming their western sides. Some sheltered sites, such as Connemara's lake islets, hidden in depressions, and the wizened stands of oakwood behind Croagh Patrick and Old Head, hold the few remnants of native wood in this great expanse of bare ground. In the better climatic conditions of the past these parts were densely covered by coniferous forest, and cutaway bogs often expose great numbers of *in situ* stumps, which grew anything up to 7,000 years ago, rooted in the soil beneath.

The oakwoods of Killarney around Lough Leane, those in Donegal by Lough Easke, and the woods west of Lough Conn in Mayo are examples of the deciduous forest which represents the natural vegetation of Ireland's lowlands. The sheltered valleys of east Wicklow – Clare, Glendalough and Glen of the Downs – are others. Such woods have the characteristic ground flora which marks centuries-old, primary forests. Plants such as Bluebell, Wood Sorrel and Wood Anemone are suited to this habitat because they flower before the leaf canopy has developed and so produce a wealth of colour in springtime. Around them, too, are still scattered some of the economically unattractive tree species, such as holly and crab apple which remain as outliers of woodland in former times. Many place names, such as Derry and Ros (as in Rosnaree) reflect the once-extensive spread of this great forest, and one notes that these relate to the better drained parts of the lowlands (marsh and bog inhibited its growth), and to sheltered valleys, for the exposed uplands seem to have been devoid of trees.

But the famous woods of Medieval times – the Dufrey in Wexford and the Royal Forest of Glencree near Dublin – have long gone, and everything that remains has been modified a great deal by human interference. Artificial grassland now dominates this natural setting and such common trees as ash, hawthorn, blackthorn and cherry are seldom found except where planted in hedgerows, where they mingle with such imports as horse chestnut, beech and poplar. In secondary woodland the more vigorous nettles, brambles and bracken tend to oust more colourful primary herbs. Some distinctive facets of the forest assemblage remain very localised, such as the hazel thickets on drained limy areas of the lowlands, for example, the esker ridges near Tullamore and Tyrellspass in the midlands, and the groves of birch and rowan in upland hollows, but there must be others which we can no longer adequately recreate.

Wherever Carboniferous Limestone rises sufficiently high in the topography to be free-draining and clear of glacial deposits, it forms a spectacular, naked-rock landscape with a quite unusual flora. The limestone plateau of the Burren in north Clare, roughly 120 square miles in area, is the most important cool-temperate limestone region in Europe, and there are smaller, less emphatic occurrences in the table mountains of Sligo, Leitrim and Roscommon as well as around Lough Gur in Limerick. The density of prehistoric settlement in such areas is often impressive and certainly the elaborate ancient field systems attached to many of the Clare cashels would be quite out of place in today's barren environment. In fact, it seems that in Iron Age times and earlier, the Burren was sufficiently clothed in soil to support vigorous agriculture.

Today virtually without cover, it carries a rich and varied assemblage of plants, tucked away in clefts in its rocky platforms. and in small grassy patches, whose blossoms produce a wonderful display throughout the warmer parts of the year. Distinctive lime-loving plants such as the Blue Spring Gentian, Bloody Cranesbill and Mossy Saxifrage are associated in places with a range of orchids. Mountain Avens, of Arctic-Alpine provenance, mingle with southern European forms such as the delicate Maidenhair Fern, and the natural hazel thickets here are the Irish stronghold of the rare Pine marten.

The low marshy country which flanks many of our major rivers inland is subject to seasonal flooding and is characterised by lush water meadows (or callows). The Shannon has much outstanding callows environment in its middle reaches below Athlone. It is a rich grassland with a wealth of colourful flowers: the Common Buttercup, Dandelion, Ox-eye, Sorrel, and the more distinctive Meadowsweet and Marsh Cinquefoil. Bird migrants, the once-common Corncrake, for example, manage to hold their own.

Dune belts and salt-marsh are special coastal environments in which grasses or related plants play a major role in stabilising the new sedimentary accumulations. They are, in fact, part of the syndrome connected with drowned coastlines. The dune belts of Dundrum Bay in County Down and Bull Island in Dublin Bay will be familiar to many. At the seaward side of the dunes creeping grasses, whose stolons or rhizomes can spread along the loose sand and form a stable environment for plants, are typical. Nearest to the tide mark salt-tolerant Sea Couchgrass is usually the first prominent coloniser. Higher up, and out of reach of the sea water, Marram Grass takes over and the dunes may reach 150 feet in height. Behind this outer belt the sheltered leeway has varied grassland with mosses and a variety of flowering plants, maybe with clumps of alder, the home of Larks and other small birds.

In brackish estuaries and muddy lagoons on the landward side of sandbars salt-marsh develops to reclaim the evolving mud-flats which are the haunt of great flocks of wading birds: Dunlins, Oystercatchers, Curlews, to mention a few, as well as migratory ducks and geese. Again, the North Bull is an outstanding example, a nature reserve of international renown which exists literally within the limits of the capital city, and salt-marsh is also present in the other tidal inlets along the north Dublin coast. It is populated by halophytic, or salt-tolerant, plants and is covered for the major part at high tide. The succulent Glasswort is the first coloniser on the mud flats to give a meadow type of vegetation but Cordgrass, introduced to the Dublin marshes for reclamation purposes, now grows in conspicuous clumps as does Sea Lavender and Sea Plantain. Beyond high water limits rushes, sedges and grasses such as Red Fescue have taken over from the halophytes. Here too, but more typically on coastal cliffs, colonies of Sea Pinks locally give a profusion of colour in summer.

Machair (machaire in Irish means "low flat country") is a Scots Gaelic word from the Western Isles which refers to a special type of plant environment occurring on exposed Atlantic coasts both there and along the west coast of Ireland. It arises on the old beach deposits which may extend considerable distances inland and carry a great deal of calcareous material: comminuted shells, pin-head skeletons of foraminifera, and coralline algae, the latter giving the misnomer "coral strand" to some Connemara beaches. This is a grassland community of Red Fescue, Meadow Grass, Vernal Grass, Cocksfoot, Yorkshire Fog, False Oat with clovers and a colourful range of wild flowers: Yellow Flags in damp places, Silverweed, Harebell, Speedwell and many others. The machair is common land and so has not been modified by improvement procedures, and hay-making is late enough to allow its bird population of Corncrakes and Larks, with waders such as Lapwing, Plover and Oystercatcher, to raise their broods successfully. Any change in conditions, however, is likely to eradicate this precarious environment.

Bogs, by far the most widespread type of natural vegetation remaining in Ireland, were formed around 9,000 years ago, until recently occupying about one-sixth of the country. Shallow lake basins in the lowlands served as centres in which fen peat, made up of reeds, sedges and various water plants, started to form. As the lakes contracted and peat thickened, vegetation growing on the latter was blanketed off from the subsoil beneath and so became deprived of mineral constituents. Sphagnum Moss, which can thrive virtually without inorganic materials, took over as a consequence and has produced the increasingly acid conditions which typify our modern bogs. The moss tussocks develop a hummocky surface interspersed with bog pools and support a very distinctive range of vegetation.

Carniverous plants such as Sundew and Butterwort, get their nitrogen supplies from captured insects, while the shrubby tree growth, represented by clumps of Bog Myrtle, does so by producing root nodules in the manner of legumes. Dried-out surfaces are spread with heathers, the wide-spreading and more restricted Bell Heather giving the delicate cover of purple and pink to the bog lands in August.

On mountains such as the Wicklows one can see a range of plant associations which typify various parts of these boglands. A moss tundra with great spread mounds of Rhacomitrium is found on exposed summits where erosion is active. Wet bogland, in contrast to the drier heather moors, supports a vegetation of low, spiky Deer Grass, golden brown in autumn, associated with waving spreads of white-tasselled Bog Cotton. Marshy seepages on hill slopes are mostly dominated by rushes, while drier scree is often colonised by fraocháns (bilberries). At a lower level rocky ground and thin soils are a blaze of golden furze: the Common Gorse up to about 1,000 feet before June, and the smaller Western Gorse higher up in the hill pastures after July. Bracken Fern is a rapid coloniser of neglected hill grassland today.

In the lowlands, the Pollardstown Fell in County Kildare, a feeder of the Grand Canal, is an example of fen-type bogland, the southern borders of Lough Neagh another. The wild areas are now almost everywhere under pressure from encroaching modern development: peat working, reclamation and land drainage, coastal exploitation for holiday use. It is a matter of great concern to preserve even small pieces of these natural environments for the enlightenment of future generations.

CHAPTER TWO

ATTRACTIONS

ANTRIM

CASTLES

Carrickfergus Castle

The mighty stronghold of Carrickfergus, once the centre of Anglo-Norman power in Ulster, is a remarkably complete and well-preserved early medieval castle that has survived intact despite 750 years of continuous military occupation. From its strategic position on a rocky promontory, originally almost surrounded by sea, the castle commanded Belfast Lough and the land approaches into the walled town that developed beneath its shadow.

The core of the castle was built in the late 1180s by John de Courcy, who conquered east Ulster in 1177 and ruled as a petty king until 1204, when he was ousted by another Norman adventurer, Hugh de Lacy. Initially de Courcy built the inner ward, a small bailey at the end of the promontory with a high polygonal wall and east gate. It had a number of buildings, including a great hall, and must have been very cramped, especially after the keep was built in the north corner.

Probably built in the late 1180s, the keep is a massive four-storey tower, 90 feet high, with a second-storey entrance. Its entry chamber, originally one large, poorly lit room with a double latrine and no fireplace, served as a public room. A shaft gave access to a well below and a mural stair led down to the vaulted storage cellar. De Corcey's curia probably used the third storey; the fourth storey, a high, brightly lit room with windows in all four walls, a fireplace and a single latrine, was the principal chamber and must have served as de Courcy's private quarters.

Following its capture by King John in 1210, the castle passed to the Crown, and constables were appointed to command the place. In 1217 De Serlande was assigned £100 to build a new curtain wall so that the approach along the rock could be protected, as well as the eastern approaches over the sand exposed at low tide.

It was almost certainly Hugh de Lacy who enclosed the remainder of the promontory to form an outer ward, doubling the area of the castle. The ribbed vault over the entrance passage, the murder hole and the massive portcullis at either end of the gatehouse are later insertions, probably part of the remodelling that followed Edward Bruce's long and bitter siege of 1315–16.

After the collapse of the Earldom of Ulster in 1333, the castle remained the Crown's principal residential and administrative centre in the North. During the 16th and 17th centuries a number of improvements were made to accommodate artillery, though these improvements did not prevent the castle from being attacked and captured on many occasions during this time. When General Schomberg besieged and took the castle in 1690, its importance was already in decline. In 1760 it was captured and held by French invaders under the command of Thurot. Later it served as a prison and during the Napoleonic Wars was heavily defended; six guns on the east battery remain of the twenty-two that were used in 1811. For a century it remained a magazine and armoury before being transferred to the Government in 1928 for preservation as an ancient monument.

Carrickfergus. NGR: J 415873.

Dunluce Castle

Like something out of a Tolkien fantasy, the ruins of Dunluce Castle have a desolate, awe-inspiring grandeur as they rise dramatically from a precipitous basaltic rock standing over a hundred feet sheer above the wild and chill northern sea. Separated from the mainland by a deep chasm crossed only by a narrow bridge and penetrated below by a long cave, this precarious rocky outcrop occupied a position of great strategic importance that was fought over for centuries, eventually becoming, in the 16th century, the principal stronghold of the MacDonnells, "Lords of the Isles" and rulers of far-flung territories along the western Scottish seaboard.

Dunluce was probably used as a fort during Early Christian times and a souterrain from this period survives beneath the present ruins. Although the site is mentioned as part of the de Burgo manor of Dunseverick in the early 14th century, the earliest features of the castle are two large drum towers on the eastern side, both relics of a stronghold built here by the McQuillans after they became lords of the district (known as "the Route") in the late 14th century.

Most of the castle ruins standing today were built by Sorley Boy MacDonnell (1505–89) and his descendants, the first and second Earls of Antrim. The castle had been seized by Sorley Boy in 1558 – although twice evicted, first in 1565 by Shane O'Neill and again in 1584 by the Lord Deputy, Sir John Perrott, Sorley Boy managed, with the aid of artillery, to resume occupation after a short period.

New work carried out at this time included the turretted gatehouse and cannon ports evidently made to accommodate cannons taken from the nearby wreck of the Spanish Armada ship the *Girona* in 1588. The north-facing Italianate *loggia* probably dates to the 1560s; it is a most unusual feature but can be paralleled at a number of Scottish castles. This loggia was blocked by a thre-storey gabled house with bay windows and a great hall 28 by 10 metres. It was built in 1636 for Lady Catherine, wife of the second earl of Antrim, and from an inventory is known to have been furnished magnificently. Lady Catherine was believed to have replaced the lower yard after some of its domestic ranges, including the kitchens, fell into the sea carrying with them most of the servants in 1639. After the Royalist second Earl was arrested at Dunluce in 1642 the family ceased to reside at Dunluce Castle, which gradually fell into decay, though it remained the property of the Earls of Antrim until 1928 when it was transferred to the State for preservation.

On the Antrim coast 3.2 km (2 miles) W of Bushmills. NGR: G 904414.

GARDENS

Antrim Castle Gardens

Formal late 17th- and early 18th-century layout featuring canal with clipped lime and hornbeam hedges; also "wilderness" wood with oval pond, large mount with spiral yew path and large 17th-century-style parterre created in 1993 and planted with varieties known in the 17th century. Parterre is overlooked by terrace with a quincunx grove of hornbeam.

Antrim town.

Belfast Botanic Gardens

Established in 1829 and made a public park in 1895. Herbaceous borders, rose garden and formal bedding. Famed for curvilinear Palm House designed by Charles Lanyon and built by Turner (wings 1838–9) and Young (dome 1852). Tropical Ravine, built 1886, contains cycads, palms, pitcher plants, tree ferns, as well as camellias and bromeliads.

Stranmillis Road, Belfast.

Benvarden

Clipped box hedging is everywhere in evidence within Benvarden's walled garden, lining paths and delimiting decorative garden features. One area has a fine array of silver foliage plants, another has crescent beds filled with Kingfisher Daisies. Other features include a colourful rose garden and a long mixed double border. There is a large vegetable garden, restored greenhouses and espalier fruit trained up the garden walls. Extensive lawns separate the house from the Walled Garden and these merge into an attractive Pleasure Ground along the banks of the River Bush, where visitors can wander.

Dervock. 3.2 km (2 miles) on B67 to Ballycastle, off the Portrush–Ballybogy Road.

City of Belfast International Rose Garden

The rolling parkland of Wilmont, now known as Sir Thomas and Lady Dixon Park, is the setting of a spectacular rose garden covering eleven acres with over 20,000 roses. There are display areas, historical sections and beds for the international rose trials held here during Belfast Rose Week in mid July. Among the display beds, visitors will find sections devoted to roses bred by the world famous breeders, McGredy's of Portadown and Dickson's of Newtownards. The latter have been breeding roses since 1879, while the McGredy's have produced a virtually unbroken series of floribundas, hybrid teas and climbing roses since 1895. Other attractions include an international camellia trials ground inside the walled garden, where trials usually take place in early April. There are also some fine trees, a selection of azaleas and rhododendrons, an ice house, a yew walk and a large but unexceptional Japanese garden.

2.5 km (1.5 miles) SE of Dunmurry, Belfast. NGR: J 307677.

MUSEUMS/HERITAGE CENTRES

Ballycastle Museum

The museum in this striking town on the north Antrim coast is located in what was once the courthouse and market hall dating from the 18th century when Ballycastle was planned as an industrial town. Pioneering industries begun then included coal mining and glass-making, but none lasted. Early this century, Ballycastle played its part in the Celtic revival and the museum has samples of this work. The most significant item is one of the original banners from the first Glens of Antrim *feis*, or festival, in 1904, together with sculptures, paintings, print and craftwork from this time. Among the artists represented is Stephen Clarke, once manager of the well-known Irish Home Industries shop in Ballycastle, An Tuirne Beag.

20 km (13 miles) E of Giant's Causeway.

Bushmills Distillery

The world's oldest distillery, still working, can trace its origins back to 1276. Its original grant to distil was made in 1608. This great pedigree is fully reflected in the whiskies produced, including Bushmills Malt, Black Bush and the standard Bushmills, itself aged for up to seven years. The visitor centre consists of the Potstill bar and two shops. In the bar can be seen the old malt kilns, once used for drying the malt.

13 km (8 miles) N of Coleraine.

Irish Linen Centre

The Irish Linen Centre, part of the excellent town museum in Lisburn, traces the development of linen-making in all its aspects from the 17th century onwards, and highlights scutching and weaving. The centre also has a short audio-visual presentation on the history of a fictional linen firm. A spinner's cottage and the grim Victorian mill era are recreated. The centre also has an outstanding collection of old costumes.

Lisburn.

Larne

This port town has two heritage locations, the Larne and District Historical Centre and Larne Borough Council Interpretative Centre. The Historical Centre has a recreated traditional kitchen and blacksmith's forge, together with many old artefacts, family memorabilia and photographs, all creating a sense of Larne in the past. The interpretative centre was opened in 1992 and besides housing a tourist information office, has a three-dimensional presentation on the history of the Coast Road.
Larne.

Linen Hall Library

Founded in 1788, this is Belfast's oldest library and the last surviving subscription library in Ireland. Best known for its Irish and local studies collections, it has some 200,000 books, ranging from its unrivalled holdings of early Belfast and Ulster printing to the definitive archive of the "Troubles" which started in 1969. The library derives its name from its residence for most of the 19th century in the old White Linen Hall, which stood on the site now occupied by Belfast City Hall.
Belfast.

Ulster Museum

Described as the "mother" museum of Northern Ireland, it has a vast array of material. Collections include fine and decorative art, archaeology and ethnography, botany, zoology and geology, as well as local history and technology. The new Early Ireland Gallery details the history of the period from 10000 BC to 1500 BC. The local history galleries illustrate political, social and industrial history in Ulster since 1600, everything from maps and coins to medals. The engineering hall has an impressive display of large steam engines and waterwheels as well as machinery once used in the linen industry. The "Made in Belfast" gallery has products made in the city over the past century or so, from bricks and rope to bicycles and aircraft. The museum also has most of the material from the Spanish Armada ships that were wrecked off the Irish coast 400 years ago. Also notable among the displays is the material on Irish flora and fauna. Recently, the Ulster Museum merged with the Ulster American Folk Park and the Ulster Folk and Transport Museum to form the National Museums and Galleries of Northern Ireland. With such a vast range of collections and material assembled since 1831, the museum merits a full day's visit. Frequent exhibitions are held during the year.
Botanic Gardens, Belfast.

ARMAGH

HOUSES

Ardress

Irish country houses that have developed over the centuries have always held a special fascination and charm, and none more so than Ardress – a modest gentleman farmer's residence with aspirations of grandeur. Originally a 17th-century house, it was enlarged with a hotch-potch of extensions at various times between 1780 and 1810 – all cleverly incorporated behind symmetrically composed façades. One of these additions includes a splendid drawing-room that could belong to a sophisticated Dublin town mansion of the period; above all else this room gives Ardress its elegance and distinction.

The magnificent room was added to the house in 1780 by the Dublin architect George Ensor. This was decorated by one of the great stuccodores of the age, Michael Stapleton – the renowned Irish master of restrained neo-classical plasterwork. The decorative ceiling design at Ardress is among his best works – it comprises intertwining segments of circles embellished by delicate foliage, urn motifs and a central plaque representing Aurora in "The Chariot of the Dawn".

The house assumed its present appearance after a series of additions between 1790 and 1810, some of which were evidently made by the author George Ensor (1772–1845). Two bays of windows were added to each end of the front façade in order to impress – an exercise that involved constructing no less than five dummy windows and a partly false front but which allowed the formation of an elegant garden front with curved sweeps at right angles to the main façade. New wings were added to the north and east sides, the latter containing the dining-room which curiously was linked to the drawing-room by a colonnade along the garden front and was later removed in 1879. The room was restored in 1961 and now contains some exceptional furniture and a fine collection of paintings.

Ardress was sold to the National Trust in 1960; in addition to upgrading the house, the Trust has restored the mainly 18th-century farmyard where visitors can inspect a milking shed, dairy, boiler house, forge and threshing barn. There is also an interesting display of old farm implements.

11km (7 miles) from Portadown. NGR: H 914559

The Argory

There is a touch of the *Marie Celeste* about the Argory, as if time had stood still a century ago and its occupants might at any moment return from their vanished world, bringing the place to life. The house is neither large nor grand by 19th-century standards. Its importance lies in the remarkable survival of its interior which, unique in Ireland, evokes the atmosphere and ambience of late Victorian country house life.

The Argory was built between 1819 and 1824 by Walter McGeough, alias MacGeough. His decision to build a house here was influenced by his father's will. According to its terms only £400 a year was left to the eldest son William; the bulk of the fortune went to the younger son Walter and his three sisters. Rather curiously the will stipulated that once Walter married he was no longer allowed to live at Drumsill, the family seat outside Armagh, so long as two of his sisters remained unwed. Although one sister died early, Walter judged correctly that the others would remain husbandless and therefore decided to build his own house on the lands he had inherited at Derrycaw, overlooking the Blackwater River.

The commisssion for the new house went to two young Dublin-based architects, John and Arthur Williamson. Most of the original plans and accounts relating to the building were lost in 1898 when a fire broke out in the octagonal pavilion, but it is known that the house was originally designed as a single block with the north wing added later.

The staircase hall has been described as one of the most exciting interiors of its date in Ireland. It has a theatrical cantilevered staircase with brass banister supports, marbled walls and a large cast-iron stove. The decorative scheme of the staircase hall with its marbled walls is continued upstairs in the organ gallery extending through the width of the house with tripartite "Wyatt windows" at each end. At one end stands the very large cabinet barrel organ which is generally accepted as the most important of its kind in existence. This recently restored instrument was commissioned in 1822 from the London organ builder James Bishop; it originally had six barrels, Samuel Wesley being consulted in their selection, but now only three barrels survive.

Perhaps the most attractive of the reception rooms at the Argory is the drawing-room, which lay shrouded in dust-sheets from 1939 until 1979. The Carrara marble chimney-piece with baseless Doric columns is original; there are rich curtains and upholstery, copies of old masters in gilt frames on the walls, a Steinway rosewood grand piano bought in 1898 and a workbox nearby ready for use. The ormolu colza-lamp was converted to gas in 1906 when an acetylene gas plant was installed in the

yard for £257 17s. 6d. The Argory has never been lit by electricity, though the National Trust installed carefully concealed power points when it took over the house in 1979. Two years later the house was opened to the public following a major restoration, which included work to the stable block, designed in 1820 and surmounted by a cupola with an eight-day striking clock and a handsome weathervane. The 300-acre demesne park has many pleasant walks.
6.5 km (4 miles) from Moy on the Derrycaw Road. NGR: H 872580.

GARDENS

Gosford Castle Arboretum

Arboretum in demesne park, established 1820s, contains large specimens of Himalayan and Noble firs, also rare Prince Albert's yew. Walled garden, 19th-century beehouse and early 18th-century gatelodges.
N of Markethill.

MUSEUMS/HERITAGE CENTRES

Armagh city

The ecclesiastical capital of Ireland, handsome with its green-swarded mall, is one of the most stimulating and interesting places to visit anywhere in Ireland because of the sheer diversity of its architectural and historical legacy. St Patrick's, the Church of Ireland cathedral, is essentially an early 19th-century restoration, but is arguably the most outstanding building in Armagh. The Catholic cathedral, also St Patrick's, was built between 1840 and 1904. The library, founded by the Anglican Archbishop Robinson in the 18th century, has manuscripts by Jonathan Swift, including that of *Gulliver's Travels*, many other rare books and registers of medieval archbishops. Near the Archbishop's Palace, the Palace Stables have been converted into a heritage centre, where 18th-century scenes are brought to life. St Patrick's Trian illustrates the Armagh story from earliest times in audio-visual form. Swift's many connections with the city are highlighted and the *Land of Lilliput*, a fantasy experience for children, is based on *Gulliver's Travels*.

Another impressive development not far from the centre of Armagh is the Navan Centre, a prehistoric site which features in the Ulster Cycle of epic myths. This series of earthworks and settlement sites was the earliest capital of Ulster and the mythology of those far-off times, Ireland in Celtic and pre-Christian times, is told superbly using audio-visual and interactive techniques, narration and display devices.

The Armagh County Museum, housed in a converted schoolhouse in the historic Mall, is highly rated among the small museums of Ireland, with a fine collection of archaeological, natural history, textile and railway items, besides examples of the work of such modern artists as AE (George Russell). The museum has been refurbished and includes new galleries. Also in the Mall is the Royal Irish Fusiliers Museum, with a fine collection of medals and uniforms.
Armagh city.
Navan Centre: Killylea Road, 3 km (2 miles) W of Armagh city.

Newry Canal

The canal was opened in 1742, linking Portadown with the sea beyond Newry; the last craft to traverse the canal did so just before World War II. Near Portadown, Moneypenny's lockhouse has been restored. Visitors can see how the lock-keepers and the lightermen lived and worked, while in the stables there's an exhibition on the local wildlife and on the history of the canal. More canal lore can be explored at the

Scarva Visitor Centre where coal was once unloaded on the canalside dock for the local linen industry.
Moneypenny's Lock: 4 km (2.5 miles) S of Portadown.
Scarva Visitor Centre: 15 km (9 miles) SE of Portadown.

Newry Museum

This small museum, located in the Arts Centre, has models of the town as it was in 1761 and in the 1930s, together with old photographs of the town. The highlight of the museum is the panelled room, decorated in the Georgian style, complete with two grandfather clocks. This room, and also an adjoining archway, were taken from an early 18th-century house when the building was being demolished.
Newry.

CARLOW

CASTLES

Ballymoon Castle

Like so many Irish castles, Ballymoon has no recorded history, but on architectural grounds it must have been built c. 1290–1310 and the most likely builders were the Carew family. The castle – as striking as it is unusual – comprises a courtyard about 80 feet square, delimited by granite walls, 8 feet thick and 20 feet high.
The interior is now bare, but the walls' many embrasures, loops, fireplaces and doors bear witness to the former presence of two-storey ranges, some with cellars that delimited the enclosure. The fine double-fireplace on the north belonged to the great hall, while such features as the cross-loops allow us to date the castle. It may not have been in use for very long; indeed, some argue it was never finished.
3 km (2 miles) E of Bagenalstown. NGR: S 738615.

Carlow Castle

This great keep was formerly one of the most impressive Norman castles in Ireland. Only the western wall and two towers now survive, the remainder having been accidentally blown up in 1814 by "a ninny-pated physician of the name of Middleton" who leased the building for use as a lunatic asylum and "applied blasts of gunpowder for enlarging the windows and diminishing the walls, and brought down two-thirds of the pile into a rubbishy tumulus in memory of his surpassing presumption and folly".
The original keep was probably built between 1207 and 1213 by William Marshall. It may be the earliest example of a "four-towered" keep in the British Isles and appears to have been directly inspired by French examples, notably Nemours (Seine-et-Marne). The entrance lies at first-floor level in the north wall and access to all storeys was by way of stone stairways in the thickness of the west wall.
Ownership of the castle passed to the Crown in 1306 and was later granted to the Earls of Norfolk, who held it until 1537. It was captured by James FitzGerald in 1494, again by Silken Thomas in 1535, and changed hands a number of times before being purchased by Donough, Earl of Thomond in 1616. It fell to the Confederates in 1642 but was later returned to Thomond after being liberated by Ireton in 1650.
Carlow town. NGR: S 718767.

Huntington Castle

The first view of the attractive grey-rendered castle of Huntington leaves one in no doubt that this is a building of great character and antiquity. Approached from the village of Clonegal down a straight 17th-century lime avenue, its front seems hardly to have a straight line anywhere – the side walls gently leaning to one angle and the sash windows lying askew. Additions, alterations and a mixture of styles accumulated over the centuries add enormously to Huntington's charm, while a treasure trove of varied contents reflects family ownership spanning three and a half centuries.

The old core of Huntington Castle is a tower house built between 1625 and 1630. A remarkable yew walk nearby possibly belongs to the 17th century, though claims that these trees were planted as early as the 15th century cannot be entirely discounted. Other formal garden features include a canal and the impressive avenue of lime trees.

The castle remained largely unaltered until 1860 when Alexander Durdin began additions to the rear of the castle. He also embarked on a disastrous attempt to enlarge the castle's basement windows, causing subsidence in the walls and the collapse of the drawing-room ceiling, which he replaced with a strapwork plaster design.

Aside from the bathrooms with plumbed water – a great rarity in those days – as well as central heating, electricity was also installed in 1888, power for which was generated from a water turbine on the River Derry. Huntington was one of the first country houses in Ireland to have electricity, and in order to satisfy local interest a light was kept burning on the front lawn so that the curious could come up and inspect it.

With its marvellously atmospheric rooms, Huntington is indeed a house of profound character, filled with the spirits of the past. Among the most memorable rooms are the library, the tapestry room and the conservatory, which houses an old vine – a cutting from a plant at Hampton Court dating around 1900. The cheerful drawing-room contains a collection of porcelain including a large *famille verte* bowl looted by a soldier from the Imperial Palace in Peking.

Clonegal village. NGR: S 913607.

GARDENS

Altamont

A wonderfully picturesque Robinsonian garden, where skilled and artistic planting gives delightful all-season effects amidst the idyllic setting of an 18th-century mansion. Rescued in the 1970s by the present owner, Mrs Carona North, after a long period of decline, the gardens have now been revitalised with new features and a remarkably wide-ranging collection of plants.

The central walkway, flanked by box hedges, rose beds, clipped yew arches and plush lawns, extends from the house down to the lake. A goldfish pond shimmers below the house; to the right are beds of conifers and shrubs and to the left golden bays, tree peonies, choice buddleias and a variety of perennials. Across the lawn an octagonal pool is shadowed by a *Magnolia stellata* and beyond lies a fine fern-leaf beech, a sweetly scented balsam poplar and adjacent to the lake, a venerable *Prunus* "Ukon" with unusual creamy-green flowers. The lakeside proffers a variety of moisture-loving plants, including a good selection of hostas, candelabra primulas, astilbes, gunnera, hydrangeas and saxifrages. Passing along the Azalea Walk, a gate gives access to a pair of bridges, one being approached through an iron pergola. The walk along the opposite shore, past the Myshall Gate, leads to the new arboretum along a tributary path. From here the path winds through a glen of ancient mossy oak woods to the River Slaney where visitors will find themselves treading on carpets of bluebells and wild daffodils in the spring. The path along the river and up the granite 100 Steps leads across a field back to the house, passing a newly built rotunda temple.

Before leaving, visitors may care to visit the walled garden where plants are for sale. It has a number of greenhouses and a *potager* garden.

8 km (5 miles) S of Tullow on the Bunclody Road. NGR: S 890648.

CLARE

Bunratty Castle

The fashion for renovating castles and using them to host "medieval banquets" may be said to have begun at Bunratty, which was restored in the 1950s and filled with Lord Gort's magnificent collection of medieval furniture and tapestries. It is now one of Ireland's main tourist attractions and justifiably so – for no other castle gives a more lasting impression of later medieval life.

The castle once stood on an island in a tidal creek with a view of the water-traffic entering and leaving the port of Limerick. Not surprisingly for such a strategic site, it has had quite a stirring history with a succession of castles from 1251 onwards. The present building was erected between 1450 and 1467 by the Macnamara or MacConmara family. Although of great size, the castle is essentially a tower house. While there are only three storeys in the main body of the castle – with vaulted cellars below the hall – the towers have many floors and small chambers approached by a profusion of winding mural stairs. Many were bedrooms with connecting latrines, the castle having no less than fifteen privies.

The castle's grandeur greatly impressed Archbishop Rinuccini who came here in 1646 and wrote of its great beauty, its ponds and 3,000 head of deer. But the property suffered during the 17th-century wars and towards the end of the 19th century the roof of the great hall was allowed to collapse. It was acquired by Lord Gort in 1954 and since his death the castle and its contents have been held in trust for the nation.

13 km (8 miles) W of Limerick city on the airport road. NGR: R 452610.

Carrigaholt Castle

Set on the verge of a cliff overlooking the Shannon estuary, this is a tall, well-preserved tower house built around the end of the 15th century.

The castle was occupied by Teige Caech "the short-sighted" MacMahon, in 1588 when seven ships of the Spanish Armada anchored at Carrigaholt. The following year the renegade fourth Earl of Thomond captured it after a four-day siege and, in breach of the surrender terms, hanged all the defenders. Ownership then passed to the Earl's brother, Donal, who was responsible for inserting many of the castle's windows as well as the fireplace on the fifth floor, which bears the date 1603. Donal's grandson, the celebrated third Viscount Clare, raised a regiment of horse known as the "Yellow Dragoons" for James II's armies. After the forfeiture of his extensive 57,000-acre estate by the Williamites, the castle was acquired by the Burton family who held it until the present century.

11km (7 miles) SW of Kilkee. NGR: Q 848512.

Gleninagh Castle

Looking down from a hillside across the wide expanse of Galway Bay, this well-preserved 16th-century tower house stands guard over the northern shoreline of the Burren. It has a distinctive L-shaped plan comprising an oblong tower of four storeys with a projecting turret containing a spiral stair. The third storey is vaulted and the dark basement may have been used as a prison.

The castle was built for the O'Loughlins (O'Lochlainns), who were still resident in the 1840s. It remained occupied until the 1890s.

5 km (3 miles) NW of Ballyvaughan off the coast road to Lisdoonvarna. NGR: M 193103.

Lemaneagh Castle

The magnificent ruins of the great O'Brien stronghold of Lemaneagh stand on the fringe of that limestone wilderness known as the Burren. It is a lonely place, some call it bleak, and perhaps a surprising location for a splendid four-storey, high-gabled, early 17th-century mansion. The early part of the building at the east end is, by contrast, a rather grim five-storey tower. The castle was first mentioned in 1550 when it was granted to Donough O'Brien who was hanged in 1582. By the 1630s it had been inherited by Conor O'Brien, whose wife was the formidable Maire Rua (Maire ni Mahon), about whom there are many tales. It is said that she hung her disobedient men servants by the necks and her maids by the hair from the castle's corbels and used to accompany her husband on raids upon English settlers. When Conor was mortally wounded in a skirmish with Ludlow's army in 1651, she is said to have refused to open the gates to receive her stricken husband, declaring "We need no dead men here", but having found that he was still alive nursed him until his death a few hours later. Ludlow later stayed in the castle for two nights, but found the November weather so foul that he retreated back to Limerick. It was abandoned around 1705 and quickly became a ruin with its lower windows and doors blocked to prevent access.

5 km (3 miles) E of Kilfenora on the Carran/Ballyvaughan Road. NGR: R 233937.

Newtown Castle

Like a rocket on its launch-pad, this unusual 16th-century tower house takes the form of a cylinder impaled upon a pyramid. The castle was originally built by a sept of the O'Briens and later passed into the hands of the O'Loughlins (O'Lochlainns) – self-styled "Princes of the Burren". It was still inhabited by the family at the end of the 19th century, but later fell into ruin. In the 1990s the castle was restored as an exhibition centre for the adjacent Burren Art College.

2.5 km (1.5 miles) SW of Ballyvaughan. NGR: M 217064.

HOUSES

Mount Ievers Court

Mount Ievers Court has a dreamlike, melancholic quality that is positively beguiling. Set in lush parkland and sheltered by beech trees, its height is accentuated by a steeply pitched roof, tall chimney stacks and the subtle architectural device of reducing the width of each storey by six inches.

Work began in 1731 when Colonel Henry Ievers demolished the 17th-century tower house that his grandfather had acquired less than seventy years before; a stone fireplace dated 1648 was salvaged from the castle and re-erected in the hall. From a surviving building account we know that eleven masons and forty-eight labourers were employed – the masons earning five shillings a week and the labourers only five pence, though each received food, drink, clothing and in some cases accommodation. Slates came from Broadford 10 miles away, while the massive oak-roof timbers, thirty-four tons in weight, came from Portumna, travelling by boat to Killaloe and hauled 20 miles overland to Mount Ievers. With so much of the work relying on local labour and materials the cost of the house was only £1,478 7s. 9d. – a comparatively small amount by the standards of the time.

The interior of the house has a simple, restrained feel. Many rooms retain their contemporary panelling and the ceilings, staircase, upper hall and magnificent staircase are reminiscent of Carolinian houses. On the top floor is a long gallery possibly designed as a ballroom, a feature that is unique in Ireland – though Bowenscourt in County Cork once boasted one. The formal garden landscape around the house has now largely disappeared, although the present owner has restored the fish ponds represented in the fresco. He has also done much to ensure that this magical building will survive successfully in the twenty-first century.

Near Sixmilebridge, NE of Limerick city. NGR: R 487663.

MUSEUMS/HERITAGE CENTRES

Bunratty

The many aspects of this world-famous folk park deserve a full day's exploration, taking in the many 18th- and 19th-century buildings that have been reconstructed here with complete authenticity. They include eight farmhouses, a watermill and a blacksmith's forge. A complete village street has been recreated, with all manner of shops, from an old-style printers to a pub, post office, even a school. The interiors of all the buildings contain antique furniture and artefacts, giving a good insight into the way of life of previous generations. If you walk through the folk village to the courtyard of Bunratty Castle, you'll come to the collection of old agricultural machinery. Also at the back of the park is the Bunratty Winery Museum, where exhibits include everything from fossils to a poitín still.

13 km (8 miles) W of Limerick city on airport road.

Burren Display Centre

A fine introduction to the flora and fauna of the Burren, this centre has displays showing the archaeology, history, local treasures and unique flowers of the district, together with a large-scale model of the Burren landscape. Next to the centre are the substantial ruins of a 12th-century cathedral. The Corofin Heritage Centre, in a converted church, has a small but comprehensive museum on life in 19th-century Clare and the nearby Dysert O'Dea Castle has an archaeology centre, with local museum and audio-visual presentation.

Burren Display Centre: Kilfenora, 11 km (7 miles) SE of Lisdoonvarna.
Corofin Heritage Centre: 15 km (8 miles) N of Ennis.
Dysert O'Dea Castle: 3 km (2 miles) S of Corofin.

East Clare Heritage Centre

St Cronan's 10th-century church in the centre of the village of Tuamgraney, on the west shores of Lough Derg, is probably the finest surviving example of an early Christian church in Ireland. It is also claimed to be the oldest church still used for services in either Ireland or Britain; services are still held in the 12th-century chancel. The church has a dual purpose: the 10th-century nave houses the heritage centre, which details the history of the area, including its associations with Brian Boru, who enlarged the church in 1007 and restored the now vanished round tower beside it. The centre also has rare books and papers, plus a video presentation. Many artefacts from the offshore Holy Island, which had a large and ancient religious settlement dating back to the 7th century and earlier, have been returned to the centre. Visitors can also walk through the nearby Raheen Wood, one of the few primeval forests still left in Ireland.

15 km (9 miles) NW of Killaloe.

Killaloe Heritage Centre

Killaloe, that historic town at the south end of Lough Derg, has a fine new heritage centre at the town end of the medieval 13-arch bridge across the River Shannon. The flora and fauna of the district are highlighted, together with details of old waterways craft. An old Shannon barge has been replicated, with its captain's cabin, and is accompanied by a video presentation of these old boats. The centre also features the life of Brian Boru, Ireland's greatest High King, who was born near here.

21 km (14 miles) NE of Limerick city.

Kilrush

This small harbour town on the north shores of the Shannon estuary boasts two heritage centres. Scattery Island, just offshore, has ruins of religious buildings; its monastery was founded in the 6th century and the well-preserved round tower is unique in Ireland in having its entrance at ground floor level. The Scattery Island Centre, devoted to the island, its monasticism and wild life, is in Kilrush town. Also in the town, the old town hall has been converted into a heritage centre showing the development of Kilrush from the end of the 18th century, as a planned town owned by the Vandaleur family.

Kilrush.

CORK

CASTLES

Ballynacarriga Castle

The hall or living-room of Irish tower houses sometimes doubled up as a chapel, though rarely were the occupants so devotional as to embellish the room with religious carvings. The Hurleys of Ballynacarriga appear to have been an exception, for the top-floor window embrasures of their castle have stone carvings mostly of a religious nature. One of the windows has a representation of the Crucifixion with the Instruments of Passion nearby – the carvings are dated 1585. The opposite window has intricate carvings around a chessboard design with the figure of a woman with five roses, thought to be the Blessed Virgin, though some believe it to represent the first owner and her five children.

Despite the date on the window soffit of the top floor, the castle was probably built in the mid 16th century or earlier. There is a good sheela-na-gig above the main door, while the remnants of a round corner tower can be seen outside. During the Confederate War of 1641–52, the Hurleys supported their overlord, Lord Muskerry (MacCarthy More), and in consequence the castle was dismantled by Cromwellian troops and their lands forfeited. It is believed that the ruin continued to serve as a chapel until 1815.

7 km (4.5 miles) SW of Ballineen and 1.6 km (1 mile) S of Manch Bridge. NGR: W 290509.

Blarney Castle

Blarney is celebrated the world over for a stone on the parapet that is said to endow whoever kisses it with the eternal gift of eloquence. The origin of this custom is unknown, though the word "blarney", meaning to placate with soft talk or to deceive without offending, probably derives from the stream of unfulfilled promises of Cormac MacDermot MacCarthy to the Lord President of Munster in the 16th century. Having seemingly agreed to deliver his castle to the Crown, he continuously delayed doing so with soft words, which came to be known as "Blarney talk".

The massive castle, which looks even larger because of its picturesque situation on the edge of a cliff, was supposedly built in 1446 by Cormac MacCarthy "the Strong". The MacCarthys held onto the castle with a few interruptions until the Williamite wars, when Donagh MacCarthy supported the losing side and had his estates forfeited. It is said that before leaving he cast the family silver into the lake. The property was acquired by Sir John Jefferys, who built a Gothic-style house onto the castle; this was burnt c. 1820, but a semi-circular staircase tower still remains. Nearby the family made a megalithic garden folly and in 1874 they built a Scottish Baronial-style house overlooking the lake in the park.

8 km (5 miles) NW of Cork city. NGR: W 614753.

Carrigaphooca Castle

Perched on a high rock overlooking the Sullane River this tall tower house commands truly panoramic views of the surrounding landscape. Built by Dermot Mor MacCarthy sometime between 1436 and 1451, it is a very simple building with a single room on each of its five levels. The windows are very plain in form, small and narrow, and like other early tower houses, there are no fireplaces or chimneys.

The MacCarthys of Carrigaphooca were constantly engaged in internecine warfare. They sided with the Crown in 1602 and their stronghold was consequently attacked by Donal Cam O'Sullivan Beare. After a difficult siege the huge wooden door of the castle burned down. The garrison was set free and O'Sullivan Beare retrieved a chest of Spanish gold he had presented to the MacCarthys some months earlier in return for their support against the English. The castle was subsequently owned by the MacCarthys of Drishane until forfeited in 1690.

5km (3 miles) W of Macroom. NGR: W 293734.

Charles Fort

Charles Fort is the most outstanding example of a 17th-century star-shaped fortification to survive in Ireland. It lies on the site of a medieval castle and 1601 it was occupied by a Spanish force and subsequently stormed by Mountjoy's troops.

The construction of the present fort began in 1677. It had five bastions; the first two faced the harbour and were the main strength of the fort, but the others were overlooked by the high ground, which proved to be the fort's great weakness. In 1690 it was besieged by the Williamite general, the Duke of Marlborough, who succeeded in making a breach in the wall by placing his cannon on the high ground.

From 1694 onwards the fort was largely rebuilt by the Huguenot military engineer Rudolph Corneille, following the original outline; a barracks for over 300 men was added in the 19th century. In 1922 the army handed over the fort to Irish "Irregulars", who burnt it down. In 1973 it was declared a National Monument and was subsequently renovated.

2.5 km (1.5 miles) SE of Kinsale. NGR: W 655494.

Conna Castle

Resembling some sort of medieval skyscraper, this captivating tower house rises about 85 feet from a great limestone bluff overlooking the lovely rich countryside of the Brade Valley. It was built in the 1550s by Sir Thomas Roe FitzGerald, who by right should have succeeded to the title and vast lands of his father, the fourteenth Earl of Desmond. His claim was disallowed, however, in favour of his younger half-brother, Garrett, who was goaded into a rebellion in which he lost everything, including his life, in 1583. Thomas Roe's claim to the earldom passed to his eldest son James, who was known as the "Sugan Earl" because his claim to the title seemed sure to fail – as indeed it did. After joining the revolt in 1599, the "Sugan Earl" was betrayed by a kinsman, captured and taken to the Tower of London, where he died. That year Conna was taken by the Earl of Essex and partly dismantled. It was later granted to Richard Boyle, Earl of Cork, who repaired the property, but in 1645 it was captured by Confederate forces under Lord Castlehaven and the men of the garrison were put to the sword.

The tower's history came to a sad end in 1653 when it was destroyed by a fire in which the three daughters of the steward were burnt to death. Considering its dramatic history, the castle survives in good condition.

6.5 km (4 miles) W of Tallow. NGR: W 931936.

Coppinger's Court

The striking silhouette of this ivy-clad ruin dominates Ballyvirine – a fertile and picturesque valley west of Rosscarbery. The stronghouse was built sometime after 1612 by Sir Walter Coppinger, whose vigorous desire to develop and modernise his estates brought him into conflict with traditional rural ways. He is therefore remembered, probably wrongly, as an awful despot who lorded it over the district, hanging anyone who disagreed with him from a gallows on a gable end of the Court.

He planned to build a model village nearby, but these and other schemes foundered with the 1641 Rebellion, when the house was ransacked and partially burnt down. So impressive was this house that it was said to have had a window for every day of the year, a chimney for every week and a door for every month. Visitors often like to count them all!

3 km (2 miles) W of Rosscarbery. NGR: W 260358.

Kanturk Castle

The construction of the great semi-fortified Jacobean house at Kanturk (c. 1610) was never brought to completion after suspicious neighbours complained that it was too dangerous and powerful a place to be in the hands of a subject. The builder, Dermot MacOwen Macarthy, Lord of Dunhallow, was ordered to stop work, and in a fit of rage he had the stained glass for the windows smashed and dumped in a nearby river. The castle shell was subsequently known as "MacDonagh's Folly".

19 km (12 miles) W of Mallow. NGR: W 382018.

Mallow Castle

The old Desmond fortress on the Blackwater River at Mallow was granted to Sir Thomas Norreys who built a "goodly strong and sumptuous house, upon the ruins of the old castle, with a bawn to it about 120 foot square" sometime between 1593 and 1599. The style is essentially English and early Jacobean with its high gables, single-stepped battlements and large mullioned windows, but the place was well-adapted for Irish conditions with numerous loopholes for muskets. Mallow Castle held out against the Confederates but was severely damaged after being captured by Lord Castlehaven in 1645 and appears to have been abandoned sometime afterwards.

Mallow. NGR: W 562983.

HOUSES

Bantry House

This is a theatrical place, full of drama and character. Standing at the foot of a steep terraced garden, it commands incomparable views across the waters of Bantry Bay to Whiddy Island and the Caha Mountains beyond. Its magnificent setting is matched by the many treasures of its interior – exquisite French furniture, tapestries and *objets d'art* – which give this remote Irish house the air of a continental baroque palace.

The original house was built around 1720 and acquired by Richard White, a farmer from Whiddy Island who had amassed a fortune from pilchard-fishing, iron-smelting and probably smuggling. He acquired most of the land around Bantry including large parts of the Beara Peninsula – estates which were further enlarged by his grandson Richard White. Richard took little interest in social or political affairs, but in 1796 he was unexpectedly thrust into the limelight when a French invasionary fleet sailed into Bantry Bay to join forces with the United Irishmen. White showed great initiative during the crisis by organising local defences and placing his home at the disposal of General Dalrymple who arrived with troops from Cork. In recognition of his "spirited conduct and important service" Richard was created Baron Bantry and later the Earl of Bantry.

Substantial changes were made in 1845 by Richard, Viscount Berehaven, a passionate art collector who travelled regularly across Europe, visiting Russia, Poland, France and Italy and bringing back shiploads of exotic goods. No doubt inspired by the grand baroque palaces of Germany, he lined the walls with giant red-brick pilasters with Coade-stone Corinthian capitals. He also laid out the Italianate gardens including the magnificent terraces on the hillside behind the house.

Today, Bantry House remains much as the second Earl left it, with an important part of his great collection still intact. The rooms also retain their Victorian clutter

and nowhere more so than in the hall where visitors will find an array of bric-à-brac, including a mosque lamp from Damascus, an Arab chest, a Japanese inlaid chest, a Russian travelling shrine with 15th- and 16th-century icons, a Friesian clock and a 16th-century marriage chest. Undoubtedly the most spectacular rooms in the house are the dining-room and drawing-rooms which offer magnificent vistas across the bay. The great library retains a fine rosewood grand piano by Bluthner of Leipzig, still occasionally used for concerts. The windows of this room once looked into an immense glass conservatory, but this has now been removed and visitors will gaze out upon the recently restored gardens. The imposing stable range has been reconstructed and houses an exhibition entitled "1796 Armada Trust".
Bantry. NGR: V 988481.

Dunkathel

During the late 18th century, successful Cork merchants built a string of elegant villas along the banks of the Lee estuary. Many of these have now disappeared, but one which still survives intact is Dunkathel, alias Dunkettle, a solid neo-classical house with an idyllic parkland setting lying just below the mouth of the Glanmire River.

Dunkathel was built around 1785 in the Palladian manner. The fanlighted front door, flanked by engaged Tuscan columns, leads directly into the entrance hall which occupies the whole centre of the building. There is a fine marble chimney-piece, a magnificent gilt mirror and a rare barrel organ, designed by Imhoff and Muckle in 1880 and still played for visitors with much musical vigour.
5.5 km (3.5 miles) from Cork city on the Waterford road. NGR: W 732730.

Fota House

The demesne of Fota, or Foaty Island, contributes enormously to the beauty of the Lee estuary whose sublimity moved Lady Chatterton to write in 1838: "The sun always seems to shine brighter here than elsewhere." Fota's magnificent parkland, its gardens and splendid mansion – one of Ireland's finest Regency houses – combine to create an aura of charm and serenity apparent to all who visit.

Fota's former owners were direct descendants of Philip de Barry, a Norman settler who was granted lands in Cork in 1179. In the 1750s Arthur Smith-Barry built a five-bay hunting box on Fota and in the 1820s the Morrisons were engaged to alter and extend the old Georgian box. They added two wings, built a Doric portico and remodelled the interior in the rich classical Regency style it retains to this day.

The house was saved from an uncertain fate in 1976 when it was leased by local businessman Richard Woods, who was looking for somewhere to display his collection of 18th- and 19th-century Irish pictures. In 1983 the house was exquisitely redecorated with Irish furniture and fittings to complement the Woods collection and was opened to the public. Visitors are often surprised by the wealth of sumptuous decorative detail in the house, for the simplicity of the building's exterior gives no hint of what lies within.

The redecoration of Fota and its adaptation as the home for the Woods picture collection is undoubtedly one of the success stories of Irish conservation. Unfortunately, Fota has recently been sold to an English development company which has received planning permission to construct hotels, golf courses and numerous holiday dwellings on this lovely island. Although the house, arboretum and 70 acres of parkland were withdrawn from the developers' plans (after public protest), the future of the house remains very much in doubt. It is now managed by the Fota Trust which closed the building to the public at the end of 1990, due to the deterioration of its structure.
Fota Island 14.5 km (9 miles) E of Cork city. NGR: W 790715.

GARDENS

Annes Grove

Set around an elegant early 18th-century house overlooking the River Awbeg, this 30-acre garden is filled with thousands of thriving plants in a wild "Robinsonian" layout that merges unobtrusively into the landscape. Created from 1900 onwards by Richard Grove Annesley, one of the great plantsmen of his time, Annes Grove contains many plants brought back from the wild by Forrest, Ward and other famous plant hunters.

The garden is divided into three contrasting areas: the Walled Garden, the Glen and Riverside Garden. The Walled Garden, formerly devoted to kitchen produce, was transformed into a number of ornamental compartments flanking an axial path, with long yew-backed herbaceous borders focussed on a Victorian summer house. There is a rose garden, an area of box-edged "ribbon beds" containing annuals and a remarkable water garden; this is laid out around a serpentine pool with a wealth of aquatic and marginal plants, all contributing to an almost tropical atmosphere in this secluded part of the garden.

The woodland walks contain many rhododendrons ranging in size and colour with some exceptional *R. cinnabarinum* and *R. griersonianum*. A winding and rather dangerously steep path leads down into the wooded limestone gorge, passing fine specimens of Wilson and Watson magnolias, a drooping *Juniperus recurva* "Castlewellan" and a number of fine azaras. The Water Garden in the gorge was begun in 1902 when a battalion of soldiers from the nearby barracks were employed to divert the river and build an island, weirs, rapids and bridges. Conifers grow in the glen and screens of bamboo stand by the waterside with a profusion of gunnera, day lilies, polygonums, rodgersias and candelabra primroses.

16 km (10 miles) NW of Fermoy and 3 km (2 miles) N of Castletownroche. NGR: R 682048.

Ballymaloe Cookery School Gardens

Darina Allen's internationally famed cookery school is based at Kinoith House, near Ballymaloe. Initially the gardens here were designed simply to provide herbs and vegetables for the school, but over recent years have been developed and are well worth visiting. Hidden behind a compartment of old beech hedges, visitors will find a flower garden with herbaceous borders. There is a wonderful herb garden, whose design can be admired from a specially created platform and an organic vegetable garden in a formal layout that is itself a work of art. A fine double herbaceous border leads to a pleasant Gothic summer house, whose interior has been decorated with thousands of shells set into wonderful patterns.

Kinoith House, near Ballymaloe.

Creagh

A delightfully romantic garden set in the grounds of a pleasant Regency house overlooking a sea estuary. It contains an extensive network of paths, meandering their way through the woodlands, across glades and along the strand, enabling the visitor to view a wide range of tender plants, notably camellias, azaleas, rhododendrons, fuchsias, magnolias, telopeas and abutilons. An ornamental serpentine pond, fringed with gunnera, hydrangea and cordyline, evokes scenes reminiscent of a Henri Rousseau landscape and nearby, the Gothic windows of a ruined gazebo peer out through the undergrowth. Elsewhere, there is a charming thatched summer house, a long herbaceous border and an old walled garden with vegetables, fruit, newly built greenhouses and exotic varieties of fowl.

5.5 km (3.5 miles) S of Skibbereen. NGR: W 077312.

Fota Island Arboretum

Forming part of the ornamental grounds of a splendid Regency mansion, this arboretum is filled with plants from all over the world, especially Chinese and South American species, and benefits enormously from a mild and sheltered micro-climate. A magnificent demesne, now partly damaged by a golf course, surrounds the house and arboretum, occupying the whole of the 780-acre island in Cork Harbour.

Planting began in 1825 and amongst the original trees is a marvellous Lebanese cedar undercarpeted with cyclamen. The Walled Garden has a magnificent specimen of *Magnolia grandiflora* "Goliath" shading a charming little temple, and visitors can visit the Orangery, Water Garden and Fernery. A towering Sequoia dominates the arboretum, while beautiful weeping spruces, silver firs, a colossal fern-leafed beech and exceptional specimens of melaleuca and pseudopanax also take pride of place. A *Phyllocladus trichomanoides* from New Zealand, planted in 1941, is now the tallest in the British Isles, while a *Cryptomeria japonica* "Spiralis", planted in 1852, is the tallest in Europe. Here also is a *Torreya californica* some 35 feet high and a charming *Dacrydium franklinii* from Tasmania, planted in 1855 and now, at 28 feet, the largest in the British Isles.

14.5 km (9 miles) E of Cork city. NGR: W 790715.

Ilnacullin (Garinish Island)

An enchanted garden island in Bantry Bay, blessed with spectacular sea and mountain scenery as well as a balmy climate brought by the waters of the Gulf Stream. From 1911 to 1914 this island of 37 acres was transformed from a barren rock into a seductive mixture of formal and informal gardens superbly filled with a rich and wonderful variety of plants. The horticulturist Harold Peto undertook the work but additions continued to be made until the garden was acquired by the State in 1953.

Boats bringing visitors to Ilnacullin pass basking seals and arrive at the north side of the island. The route to the Italian gardens winds past a variety of magnolias, abutilons, camellias and a fine specimen of the tender Kauri pine. The wisteria-covered colonnades of the Renaissance-style Casita gaze down over a formal sunken garden featuring a reflecting pool, a pavilion and the distant landscape beyond. The varied planting here includes a variety of magnificent sun-loving callistemons and unusually large leptospermum shrubs, while around the pool are a venerable collection of bonsai specimens. The path south winds through more exotic planting to a long, grassy vista known as the Happy Valley with a small temple overlooking the sea at one end. Passing a lily pond, steps lead up to a Martello tower, built in 1805 on the highest point of the island. From here visitors descend to a walled garden dominated by a tall folly built in one corner. The main path, with matching gates at each end, is flanked by wide herbaceous borders, while the garden walls support a fine collection of climbing plants.

On an island near Glengarriff. NGR: V 935550.

Timoleague

At Timoleague no less than five successive generations have left their mark on these charming gardens on the banks of the Argideen River. A long terraced lawn separates the site of the old Travers family mansion, burnt in 1922, from the later house close to the ruins of a medieval castle. Some of the most interesting plants include a collection of spring-flowering azaleas and magnolias. There is a recently restored sunken garden with formal beds and lily pond and above, steps overhung with a lime arch lead to the Lower Garden with its herbaceous border. Another walled garden contains a variety of fruit and vegetables, while beyond the castle ruins, a river garden has been developed.

Timoleague, 12 km (8 miles) S of Bandon. NGR: W 471439.

MUSEUMS/HERITAGE CENTRES

Bandon Heritage Centre

The West Cork market town of Bandon has one of Ireland's oldest Protestant churches, Christ Church, originally built in 1610 (the oldest is reckoned to be St Patrick's Church of Ireland in Newry, built in 1575). Bandon was once a strongly Protestant town, but Christ Church, long deconsecrated, now houses a heritage centre with a number of disparate themes. The distilling and brewing section recalls Allman's whiskey distillery in the town and includes some old bottles from the company. Another section features a traditional grocery store with wooden packaging and old advertisements, also a traditional country pub, complete with wooden counter and old bottles. The schoolroom faithfully recreates the old style of learning, with rows of wooden desks, a blackboard and even satchels hung up. The centre also has a wildlife section and 19th-century material from the Orange Order in the town, as well as a complete set of old weights and measures, together with the old Irish and English Acts on the subject.
Bandon.

Bantry House and French Armada Centre

Bantry House, one of the finest 18th-century stately homes in Ireland, is complemented by the new French Armada centre, commemorating the abortive French landings in Bantry Bay in 1796. Models of the ships that took part, old medals, lithographs and paintings, besides reconstructions of incidents, help tell the story in an attractive modern format. The centrepiece of the exhibition is the 1:6 scale model of the frigate Surveillante, scuppered off Whiddy Island, while another depicts Wolfe Tone in his cabin.
Bantry.

Bealick Mill Museum

Set on the outskirts of Macroom, this four-storey 18th-century riverside mill has been well restored and has much material on local industrial history.
Macroom.

Cape Clear Island Museum

The island has a wealth of folklore tradition and an Irish-speaking resident population of about 135 that increases to nearly 1,000 in the summer. The many facets of this diverse island can be seen in the museum, housed in a former schoolhouse. Few parishes anywhere in Ireland can claim to have such an assiduous collection of local material, which includes household items such as a dresser from an island kitchen. Cape Clear's rich fishing tradition is recalled, along with the numerous shipwrecks in the area. Material from some of those wrecks, everything from delft to saloon doors, is on display. Fishing is the island's main economic activity and is reflected in the museum's contents. More history can be seen in the island's three pubs, one of which has remained virtually unchanged during the past century.
11 km (7 miles) off West Cork coast. Ferries from Baltimore and Schull.

Céim Hill Museum

This West Cork museum is unique in that it is a one-person collection, reflecting the many local history interests of Therese O'Mahony. She describes the museum as telling the story of her townland from the time of the dinosaurs to her own period and the collection even boasts some fossilised dinosaur droppings! Jawbones and teeth that once belonged to an Irish elk nestle side by side with more recent exhibits, including a soup pot from the Famine era, old farm implements, artefacts from the War of Independence and various local historical costumes. The location of the

museum is quite spectacular, overlooking Castletownshend and its estuary.
15 km (9 miles) SW of Rosscarbery.

Clonakilty

The Model Village, set overlooking the estuary, depicts in miniature form the West
Cork railway which closed down, amIdst much chagrin, over thirty years ago, and the
main towns of the region. A highlight are the models of Clonakilty houses painted in
bright Mediterranean colours.

Also in Clonakilty, the West Cork Regional Museum, in a former schoolhouse, has
memorabilia relating to Michael Collins, records from Clonakilty Corporation dating
back to 1675 and material on the local post office.
Clonakilty.

Cobh

This seaside town, developed in the 19th century, was once the main emigration port
for people sailing to North America. The story of that relentless emigration is told in
the fine Queenstown Story Centre. Using audio-visual techniques, artefacts and
models, the centre recreates emigration history and recalls the appalling conditions
on the aptly named coffin ships that crossed the Atlantic in the 19th century.
Conditions aboard the convict ships that went to Australia is also detailed while, more
genteelly, the centre tells the story of the great ocean liners that once called at Cobh.
Among them were the *Titanic*, which sank in 1912, subject of a new audio-visual
presentation in the centre, and the *Lusitania*, torpedoed off the Old Head of Kinsale in
1915. In the old cemetery, a mile north of the town, many victims of the *Lusitania*
sinking are buried.

Also in Cobh, the former Presbyterian church was opened as a museum in 1973.
It has many interesting artefacts from former industries, including the Belvelly
Brickworks. Models of Cork harbour coasters, marine paintings and maritime
photographs are also in the collection.
Cobh.

Cork City Gaol and Broadcasting Museum

This jail received its first prisoners in 1824 and was last used as such in 1923. The
magnificent architectural set piece languished in dereliction until it was reopened as a
visitor attraction in 1993. The west wing, with cells on three floors, has been
thoroughly and convincingly restored. A spectacular multimedia presentation depicts
Cork social history in the 19th century, explaining why so many people in the city
were driven to crime. The penal regime they encountered is well documented,
including the infamous Cork treadwheel, while the governor and his officers have also
been recreated in life-size model form.

When the first Cork radio station was set up in 1927, the top floor of the
governor's house was used for studios, and this same floor now houses RTÉ's
broadcasting museum (the Radio Museum Experience) which traces the history of
radio in Ireland. It has details of noted presenters and performers and many
broadcasting artefacts, including wireless and radio sets from the days of the cat's
whisker in the 1920s. A selection of microphones includes one used by John F.
Kennedy during his visit to Ireland in 1963. Valentia Island telegraphic equipment is
also included.
Sunday's Well, opposite Fitzgerald Park and Western Road.

Cork Heritage Park

This recently developed centre is most attractively set in park grounds once part of a
great estate. A central point of interest in the park is the bell tower that once stood
atop the Beamish and Crawford brewery in South Main Street, Cork, to summon the
workers. In themed exhibition areas the history of the port of Cork is detailed, with a

large model of the whole area made by the Cork Harbour Commissioners in 1932, restored and updated. Many other maritime relics include photographs of Cork harbour around 1890, ships' models and the free pass given by the Cork Steam Packet Company to Winston Churchill in 1922.

A key feature of the centre is the elaborate section on fire brigades; it is reckoned to be the only fire service museum in Ireland. Fire-fighting is traced back to the 18th century, when insurance companies ran primitive fire brigades (only for those who had paid their premiums) through to early breathing apparatus. The burning of Cork in 1920 by the Black and Tans is recalled. Two new attractions have been opened – an animal farm and a garden of reflection.

Bessboro, Blackrock, SE Cork city.

Cork Public Museum

Founded in 1945, the city museum, set in Fitzgerald Park by the River Lee, is very much a traditional-style museum, but well maintained and presented. Beside its entrance is the coat of arms, carved in stone, of the City of Cork, rescued after the Black and Tans burned the city centre in 1920. Rooms display the prehistory of the Cork region, details of the War of Independence and many examples of Cork crafts. These include 18th-century silver, now much prized, besides the even rarer Republican silver, assayed in Cork in 1922, when times were too troubled for it to be sent to the Assay Office in Dublin. Cork glassware and Youghal needlepoint lace are also featured.

Fitzgerald Park, off Western Road.

Gunpowder Mills

These old mills, once used to make gunpowder, were built in the late 18th century, on the banks of the River Lee. After the Napoleonic Wars, they were closed down for twenty years before reopening and becoming a major employer in the area; in 1903, after the Boer War, they were finally closed. Now the mill has been reconstructed, showing just how gunpowder was made 150 years ago.

8 km (5 miles) W of Cork city on Killarney Road.

Jameson Whiskey Heritage Centre

The old distillery here has been marvellously restored. Whiskey distillation began here in 1825 and continued for 150 years before being moved to the modern distillery nearby. The world's largest pot still and many other facets of the old distillery can still be seen. Visitors can tour the complex of old buildings and inspect the maltings, corn stores, stillhouses and warehouses. The story of whiskey is graphically told, with audio-visual presentations, demonstrations, display cabinets, artefacts and working models.

Midleton, 25 km (15 miles) E of Cork city on N25.

Kinsale

Kinsale Museum, on the first floor of the 17th-century former town hall, is packed with memorabilia relating to the town and its industries, everything from royal charters to the *Lusitania* disaster. Town crafts, including silver-making and lace-making, are featured, while the museum also has details on the black cloaks that were worn by women in the town until the 1950s. Agriculture and shipbuilding are also commemorated in the museum.

A newer museum in the town is the Wine Museum in the Desmond Castle. This celebrates the Irish wine experts and growers, the "Wine Geese", who contributed to the wine industries in such locations as Bordeaux in France, Jerez in Spain, Chile and California in the 18th and 19th centuries. Also worth seeing in Kinsale is the historic St Multose Church.

Kinsale.

Mizen Head Signal Station

The old signal station at the tip of Mizen Head peninsula has been turned into a visitor centre. The fog signal sounded out here until the 1970s, when the last keepers left. The station is reached by an early 20th-century suspension bridge.
25 km (15 miles) SW of Schull.

Youghal

The story of this medieval sailing port, from Viking times and continuing through the building of the Anglo-Norman town walls, is told well in the new Youghal Heritage Centre on the quays. Sir Walter Raleigh, who was the Mayor of Youghal in 1588–9, planted the first potatoes in Ireland here, and also introduced tobacco smoking. Youghal had a strong tradition of sailing schooners which lasted until the 1930s and the centre has a fine model of a square-rigged ship. The development of the town as a seaside resort in the 18th century is also highlighted.

Many interesting places can be visited in the town, for example, the Moby Dick pub, with photographs taken when *Moby Dick* was filmed in Youghal in 1954. The town walls on the heights behind the Main Street are, Derry's excepted, the finest in Ireland. Myrtle Grove, once Raleigh's house, can also be visited. Many medieval buildings, including the 1777 Clock Tower, are dotted along Main Street. Finally, it's worth seeing the old photographs of the schooners on display in the Devonshire Arms Hotel.
Youghal.

DONEGAL

CASTLES

Castledoe

On a remote rocky promontory by the upper reaches of Sheephaven Bay, stands the grim four-storey tower house of Castledoe – one of the most fought-over and disputed castles in Ireland. It was built in the 1520s by MacSweeney Doe, head of a fiery and quarrelsome tributary sept of the O'Donnells, who were constantly engaged in internecine wars usually over possession of the castle, which was besieged and captured at least twenty times before being abandoned at the close of the 17th century.

The halcyon years at Castledoe came during the chieftancy of Eoghan Og II MacSweeny, the foster-father of Red Hugh O'Donnell, who was famed for his hospitality, patronage of the bards and for harbouring shipwrecked sailors of the Spanish Armada. In 1596 the castle passed to Mulmurry MacSweeney Doe, an unsavoury tyrant who tried disobedient vassals in the castle's great hall; those of the condemned he wished to honour he brained with his club, while the less fortunate were strung up on meat hooks from the castle's parapets. It is said that in order to prevent the marriage of his daughter to Turlough Oge O'Boyle, the unfortunate man was cast into the dungeon and starved to death.

The castle was in ruins by the 1790s, when it was repaired by General Vaughan Harte, and sold in 1864. It was occupied by tenants until the end of the century, but afterwards allowed to fall into ruin again.
3 km (2 miles) NE of Creeslough on the coast. NGR: C 085318.

Donegal Castle

The site of Donegal Castle at the mouth of the River Eske was chief seat to the great clan O'Donnell; the original tower house is believed to have been built in 1474, but existing detail suggests a mid 16th-century date. In 1566 the castle was visited by Sir Henry Sidney, who described it as "...one of the greatest that I ever saw in Ireland in

any Irishman's lands and would appear in good keeping one of the fairest". It was burnt in 1589, partly demolished in 1595 and remodelled after 1623. During the Williamite wars the castle was successfully defended against the Jacobite forces. It subsequently fell into decay during the 18th century.
Donegal town.

Greencastle (Northburgh)

At first glance the shattered remains of this castle resemble the magnificent Edwardian fortress at Caernarfon. Indeed, it may have been designed by the same person, though Greencastle – called Northburgh by the Normans – was not a royal castle but was built by the "Red" Earl of Ulster, Richard de Burgo, in 1305 to help subdue the O'Neills and O'Donnells and control the entry into Lough Foyle.

The castle encompasses a lofty rock platform, whose cliffs afforded good protection on the seaward side. Like Caernarfon, it has an oblong plan with the gatehouse at one end and a large polygonal tower dominating the north-east corner. The three-storey gatehouse, which projects from the side of the rock platform, is the most impressive part of the castle and contained the main apartments.

Once completed, the castle quickly became an important port of supply for the English armies in Scotland. Consequently, in 1316 Edward Bruce lost no time in capturing it after he had invaded Ireland. Two years later it reverted back to the Red Earl and later passed to his grandson, William, who was murdered in 1333 – an event that brought about the end of de Burgo power in Ireland. The murder was an act of revenge for the death of his cousin, Walter Burke, whom William had imprisoned at Northburgh the previous year and left to starve to death. It is said that William's sister, moved by Walter's fate, endeavoured to bring him food but was detected and thrown over the battlements to the rocky shore beneath.

A small garrison was maintained here until the 17th century, when it was completely abandoned to the ivy, jackdaws and turf-scented salty air.
E of Greencastle village on the Inishowen shore of Lough Foyle. NGR: C 653403.

GARDENS

Glenveagh Castle Gardens

A remarkable garden set amidst the operatic setting of a baronial castle in the Donegal highlands. Begun on a bare hillside in the 1870s, the garden now covers 10 acres of formal and informal areas with a wealth of vegetation, almost tropical in luxuriance. It owes its present appearance to Henry P. McIlhenny, who gave the castle and its gardens to the nation in 1983 to form the centrepiece of the 28,000-acre National Park.

To the north of the castle lies the Pleasure Ground, a broad sweep of lawn with bordering trees and shrubs planted to resemble the shape of the adjacent lough. Among its tender plants are the tree fern *Dicksonia antarctica* and a very beautiful *Magnolia tripetala*. Above lies the Belgian Walk, laid down by convalescing Belgian soldiers in 1915 and noted for its rhododendron varieties. A stone-flagged Italian terrace along this walk has an air of timeless serenity with antique sculpture and massed terracotta pots. The formal Walled Garden beside the castle contains, in addition to herbaceous borders, a mixture of fruit, vegetables and flowers in the *jardin potager* style and a Gothic orangery. To the south lies the View Garden and the Swiss Walk, both of which offer lovely vistas.
Near Churchill, 15 km (9 miles) W of Letterkenny.

MUSEUMS/HERITAGE CENTRES

Ardara Heritage Centre

This small West Donegal town once had a great weaving tradition, with over one hundred weavers turning out the tweeds for which Donegal is justly renowned. These skills were practised in the area for about 200 years until around 1970. Now the town's former courthouse has been turned into a heritage centre that neatly weaves the story of this craft, complete with a hand weaver working a loom. Visitors can follow the story of Donegal tweed from the shearing of the sheep to the completion of the woven cloth with the help of documentation, old photographs and models.
40 km (25 miles) NW of Donegal town.

Flight of the Earls Centre

In 1607, the great exodus of nobility, known as the Flight of the Earls, took place from Rathmullan harbour. This saw the end of the old Gaelic order in Ireland and within two years the plantation of Ulster began. The story of the earls is dramatically told in the centre at Rathmullan using models, artefacts, extracts from literature and stained glass. Wax figures of the two leading earls, Hugh O'Neill and Rory O'Donnell, stand at the entrance to the exhibition hall. The centre is housed in a fort dating from Napoleonic times; a similar one on the opposite shore of Lough Swilly houses the Fort Dunree military museum. Flight of a different kind is illustrated at Ramelton Heritage Centre, where Francis Makemie was born in 1658; he emigrated and founded the American Presbyterian Church. The centre has a library, artefacts and displays.
Rathmullan: 26 km (16 miles) NE of Letterkenny.
Fort Dunree: 16 km (10 miles) NW of Buncrana.
Ramelton Heritage Centre: 13 km (8 miles) NE of Letterkenny.

Glebe House and Gallery

This Regency house with Victorian decorations housing the works of many 20th-century artists is beside the Glenveagh National Park and castle.
Churchill, 15 km (9 miles) W of Letterkenny.

Glencolumbkille Folk Museum

The brainchild of the late Fr James McDyer, the museum was set up to help preserve the area's strong cultural traditions. The heart of the museum consists of three reconstructed houses, one from 1700, another from 1850 and the third from 1900. The 19th-century house has a flagstone floor and includes tools once used by a shoemaker. The early 20th-century house is altogether more grand and includes a parlour, complete with wooden floor, linoleum, a sofa and a gramophone.
25 km (16 miles) SW of Ardara.

Lifford Heritage Centre

Just across the River Foyle from Strabane, the Centre is located in the old courthouse (built 1746). Upstairs, a storyboard area depicts the history of Lifford until the present century, with historic items in display cases. This history is amplified by a short audio-visual presentation in the Manus O'Donnell Room. A further display area tells the story of Lifford during the Plantation. The courtroom scene recreates famous trials held here. Finally, the centre houses many geneaological records on the O'Donnells and other Donegal clans.
24 km (15 miles) SW of Derry city.

Newmills

A rare venture into industrial archaeology by the Office of Public Works has seen the restoration of this milling complex, the oldest part of which is said to be between 300

and 400 years old. The mill race has been restored and so too have the two mills; one was used for flax and still has much of its old machinery, while the lower mill was used for grinding barley and oats.
3 km (2 miles) NW of Letterkenny.

St Conal's Museum

This museum, named after the saint who brought Christianity to West Donegal in the 6th century, is housed in two buildings. The older one is the 1843 courthouse (still used as such once a month), while a modern building was opened in 1994. There's a good collection of artefacts from the narrow gauge County Donegal Railways, including many old photographs and posters. Noted writers from the North-West, including Brian Friel and Patrick McGill, are commemorated. Nearby is the Fintown railway, Donegal's only narrow gauge railway, which runs beside Lough Finn.
Glenties, on the Ardara Road.

Vintage Car and Carriage Museum

This small but intriguing collection, about twenty items in all, covers vintage and veteran cars, horse-drawn carriages and vintage motor cycles, plus model cars and railways. Among its exhibits is a 1929 Rolls-Royce Landaulette, which has never needed restoring, a 1935 Austin Seven, also in perfect condition, and a 1957 Chevrolet, the classic American car of the 1950s.
Buncrana.

DOWN

CASTLES

Audley's Castle

From its rocky vantage point overlooking the narrow entrance of Strangford Lough, this tower house is a striking landmark whose natural advantages no doubt played a key role in its siting. It was built in the 15th century by the Audleys, one of the families introduced into Lecale by De Courcy in 1177. Internal features include a murder hole in the stair, fireplaces, window seats, cupboard niches and drain holes for slops, while unusually there is a stone vault roofing on the first floor rather than the ground floor.

In 1765 the Wards purchased the property from the descendants of the Audleys, some of whom continued to reside in Audleystown village. During the 1850s, however, the inhabitants of this settlement were shipped to America by the Wards and the area was incorporated into the landscape park.
Audleystown. NGR: J S78506.

Dundrum Castle

One of Ulster's most evocative medieval ruins, Dundrum Castle was founded by the legendary Norman adventurer John de Courcy following his invasion of Ulster in 1177. The site occupies the summit of a rocky hill commanding fine views over Dundrum Bay and the plains of Lecale, controlling access into east Down from the south. De Courcy's original castle may have had defences of earth and timber.

In 1204 de Courcy was expelled from Ulster by Hugh de Lacy who proceeded to strengthen the castle, probably employing master masons from the Welsh Marches. The castle was captured by King John in 1210 and remained Crown property until de Lacy was allowed to return in 1226.

The Maginnis family held it intermittently from the 14th century until the Parliamentarians dismantled it in 1652. The dwelling was ruined by the time it passed to the second Marquess of Downshire in the early 19th century, though the trees on the hill were probably planted at this time. The castle and grounds were placed in State care in 1954.

Dundrum village. NGR: J 404370.

Greencastle

A popular 19th-century travel handbook exclaimed of Greencastle, "You would go into ecstacies if you saw such ruins on the Rhine, and quote 'Childe Harold' by the canto." The fortress is impressive, though its dramatic setting at the mouth of Carlingford Lough adds much to its appeal, with views over a sweeping landscape and towering mountains beyond.

The castle was built by Hugh de Lacy almost certainly during the 1230s and from 1280 to 1326 was a favoured residence of the most powerful man in Ireland, Richard de Burgh, the "Red Earl" of Ulster. His daughters were raised here, including Elizabeth, who married Robert Bruce, King of Scotland, although this did not dissuade Edward Bruce from sacking it in 1316. In 1505 it was granted to the Earls of Kildare, but after their downfall in 1534 quickly deteriorated into a "wretched condition". The place was later destroyed by Parliamentary forces in 1652.

Remodelling of the hall in the 15th and 16th centuries gave it much of its present keep-like appearance. For centuries the green below the castle played host to a great fair every August. It was often called "Ram Fair" as a great ram was customarily enthroned on top of the castle's walls.

6.5 km (4 miles) SW of Kilkeel. NGR: J 247119.

Jordan's Castle

Ardglass was an important seaport in post-medieval times, whose defence depended upon a ring of fortified merchants' houses. The largest of these is 15th-century Jordan's Castle overlooking the harbour. Little is known of its history except that it withstood a lengthy siege during the Tyrone Rebellion, when Simon Jordan defended his castle for three years until relieved by Mountjoy in 1601. It probably remained a dwelling until the 17th century, but was a ruin when purchased by the antiquarian F.J. Bigger in 1911, who restored it and bequeathed it to the State in 1926.

Near Ardglass Harbour. NGR: J 560372.

Kilclief Castle

Kilclief was built sometime between 1412 and 1433 as the summer residence of John Sely, the last Bishop and Abbot of Down. Few tower houses can be dated so precisely, but Bishop Sely gained much notoriety for openly living in "castro de Kylcleth" with a married woman. Although the Primate threatened him with suspension and excommunication, the Bishop obstinately persisted and was expelled from his offices. The castle was later garrisoned by the Crown and more recently was used as a farm granary. There is a blocked fireplace with a re-used 13th-century coffin-lid serving as a lintel.

4 km (2.5 miles) S of Strangford. NGR: J 597457.

Narrow Water Castle

Situated on a strategically important site where the Newry River narrows, this tower house was built by the Government around 1568 at a cost of £361. In 1570 it was described as having "two chambers and a cellar and a hall covered with straw and a stable nigh unto the said castle ... and nine cottages covered with earth within the precinct of the said castle". The walled bawn was extensively restored in the 19th century, but the modern entrance probably perpetuates the site of the original gate.

8 km (5 miles) SE of Newry. NGR: J 128194.

HOUSES

Castle Ward

One of the most interesting aspects of country house design lies in the decorative schemes adopted for the male and female spheres of the building; the drawing-room and boudoir are often feminine and adventurous in taste, while the hall and dining-room are predominantly conservative. Such divisions were generally confined to plasterwork and furnishings, but at Castle Ward they have been incorporated into the architecture itself.

Sadly, little evidence has survived relating to the building of the house, though it is clear that work began in 1761. It was commissioned by Bernard Ward, first Viscount Bangor, who began creating a "naturalistic" landscape park as a setting for his new house. Work was well underway when Mrs Delany visited in 1762 and expressed concern that its magnificent setting "should not be judiciously laid out. He wants taste and Lady Anne is so whimsical that I doubt her judgement. If they do not do too much they can't spoil the place for it hath every advantage from nature that can be desired." Mrs Delany need not have worried for the park was laid out in excellent taste, while the house is an attractive and highly accomplished piece of architecture.

After Bernard's death the estate was placed in Chancery due to the insanity of Nicholas, the second Viscount. Nicholas continued to live at Castle Ward with the second son, Edward, who had little money of his own and sank increasingly into poverty. He resorted to farming the park to make money and at one stage even tried selling bread at the gate. By 1827 the demesne was in a state of ruin. Much of the present decoration and furnishing consequently dates from the 1830s when the third Viscount refurbished the interior.

A special room is dedicated to the memory of Mary Ward (1827–69), one of the most fascinating people associated with Castle Ward – she was a botanical artist and outstanding naturalist who published a number of books connected with the microscope. In 1950 Castle Ward was given to the National Trust.

1.6 km (1 mile) W of Strangford. NGR: J 573494.

GARDENS

Castle Ward Park

An idyllic 800-acre landscape park overlooking Strangford Lough and the setting for the 1760s mansion. It includes yew terraces, the site of a canal between two replanted rows of limes and a long canal known as the Temple Water – the largest garden feature to survive from early 18th-century Ireland. The sunken Windsor Garden, close to the present house, once held an elaborate parterre, but the colourful bedding on its terraces largely retains its Victorian layout. Rows of cordylines and yews lead to a pinetum and rockery.

0.6 km (1 mile) W of Strangford. NGR: J 573494.

Castlewellan National Arboretum

Undoubtedly Ireland's foremost collection of mature trees, this arboretum was established by the fifth Earl of Annesley (1831–1909) in the Walled Garden close to his huge baronial castle. Subsequently it has expanded to cover over a hundred acres and is managed by the Forest Service. Now called the Annesley Garden, the Walled Garden is divided into two portions: the Upper Garden, originally built in the 1740s to cultivate kitchen produce, and the Lower Garden, laid out in the 1850s as a pleasure ground with terraces, a fountain and ornamental trees. The two areas are united by a formal axis down the centre, which in the Upper Garden is lined with herbaceous borders backed with clipped yew hedges.

The oldest trees in the garden are a pair of *Wellingtonia* planted in 1856, no less than three years after the species was first introduced. Close by is the mother tree of the golden Leyland cypress that came from here, but if that is not to every visitor's taste, there are countless other remarkable plants, including many old species of podocarpus, juniper, silver fir and picea. A magnificent avenue of late summer-flowering eucryphia and greenhouses with fuchsia, passiflora, ferns and phormiums are other features, while outside the walls is a large rhododendron garden, an extensive collection of spring-flowering trees and prodigious groupings of dwarf conifers. Signposts from here lead into the forests and around the magnificent lake. *Castlewellan, 6.5 km (4 miles) NW of Newcastle. NGR: J 335371.*

Mountstewart

Acknowledged as one of the premier gardens of Western Europe, Mount Stewart has an incomparable plant collection the youth of which is disguised by the exceptionally high humidity from the sea. It is largely the creation of Edith, Marchioness of Londonderry, who left behind a garden of 78 acres comprising formal garden areas, terracing, pergolas, pavilions, woodland gardens and a water garden encircling a large lake in the park, all still beautifully maintained by the National Trust.

The formal gardens surrounding the neo-classical house include the Italian Garden; it is divided by a wide grassy verge into two identical parterres and flanked on one side by the Dodo Terrace, decorated with amusing stone ornaments depicting political figures. Beyond is the Mairi Garden and the Spanish Garden with its oval pool, loggia and arches of Monterey cypress. South of the house lies the sunken garden, designed by Jekyll, and the Shamrock Garden, with topiary which includes the shapes of an Irish harp. From the adjacent Memorial Glade a path leads to the informal gardens, with many trees and shrubs which are universally envied. Here one can admire the many pittosporum varieties, the great banks of rhododendrons, the vigorous growths of *Weinmannia* and the masses of maples around the lake. On the slopes below the family cemetery there are many rare tender plants and marvellous views across the lake back towards the house. Before leaving, a visit should be made to the Temple of the Winds (c. 1785), magnificently sited above Strangford Lough. *8 km (5 miles) SE of Newtownards. NGR: J 552698.*

Rowallane

The impressive range of plants in this 52-acre garden are so skilfully grouped that they are as much a joy to the plantsman as to the artist. Although normally associated with spectacular spring-colour displays, Rowallane also has extensive collections of summer-flowering plants and boasts a fine collection of trees and wildflower meadows. Some of the most colourful displays lie in the Walled Garden beside the house, where there is a splendid collection of herbaceous plants, notably great clumps of *Meconopsis* and the National Collection of large-flowered *Penstemons*. There are some fine magnolias, *Viburnum plicatum tomentosum* "Rowallane", a collection of hydrangeas and a great display of primulas, including the vigorous hybrid *Primula* "Rowallane Rose". Visitors will also find the original *Chaenomeles x superba* "Rowallane" here, as well as the famous yellow cupped *Hypericum* "Rowallane" hybrid.

The undulating slopes outside the Walled Garden is home to a series of informal gardens all bursting with blossom. The Spring Ground is noted for its banks of azaleas and rhododendrons and the Stream Ground for its royal ferns and bog arums. The Hospital has a fine handkerchief tree and an immense *Desfontainea spinosa*, while through the Old Wood lies the restored Rock Garden accommodating a wide range of alpines, heathers and dwarf rhododendrons. Brilliant orange *Embothrium coccineum* flower at the Trio Hill, while wildflowers are profuse in the Pleasure Ground behind the house, amidst old trees and a restored Victorian bandstand. The house is the headquarters of the National Trust in Northern Ireland. *1 km (0.6 miles) S of Saintfield on the Downpatrick Road. NGR: J 109576.*

Seaforde

The Seaforde garden was created during the 1970s on the site of a walled Victorian flower garden on the perimeter of a beautiful demesne park. A good selection of echiums grow on the site of the former greenhouses and nearby stands a Mogul-style tower, a herb garden and Gothic arbour. A hornbeam maze occupies the central area and those reaching the centre will find an arbour with a statue of Diana. Flanking the maze are two avenues of shrubs containing the National Collection of eucryphias; at present there are nineteen cultivars of these fragrant, white-flowering shrubs. In the adjacent Pheasantry there is a magnificent Crimean pine, and visitors will find a butterfly house filled with tropical plants.
Near Seaforde on the Ballynahinch Road. NGR: J 403433.

Tollymore Arboretum

Arboretum in old demesne pleasure grounds with many stately trees: large silver firs, Douglas firs, tall giant redwood, Monterey pine, original *Picea abies* "Clanbrassilliana".
3 km (2 miles) N of Newcastle.

MUSEUMS/HERITAGE CENTRES

Ballycopeland Windmill

In the 18th and 19th centuries, the Irish countryside was dotted with windmills, their sails powering the millstones that ground the grain. Today only two restored windmills are left in Northern Ireland. The white-painted Ballycopeland Windmill, complete with majestic sails, is the only survivor of the many that once stood on the Ards peninsula, an ideal site. Built in the 1780s, this windmill was in operation until 1915.
1.6 km (1 mile) W of Millisle.

Brontë Homeland Interpretative Centre

Patrick Brontë, father of the famous Brontë sisters, was born near Rathfriland, County Down, in 1777. The story of the family is told at Drumballyroney church and schoolhouse, where Patrick first preached and taught. The centre includes displays on the Brontë family's history and connections with the area, complete with photographs and models. After seeing the centre, visitors can go on a tour of nearby sites connected with the family, including the remains of Patrick's birthplace cottage at Emdale, the site of the school where he taught at Glascar, and the cottage where his mother was brought up. The picnic site at Knockiveagh gives excellent views of the surrounding hills and landscapes where Patrick grew up.
Drumballyroney; 5 km (3 miles) NE of Rathfriland.

Burren Heritage Centre

Not to be confused with the Burren in County Clare, this converted national school, sited at the foot of the Mountains of Mourne, uses interpretative models, exhibitions and audio-visual aids to tell the story of the locality. In the main exhibition hall are models of prehistoric sites in the area and Neolithic tools. Many 18th- and19th-century artefacts recall social history. Also worth seeing in the area is the Mullaghbawn Folk Museum in the Ring of Gullion in south Armagh. The two-roomed thatched cottage highlights local history, landscape and wildlife.
Burren Heritage Centre: 3 km (2 miles) from turn-off between Narrow Water Castle and Warrenpoint. Mullaghbawn Folk Museum: 20 km (12 miles) SW of Newry.

Down County Museum

The museum, opened in 1984, is in the old Down County gaol, built between 1789 and 1796, the most complete surviving Irish gaol of its period. The gatehouses of the museum are occupied by the St Patrick Heritage Centre, which tells the story of

Ireland's patron saint through large-scale illustrations. St Patrick is reputedly buried in the graveyard of nearby Down Cathedral, while nearby is the reputed site of his first church at Saul. The nearby Downpatrick steam railway recreates the long-gone era of steam trains. There is also a railway museum.
Downpatrick.

Fergusons Linen Centre

Three separate centres tell the story of linen, once a mainstay of textile manufacturing in Northern Ireland and now enjoying a revival. Fergusons in Banbridge is the only maker in the world of double-damask linen and its exhibition centre relates both the story of linen and of the firm itself.
Banbridge.

Newry Museum

This small museum, located in the Arts Centre, has models of the town as it was in 1761 and in the 1930s, together with old photographs of the town. The highlight of the museum is the panelled room, decorated in the Georgian style, complete with two grandfather clocks. This room, and also an adjoining archway, were taken from an early 18th-century house when the building was being demolished.
Newry.

North Down Visitors and Heritage Centre

The outbuildings of Bangor Castle make an excellent setting for this historical endeavour, which is divided into several sections. In the early Christian section, the most important artefacts are the 9th-century Bangor bell and a handbell from the old monastic foundation. The centre also details the arrival of Scottish settlers in this area over 300 years ago and has an important collection of folio maps from that time. Nearer the present, Bangor's heyday as a seaside resort is recalled.
Bangor.

The Somme Centre

This centre, opened in 1994, examines Ireland's role in World War I, especially that of the three volunteer divisions raised in Ireland, the 10th and 16th (Irish) Divisions and the 36th (Ulster) Division. Visitors are taken on a guided tour, beginning with the Home Rule crisis in 1910. An audio-visual presentation then charts the development of the war between 1914 and 1916, focussing on Gallipolli and the Battle of the Somme. A front-line trench has been realistically created and visitors can also see a dramatic audio-visual recreation of the latter battle.
4 km (2.5 miles) N of Newtownards on Bangor Road.

Ulster Folk and Transport Museum

This extensive museum, much of it outdoors, tells the story of the North of Ireland's social and economic development, often through the recreation of old buildings and workshops. The outdoor museum covers over 60 acres and includes an 1820s' farmhouse from County Armagh, cottiers' houses from County Derry and County Tyrone, and a 19th-century farmhouse with outbuildings from County Antrim. Many examples of workshops have been transposed here. Other buildings include a rectory, a church and a market/courthouse. Since all the buildings were moved from their original sites and reconstructed here, they are totally authentic. A town area is being assembled to portray a small Ulster town with houses, shops, churches and school. The museum's farmland has many old implements and rare local breeds. There is also a strong textiles collection.

Transport is well represented, with one of the highlights being the schooner Result, built in Carrickfergus in 1893. A road transport gallery is being developed, while perhaps the single most impressive part of the whole site is the new Irish

Railway Collection. Not only have buildings been preserved, including sales kiosks from Portrush station and York Road station, Belfast, but also an impressive array of carriages and locomotives from all parts of Ireland. But of all this vast collection of railway material, by far the most extensive in Ireland, the star is undoubtedly "Maeve", the great steam locomotive built at Inchicore railway works, Dublin, in 1939. It ran until 1958, mostly on the Dublin–Cork line and achieved a record speed of 154 kph (96 mph). Road transport and aviation are also recorded in the Dalchoolin Gallery. Frequent themed exhibitions are held.

10 km (6 miles) NE of Belfast.

DUBLIN

CASTLES

Drimnagh Castle

Founded during the 13th century, Drimnagh Castle remained continuously occupied until 1953. It is a picturesque and modest-sized building, and its large flooded moat has recently been repaired as part of the castle's programme of restoration.

The moat probably dates from the late 13th century, but the castle is quite a hotch-potch of different periods. The gateway tower belongs largely to the 16th century, the stone mullioned windows are 17th century, while the entrance porch and stone staircase were added a century later. The great hall was restored in 1988 with a minstrel's gallery, arched sandstone fireplace and trussed oak roof. The formal garden was created in 1990 featuring plants known in Ireland during the 17th century.

1 km (0.6 miles) W of Crumlin Children's Hospital, Long Mile Road.

Dublin Castle

Fragments are all that remain of the great medieval fortress that once served as a symbol of Royal authority in Ireland and the centre of administration. Its construction began in 1204 when King John directed Meiler FitzHenry to make a castle "with good ditches and strong walls". Meiler chose a site on a ridge at the south-east corner of the city walls that was previously occupied by Henry II's "royal palace roofed with wattles" and possibly by a Hiberno-Norse forerunner. It was completed around 1228 and remained more or less intact until the 17th century when it was extensively rebuilt.

The castle was an outstanding example of a "keepless" castle and has been compared to contemporary French castles such as Le Coudray-Salbart. Its east and south walls rose above the natural fosse provided by the River Poddle (now underground), whose waters also fed an artificial moat on its north and west sides.

The castle had a comparatively uneventful history and only ever had to endure one siege, when Silken Thomas made an unsuccessful and rather disorganised attempt to capture it in 1534. For many centuries it was the official residence of the Lords Deputy and Lords Lieutenant of Ireland, the home of State councils, and sometimes Parliament and the Law Courts.

Off Castle Street, Dublin 2. NGR: O 154339.

Dunsoghly Castle

Considering the enormous number of castles in Ireland, it is perhaps surprising that only Dunsoghly has retained its original medieval trussed roof. This has survived because the castle, built around 1450, was continuously occupied until the 1870s by descendants of the same family, despite being cramped and uncomfortable by post-medieval standards. The topmost chamber of the south-west turret was used as a prison and is only accessible through an opening in the vault above it.

There is a small chapel to the south bearing the year 1573 over the door, the Instruments of the Passion and the initials of John Plunkett and his wife Genet Sarsfield. On the west and south are remains of earthwork defences put up during the warfare of the 1640s.

4 km (2.5 miles) NW of Finglas off the Slane Road. NGR: O 118430.

Swords Castle

Swords Castle was built as the manorial residence of the Archbishops of Dublin around 1200. It was never strong in the military sense, but covers a large walled area of nearly 1.5 acres. The adjoining chapel, built in the 13th century, was probably used as the Archbishop's private oratory. Other buildings, recorded for an inquisition in 1326, have now vanished, including the great hall.

The Archbishop abandoned Swords once a new palace was built at Tallagh in 1324 – a move no doubt encouraged by damage sustained during Bruce's campaign of 1317. By 1583, when briefly occupied by Dutch Protestants, it was described as "the quite spoiled old castle". It was used as a garden in the 19th century and sold after the Church of Ireland was disestablished.

Swords. NGR: O 182469.

HOUSES

Malahide Castle

Such was the troubled state of Ireland's past that few Irish country houses were ever continuously inhabited by the same family for more than a few centuries. A rare exception to this rule was Malahide Castle, home of the Talbots for 791 years from 1185 until 1976 when it was acquired by Dublin County Council.

The core of the medieval castle is the oak room approached by a winding stone staircase and lit by Gothic windows added in 1820; the room contains fine carved panelling, mostly of 16th-century date, which has darkened to a gleaming ebony. According to tradition, the Flemish carving of the coronation of the virgin over the mantelpiece disappeared when the castle was occupied by the Cromwellian Miles Corbet between 1653 and 1660. Fortunately for the Talbots, the unsavory Corbet was one of the regicides who signed the death warrant of Charles I and after the Restoration he was duly hung, drawn and quartered at Tyburn. The Talbots returned to Malahide and the figure of the virgin made a miraculous reappearance above the fireplace.

The great hall was added to the castle around 1475; unique in Ireland, it not only retained its original form but also remained in domestic use as a dining-room until 1976. On the morning of the Battle of the Boyne fourteen Talbot cousins, all followers of James II, gathered here to dine – none survived the carnage of the day. The magnificent 35-foot table comes from Powerscourt but many other items are original, including the nucleus of the Talbot ancestral portraits. Two fine drawing-rooms, with splendid rococo plasterwork ceilings, are famous for their wonderful 19th-century painted orange-terracotta walls that many have apparently attempted to reproduce without success over the years.

The famous gardens around the castle are largely the creation of the late Lord Talbot de Malahide; they have been well restored by Dublin County Council and are certainly worth visiting. Also in the castle yard is the Cyril Fry Model Railway Exhibition with its model engines, rolling stock and replicas of railway stations in Dublin, Belfast and Cork.

Malahide, 14 km (9 miles) N of Dublin. NGR: O 220452.

Newbridge House

Although located within a few miles of Dublin's advancing urban sprawl, Newbridge House still manages to preserve its character of a secluded 18th-century gentleman's residence set in a wooded demesne. The house features a series of beautifully proportioned rooms, each retaining their original furnishings thanks to an agreement between the Cobbe family and its new owners, Dublin City Council, who acquired the property in 1986 and have since embarked on a major restoration of the house, yards and parkland. The front façade is particularly attractive, a facing of pink ashlar giving it a lovely warm glow.

For many years Newbridge was believed to be the work of Richard Castle, but we now know that it was designed by the prominent Dublin architect George Semple and built between 1749 and 1750 for Archbishop Charles Cobbe. Despite a limited intellectual capacity, Cobbe enjoyed rapid promotion and became Archbishop of Dublin in 1742. His portrait hangs in the hall and shows him wearing a long grey wig and a black sleeveless surplice over the full lawn sleeves of a bishop.

The dining-room is dominated by an original black Kilkenny marble chimney-piece and a magnificent chandelier. Other rooms include the library, with its baroque ceiling depicting the four seasons, and the "Mr Cobbe's Museum or Cabinet of Curiosities" – a curio room dating from 1790 and containing a remarkable display of souvenirs and trophies collected by various members of the family on their numerous travels abroad, particularly in India. The red drawing-room is a vast room, 42.9 feet by 25.6 feet, with no less than forty-five pictures, many bought on the advice of art connoisseur Matthew Pilkington. A friend of Cobbe's, he is best remembered for his spectacular divorce suit with his wife, the amusing and naughty Laetitia, who was described by Virginia Woolf in an essay as "shady, shifting and adventurous". Mrs Pilkington's autobiography is on display in one of the glass cases in the house.

The kitchen is fitted with its original screen wall, dresser with jugs and dishes, 19th-century iron range, whiskey still, duck press, rat traps, numerous copper pots, jelly moulds and wooden tubs for salting meat. In the laundry visitors can inspect a range of equipment used to wash, dry, iron and mend clothes. In the cobbled yard lies the dairy with its marble niches for maturing cheeses, the demesne workers' kitchen, a forge and a carpenter's shop. On display in the coach house is the state carriage made in London in 1790 for "Black Jack" FitzGibbon, the Lord Chancellor of Ireland and a relation of the Cobbes. The coach was itself black until restored to its former gold magnificence – even the fresco panels had been painted out, probably for the funeral of Queen Victoria.

Donabate, 17.5 km (11 miles) N of Dublin. NGR: O Z14501.

GARDENS

Ardgillan Demesne Gardens

Once appropriately named "Prospect House", this charming neo-Gothic country house gazes out to the open sea across a sweeping parkland. The approach to the Walled Garden passes a large rose garden overlooked by fine Victorian conservatory, recently rescued and brought here from a nearby house. The Walled Garden is subdivided by walls and hedges into a series of compartments containing, among other things, a herb garden, an Alpine garden, a *potager* laid out in neat box hedges, a Robinsonian garden and a four-seasons garden. There is also a cottage garden, a fine herbaceous border and a remarkable alcove wall, intended to provide protection for the fruit trees. A small garden museum is presently being added to this well-maintained garden.

Lusk, 24 km (15 miles) N of Dublin off the Belfast Road.

The Dillon Garden

This long rectangular walled garden is screened with trees and is focussed around an immaculate central lawn; there are mixed borders of shrubs and herbaceous perennials with raised beds provided for such floral rarities as lady's slipper orchids.

A plantsman's garden of international fame completes the arrangement.
45 Sandyford Road, Ranelagh, Dublin 6.

Fernhill

The great banks of rhododendron species and cultivars are undoubtedly the great glory of Fernhill in spring and early summer, but this 40-acre garden has much to offer, not least its superb location overlooking Dublin Bay. It contains a comprehensive collection of trees and shrubs, a water garden, rockery, heather bank, fernery and large drifts of spring bulbs. A lovely light woodland includes splendid Wellingtonias, Scots pines and other impressive trees, such as a 79-foot-high *Tsuga heterophylla*. Some of the best rhododendrons can be found – aside from the older *R. arboreum* varieties, the area has fine examples of *R. Genestierianum*, bright blue forms of *R. augustinii* and the pink flowering R. "Fernhill Silver". There is a well-developed *Michelia doltsopa* from China, outstanding specimens of camellia, leptospermum, pieris and magnolia, and a laurel lawn – a rare survival from Victorian days. An amazing mixture of pieris, cordylines, bulbs, perennials, rhododendrons, azaleas, as well as a variety of alpines can be found on the rockery, while the adjacent heather bank has amongst the erica, varieties of bergenia, most notably the local *Bergenia* "Ballawley". Mrs Walker's famed collection of primulas lies near the Water Garden, whose banks proffer verdant plantings of ferns, pulmonarias and many candelabra primulas. The herbaceous borders in the hedged Kitchen Garden offer additional summer colour, as does a small Edwardian rose garden whose clipped box hedges contain beds of floribunda and old hybrid tea varieties.
Sandyford, 13 km (8 miles) S of Dublin on the Enniskerry Road. NGR: O 183257.

Iveagh Gardens

Gardens designed by Ninian Niven for the International Exhibition Palace of 1865. The great exhibition building was subsequently demolished and the gardens became attached to Iveagh House. Niven's gardens were all but lost until recent years, when an extensive programme of restoration has been embarked upon. Victorian fountains have been restored, the maze and rosarium replanted and work is ongoing upon the American Garden, rooteries, the Italian parterre and a huge rockery.
Clonmel Street, Dublin 2.

Malahide Castle Gardens (Talbot Botanic Garden)

At Malahide the alkalinity of the soil has given prominence to the many lime-tolerant genera so often bypassed in Irish gardens. The enormous range of non-ericaceous plants is particularly admired for its collections of ceanothus, clematis, crocosmia, eryngium, escallonia, euphorbia, hebe, hypericum, olearia and pittosporum. The gardens cover 20 acres, including a 4-acre walled garden, forming part of a 250-acre park acquired by Dublin County Council in 1976 following the death of the garden's creator, Lord Talbot de Malahide.

From the West Lawn in front of the castle, passing just beyond a blue conifer, *Cupressus glabra* "Pyramidalis", visitors will enter the main shrubberies, divided by a network of grass rides and interlinking paths. Here lies a large-leaved *Meliosma dillineifolia* and the rarely seen *Aralia spinosa*. The Walled Garden, subdivided into separate sections, has cottage-type plants, climbers and a small collection of tender species. There are raised beds for alpines, a reconstructed sunken greenhouse and a lawn of shrubberies with a number of garryas raised by Lord Talbot, including *Garrya x issaquahensis* "Pat Ballard". A peach house with a selection of tender climbing plants lies along the south wall in addition to a shrubbery of exotic plants: *Clematis* "Etoile Rose", *Azara dentata*, the silk tree *Albizia julibrissin* "Rosea" and the yellow-flowering *Fremontodendron* "California Glory".
Malahide, 14.5 km (9 miles) N of Dublin. NGR: O 220452.

National Botanic Gardens

Ireland's premier botanical and horticultural establishment occupies a beautiful 48-acre site on the banks of the Tolka with over 20,000 different plant species and cultivars. The soil is heavy alkaline boulder clay, which confines the growing of calcifuge plants such as rhododendrons to specially prepared peat beds, but the garden includes a wide range of habitats with special areas devoted to roses, ground-cover plants, economic and poisonous plants, native plants and herbs and vegetables. Glasnevin also houses a large rockery, a bog garden, a wild garden and a double, curving herbaceous border which is a marvellous sight in summer.

More plants are grown in the Victorian glasshouses, including the recently restored curvilinear range, built by Richard Turner and completed in 1848. The Great Palm House, built in 1884, contains a tropical tree collection and is notable for its cycads. Flanking the Aquatic House with its Amazonian water lily lies the Cactus and Succulent House and the Fern House, the latter being divided into separate compartments for tree ferns and tropical species. Here grows the native but rare Killarney fern *Trichomanes speciosum* and the Australian tree fern *Todea barbara*, reputed to be 400 years old. One of the most popular sights is a cultivar of the China rose *R. chinensis* "Old Blush", raised from a cutting which, according to tradition, was the rose that inspired Thomas Moore to write his famous ballad.
Glasnevin, 1.6 km (1 mile) N of Dublin. NGR: O 152373.

National War Memorial

Remarkable war memorial garden designed by Lutyens in 1930, restored and replanted in 1988. The War Memorial Gardens are dedicated to the nearly 50,000 Irish soldiers who died in World War I. All their names are listed in the Book Rooms.
Kilmainham/Islandbridge.

St Anne's Rose Garden

Several acres of a well maintained formal rose garden set in old parkland.
Clontarf, Dublin.

MUSEUMS/HERITAGE CENTRES

Chester Beatty Library and Gallery of Oriental Art

This repository of Islamic and Asian art, one of the most important in the world, is now located in Dublin Castle (see below).

Civic Museum

One of this small museum's claims to fame is the head of Lord Nelson, from the O'Connell Street statue blown up in 1966. Once the city's Assembly House, the museum, run by Dublin Corporation, has despite its lack of size frequent and interesting exhibitions on many aspects of Dublin life.
South William Street, beside Powerscourt Town House.

Custom House

The Custom House, beside the River Liffey in central Dublin, is one of Ireland's great architectural masterpieces, designed by James Gandon and completed in 1791. The visitor centre details the history of the building and the Customs service.
Custom House Quay, Dublin 1.

Dalkey Heritage Centre

A 15th-century castle in Castle Street in the centre of Dalkey has been restored. The centre tells the story of Dalkey's progression from ancient to modern times.
Dalkey, 5 km (3 miles) SE of Dun Laoghaire.

Dublin Castle

Originally built in the 13th century on a Viking site, the castle served as a military fortress, prison, courts of law and centre of British administration in Ireland for 700 years. Visitors can see the State Apartments, which include the grand staircase leading up to the Battleaxe Landing, and the Church of the Most Holy Trinity, designed by Francis Johnston, architect of the GPO. The Company of Goldsmiths, the last remaining medieval guild in the city, is housed in the complex and has interesting memorabilia, including paintings and documents. Dublin Castle is already the new location for the Garda Siochana Museum, with many fascinating relics of Irish police history.
Off Castle Street, Dublin 2.

Dublin City Libraries

Dublin has a remarkable collection of libraries and archives, enough material to satisfy any search for information. Dublin Corporation City Archives, located in the Civic Museum, offer access to considerable material about Dublin. The archives' stock includes a complete set of Thom's directories on the city from 1846 to the present day, and Wilson's directories, the predecessor to Thom's, begun in the 18th century. The Irish Architectural Archive has books, newspaper and magazine clippings on Ireland's architectural heritage, not just the golden era of the 18th century, but right up to present times.

Marsh's Library, near St Patrick's Cathedral, was built in the early 18th century as the first public library in Ireland and has a collection of 25,000 books, many of them rare. Marsh's also has an interesting conservation section. The National Library has many first editions of works by Irish writers, practically every book ever published in Ireland and almost every newspaper and magazine. Themed exhibitions are staged here. The National Archive has many State papers and documents. Pearse Street Library has a wealth of printed information on Dublin history and the Gilbert Collection of 18th-century books on the city. The Royal Irish Academy, whose elegant building near the Mansion House has been thoroughly refurbished, has many rare medieval manuscripts and other early Irish material. Trinity College has two main libraries, the old and the new; the Long Room in the early 18th-century library is the most impressive. Its most famous treasure, the Book of Kells, is on show in the Colonnades Gallery beneath the Long Room. The Dublin Writers' Museum details many famous writers with Dublin connections.

City Archives: Civic Museum, South William Street, Dublin 2.
Irish Architectural Archive: 73 Merrion Square, Dublin 2.
Marsh's Library: St Patrick's Close, Dublin 8.
National Archive: Bishop Street, Dublin 8.
National Library: Kildare Street, Dublin 8.
Pearse Street Library: Dublin 2.
Royal Irish Academy: Dawson Street, Dublin 2.
Trinity College: Dublin 2.
Dublin Writers' Museum: Parnell Square, Dublin 1.

Dublinia

Between 1875 and 1983, Irish bishops gathered in the Church of Ireland Synod Hall beside Christ Church Cathedral. This now houses the Dublinia Heritage Centre which depicts life in medieval Dublin from 1170 to the closure of the monasteries in 1540. The entrance to the exhibition area features such topics as the Black Death plague, the languages used in medieval Dublin and the building of Dublin Castle. Some of the models are decidedly life-like, especially that of the plague sufferer, while the background audio of old Dublin sounds is also realistic. Life-size reconstructions include a merchant's house, with a leather-worker outside making shoes, and a quayside setting.

More Dublin history, 1,000 years of it, can be seen in the Dublin Experience, the elaborate audio-visual presentation in Trinity College.

Dublinia: beside Christ Church Cathedral.

The Dublin Experience: Thomas Davis Theatre, Trinity College.

Findlater's Museum

Findlater's grocery stores were renowned in the Dublin area from the late 19th century to the 1960s, but were superseded by the supermarket era. Many artefacts from the old counter service stores are preserved in the museum at present-day Findlater's, a wine company located in the vaults beneath the old Harcourt Street railway station. The museum details the Findlater family's Scottish antecedents, its connections with Robert Burns the poet, and contains many photographs and other memorabilia from its chain of shops. The atmosphere of old-style shopping is enhanced at the entrance to the company's premises, where a double-fronted shop façade has been recreated in replica.

Harcourt Street, Dublin 2.

Guinness Hopstore

Guinness and Dublin are synonymous; the dark brew has been produced on this site since 1759. The Hopstore is an ingeniously converted warehouse that contains an impressive multimedia presentation on the history of Guinness, which highlights its contribution to Irish social and literary life. This presentation is complemented by the brewing gallery that depicts the traditional and contemporary methods of making Guinness and an extensive display of Guinness advertising material, past and present. Although the centre has a lot of old equipment and a fair amount of technical information, it all slips down as easily as the familiar pint. On the ground floor, visitors can enjoy a free sample. The building is also used for frequent visiting exhibitions.

Crane Street, off Thomas Street, Dublin 8.

Howth Transport Museum

This museum, in the grounds of Howth Castle, has fine examples of old vehicles crammed into every corner: public transport, commercial and public utilities and military transport. Most striking exhibit is the fully restored double-deck tram, Number 9, from the Hill of Howth tramway, which ran from 1902 until 1959. Alongside it, but less glamorous, is a standard Dublin double-deck tram which was in service from 1928 until the Dublin tramway system closed down in 1949. One of the world's oldest electric tramway cars is being restored; it dates from about 1883 and was used on the Portrush and Giant's Causeway tramway, which also closed in 1949. A double-deck green-painted Dublin bus, once part of a familiar fleet in the city through the 1950s and 1960s, is complemented by two buses (painted blue and cream), one double-deck, the other single-deck, that once belonged to the Great Northern Railway Company.

On Dublin side of Howth village, 0.8 km (0.5 miles) past turn for Howth Lodge Hotel.

James Joyce Museum

The James Joyce industry is flourishing in Dublin as never before. Following the Joycean trail through Dublin can provide an interesting if arduous itinerary, but one essential is the Joyce Museum at Sandycove, County Dublin. Once a Martello tower, built in the early 19th century against the threat of a Napoleonic invasion, Joyce lived here briefly in 1904 and described it in the first chapter of Ulysses. Thanks to Sylvia Beach, the first publisher of the book, the tower was reopened as a museum in 1962. In a recent refurbishment, the upstairs room has been reconstructed to look exactly as it did in Ulysses. The new James Joyce Cultural Centre in Dublin city centre, in a restored 18th-century town house, also has material on Joyce, plus an ongoing cultural programme on his work.

Joyce Museum: Sandycove, 3 km (2 miles) S of Dun Laoghaire.
Joyce Cultural Centre: 35 North Great George's Street, Dublin 1.

Kilmainham Gaol

This grim building has been restored, although the cells have been left as they were; a new exhibition building has been added to help tell the story of Ireland's struggle for independence between the 1780s and the early 1920s.
Kilmainham Gaol, near the Royal Hospital.

Malahide Castle

This great castle, now in public ownership, was home to the Talbot family for nearly 700 years. The house includes the original 14th-century tower, the 15th-century Great Hall and the reception rooms dating from the 18th century. The rooms are hung with many portraits of Irish notables and many original furnishings are still in place.

In a nearby building the Fry Model Railway Museum has many models of old trams, steam locomotives and boats on a huge working circuit, together with details on the development of transport in Ireland over the past 150 years.
Malahide, 14 km (9 miles) N of Dublin.

National Museum

The National Museum has two main sites, the original museum in Kildare Street in the city centre, and the converted Collins Barracks in Benburb Street, near Heuston Station. The museum in Kildare Street has a façade that exactly mirrors that of the National Library, from which it is separated by the entrance to Leinster House, home of the Dáil and Seanad.

The emphasis here is on prehistoric material, including the Lurgan bog boat, dug out of a bog in County Galway early in the 20th century, and the oldest surviving Irish boat, made about 2500 BC. The museum also concentrates on AD 800 to 1200, which includes the Viking period. Medieval treasures include the Ardagh hoard from County Limerick, 12th-century book shrines, and a collection of highly decorated croziers, including one from Lismore, County Waterford, made about 1100. There's another entrance to the museum from Merrion Row, while the approach to the Natural History Museum is from Merrion Square West. The new site was once Europe's oldest military barracks and it has been imaginatively transformed into a brand new museum, containing such sections as Irish furniture, silver and military memorabilia.
Kildare Street, Dublin 2; Benburb Street, Dublin 7.

National Print Museum

This museum recalls the long and now defunct history of traditional hot-metal printing. It's set in the former garrison chapel at Beggar's Bush; the barracks here were used by the British military until their withdrawal in 1922. The ground floor of the museum has examples of old printing machinery, including hand presses, hot-metal typesetting machines and proofing presses. The earliest piece of equipment is from the 18th century, one of the first examples of automation in the printing craft – a hand caster which produced a single letter of type. The mezzanine floor shows the progression of printing right up to the present day, using display cabinets of material and videos.

Also in the Beggar's Bush complex is the Irish Labour History Society museum, which depicts episodes from trade union history, with photographs, news clippings and other archive material.
Beggar's Bush, Haddington Road, Dublin 4. (Off Northumberland Road.)

Number 29

This four-storey house, complete with basement, has been completely restored and recreated in the style of the 1790–1820 period when it was the home of a well-off wine merchant's widow. The house is owned by the Electricity Supply Board and the restoration was supervised by the National Museum of Ireland. Totally refurbished from the kitchen in the basement to the attic, the house includes servants' quarters, nursery and more formal rooms.

29 Lower Fitzwilliam Street, corner of Merrion Square and Upper Mount Street, Dublin 2.

Old Jameson Distillery

Anyone who remembers the old Irish Whiskey Corner just off Smithfield will be amazed at this new museum, which has far more space and is far grander in concept. A whole whiskey distillery has been recreated and you can see all the old equipment for yourself, including a working mash tun, original copper stills, an old wooden fermentation vessel, a working bottling line and a reconstructed maturing warehouse. There's also an audio-visual presentation. The whole history of Irish whiskey since the 6th century is traced and you can taste the modern product.

Bow Street, Smithfield, Dublin 7.

Pearse Museum

This museum, in St Enda's Park, once housed the school run in the early 20th century by Patrick Pearse, leader of the 1916 Easter Rising. The museum includes historical data and documentation, as well as displays on Irish flora and fauna and an audio-visual presentation on Pearse, the man and his work.

Grange Road, Rathfarnham, Dublin 16. 10 km (6 miles) S of city centre.

Phoenix Park Visitor Centre

The centre tells the story of Phoenix Park, Europe's largest park, which was created as a deer park in 1662 by the Duke of Ormond. A audio-visual presentation introduces visitors to the centre, which details the many historical events that took place in the park, including the assassination of Lord Frederick Cavendish, Chief Secretary of Ireland and his deputy, Thomas Henry Burke, in 1882. The many great meetings that have taken place here are also highlighted, including the Land League meeting of 1880, attended by 30,000. At the 1932 Eucharistic Congress, a quarter of a million men walked in procession to the Mens' Mass, while when Pope John Paul II came to the park in 1979, over a million people attended. The Papal cross can still be seen. The park still has its deer herds; the flora and fauna are well documented. Exhibition area. Nature trails.

Nearby is a restored early 17th-century tower house, once part of the old Papal Nunciature. The recreation of the roof timbers, using oak from the park, is impressive.

Phoenix Park, Dublin 7.

Plunkett Education Museum

This small museum in the former stables of Rathmines Castle, which now houses the Church of Ireland College of Education, gives a useful insight into 19th-century classroom life. The museum is named after William Plunkett, the Archbishop of Dublin who brought the Protestant schools into the national school system. The recreation of an old classroom is complete with desks, a peat fire and attendance book.

Upper Rathmines Road, Dublin 6.

Waterways Visitor Centre

The first artificial waterway in Ireland was dug near Lough Corrib in the 12th century. Subsequently 18th- and 19th-century canal builders constructed waterways all over the country, including the Grand and Royal canals, linking Dublin and the Shannon, and the Ulster Canal, connecting Lough Neagh with the Erne system. Interest in inland waterways has greatly revived and the Royal Canal, closed for navigation in 1961, is now fully restored for most of its length. The three-storey Waterways Centre, modernistic in its exterior and interior design, sits in the Grand Canal basin just off the River Liffey. A large relief map of Ireland shows all existing canals and also the nine canals for which restoration is planned. Other topics include canal breaches, the life of a canal family and recreations, fish and wildlife on canals. There's even a model of a Boyne coracle.

Also on a waterborne theme, the National Maritime Museum is located in the former Mariners' church overlooking the great harbour of Dun Laoghaire. Its exhibits include a French longboat captured during the abortive Bantry Bay invasion in 1796, the great optic, still working, from the Baily lighthouse on the other side of Dublin Bay and many models of different types of ships and boats, plus much memorabilia.
National Waterways Centre: off Pearse Street, Dublin 2.
National Maritime Museum: Dun Laoghaire.

FERMANAGH

CASTLES

Castle Balfour

When Captain Nicholas Pynnar visited Lisnaskea in 1619 he found "great numbers of men at work" building a 70-foot-square bawn and a "castle of the same length, of which one half is built two storeys high, and is to be three storeys and a half high". No definite trace of the bawn survives, but the gaunt ruins of the castle, built by the Scottish planter Sir James Balfour on the site of an important Maguire stronghold, still dominate the town. Just inside the entrance lies a timber stair giving access to the great hall on the first floor. On the ground floor are barrel-vaulted service rooms including a kitchen with a big fireplace and circular brick-built oven.

The castle was refortified in 1652 by Ludlow, the famous commander-in-chief of Cromwell's Irish armies. It was dismantled during the troubles of 1689 but reoccupied by the Balfours and later passed to the Townleys. The building ceased to be inhabited after a fire in 1803 and was acquired by the Crichtons of Crom in 1821.
Lisnaskea. NGR: H 362337.

Crom Castle

Romantic ensemble of ruins and sham ruins set in exquisite parkland on the shores of Lough Erne. At the core of the complex are the remains of a castle built in 1611 by a Scottish planter, Michael Balfour, which in 1629 comprised a bawn 61 feet square with walls 15 feet high, two flankers and a house of "lime and stone" 22 feet square. In 1644 it was acquired by the Crichtons, ancestors of the Earls of Erne, and later enlarged so that the dwelling occupied the whole area of the bawn. It successfully withstood two ferocious Jacobite sieges in 1689, but later succumbed to an accidental fire in 1764 and was never rebuilt.

Today the remains of the castle comprise two gables and a flanker, with the remainder surviving only as foundations. In the 1830s these ruins were transformed into a picturesque folly with the addition of ruined walls and towers forming a sham bawn. Impressive battlemented terraces were also built around the garden to the south, where the famous pair of 400-year-old yews stand, one male and one female, at the site of the original entrance to the plantation castle garden.
Crom Demesne 6.5 km (4 miles) W of Newtownbutler. NGR: H 363238.

Enniskillen Castle

All roads in Fermanagh converge on Enniskillen, which commands a vital strategic crossing of the Erne between the Upper and Lower lakes. The first castle was built here around 1415 by Hugh "the Hospitable" Maguire but was retaken many times by the O'Donnells, the O'Neills and the English, until wrecked by Niall Garbh O'Donnell in 1602. The castle became the focus of a plantation town after 1607, when William Cole proceeded to build "a fair house upon the foundation of the old castle with other convenient houses for store and munition". This withstood a Jacobite siege in 1690 and remained the Cole family residence until a fire in 1710; the ruined castle was refurbished as a barracks during the 1790s and remained in military occupation until 1950.

The bawn had two circular and two rectangular flanker towers, but only the south flanker now survives – the so-called Watergate – one of the most photographed buildings in Ulster. It has a three-storey façade with stepped Irish battlements and a pair of round conical-roofed turrets. As tall turrets are a feature of late 16th-century architecture in Scotland, it has been argued that the Maguires built it in the 1580s using Scottish masons. Most authorities, however, believe the Watergate was constructed around 1616–19, though it is difficult to imagine a planter like Cole, who did not even own the castle until 1620, spending much-needed resources on such a refined architectural feature just to make the castle look more impressive from the water.

The castle keep now appropriately houses the regimental museum of the Royal Inniskilling Fusiliers. On the east side of the complex stands the recently constructed Heritage Centre.

Enniskillen. NGR: H 231442.

Monea Castle

Few castle ruins so readily engage the imagination as the picturesquely sited Monea – undoubtedly the most complete and best-preserved of all the Plantation castles of Ulster. Building commenced in 1616 by the Reverend Malcolm Hamilton. Shortly afterwards it was described by Pynnar as "a strong castle of lime and stone being 54 feet long and 20 feet broad". The bawn, comprising "a wall 9 feet in height and 300 feet in circuit" was added shortly before Hamilton was promoted to become Archbishop of Cashel in 1623.

Monea's history is less dramatic than nearby Tully. During the 1641 rebellion it was attacked by Rory Maguire, who "slew and murthered eight Protestants" here, but evidently failed to capture the castle. In 1688 it was occupied by Gustavus Hamilton, the Governor of Enniskillen, who had incurred enormous financial losses in the Williamite wars. His greatly impoverished wife and children continued to live at Monea, but had to sell the estate in 1704. A few decades later the castle was gutted by fire and was subsequently abandoned. In the last century "a weird woman named Bell McCabe took her residence in a vault beneath one of the towers" until she was evicted by the proprietor, who feared she "might be found dead on the wretched premises" and that some inquiries might ensue.

9.5 km (6 miles) NW of Enniskillen and 1.6 km (1 mile) E of St Molaise's Church. NGR: H 165494.

Tully Castle

Ireland is full of roofless ruins, but few have had such a tragically brief history as the beautifully sited Plantation castle of Tully. Built between 1612 and 1615 for Sir John Hume, it was gutted and abandoned in the 1641 rebellion. The castle had been surrendered to Rory Maguire on Christmas Eve 1641 by Lady Hume on condition of safe conduct for the local Protestant settlers who had sought refuge with her. However, the "rebels having stripped the inhabitants, except Lady Hume, of all their clothes, imprisoned them in the vaults and cellars" of the castle. The men were bound hand and foot and "thrown into the courtyard where they lay all night". The next day (Christmas Day) the Maguires massacred all sixteen men and sixty-nine women and children, sparing only the Humes. They then pillaged and burnt the castle, which has remained a ruin to this day.

The Maguires would have had difficulty investing the castle by force as it was well protected. When the Commissioners visited the place in 1622 they found it had "a bawne of stone and lime 99 feet long, 9 feet broad, 10 feet high, with 4 flankers.

There is also within the bawne a strong castle 54 feet long, 19 feet broad, 3 storeys high, covered with thatch." Of this, the stronghouse survives to almost full height, while the bawn wall and its rectangular flankers are ruined except for the north-east side.

A ten-year programme of repair followed the acquisition of the castle by the Department of Environment in 1974. Excavation revealed that the bawn was divided up by cobbled paths suggesting the use of this area as a garden. In 1988 formal beds were created within these paths using plants known in Ireland during the 17th century. *On the shore of Lough Erne, 5 km (3 miles) N of Derrygonnelly off the Belleek road. NGR: H 186599.*

HOUSES

Castle Coole

By the end of the 18th century the classicism of Palladio with its Renaissance interpretations of Roman buildings had been replaced by the neo-classical movement proclaiming the primitive virtues, simplicity and tranquil grandeur of Greek architecture. Although Castle Coole still has echoes of Palladianism in its balustraded roof parapets, Venetian windows and centre block with wings, it is without doubt the most perfect neo-classical country house in the British Isles, the masterpiece of James Wyatt whose brilliant adoption of earlier designs resulted in a monumental, masculine and chaste house enhanced by a gleaming white façade of Portland stone. Its magnificence so impressed the French traveller de Latocraye in 1797 that he considered this "superb palace" to be too splendid for ordinary mortals, remarking that it was better "to leave temples to the gods".

The demesne lands of Castle Coole originally belonged to the Maguires; Roger Atkinson, an English adventurer, built a castle close to the lake shore. The property changed hands a number of times until James Corry replaced the castle in 1709 with a fine Queen Anne house, whose garden layout is still visible from the present house together with its canal and splendid oak avenue, planted in 1725.

Armar Lowry-Corry, later Earl of Belmore, determined to build a much grander house and work levelling the site began in 1788; the following year Dublin architect Richard Johnson submitted plans and work commenced. Seven months later, Lord Belmore transferred patronage to James Wyatt, who adopted Johnson's plan. No expense was spared in getting the finest materials and craftsmen available. Portland stone was specially shipped from Dorset for the exterior cladding, and the gangs of imported artificers on site must have seemed like a veritable factory – fourteen joiners, twenty-five stone cutters, twenty-six stone masons, ten stone sawyers, seventeen carpenters and eighty-three labourers. When completed the cost amounted to £54,000, nearly twice the original estimate, with the result that the first Earl found himself in debt and unable to furnish all of the principal rooms. This task was thus undertaken by his son, who brought up the leading Dublin upholsterer of the time, John Preston of Henry Street, at a cost of over £17,000. The house was furnished and decorated "in a bold and opulent Grecian manner" between 1807 and 1825. In 1817 Sir Richard Morrison was engaged to build the impressive stableyard, though the vaulted tunnel linking the yard to the basement had been completed in 1790.

The sense of proportion, spaciousness and high-quality craftsmanship that visitors will experience in the entrance hall is repeated throughout the house. Flanking the saloon are the elegant dining- and drawing-rooms which interconnect to form an enfilade, or cross axis. The decoration of the dining-room seems to have changed little since Wyatt's day and still contains much of the furniture. The drawing-room has been restored by the National Trust to its Regency appearance. The boudoir, which was used by the women of the house for sewing, reading, talking and playing the piano, is an intimate and particularly attractive room whose original early 19th-century wallpaper, curtains, draperies and valance have been faithfully reproduced by the National Trust. Opposite lies the sumptuous state bedroom with its magnificent canopied bed and flame silk hangings supplied in anticipation of a visit by King George IV in 1821. Closed for over four years, this room is happily once again on public view and is one of the wonders of Castle Coole.

The National Trust acquired the house in 1951 and between 1980 and 1991 spent over four million pounds restoring the building and redecorating the interior. The present Earl of Belmore lives in a new house sited in the walled garden. It is said that the Grey-lag Geese, which have been at Castle Coole since 1700, will only go when the Belmores do. Except for some hardship during Hurricane Debbie in 1961, the flock has never shown any desire to leave, and the geese remain a wonderful sight on the lake. *Just SE of Enniskillen on the main Belfast road. NGR: H 260430.*

Florence Court

Few country houses can rival the wildly romantic parkland setting of Florence Court or its irresistibly attractive golden-grey façade, whose baroque composition of rustications, balustrades, pedimented niches, lugged surrounds and deep-set quoins has an ethereal, almost bucolic quality.

The original house at Florence Court was begun around 1718 by Sir John Cole, whose ancestors came from Devonshire during the reign of Queen Elizabeth and lived at Enniskillen Castle until it was burnt in 1710. Cole's "very costly and sumptuous building", which he named after his wife Florence Wrey, was built in what was then "a majestic wildness ... so wild that it was scarce inhabited by any human creatures but ye O's and Mac's, who ranged through the woods like so many freebooters pillaging all that came in their way".

The building's early appearance is conjectural, but its basement was evidently retained for the present house, which was erected some time during the 1750s by the first Cole's son, John Cole, the first Lord Mount Florence. His tall three-storey seven-bay block, which appears to have been built in two stages and completed by 1764, has a heavily enriched front façade, while the sides and back are plain by comparison – a characteristic feature of 18th-century Irish houses. Once completed, the house was given an appropriate Brownian parkland setting between 1778 and 1780 by William King, probably the head gardener at the time, replacing straight tree-lined avenues and other features of a formal layout that had been created in the 1720s.

The large segmental arch at the rear of the hall, which opens onto the magnificent grand staircase, once had a partition wall and double doorcase, but in 1955 this was removed in the mistaken belief that it was a 19th-century addition. In fact, this arch was probably blocked around 1760 when the rear of the house was remodelled. Great panels of swirling foliage decorate the walls of the staircase hall with a Gothic cornice of cusped and ogee arches. Sadly, the elaborate drawing-room ceiling was lost in the fire of 1955, but the ceiling in the dining-room survives and is one of the best examples of rococo plasterwork outside of Dublin. It is composed of symmetrically arranged and naturally rendered scrolls of foliage, birds, rocaille work, shells and flamboyant palmiers. The centrepiece is an oval panel containing an eagle in high relief representing Zeus, who holds his thunderbolt and hovers in the midst of a stormy empyrean, surrounded by the heads of four cherubs vigorously puffing the winds to the four corners of the earth.

Visitors who look closely at the dining-room ceiling will notice some of the small holes drilled during the 1955 fire to allow the water pumped into the room above to drain away. These holes were the result of quick thinking on the part of the late Duchess of Westminster, Viola Grosvenor, who arrived during the fire to find little urgency about saving family treasures and discovered the old butler on the stairs removing a pair of his master's socks. She managed to get the servants to form a human chain and thus saved much of the house's contents. Unfortunately, the fire destroyed the fine plasterwork of the bedroom landing lantern, the martial decorations of the schoolroom ceiling and the Chinese wallpaper in the red rooms while the grand staircase with its wonderful joinery was miraculously only slightly damaged. The plasterwork ceilings in the Venetian room and the entrance hall, which had been completely destroyed, were later expertly restored.

The National Trust acquired Florence Court as a gift in 1954 and has since successfully refurnished the building. The emphasis has been on acquiring 18th-century Irish furniture – an admirable policy considering the quintessentially Irish character of this endearing house.

13 km (8 miles) SW of Enniskillen on the Swanlinbar Road. NGR: H 175343.

GARDENS

Florence Court

Set amidst the splendour of superb parkland and majestic mountain scenery, Florence Court can boast a fine Victorian pleasure ground, a walled garden and the original Irish yew *Taxus baccata* "Fastigiata". The 250-year-old mother plant of millions of Irish yews grows half a mile from the house and is well worth the walk. Some outstanding specimens of weeping beech, old rhododendrons, magnolias and maples can be found in the pleasure grounds set out amidst a network of meandering footpaths and mowed grass. Azaleas, viburnums and dogwoods also grow here, while the stream bank has a variety of plantings, notably primulas. There is a rose garden, long ornamental ponds and an attractive cottage in the Walled Garden.

13 km (8 miles) SW of Enniskillen on the Swanlinbar Road. NGR: H 175343.

Tully Castle

Formal garden created in bawn of plantation castle, built 1618, using plants known in Ireland in early 17th century.

On the shore of Lough Erne, 5 km (3 miles) N of Derrygonnelly off the Belleek road. NGR: H 186599.

MUSEUMS/HERITAGE CENTRES

Belleek Pottery

The flamboyantly decorated Parian ware made at Belleek, a tiny village in south-west Fermanagh, since 1857 has become world-renowned. At the pottery, visitors can see the production process for themselves, including the hand-crafting of the basketware designs that characterise Belleek and the hand-painting of the designs. The museum, with its classical-style columns, has many examples of Belleek pottery made since the pottery's foundation, including the earthenware which was produced for its first ten years. A presentation in the audio-visual theatre completes the tour.

8 km (5 miles) E of Ballyshannon.

Carrothers Family Museum

This family-run collection has an informality that cannot exist in larger museums. In the best family tradition, it has a little bit of everything, including farming and household utensils, as well as mementoes of family life going back 200 years. The museum has much 19th-century documentation including wages books and deeds, besides letters written home by members of the family who emigrated to North America, and from the front during World War I.

11 km (7 miles) SE of Enniskillen on the Lisnaskea Road.

Enniskillen Castle

Parts of the castle, surrounded by a wide moat, date back to the 15th century and include several attractions. The castle keep, in the original Maguire stronghold,

houses the regimental museum of the Royal Inniskilling Fusiliers, a regiment formed in the late 17th century. Weapons, uniforms and medals are included in the collection. There are also displays on the natural history, folk life and archaeology of County Fermanagh, besides an audio-visual programme on the history of the Maguire clan and the town of Enniskillen.
Enniskillen.

GALWAY

CASTLES

Aughnanure Castle

The "ferocious O'Flaherties", masters of the whole territory of west Connaught, built this fine castle in the early 16th century, possibly on the site of a 13th-century Norman fortification. It occupies a position of some strength close to Lough Corrib on what is virtually a rocky island formed by the Drimmeen River, separating into two branches and reuniting at the other side – a circumstance that gave rise to the old phrase "Aughnanure, where the salmon come under the castle".

A natural bridge of rock gives access to the inner bawn and tower house on the west. The well-built six-storey tower with a gracefully battered base imparts a very picturesque appearance and commands a wonderful view over Lough Corrib. Aughnanure is unusual in having a double bawn. Its riverside walls have survived whilst an outer wall has collapsed into an underground tributary river (now dry as its course has been changed). However, its pretensions to style are evident from the carvings on the soffits of the window embrasures depicting elaborate vine leaves and clusters of grapes in low relief.

The castle was the seat of the O'Flaherty chiefs until 1572, when it was captured by Sir Edward Fitton. Its position at the head of the lake allowed the castle to play an important role in the Cromwellian blockade of Galway, but afterwards it was forfeited and granted to the Earl of Clanrickard. Somehow the O'Flahertys remained in residence and in 1719 regained ownership, but later the castle passed to Lord St George on the foreclosure of a mortgage. In the 19th century a member of the Leconfield branch of the O'Flahertys planted yew trees about the castle to perpetuate its Gaelic name – the field of the yews.
3 km (2 miles) SE of Oughterard. NGR: M 1544.

Ardamullivan Castle

Standing on the brow of a secluded valley and surrounded by trees, this is a well-preserved early 16th-century tower house of the O'Shaughnessys. The castle is first mentioned in 1567 on the death of Sir Roger O'Shaughnessy. He was succeeded by his brother Dermot, "the Swarthy", known as "the Queen's O'Shaughnessy" for his support of the Crown. He became very unpopular in the district and indeed among his own family after he betrayed Dr Creagh, the Roman Catholic Archbishop of Armagh, who had sought refuge in the woods on O'Shaughnessy territory. In 1579 his nephew John, popular heir to the family estates and title, fought with Dermot outside the south gate of the castle and both claimants were killed. In the last century the ruin was renovated.
8 km (5 miles) S of Gort due W of the main Ennis Road. NGR: R 443950.

Athenry Castle

The great fortress and walled town of Athenry played a vital role in the Anglo-Norman control of East Connaught. Construction of the castle can be dated to between 1235–41 and was undertaken by Meiler de Bermingham after being granted a charter by William de Burgo, the Anglo-Norman conqueror of much of Connaught. It comprises a particularly well-preserved first-floor hall standing isolated within a walled enclosure, which forms part of the town's mural defences. The bailey has been much restored, and there is a round tower at the south-east corner and fragments of another on the north-east. Excavations in 1989 did not resolve the problematic question of the exact location and nature of the entrance, which presumably lay in the south-west corner.

The town's walls were begun in 1312 and considerable lengths can still be seen. Not long after the completion of their walls one of the bloodiest battles of medieval Ireland was fought outside the town between Phelim O'Connor, King of Connaught, and the Anglo-Normans. The defeat of the Irish was so decisive that the constant struggle with the O'Connors came to an end – a process that seems to have resulted in a decline in the importance and strength of the town. It fell an easy prey to Red Hugh O'Donnell in 1596 and never recovered from the damage he inflicted.
Athenry. NGR: M 512288.

Ballylee

The poet W.B. Yeats was so enchanted with this 16th-century tower house beside the Cloon River that he purchased the property in 1916 and restored it. For twelve years Yeats made "Thoor Ballylee" his summer home which he found so "full of history and romance" that he was inspired to write "The Winding Stair" and "The Tower Poems". He once said: "To leave here is to leave beauty behind", and in a letter to Olivia Shakespeare wrote: "We are in our Tower and I am writing poetry as I always do here, and as always happens, no matter how I begin, it becomes love poetry before I am finished with it", and remarked "as you see I have no news, for nothing happens in this blessed place but a stray beggar or a heron."

The castle originally belonged to one of the Burke septs – it stands four storeys high and its original windows still survive in the upper part, though Yeats and his architect installed larger windows in the lower floors. The ground-floor chamber was described by Yeats as "the pleasantest room I have yet seen, a great wide window opening over the river and a round arched door leading to the thatched hall". He also loved the mural stair, symbolically declaring "This winding, gyring, spring treadmill of a stair is my ancestral stair; That Goldsmith and the Dean, Berkeley and Burke have travelled there."

Ballylee was abandoned and started to fall into ruin in the early 1930s. For the centenary of the poet's birth in 1965, however, the place was fully restored to appear as it was when he lived there. It now also houses an interpretative centre on his life and works. Lest it be forgotten that this was once the poet's home, there is a tablet on the wall commemorating his sojourn here:

I, the poet William Yeats,
With old mill boards and sea-green slates,
And smithy work from the Gort forge,
Restored this tower for my wife George;
And may these characters remain
When all is ruin once again.

6.5 km (4 miles) NE of Gort on a minor road to the W of the Loughrea Road. NGR: N 481062.

Derryhivenny Castle

The building of true castles came more or less to an end in Ireland with the outbreak of war in 1641 – one of the very last being the tower house and bawn at Derryhivenny. Its date is known from an inscription on one of its bartizan corbels which reads "D:O'M ME:FIERI:FECIT 1643" and states that Donal O'Madden built the castle in 1643.

A late date is supported by the absence of vaults on all four storeys of the tower and by its picturesque diagonally disposed Jacobean chimney-stacks. The upper

rooms have two- and three-mullioned windows with good fireplaces, including one fine example with a plain chamfered lintel, curved downwards at each end and covered by a chamfered cornice. Along one side of the enclosure opposite the tower there are fragments of a one-storey gabled building, possibly a stable block.
6 km (3.5 miles) N/NE of Portumna, off a minor road lying E of the Eyrecourt Road.
NGR: M 872085.

Fiddaun Castle

Fiddaun is a lofty tower house that is best known for having one of the best-preserved bawns in Ireland. Built during the 16th century for the O'Shaughnessys, it comprises an oblong six-storey tower with vaults over its first and fifth floors. There are square bartizans placed very low down at third-floor level, a peculiarly Irish feature that was brought about by the introduction of firearms, which changed the axis of defence from the vertical to the horizontal.

Most of the O'Shaugnessy estates were forfeited in 1697 when the castle's owner, Sir William O'Shaughnessy, fled to France. Though only fifteen in 1690, he had fought as a captain in the Jacobite cause and later in exile pursued a brilliant military career, becoming a Mareschal de Camp in 1734. The castle was continuously inhabited by O'Shaughnessys until 1727.
8 km (5 miles) SW of Gort off the Tubber road, lying on a low-level plain between two lakes.
NGR: R 409949.

Glinsk Castle

In the decades preceding the 1641 Rebellion, a number of Irish landowners were building houses that tried to combine the need for spacious and luxurious living with an adequate means of positive defence. Inevitably, such houses differed from contemporary English manors in having fewer windows, high basements, musketry loops, bartizans and other defensive features. Nonetheless, many succeeded in projecting the air of a gentleman's residence, and few more successfully than Sir Ulick Burke's handsome strong house at Glinsk, probably begun around 1628.

Glinsk was gutted by fire at an early stage and survives as an exceptionally well-preserved ruin. It has a three-bay rectangular plan of three storeys over a raised basement with an attic floor in its high gabled roof. The exact plan of the interior is unknown as there were only timber divisions, but the fireplaces were in the end walls where the stacks rise with tall, elegant shafts that are undoubtedly the best examples of their kind in Ireland.
6.5 km (4 miles) SE of Ballymoe off a minor road to Creggs village. NGR: M 717681.

Pallas Castle

The remarkably complete and well-preserved tower house was built by the Burkes sometime around 1500. It has four storeys and an attic, the third floor being vaulted and the thick end wall containing a tier of mural chambers and a winding stair. There are attractive mullioned windows in the fourth floor and a number of fine fireplaces on various levels, though the oven on the ground floor is a secondary addition. The roof was still thatched in the early part of the present century, the bottom being covered with stone flags for protection.

The tower stands in one corner of a large well-preserved bawn, which has internal steps and parapets, a two-storey gatehouse (rebuilt) and a pair of round flankers with gun ports. Near the tower at the west end, there is a rectangular flanker, an 18th-century malt-house and the remains of a large 17th-century gabled house.
3.2 km (2 miles) E/SE of Duniry off the Portumna Road. NGR: M 757074.

Portumna Castle

It is no exaggeration to describe Portumna as the most important residence to be built in Ireland until Castletown a century later. In grandeur and scale it was without equal when constructed in 1616–18 and like Castletown introduced a new sophistication to Irish architecture. The builder – not surprisingly a man of great wealth and power who moved in court circles – was Richard Burke, fourth Earl of Clanrickarde, Lord President of Connaught and descendant of a Gaelic chieftaincy of Norman origin that ruled much of Connaught for centuries. His house survived the wars of the 17th century, only to be gutted by fire in 1826. In recent years its great shell has been re-roofed by the State.

The building belongs to a distinctive group of spacious semi-fortified rectangular houses with flanking towers at each corner. It rises to a height of three storeys, plus attics, above a raised basement and has an attractive symmetrical fenestration of regularly placed two- and three-mullioned windows and a skyline of battlements of small curved gables with pedestals and balls. At first glance it may not appear fortified, but it was surrounded by a bawn, whose wall and flankers still survive on the north side.

From mid 18th-century plans, we know that the interior was laid out in sets of state apartments in the French taste. From accounts of visitors in 1808 it is apparent that the state rooms were fabulously decorated with rich stucco ceilings and friezes, handsome panelling and magnificent furnishings.

The great house was requisitioned in 1634 by the unpopular Lord Deputy Stafford to hold the celebrated inquisitions into the titles of lands in Connaught. It was lost to Henry Cromwell from 1652 to 1660 and again forfeited by William III, but restored to the tenth Earl by Queen Anne. The family continued here in great pomp until the 1826 fire. The castle laid out a fine approach from the north, with its Gothic gates leading into the two great courts in front of the house. The inner court now has a restored Jacobean-style garden, though this would originally have had cut grass and statues. *Portumna. NGR: M 852040.*

HOUSES

Kylemore Abbey

Kylemore Abbey is an intensely romantic place, an enchanted fairytale castle in the neo-Gothic style that stands dramatically at the foot of a barren mountain in a remote and beautiful part of Connemara – its numerous battlemented and machicolated towers and turrets reflected in the waters of the lake below. For years this amazing house, now a convent, has been the most admired and photographed building in the West of Ireland.

The castle was built between 1863 and 1868 for Mitchell Henry, a highly successful Manchester financier and MP, to the design of James Franklin Fuller and Ussher Roberts. The story of its building began in 1852 when Henry was on honeymoon with his bride; stopping near Kylemore Pass for an al fresco lunch, the young Mrs Henry looked up and saw a small shooting-box on the opposite hillside, the only dwelling in sight, and exclaimed: "How I would love to live there." Ten years later, Mitchell Henry, by now a rich tycoon, purchased the property with its 9,000 acres of moorland, mountain and lake and embarked upon a dream house for his wife.

The building took five years and cost over one and a quarter million pounds – a staggering sum in those days. The completed castle was on a "Citizen Kane" scale, boasting many splendid reception rooms including a ballroom with a sprung floor, a magnificent staircase, a library, a study and thirty-three bedrooms. There were only four bathrooms, but the house was equipped with a Turkish bath, its water pressure ensured by an elaborate system of hydrants. He also built a model farm, laundry, dairy, saw mill, ornate chapel and a Gothic church, which was in part a replica of Norwich Cathedral. There was a 6-acre walled garden and thanks to 3 miles of hot-water piping, twenty-one greenhouses containing tropical fruit, vineries, peaches, pineries and orangeries. Three hundred thousand trees were planted a year to protect the castle and gardens from constant gales and many of these grew successfully despite the harsh weather conditions.

For ten years the Henrys and their nine children lived at Kylemore, entertaining on a lavish scale. Tragedy struck in 1875 when Mrs Henry died on a visit to Egypt. She was buried in a mausoleum at Kylemore, but afterwards her husband could no longer bear to spend much time there. Later his daughter was killed when driving a pony-trap at Derryinver and shortly afterwards Henry's financial empire started to collapse. In 1902 Kylemore was acquired for a twentieth of its value by Mr Zimmerman, a Chicago businessman, as a present for his daughter who had married the Duke of Manchester. During their tenure from 1902 to 1913, when the estate was mortgaged to money lenders, they made many unfortunate changes, including transforming the lovely ballroom into an enormous kitchen. This conversion was undertaken to satisfy the cook who was expecting to prepare a meal for Edward VII and Queen Alexander on their visit to Connemara in 1903. Their Majesties did, in fact, come – but only for a cup of tea.

The old ballroom is now the chapel of the Irish Dames of Ypres who acquired Kylemore in 1920. This Benedictine congregation came to Ireland after their abbey in France was destroyed during World War I and settled at Kylemore, where they established a famous girls' school.

Between Letterfrack and Recess, 20 km (12 miles) NE of Clifden. NGR: L 748585.

GARDENS

Kylemore

A 6-acre Walled Garden set into the side of the mountain about a mile from the castle. Built in the 1870s, the garden formerly contained a kitchen garden and magnificent pleasure grounds, dominated by an enormous range of glasshouses. The garden was abandoned in the 1920s, becoming an impenetrable jungle until 1994, when work began on its restoration. After painstaking research and archaeological investigations, the pleasure gardens are now beginning to regain their lost glory. Extensive flowerbeds dot the lawns and the fine trellised rose garden has been restored. The greenhouse bases have been exposed and work will shortly begin rebuilding the wooden frame of the peach house. This exciting project is ongoing and is well worth a visit.

Between Letterfrack and Recess, 20 km (12 miles) NE of Clifden. NGR: L 748585.

MUSEUMS/HERITAGE CENTRES

Aran Islands Interpretative Centre

The unique history, spirit and landscapes of the Aran Islands are well documented in this centre in Kilronan (the "capital" of the islands) on Inishmore. The centre details the geology, history and present lifestyle of the islands. Visitors can see how the legendary currachs, those open-topped, often tar-coated, boats that skim over the waves, are made. Also on display are details of the fish species off the islands and how the islanders have long used seaweed to create patches of soil, that could be cultivated for crops, in between the dry stone walls that criss-cross the islands and divide their tiny fields. The islands' other craft traditions, including weaving of the famous Aran sweaters, are also documented. There are daily showings of the famous 1934 film, *Man of Aran*.

Inishmore.

Battle of Aughrim Centre

Visitors can relive the day that changed Irish and European history, the battle fought in 1691. A total of 45,000 soldiers from eight European countries came to fight; by nightfall some 9,000 had been slain. The victory of Williamite forces over Jacobite troops had profound effects on the course of European history, as had the Battle of the Boyne, fought a year earlier.

Aughrim, 6 km (3.5 miles) SW of Ballinasloe.

Galway City Museum

This small museum, with a quayside location beside the Spanish Arch, has a mixture of folk and medieval artefacts and documentation recalling the city's development since the 12th century. The displays include a copy of the famous 1691 map of Galway, while the city's most famous district, the Claddagh, is also recalled. Its cottages have long since been swept away in the name of modernisation, but the name lives on, especially in Claddagh rings. Early photographs and other memorabilia recall the earlier days of the Claddagh, while other long vanished Galway "institutions", like the Salthill tram, are also recalled.

City quaysides near Spanish Arch.

Inis Oírr Heritage House

Innis Oírr (Inisheer) is the smallest of the three Aran Islands and the Ceárd Shiopa Inis Oírr on the island promotes Aran culture and art. Next door is the heritage house, built as a traditional Aran Islands house with sturdy stone walls and a thatched roof tied down against the wind. The folk collection inside the museum details the history of island life up to the present and includes old photographs.

Aran Islands.

Nora Barnacle's House

Nora Barnacle, wife of James Joyce, was brought up in this one-up-one-down house with no kitchen or bathroom and a tiny walled-in back yard, near Galway city centre. Despite its lack of size, the house has some artefacts, including photographs, and great atmosphere. Stories about this remarkable couple flow freely, as if they had just visited yesterday.

Bowling Green, near St Nicholas' Church, Galway

KERRY

CASTLES

Carrigafoyle Castle

Carrigafoyle has had a stormy history and, although wrecked by a series of bloody sieges, remains a remarkable castle. Cleverly located between the high- and low-water marks on the shore of the Shannon estuary, it comprises a large tower built towards the end of the 15th century by the O'Connors. The tower was protected on the landward side by two square bawns; these extended into the water and enclosed a small dock, so that boats could sail right up to the castle – a rather useful if not unique feature.

The tower has five storeys rising to a height of 86 feet and is beautifully constructed of specially selected small stones laid in neat courses.

In 1580 Sir William Pelham besieged the castle, held by the Earl of Desmond, with fifty Irishmen and sixteen Spaniards. Pelham used artillery brought by sea and within two days had battered down the bawn and the landward side of the castle. All the surviving members of the garrison were hung and the Earl of Desmond's plate, stored in the castle, was sent to Queen Elizabeth I. The castle was later recovered by the O'Connors, only to be surrendered again to Sir George Carew in 1600. It is known to have had a garrison of forty men in 1659 to protect the south shore of the Shannon. Despite its wrecked condition the castle was occupied in the last century by a Dr Fitzmaurice and his family.

3 km (2 miles) N of Ballylongford in the channel between the mainland and Carrig Island. Accessible from the road across a raised path of stones liable to be submerged at very high tides. NGR: Q 988474.

Ross Castle

There are few castles anywhere in Ireland that can boast such a dreamlike enchanted setting as this ruined tower house on the shore of Killarney's Lower Lake. Built in the late 15th century, it is fairly typical of its type, with square bartizans on diagonally opposite corners and a thick end wall containing a tier of chambers and a winding mural stair. The tower stands within a square bawn defended by round corner towers, two of which survive, the others having been removed in 1688 to make room for an extension, the ruins of which remain on the south side of the castle.

The castle was the chief seat of the O'Donaghue Mors, hereditary rulers of this district and descendants of the ancient kings of Munster. After the Desmond rebellion, their fortified lands were acquired by the MacCarthy Mors and later Sir Valentine Browne, ancestor of the Earls of Kenmare. In 1652 the castle was held by Lord Muskerry against a Cromwellian force of 1,500 foot and 700 horse soldiers. It fell after floating batteries were brought over land to bombard it from the lough as well as from the land. The Brownes, who retained the old faith, remained in the castle until they lost their estates in 1690 for supporting the Jacobite cause. Although their lands were recovered around 1720, they were unable to regain possession of the castle, which had been taken over as a military barracks.

2.5 km (1.5 miles) SW of Killarney on Ross Island. NGR: V 949887.

HOUSES

Muckross House

Muckross House is best known for its magical parkland setting beside the Lower Lake at Killarney, but the house is also worthy of its location. It was built between 1839 and 1843 for Colonel Henry Herbert to a design by the great Scottish architect William Burn, who was just beginning to establish himself as the most influential country house architect of his generation. Burn's brilliance lay principally in his ability to produce comfortable, well-organised houses, but Muckross is also a highly successful example of the Elizabethan Revival style, then very popular in Ireland. Its great array of tall chimneys, oriels, stepped gables, finials and mullioned windows are all skilfully integrated into a crisp, uncluttered composition that gains much from being faced with lavish quantities of Portland stone, shipped at great expense from Dorset and hauled by cart over the mountains from Kenmare.

The interior was built with the same magnificence of the exterior, though sadly the rooms have now lost most of their original Victorian furnishings. Major Herbert, whose family had lived at Muckross since the early 18th century, was forced to sell the property in 1899 after he ran into serious financial difficulties. It was bought by Lord Ardilaun, a member of the Guinness family, and sold again in 1910 to William Bourn, a rich American gold miner who gave the house as a wedding present to his daughter Maud. Maud died in 1929 and three years later her husband bestowed Muckross together with the 11,000-acre estate upon the nation on the understanding that its peace and tranquillity would never be disturbed by the sound of motor cars.

The entrance hall is presided over by an impressive set of antlers of the long-extinct Irish elk – an inevitable status symbol of all large Irish country houses. The main hall is a spacious room that serves as a focus for the whole house with an array of stags' heads and portraits. In common with most houses of that period the main hall is flanked by the principal reception rooms along the garden front. All have immense bay windows which allow for marvellous views across sweeping lawns to the lake and mountains beyond. The dining-room is the only room in the house that really retains its authentic country house atmosphere. A good mahogany dining-room table with a set of twelve Chippendale chairs occupies the centre of the room, while at one end stands a large walnut sideboard carved in Italy and bearing the Herbert crest. The curtains, fragile and still quite beautiful, are original to this room and were woven in Brussels specifically for the visit of Queen Victoria and Prince Albert to Muckross in 1861.

On the first floor of the upper landing a few bedrooms, dressing-rooms and children's rooms are open to the public. The main bedroom has a large Sheraton wardrobe and bed, while the pretty children's bedroom contains miniature furniture and toys. The basement still features its old wine cellar, dairy, boiler room, kitchen and laundry, while the remaining rooms are used as regional craft workshops. There is also a blacksmith's forge and a representation of an early public house.

5 km (3 miles) S of Killarney on the Kenmare Road. NGR: V 965850.

GARDENS

Derreen

A woodland garden of luxuriant vegetation lying in a sheltered inlet amidst the splendour of the Caha Mountains. Created by the fifth Marquis of Landsdowne over a sixty-year period from 1870, the garden is designed around a pleasant house, whose plush, undulating lawns sweep down to the woodland below. Here, wide grassy vistas give way to a labyrinth of narrow mossy paths, which weave their way through groves of bamboo, towering eucalyptus, tree ferns and a wide variety of conifers, some planted as specimens, some in small groups. Kalmia and leptospermum thrive, as do olearias, azaleas, gaultheria, drimys and, above all, the rhododendrons which are found everywhere in profusion, some of enormous size. One path with the evocative name of King's Oozy leads past a majestic *Thuja plicata* to a remarkable grove of tree ferns (*Dicksonia antarctica*) planted here around 1900, which have become completely naturalised, constantly renewing themselves by self-sown spores. On the way back to the house along the Rock Garden Walk visitors will be impressed by an outstanding specimen of the beautiful Japanese cypress (*Cryptomeria japonica* "Elegans"), now unhappily lying in a near horizontal position almost blocking the walk. Wellington boots are advised for full enjoyment of this lush paradise.

Near Lauragh, 15 miles SW of Kenmare. NGR: V 775585.

Dunloe Castle Gardens

With magnificent panoramic views of the towering MacGillycuddy Reeks, these gardens contain an exceptionally rich variety of trees and shrubs, including many species that are rarely if at all found elsewhere in Ireland. Visitors arriving in the Walled Garden will find beds and borders of rhododendrons, magnolias and camellias planted closely beside many rare and tender plants. Along the main path through the garden, there are specimens of the shrub *Banksia marginata*, the Chilean hazel *Gevuina avellana* and a magnificent *Viburnum odoratissimum* from China. The north wall of the garden provides a suitable environment for the magnificent Chilean foliage plant *Lomatia ferruginea* and the remarkable *Camellia granthamiana*, now endangered in the wild.

The path out of the Walled Garden leads to the shell of the old 13th-century castle where a handsome strawberry tree can be admired. A series of paths on the east reveal a whole range of shrubs, such as the heavily scented *Ozothamnus ledifolius* from Tasmania and the Gippsland waratah *Telopea oreades*. Another route leads to a Chinese pond cypress (*Glyptostrobus lineatus*), possibly the largest of its kind in Europe. Back at the hotel, visitors can venture into an arboretum boasting a variety of

rare maples, rare cherry trees from China and such curious specimens as a small hornbeam from Asia, *Carpinus cordata*, a white-flowering ash from the Himalayas, *Fraxinus floribunda* and the distinctive but rarely seen conifer from Taiwan, *Calocedrus formosana*.
8 km (5 miles) W of Killarney and 1.6 km (1 mile) S of Beauford. NGR: V 808901.

Muckross Gardens

Demesne gardens with sweeping lawns and clumps of old rhododendrons near house; woodland garden, rock garden, arboretum and magnificent lake views.
5 km (3 miles) S of Killarney on the Kenmare Road. NGR: V 965850.

MUSEUMS/HERITAGE CENTRES

Blasket Centre

This centre commemorates the heritage of the nearby Blasket Islands. The islands had a strong cultural tradition, reflected in the creation of various literary masterpieces in Irish, and a distinctive way of life which endured until the last of the islanders abandoned their homes on Great Blasket Island in 1953. The new centre describes in detail the old island way of life, its social and literary traditions and the flora and fauna of the islands. The extensive research on the islands' history is available in the centre's library, which also has display areas and a room where the sounds of the islands are recreated.
25 km (15 miles) W of Dingle.

Blennerville

The locomotive once ran on the old Dingle–Tralee narrow gauge railway and was returned home from a museum in Vermont. In Blennerville, the 200-year-old five-storey windmill has been restored to working order. One of only two restored windmills to be seen in the Republic, the tall, white-painted structure is well worth a visit. There's also a display about 19th-century emigration through Blennerville port – you can see over a replica of an emigrant ship, *Jeanie Johnston*, an exact replica of Kerry's most famous emigrant ship.
Blennerville, 3 km (2 miles) SW of Tralee.

Derrynane

Once the home of Daniel O'Connell, the "Liberator" responsible for Catholic Emancipation in Ireland in the 19th century, Derrynane is now a place of reverential remembrance. The house itself is most attractive, with its slate-faced exterior, while the interior is surprisingly homely and comforting for a grand house. The dining- and drawing-rooms are packed with furniture, paintings and other mementoes relating to O'Connell, including a table decorated with carvings of Irish wolfhounds and a harp presented to him by Dublin Corporation when he was an alderman of that city. The centrepiece of the museum is O'Connell's grand and elaborate ceremonial coach, which had lain forgotten for a century and has now been magnificently restored. The story of the great man and his works is narrated in an audio-visual presentation. The surrounding national park extends for 298 acres.
2 km (1 mile) W of Caherdaniel on the Ring of Kerry Road.

Kenmare Heritage Centre

This details many facets of local history, including the establishment of the town and its mine by Sir William Petty in 1670. The centre also uses modern audio-visual and display techniques to detail the effect of the Famine in the late 1840s on the town and the lace once made by the local nuns. A separate lace display is upstairs.
Kenmare.

Muckross House

This Elizabethan-style mansion, built in the early 1840s, retains much of its original decor. In the basement there is an old wine cellar and dairy. Craft skills are practised here, including bookbinding, printing, woodcarving, harness-making, shoemaking, basketry, stonecutting, pottery and weaving. Outside, you can visit the three working farms that make up Muckross Traditional Farms and are designed to show the lifestyles, farming traditions and livestock of Kerry in the 1930s. Muckross House and the traditional farms are in the Killarney National Park, where other sites to be seen include Muckross Abbey, founded in 1448.

5 km (3 miles) S of Killarney on the Kenmare Road. NGR: V 965850.

Museum of Irish Transport

This museum is a veritable cornucopia of transport memorabilia. Not only does it have many vintage and veteran cars, but also an 1825 hobby horse, bicycles and fire engines. A vintage garage workshop has been reconstructed, complete with tools and spare parts. The display of sparking plugs goes back to 1899 and is complemented by other automobilia and old posters. Cars on display include an 1898 Benz, the very first car to take to Irish roads. Also on show is a 1904 Belgian-made Germain, a true luxury car, but one of only four survivors of this marque. Other models include an Austin Seven from 1930 and an Austin Ten from 1934. The 1952 Volkswagen was one of the first Beetles to be assembled in Ireland, by the O'Flaherty group, at Shelbourne Road, Ballsbridge, Dublin. The cycle collection has about twenty machines dating from 1850 to the 1930s and includes a bone shaker, made about 1865, and claimed as Ireland's oldest bicycle.

Scott's Gardens, Killarney.

Reidy's Shop

Reidy's traditional grocery shop has been trading for well over a century and is one of the very few such shops in Ireland not to have succumbed to modernisation. The customer (every visitor will buy something) experiences shopping as it should be. The goods are still packed in wooden cupboards and shelves, the floor is wooden and the counter runs the length of the shop to the bar at the back. Hooks for the Christmas turkeys and hams are still embedded in the ceiling. The shop also has one hundred varieties of sweets, sold by the quarter-pound. Reidy's, which is run by the Sheehan family, even has five varieties of snuff. The shop is a marvellous and rare example of how grocery shopping used to be.

Killarney.

Skellig Experience

The centre is unique in Ireland in that it includes a boat trip. The building itself is unusual, with Valentia stone used for facing the external walls and a roof made of natural grass. The centre depicts different themes. Firstly, there's the history and archaeology of the early Christian monastery that sits atop Skellig Michael, one of the two Skellig Islands off the nearby coast. Models, photographs and old artefacts, like a brass chronometer from a lighthouse, make up the exhibition, while visitors can also see an audio-visual presentation on the Skellig Michael monastery. After touring the Skelligs Centre, visitors can take to the open seas in a specially designed boat to see the Skelligs at close quarters.

Valentia Island.

Sliabh Luachra Centre

This centre details the fine traditional music heritage of this part of Kerry and includes venerable old musical instruments.

Near Castleisland.

Sneem Museum

This small museum, run by Tim O'Reilly, has a wonderfully eclectic collection of local material. The museum is housed in the former courthouse and was opened in 1987. It now has around 1,500 items, from candle moulds and old furniture to school roll-books and photographs of former generations of Sneem people. It has memorabilia of a former President of Ireland, the late Cearbhall Ó Dálaigh, who had strong connections with this part of Kerry. Examination of this diverse material will be enhanced by conversation with Tim, a former wheelwright and long-time collector.
27 km (17 miles) W of Kenmare on the Ring of Kerry Road.

Tralee

The Ashe Memorial Hall in the centre of Tralee is home to three centres collectively known as Kerry the Kingdom. First, "Kerry in Colour" is an extravagant audio-visual presentation on the history of the county from prehistoric times. Kerry County Museum uses artefacts, scale models and video displays to tell the story of the county from over 7,000 years ago to the present day and includes interactive videos of Kerry's Gaelic football triumphs, plus a documentary newsreel covering the period from 1914 to 1965. Thirdly, "Geraldine Tralee" recreates the town in the Middle Ages. Visitors can then take the steam train from Tralee to Blennerville (see above).
Tralee.

KILDARE

CASTLES

Maynooth Castle

The tides of war have left their mark on the great castle of Maynooth – the chief residence of the all-powerful Earls of Kildare from the early 14th until the 16th century. Most of the curtain walls have now vanished, but the entrance gate and hall-keep still testify to the castle's former glory.

The massive keep, one of the largest of its kind in Ireland, probably occupies the site of an earlier castle built soon after the conquest by Gerald FitzMaurice, one of Strongbow's associates. Begun sometime around 1210, the building was much altered in 1426 by the sixth Earl of Kildare. What remains now are its eastern walls and towers, together with the main entrance gate on the south – the present entry to the castle.

In one of the first recorded uses of siege guns in Ireland, Sir William Skeffington, Henry VIII's Lord Deputy in Ireland, took Maynooth Castle in 1535 after a week's bombardment. In the "Pardon of Maynooth" – a byword in contemporary Ireland – he put the garrison to the sword despite their having surrendered unconditionally. It was restored to the eleventh Earl of Kildare in 1552, repaired in 1630, taken by the Confederates in 1641 and dismantled at the end of the war.
Maynooth. NGR: N 938377.

HOUSES

Castletown House

It may justly be said that Castletown is the largest and most splendid country house in Ireland, but it is also arguably the most important, for it introduced sophisticated Palladianism from the continent and brought about a revolution in Irish architecture. The building was begun in 1721 for William Conolly, the son of a Donegal innkeeper who, through astute dealings in forfeited estates after the Williamite wars, had become the richest man in Ireland. The house is an obvious manifestation of his wealth, but it also reflects the enormous political power that Conolly achieved following his election as Speaker of the Irish House of Commons in 1715 and his appointment as Lord Justice in 1716. Proud of his Irish identity, he consistently used his power to promote Irish interests. It was Conolly who instigated building the Parliament House on College Green, the first of its kind in Europe. Undoubtedly there were similar patriotic and political motivations underlying the building of his house at Castletown.

The design of the house was entrusted to the Florentine Alessandro Galilei, best known for his work on the Lateran Basilica in Rome. Although Galilei returned to Italy in 1719 having spent only a few months in Ireland, work on the building designs did not materialise until a few years later. Building was evidently well underway in 1722, but with Galilei in Italy it is not clear who was supervising the operation. In 1724, however, the project was taken over by Edward Lovett Pearce who had just returned from Italy where he was studying the work of Palladio. Pearce had been in close touch with Galilei in Italy and possibly helped him transmit designs back to Conolly in Ireland. Building operations at Castletown continued after Conolly's death in 1729 but came to a halt in 1733 with the early death of Pearce, by now the most outstanding architect of his generation.

It is not known precisely how much of Castletown is Galilei's work, but he was certainly responsible for devising the overall scheme of the centre block, which was flanked by colonnades in the manner of Palladio's villas in the Veneto – a concept that was completely new in Ireland and later became the prototype and inspiration for numerous houses. The classically correct and regimented main façades of the centre block, both of which are almost identical, have the character of an Italian Renaissance town palazzo and are clearly also Galilei's work; their beauty and serenity are enormously enhanced by the silvery-white limestone which, unlike other Irish limestones, is free from age-darkening and blackening from the rain. The pavilions, designed by Pearce, are composed of a coarser and less dazzling golden-brown limestone; together with the curved colonnades they have the effect of focussing the eye upon the centre block.

Castletown's interior was largely created during the time of Tom Conolly, the Speaker's great nephew, who inherited the property in 1758; that same year he married the fifteen-year-old Lady Louisa Lennox. By all accounts Tom Conolly had a weak, indecisive character, but Louisa was extremely dynamic and immediately set about completing the house.

The staircase hall was Louisa's first objective. She employed the Dutch-Italian sculptor and stonemason Simon Vierpyl to install the magnificent cantilevered staircase in Portland stone. As substantial payments were made to the famous Swiss-Italian stuccodores – the Francini brothers – in 1765, it may be assumed that the plasterwork in the staircase hall was applied then, except for the cornice and coffered ceiling which belong to Pearce's time. The Francini brothers first came to Ireland in 1739 and are credited with the introduction of human figures into plaster decoration; character-istically, their plasterwork on the staircase incorporates a number of family portraits.

Alterations and improvements to the house during the 1760s included the creation of the dining-room. It was in this room that legend has it Tom Conolly entertained the devil, whom he had met out hunting and invited back, believing him to be a "dark stranger" but realising the truth after his guest had removed his boots to reveal hairy feet shaped like cloven hooves. A priest was summoned in haste; he hurled his breviary at the devil, missed and cracked a mirror, whereupon the devil took fright and vanished up the chimney, leaving behind a split hearthstone and a cracked mirror to this day.

The green drawing-room, formerly the saloon, has been restored with green silk copied from the original fabric and contains a japanned lacquer cabinet that belonged to old Mrs Conolly. The adjacent print room was created by Lady Louisa Conolly with the help of her sister; the fashion for pasting engravings and mezzo tints onto walls during the long winter days became very popular at that time. The print room at

Castletown is possibly the earliest to survive – it is certainly the only one that still exists in Ireland. Used as the billiard room in the last century, it now contains Louis XVI furniture with Aesop's fables in tapestry, a gift to Castletown which looks very well here.

Apparently inspired by her success in the print room, Louisa Conolly decided to redecorate the long gallery – an 80-foot room on the first floor. She had the old plaster panels "knocked off smack smoot" and Pompeiian decoration painted onto the walls. The glass chandeliers from Murano near Venice were bought to match the room's colour, though Louisa was disappointed when they arrived, claiming they were the wrong blue. A visitor in 1778 found the room furnished "in the most delightful manner with fine glasses, books, musical instruments, billiard table – in short, everything that you can think of ... and though so large it is so well fitted that it is the warmest, most comfortable looking place I ever saw and they tell me they live in it quite in the winter, for the servants can bring in dinners at one end without anyone hearing at the other."

Tom Conolly died in 1803 but Lady Louisa lived on for many years. She eventually died in 1821, seated in a tent erected on the lawn in front of Castletown, for it was her wish that she should go looking at the house she had loved so much.

Castletown was eventually inherited by Lord Carew who put it up for auction in 1965. The land was bought by property speculators who proceeded to build a housing estate beside the 250-year-old lime avenue. In 1967 the decaying house and 120 acres were bought in the eleventh hour by Desmond Guinness in order to save Castletown for posterity. It became the headquarters of the Irish Georgian Society, who with the help of weekend volunteers and money raised at home and abroad managed to repair the building and refurnish some of the rooms. In 1992 it was acquired by the Office of Public Works and its future is now finally assured, although the battle to recover its dispersed contents may be waged for generations to come. *1.6 km (1 mile) NE of Celbridge. NGR: N 980342.*

GARDENS

Tully Japanese Gardens

Tully is a product of the Edwardian vogue for Japanese garden-making and is one of the most successful of its kind. Devised by Colonel Hall-Walker, later Lord Wavertree, it was laid out by a Japanese landscape designer, Tassa Eida, from 1906 to 1910. A shipload of plants, bonsai, stone ornaments and even a geisha house were imported from Japan and the garden was designed to symbolise the vicissitudes of man's life from cradle to grave. It incorporates a dark tunnel, cave, blind paths, lawns, shady trees and a wide, slow-moving stream. Now in the possession of the Irish National Stud. *1.6 km (1 mile) E of Kildare town. NGR: N 735109.*

MUSEUMS/HERITAGE CENTRES

Ballitore Quaker Museum

The tiny village of Ballitore, a substantial Quaker settlement in the 18th century, has a Quaker museum, where Quakers still meet. Inside are Quaker relics, including a late 18th-century wedding gown and bonnet, lace, tapestry and embroidery, plus documentation on the Quaker community. Ballitore was renowned for its school; among its pupils was the 18th-century philosopher, Edmund Burke. The village also has a Quaker burial ground. Nearby Crookstown Mill and Heritage Centre is in a converted 1840 cornmill and details the baking and milling trades and local history. *30 km (18 miles) S of Naas, off the Carlow Road.*

Irish Horse Museum

This museum, part of the National Stud and the Japanese Gardens adjacent to Kildare town, tells the story of the animal that has achieved mythological status in Ireland. The museum is compact but tells the history of the horse from prehistoric times to the present in a logical and appealing manner. Many medieval relics include bronze rowel spurs from the 15th century, Anglo-Norman horseshoe nails, a 12th-century iron horseshoe, horse bones (12th-century or earlier) from Wood Quay in Dublin and a 13th-century horse skull found near Christ Church Cathedral in the city. Bianconi and his mail coaches are detailed; the latter was the first mode of public transport in Ireland. At its peak, the service had 100 vehicles and 1,400 horses. Amid all the horse memorabilia, one exhibit stands out, that of the skeleton of Arkle, arguably the greatest ever racehorse, born in 1957. It ran its last race in 1966. St Fiacre's Millennium garden opened here 1999.

1.6 km (1 mile) from Kildare town.

Maynooth College Museum

This museum is largely devoted to science; it features the work of the Rev Nicholas Callan, professor of natural philosophy here between 1826 and 1864, who invented many items of electrical equipment, including batteries and induction coils. The centre also includes primitive wireless equipment used by Marconi in Ireland a century ago and a large collection of scientific instruments made in Dublin in the late 19th century. There are also some religious artefacts. The college's own fascinating history over the past 200 years is told in a separate visitor centre.

25 km (15 miles) W of Dublin.

Peatland World

The esoteric world of the midlands bogs is well recaptured in this museum, housed in restored stableyard buildings. The displays include the kitchen and hearth of an old cottage, scale models of old and new peat-fired power stations and briquette works, and presentations on the flora and fauna of the boglands. Animal, bird and insect species have been preserved. Mementoes of old turf cutting, besides implements and equipment, are shown. Many old photographs complete the display. The nearby Lullymore Heritage Park recreates early Christian settlements.

24 km (15 miles) N of Kildare.

Steam Museum

This museum is housed, appropriately, in a church that once stood in the Inchicore railway works in Dublin. Inside the museum, there's a fine collection of models of steam locomotives, including two used in the late 19th century by the Great Northern Railway. The museum also has a fine selection of steam engines used for industrial propulsion, including a huge beam engine used in the Midleton whiskey distillery in County Cork, a pumping engine employed in Jameson's distillery in Dublin, and a large beam engine installed in Smithwick's brewery, Kilkenny, in 1847.

Straffan, 32 km (20 miles) W of Dublin.

KILKENNY

CASTLES

Burnchurch Castle

Many tower houses have an abundance of mural chambers and passages hidden away within their walls, though few have the number and complexity of those found in the early 16th-century castle of the Burncourt FitzGeralds. This well-preserved tower house, occupied until 1817, has four storeys beneath a vault with the principal chamber above, lying just below a gabled roof. Apart from its mullioned windows, this chamber is noteworthy for its finely carved chimney-piece; it has a tall, round chimney, while the roof's gable walls have been extended so that both ends of the tower are carried up an extra stage to provide high battlemented fighting platforms.

A great hall was formerly attached to the tower's outside wall, but this has now vanished, as has most of the bawn. A curved outside staircase still provides access to the three upper floors of this little tower.

6.5 km (4 miles) SW of Kilkenny off the Clonmel Road. NGR: N 472474.

Clara Castle

Anyone with a serious interest in Irish tower houses is sure to be familiar with this well-preserved example, which still retains many of its original oak doors and floor beams. Its survival owes much to having been continuously occupied from the early 16th century, when built by the Shortall family, until the early part of the present century.

The building has four storeys below a vault with a hall, and the entrance leads into a small lobby with a murder hole above. A winding stair occupies the north-east angle of the tower, and a door leads into a dimly lit square room, doubtless used as a store.

On the second floor, in what must have been the lord's chamber, there is a fine hooded chimney-piece, as well as a mural passage, latrine and a small room to the north, probably a bedroom. More sleeping room was available in the floor above, lying just beneath the vault, where there is also a remarkable secret chamber or strong box only reached through an opening masquerading as a lavatory seat off the top floor chamber. This latter chamber, the largest and best-lit room in the castle, was used for general family living. Its large lintelled fireplace is a secondary insertion, so the fireplace in this room must originally have been in the centre of the floor. The small window beside the fireplace has a sink or slop-stone below, suggesting that dishes were washed and perhaps food was cooked up here. The roof above is a modern erection, while the parapets, which are crenellated in the Irish fashion, are pierced by a large number of pistol- or musket-loops.

9.5 km (6 miles) NE of Kilkenny on a minor road 3 km (2 miles) off the main Carlow Road. NGR: N 573579.

Granagh Castle

Founded by the Le Poer family in the late 13th century, the castle stands dramatically on the north bank of the River Suir just above Waterford. After the attainder and execution for treason of Eustace FitzArnold Le Poer, the castle was granted in 1375 to James, second Earl of Ormonde, whose family retained possession until 1650, when it was captured by the Cromwellian regicide, Colonel Axtel, and subsequently dismantled.

The castle comprised a large, square, walled enclosure with cylindrical corner towers. The landward side was later rebuilt by the Butlers of Ormonde, but the old river façade survives complete with its south-west tower, parts of the north-east tower, the connecting curtain wall and latrines. An adjacent walled enclosure has now largely disappeared, save for a riverside drum tower. In the late 14th century the Butlers built a tall tower house in the north corner of the old castle and this was truncated later in the 15th century by a two-storey hall block built against it. The latter has vestiges of beautifully sculpted ornamentation, including an angel holding the Butler arms which decorates the inside arch of the window from which Margaret, the great Countess of Ormonde, hung rebels.

3 km (2 miles) NW of Waterford on the Carrick-on-Suir Road. NGR: S 171145.

Kilkenny Castle

The imposing ancestral castle of the Ormonde Butlers stands in the south-east corner of the medieval city of Kilkenny in a magnificent location over the River Nore. This great Norman castle has undergone many alterations over the centuries. Strongbow built a castle here as early as 1172 but this structure was destroyed by Donald O'Brien, King of Thomond. It was rebuilt between 1204 and 1213 by Strongbow's son-in-law and successor, William Marshall, Earl of Pembroke. The shape of his superb "keepless" castle – built to a trapezoidal plan with massive drum towers – has been largely preserved despite the many subsequent reconstructions. Excavations in the 1990s indicate that Strongbow's fort determined the basic outline of Marshall's fortress.

After the death of Earl Marshall, the castle was assigned to his eldest daughter and passed through her to the Despencers, who did not reside in Ireland. Parliament often met in the castle during the 14th century, which in 1307 comprised "a hall, four towers, a chapel, a motte, and divers other houses necessary to the castle". In 1391 it was sold to the Butlers, Earls of Ormonde, who after the Restoration of 1660 carried out a major rebuilding of the old castle after it had been damaged in Cromwell's siege of 1650.

Except for the classical-style gateway, the whole castle was again rebuilt during the 1820s in an uncompromisingly feudal-revival style for the first Marquess of Ormonde. Largely the creation of William Robertson, the building owes more to the spirit of romance than to historical accuracy. Nonetheless, it retains portions of earlier buildings, including the basic plan and shape of the great medieval fortress – a castle that has served as a princely residence for over eight centuries and played a major role in the country's history.

As befitting a potentate of enormous wealth and power, the new castle was erected on an impressive scale. According to tradition, its remodelling came about in 1826 when the Kilkenny architect William Robertson, who had been walking in the castle courtyard with Lady Ormonde, suddenly paused and pointed out that the main wall was out of alignment and consequently unsafe. This observation gave him the commission to rebuild the castle on a massive scale; as the Marquess of Ormonde was one of Ireland's richest landlords, no expense was spared. The building of sham castles was all the rage at the time, so it was hardly surprising that Robertson should have chosen to recreate the romantic appearance of the medieval castle. He duly swept away all of the first Duke's charming buildings, fortunately leaving the second Duke's classical gateway. The castle that emerged was externally a rather grim essay in neo-feudalism and internally distinguished only by its dullness.

Subsequent alterations to the castle from 1859 to 1862 by Benjamin Woodward and Thomas Deane improved the castle, though it was always the magnificent collection of tapestries, portraits, furniture and above all the famous Ormonde gold plate which redeemed the dark rooms of the interior. It was therefore a tragedy when the contents were sold in 1935 when the Ormondes ceased to live in the castle, bringing to an end the centuries-old occupation. In 1967 the sixth Marquess gave the castle to a local preservation society who two years later transferred it to the State to be restored and managed on behalf of the nation.

Extensive restoration began in 1973, but as yet only portions of the castle are open to the public. This includes the hall, which retains its fine 18th-century flagged floor and walls that were once covered with gilded Spanish leather, while its elaborate ceiling is a modern replica of the original. The great mahogany staircase brings the visitor to the dining-room, located in the circular north-east tower with its 12-foot-thick walls; a further set of stairs winds upwards to a corridor leading to the principal restored room of the castle – the picture gallery. Occupying the entire length of the castle's east wing, it measures 150 feet long, 27 feet wide and 30 feet high to the apex of the hammer-beamed roof. Between 1859 and 1862 Benjamin Woodward introduced a partly glazed roof so that this immense space could be lit, while John Hungerford Pollen painted the roof trusses in the pre-Raphaelite style. Pollen was also

responsible for the white Carrara marble double chimney-piece which he carved himself, complete with a series of bas-reliefs illustrating important events in the Butler family history. The walls of this room are again lined with pictures, and although these are but a few compared to the 184 paintings it once contained, some of the magic and grandeur of this room has now been restored.
Kilkenny city. NGR: S 509557.

GARDENS

Kilfane Glen

A romantic wooded garden ravine with a fairytale cottage, a hermit's grotto and a waterfall – all long lost until rediscovered and restored by Nicholas and Susan Mosse, the well-known Kilkenny potters. The layout was created at the turn of the 18th century, during the height of the "Picturesque" movement, when it was fashionable to display nature in all her rugged beauty. Cliffside paths and rustic bridges provide the approach to the charming thatched cottage, which looks out across lawns to the dramatic waterfall, created by diverting a nearby stream. A unique experience and well worth the walk.
6.5 km (4miles) from Thomastown, 3 km (2miles) off the N9 to Dublin.

Woodstock

Eyeless sockets of this great house, built 1746–7 by Frances Bindon, stare out over what was once one of Ireland's finest gardens. After the house was burnt in 1922 the gardens became an overgrown and forgotten jungle, while the magnificent parkland vistas across the Nore Valley were blocked with coniferous plantations. Some garden clearance was undertaken in the 1970s, but in 1999 the local council embarked on an ambitious programme of restoration.

Some of garden's features included a large formal parterre in front of the house (the Winter Garden), a long flower garden terrace with domed conservatory at one end, a rose garden, a grotto, a huge rockery with ponds, the Walled Garden and extensive pleasure grounds, which still boasts some fine trees including outstanding specimens of fern-leaved beach, weeping Himalayan spruce, Monterey pine and a giant redwood with the biggest bole in Europe. The avenue of silver fir is breathtaking and the avenue of monkey puzzles the finest of its kind in Europe. There are also pleasant walks along the banks of the Nore, overhung with beech woods, down to the pretty Red House. Above lies the ravine with its waterfalls and ruins of a Regency period "Swiss Cottage".
Near Inistioge village.

MUSEUMS/HERITAGE CENTRES

Kilkenny

Ireland's most perfect medieval town is packed with fascinating sites. Best place to start is Kilkenny Castle (see above).

In Parliament Street, Rothe House, built between 1594 and 1610, is now a museum. The collection includes furniture, pictures, costumes, and many local curiosities, including old musical instruments and details of the first ever Irish aeronautical patent, taken out in 1856.

St Canice's Cathedral is one of Ireland's finest churches; its library has around 3,000 books printed in the 16th and 17th centuries, while the top of the round tower beside the cathedral is the best vantage point for an overview of this historic city.
Kilkenny.

Nore View Folk Museum

This personalised museum, looking over the River Nore towards Mount Leinster and the Blackstairs Mountains, has an amazing variety of items, over 10,000 in all. The man who owns it, Seamus Lawlor, has made a collection representative of modern Irish history, although it has some items dating back to 2000 BC. The penal laws, the Famine, the 1916 Rising and the War of Independence, all feature. Included in the display are an old kitchen and pub, carpenter's workshop, forge and dairy, and most unusually, an old-style petrol station. Individual artefacts of antiquity include bicycles, books, church items, musical instruments and prams.
Bennettsbridge, 9.5 km (6 miles) SE of Kilkenny city.

Tullaroan Centre

This heritage centre, known as the Brod Tullaroan Centre, has several aspects. The most dramatic is the 17th-century thatched house in which Lory Meagher, once known as the "Prince of Hurling", lived. The house has been restored to its condition of 1884, the year in which the GAA was founded. In one bedroom of the house, the underside of the roof can be seen, complete with sods of turf lining the thatch. Beside the house is a museum devoted to the history of Gaelic games in County Kilkenny, while other aspects of the centre include a farm museum and a cultural centre.
14.5 km (9 miles) W of Kilkenny city.

LAOIS

CASTLES

Dunamase Castle

The battered remains of this once-strong castle crowns a massive rock with superb views over the pass through the west Wicklow hills. It was built in the 13th century by William Marshall and his son-in-law William de Braose on the site of an Irish fort that Strongbow had obtained. It had a number of owners, notably Roger de Mortimer – who further fortified it – before it fell into the hands of the O'Mores in the 14th century. In 1641 it was taken from the O'Mores by Sir Charles Coote, retaken by Eoghan O'Neill in 1646 and finally captured and dismantled by the Cromwellians in 1650.

William Marshall probably began the enormous rectangular tower on top of the hill. Much of the southern part has now vanished, while the northern portion was remodelled to form a stronghouse in the 16th century and a tower was added to the west wall flanking the entrance. The surrounding walls of the inner bailey were probably built by William de Braose around 1250. These are strongest on the vulnerable east side where there is a gateway flanked by oblong towers containing guard rooms.
5 km (3 miles) W of Stradbally off the N80 Portlaoise Road. NGR: S 523980.

Lea (Leghe) Castle

Cromwellian troops dismantled some of Ireland's finest castles – not least of which was the great fortress of Lea. The core of the castle is a massive four-towered keep that bears such a striking resemblance to Carlow Castle that they must be contemporary, especially as both were owned by William Marshall. It therefore belongs to the early 13th century and if so, it must be one of the earliest of these distinctive castles comprising a rectangular block with cylindrical corner towers. Sadly, only one tower now stands to any height, but the main block had three storeys over a basement and like Carlow has a first-floor doorway by the north-east tower and a straight stair in the north wall. Few castles have had such an active history. Lea was burnt in 1285 by the O'Connors, in 1307 by O'More and in 1315 by Bruce, after which the adjacent town was abandoned. The castle was subsequently captured on many occasions and passed to the O'Mores, the FitzGeralds, the Earls of Ormonde and the O'Dempseys, before Cromwellian troops finally wrecked it in 1650. In the 18th century the celebrated horse-thief James Dempsey used the vaults of the keep as his stables.

4 km (2.5 miles) E of Portarlington on a minor road N of the Monasterevin Road. NGR: N 571121.

HOUSES

Emo Court

This spectacular mansion, with its fine garden and parkland setting, is perhaps best known as James Gandon's sole venture into the field of monumental domestic architecture. It was designed around 1790 on the same magnificent scale as his Custom House and Four Courts, and in common with these was built in the neo-classical style – the style in which Gandon had established himself as the pre-eminent architect of late 18th-century Ireland.

The house was commissioned by John Dawson, Viscount Carlow and the first Earl of Portarlington, a man of undoubted architectural knowledge who was instrumental in bringing Gandon to Ireland. Dawson engaged Gandon primarily to design the nearby church at Coolbanagher; later he requested plans for a new county seat to replace Dawson Court, built in the early 18th century. A new site was chosen for the house which was named Emo – an Italianised version of Imoe, the original Irish name of the demesne. As designed by Gandon, it has a giant pedimented Ionic portico dominating the centre of the entrance front, flanked by two end pavilions making it in all a nine-bay composition with two storeys over a basement. Panels containing Coadstone reliefs of putti representing the Arts and a pastoral scene, dated 1794, crown the blind attics of the pavilions.

Sadly, Gandon's building was never completed as Lord Portarlington died of an illness when out campaigning during the 1798 rebellion. Despite their motto 'Virtue is the Way of Life', the family fortune was subsequently dissipated through gambling and the second Earl was unable to finance further building until 1834 when he employed the English architect Lewis Vulliamy, assisted by Arthur and John Williamson of Dublin, to make improvements. They worked on the interior as well as completing the garden front giving it a portico of four tall Ionic columns with a balustraded entablature to complement Gandon's front elevation. Finally in 1861, after the Encumbered Estates Court came close to ordering a compulsory sale of the estate, the third Earl somehow found enough money to build the great rotunda, whose copper-clad dome rising from behind the garden front was designed by William Caldbeck of Dublin. The mile-long Wellingtonia avenue was planted at this time and formal gardens laid out around the house. Unfortunately, much of Gandon's interior at Emo failed to survive 19th-century alterations. An important exception is the entrance hall – an attractive room whose apsidal ends were painted with trompe l'oeil paintings in the 1970s to represent plaster decoration that Gandon had originally intended.

The Portarlingtons sold Emo in 1930 to the Society of Jesus for use as a seminary. In 1969 the property was bought from the Jesuits by C.D. Cholmeley-Harrison who has subsequently carried out a magnificent restoration and refurbishment of the house. He has also admirably restored the gardens, planting many new trees and shrubs. In an area of the demesne park now owned by the Forest Commission stands the ruin of a building known as the Temple – a remarkable gazebo built around 1760 on alignment with Dawson's Court. It consists of a triumphal arch surmounted by an octagonal turret that was formerly domed. No doubt it was used for entertaining as it had a kitchen in the basement. A short distance away on Spike Hill is an obelisk.

9.5 km (6 miles) S of Portlaoise. NGR: N 539066.

GARDENS

Emo Court

Gandon's monumental neo-classical country house provides the focus for 55 acres of gardens that include spreading lawns, statuary, shrubs, a wealth of trees, a lake and a series of attractive walks, each with a different theme to explore. Avenues of dignified Irish yews planted in Victorian times criss-cross the lawns around the house from where paths lead to an attractive arboretum, crossed by a series of walks with such evocative names as the Everglade and the Apiary. An area of light woodland contains some fine trees including large examples of *Cedrus deodara*, *Pinus radiata* and *Picea smithiana*. Beneath the tree canopy is a wide selection of azaleas, rhododendrons and other shrubs. The garden looks best in spring but there are plenty of maples to give colour in autumn.

9.5 km (6 miles) S of Portlaoise. NGR: N 539066.

Heywood

Designed by Sir Edward Lutyens and Gertrude Jekyll between 1909 and 1912, this garden overlooks a spectacular 18th-century landscape park. The associated Georgian house has now gone, but the gardens have been restored to their original state. The main feature is a large elliptical enclosure with terraced borders and an oval pond encircling a stone fountain. A pavilion stands at one end, while opposite, an alley of pleached limes leads to a terrace with a lawn and borders. Beyond lies a pergola terrace whose Ionic columns were taken from one of the follies in the park. Other parkland follies still stand, notably a sham Gothic ruin on the main driveway.

Near Ballinakill, 5 km (3 miles) from Abbeyleix. NGR: S 472817.

MUSEUMS/HERITAGE CENTRES

Donaghmore Workhouse Museum

This mid-19th century workhouse has been meticulously brought to chilling life. Donaghmore was a thriving industrial community in the 19th century but now only has a dozen houses.

20 km (12 miles) W of Abbeyleix.

Morrissey's Pub

Very little has changed in this pub on the Main Street of Abbeyleix over the past century, yet it's still a lively meeting place for local people and visitors. The old mahogany counters are still in place, together with the shelves (most Irish pubs once doubled as grocery stores). The old packets, tins and advertising posters date back to the early years of this century. Beside the pot-bellied stove, the delivery bicycle, complete with bell and basket, awaits the call. Abbeyleix also has its own heritage centre, which highlights the town's long vanished carpet factory, which made carpets for the *Titanic*. Also in the town you can visit the sexton's house, a mid 19th-century cottage restored to its original style.

Abbeyleix, 14 km (9 miles) S of Portlaoise.

LEITRIM

CASTLES

Parke's Castle

Rising from the tranquil waters of Lough Gill, this attractive Plantation castle has recently undergone an extensive restoration. It now appears much as it did around 1610 when Robert Parker completed his fortified manor house on the site of a 15th-century O'Rorke castle. The walls of the original bawn were retained, but the O'Rorke tower house in the centre was demolished and its stones used to build the three-storey manor. This has now had its window glazing reinstated, while local craftsmen have successfully restored the timber stair, as well as the mortice and tenon oak roof. One of two round flankers forms one end of the manor, while at the other end stands a gatebuilding with an arched entrance leading into the enclosure. There is also a postern gate and a sally port, though there are no flankers on the lake shore probably as the water level was 10 feet higher in the 17th century and lapped up against the bawn walls. No doubt these waters fed the moat that formerly surrounded the bawn.

Excavations in the 1970s revealed the base of the O'Rorke tower house beneath the courtyard cobbles and this is now exposed to view. It was in this tower that Francisco de Cuellar, the shipwrecked Armada officer, was entertained by Brian O'Rorke. In later years de Cuellar was to write of his host: "Although this chief is a savage, he is a good Christian and an enemy of the heretics and is always at war with them." He was eventually captured, indicted and executed for high treason in London in 1591. The Parkers, who subsequently acquired his confiscated property, remained at Newtown, or Leitrim Castle – as it was formerly known – until the end of the 17th century, when it was deserted.

6.5 km (4 miles) NW of Dromahaire on the Sligo Road beside Lough Gill. NGR: G 783354.

MUSEUMS/HERITAGE CENTRES

Dromod Railway Heritage Centre

The Cavan and Leitrim narrow gauge railway opened in 1887 and closed in 1958. It ran from Dromod, on the main Dublin–Sligo line, to Belturbet in County Cavan, with a branch from Ballinamore to Drumshanbo and Arigna coal mines. Fondly remembered even today, the railway was as renowned in its day as the West Clare railway and, in the first stage of restoration, rails that originally came from the West Clare railway were used. The plan is to extend the line to Mohill. The old Cavan and Leitrim railway was slow but sure, with a maximum speed of 19 km (12 miles) per hour. The original station at Dromod, complete with ticket office and waiting room, has been restored, as have been the engine shed and water tower. Many relics of the line still exist, including hundreds of photographs taken during the 1950s by an English railway enthusiast, Michael Davies.

Dromod, on the main Dublin–Sligo line.

LIMERICK

CASTLES

Adare Castle

The time-worn remains of this Anglo-Norman fortress on the banks of the River Maigue may be counted among the most impressive castles in Ireland. It was first mentioned in 1226 as being held by Geoffrey de Marisco, but later passed to the FitzGeralds, possibly as early as 1240. The Earls of Kildare retained ownership for nearly 300 years until Silken Thomas's rebellion of 1536, when it was forfeited and granted to the Earl of Desmond. Barely forty years later, in 1578, the Munster Geraldines were themselves in rebellion and lost the castle to English troops after an eleven-day siege. Attempts to retrieve the castle resulted in a series of notably bloody sieges in 1579, 1581 and 1600, leaving the fabric badly damaged. It was finally dismantled by Parliamentary troops in 1657.

The castle was probably begun in the 1190s and initially comprised a large square tower; this was remodelled in the 15th century and is thus difficult to assess confidently. No doubt it served as the lord's accommodation and thus complemented the more public function of the Great Hall by the river, which was clearly built to entertain visitors.

The curtain walls around the inner ward and along the west side of the outer ward were possibly built around 1240, no doubt replacing timber palisades. The very ruined aisled Great Hall may have been added in 1326 when the second Earl of Kildare undertook extensive works at the castle. It is flanked by kitchens and service rooms, which extend to the eastern perimeter of the outer ward – whose well-preserved battlemented walls may be largely 15th century in date.

14.5 km (9 miles) SW of Limerick city. NGR: R 471467.

Askeaton Castle

The splendid castle of the Munster Geraldines at Askeaton, the principal seat of the last Earls of Desmond, rises majestically above the River Deel on a small rocky island. Most of the ruins belong to the 15th century, though they incorporate parts of a much older fortress that was founded here by William de Burgo in 1199. The Earls of Desmond had many changes in fortune after they acquired the place in the 1340s, but the heyday of their great wealth and power undoubtedly came when the King, otherwise engaged in French wars, surrendered his royal rights in Munster to the seventh Earl of Desmond. It was during this time from 1420 to 1457 that most of the castle and nearby Franciscan friary were built.

The castle extends over two courtyards – an upper ward crowning the rock and a lower ward surrounding it. The upper ward still retains fragments of its 13th-century polygonal wall with footings of a gateway on the east side. At the northern end stands a large 15th-century hall and chamber block, probably on 13th-century foundations. In the outer ward, built against the ramparts on the west side, stands the celebrated banqueting hall – perhaps the finest secular building of its period in Ireland. Its foundations are early medieval, but the ground floor vaulted chambers, cellars and kitchens all belong to the 1430s, when the seventh Earl built the hall above – a magnificent room 72 feet long and 30 feet wide. A striking feature are the large windows with decorated carvings, while the south end is decorated with a blind arcade, behind which stands the remains of a chapel block.

During the Desmond rebellion in 1580, the castle fell to Pelham after two days' bombardment, and shortly afterwards was handed over to the Berkleys. In 1599 the Earl of Essex came to its relief after it had withstood a 147-day siege by the "Sugan" Earl of Desmond. It was captured by the Confederates in 1642 and ten years later dismantled by Cromwellian troops.

25.5 km (16 miles) W/SW of Limerick city on the T68. NGR: R 341501.

Carrigogunnell Castle

From its superb vantage point on a volcanic crag, this fortress is a striking landmark which demonstrates an excellent use of natural defences. It is mentioned in 13th-century contexts, but the greater part of the present remains belong to the period after 1449 when the sixth Earl of Desmond conferred it on Brien Duff O'Brien, son of the Prince of Thomond. It has a rather complex range of buildings, including a four-storey tower, a circular bastion and a gabled house. In 1536 the castle was surrendered to Lord Deputy Grey, after he used his artillery to blow up the gate of the outer court. The men of the garrison, who were found huddled in the dungeon, were all taken out and executed. The O'Briens later lost the castle in the Cromwellian forfeitures. In 1691 it was mined and blown up with an enormous quantity of gunpowder by order of General Ginkel, after it had surrendered with its Jacobite garrison of 150 men.

Located 2 miles NW of Mungret. NGR: R 499552.

Limerick Castle

This striking landmark in Limerick, known as "King John's Castle", stands on the east bank of the Shannon within the city walls, commanding a strategically important river crossing. It was built as a royal fortress in the early 13th century and is an outstanding example of a "keepless" castle, similar in many respects to contemporary castles at Kilkenny and Dublin. It has a pentagonal plan with massive drum towers defending each of the four main angles – one of which was replaced by a diamond-shaped bastion in 1611.

The Normans appear to have attempted to secure control of Limerick around 1202 when the Annals record a "castle there". Stone-revetted earthen banks, recently discovered during excavations, may be part of this early Norman fort. Work on the stone castle may have begun a little later, perhaps around 1210, as the Pipe Rolls record an expenditure of £733 on the site in 1212.

For most of its history the castle remained in Crown control and had an uninterrupted line of constables from 1216 until the death of Lord Gort in 1842. Despite this continuity, the castle did not escape being captured on many occasions. It fell to Bruce in 1316 and later again to the O'Briens and MacNamaras in 1369. In 1642 it was taken by a strong force of Irish, after they ignited mines and breached the walls. Recent excavations in the vicinity of the east curtain wall have uncovered a fascinating series of mines and countermines dug during this siege. The castle was captured by Cromwellian troops in 1651 and by Williamite troops in 1691.

In the 18th century the towers were reduced in height and fitted to bear artillery. Barrack buildings were also completed in 1751 and remained in use until 1922. These were partly replaced by Corporation houses in 1935, but in 1990 the whole interior was cleared and a new visitor centre erected. Ongoing archaeological excavation, supported by Shannon Heritage, continues in the castle every summer.

Limerick city. NGR: R 582576.

Shanid Castle

The famous war-cry and motto of the Earls of Desmond "Shanid aboo", echoed a belief that this little castle was "Desmond's first and most ancient house". It was built by Thomas FitzGerald, after he had been granted the land around 1198. The castle comprises the shattered shell of a polygonal tower spectacularly clinging to the summit of a large earthen motte with surrounding fosse and bank. The tower is circular internally and only half survives to full parapet height. It was surrounded by a curtain wall around the summit of the earthwork; the remains on the south side still retain some of their battlements and loop-holes. A small kidney-shaped bailey on the east side has no sign of an enclosing wall. It was captured by Red Hugh O'Donnell in 1601 and wrecked in 1641.

13 km (8 miles) N of Newcastle West. NGR: R 243452.

HOUSES

Glin Castle

The late Georgian Gothicisation of Glin Castle is only skin deep, but its pasteboard-like loops, crenellations and gleaming white walls have an ethereal quality that is particularly memorable. The castle's magic is further enhanced by a serene parkland setting, delightful gingerbread Gothic gatelodges and a lush location facing across the Shannon estuary. The romantically titled Knights of Glin have retained ownership of their lands here for seven centuries in spite of sharing a familiar history of rebellion, attainders and confiscations with the other Desmond Geraldines.

Fragments of the old medieval castle of Glin can be seen in the village and were built by one of the early Knights, whose family – a cadet branch of the Earls of Desmond – had held their rather unusual title since the 14th century. The castle was seriously damaged by George Carew in 1600 and completely destroyed following another siege in 1641. By the century's end the family was living one mile from the old ancestral castle in a thatched house known as Glin Hall. They remained true to the old faith until Edward, the twentieth Knight, conformed to Protestantism in 1737; he died soon after as a result of dancing at his wedding feast.

It was the twenty-fourth Knight who began constructing the present mansion on the site of Glin Hall in 1789. His son, John Frraunceis Fitz-Gerald, following the fashion of the time, added battlements and turrets in 1812 and rechristened it Glin Castle. He liked gambling and evidently was rather successful for he laid out much of the present park, built a hermitage made of tufa, a Gothic folly, the demesne wall (erected as a result of a bet with a local landlord) and three delightful castellated entrances to the demesne.

The interior is noted for its very fine neo-classical plasterwork and above all for its magnificent Irish furniture, much of which has been collected over the past two decades by the present Knight of Glin. It also has many interesting family portraits – one (c. 1745) is of Richard Fitz-Gerald, the duellist Knight, being challenged to a duel. Always willing to engage in personal combat, Richard offered his opponents the choice between pistols at twenty paces or the short sword wielded within a 10-foot ring – an unpleasant prospect as he was an accomplished swordsman and an excellent shot. On one occasion when engaged in a duel with a Spaniard, Richard was unable to drive his sword home until his servant cried out: "Stick him where they stick the pigs", whereupon the Spaniard was pierced through the throat and was found later to have been wearing protective chain mail under his clothing.

In sharp contrast to other Irish country houses, there is no doubt that Glin Castle looks better today than it has ever done in the past. Aside from being completely restored in recent decades, it has become home to many fine examples of Irish furnishings collected by the present Knight as part of his efforts to ensure that the finest examples of 18th- and 19th-century Irish craftsmanship remain in Ireland. Desmond Fitz-Gerald, who is the twenty-ninth holder of the title, is Christie's representative in Ireland and is well known and respected for his outstanding contribution to the study of Irish furniture, paintings, architecture and historic gardens. *1.6 km (1 mile) W of Glin village. NGR: R 123472.*

MUSEUMS/HERITAGE CENTRES

Adare

Often regarded as Ireland's most picturesque village, Adare's Main Street is lined with thatched cottages. The village, which is set on the banks of the River Maigue, has changed little since the late 19th century, while several buildings are of considerable antiquity. Desmond Castle dates back to the 14th century, while parts of the Church of the Most Holy Trinity date back to the 13th century. Adare's new heritage centre uses artefacts, models and an audio-visual presentation to portray the history of Adare from its foundation in 1233. *16 km (10 miles) SW of Limerick city.*

Limerick Museum

This excellent museum details the history of the city since 5000 BC. It's also excellent on the city in the 19th and 20th centuries, its crafts and trades, and also the Soviet set-up in Limerick after World War I. Local silverware, Limerick lace and old coinage are all part of the collection, which also has the "Nail" from the long-demolished Limerick Exchange. Traders here paid on the nail, hence the modern expression. The museum moved to new premises in Castle Lane in 1999, which gave it much more room for its extensive collections.
John's Square, Limerick city.

LONDONDERRY

HOUSES

Springhill

Considering the harsh and unappealing conditions that still prevailed in late 17th-century Ulster, it is perhaps surprising that country seats developing at that time were often pleasant and unassuming buildings exuding a feeling of warmth. Sadly, such houses from this period are now rare, though one particularly attractive and well-preserved example is Springhill – a charming and almost timeless building whose whitewashed front façade still brings to mind "something of the ancient dignity of resident landlords" as it did for Sampson, writing nearly two centuries ago.

The early history of Springhill is a little elusive, but the present house was built by William "Good-Will" Conyngham in 1680 to "erect a convenient dwelling house of lime and stone, two stories high, with necessary office houses, gardens and orchards". It is not known if a dwelling stood here previously, but the townland of Ballindrum (Springhill) had been bought for £200 by Good-Will Conyngham's father in 1658.

Although enlarged in the late 18th century, the house that Good-Will built survives much as he left it – a gable-ended block of two storeys over a basement with a steeply pitched roof, solid brick chimneys at each end and tall, thin windows in a seven-bay symmetrical front façade. Springhill faces onto a deep courtyard flanked by long, low office ranges with pointed windows (a later insertion) and curvilinear "Holborn gables" – a Flemish type which seems to have been much used in late 17th-century Ulster. Front courtyards were a standard feature of the period and Springhill was originally entered through large gates aligned upon a long, straight avenue. The main outbuildings, grouped around a series of small yards flanking the house, include a recently restored barn with an important oak roof, which like that of the main house incorporated butt purloins, rare in Ireland. Tree-ring dating by Queen's University, Belfast, revealed a date of 1694 for a lintel from this barn, while a floor joist timber from the attic of the main house produced a felling date of 1697.

The building has a tripartite plan with a centrally placed stair projection at the back. The door to the staircase hall is flanked by two pikes used in the Battle of Vinegar Hill, County Wexford, during the 1798 rebellion. The magnificent broad staircase is the real glory of Springhill and one of the earliest to survive in Ireland. The treads are made of oak while the handrail and balusters – alternately plain and spiral twisted – are made from yew. Ancestral portraits line the walls above, including one of Good-Will Conyngham, while at the foot of the stairs is a heavy oak chest inscribed "John Smith maid this in 1714".

The gun room, formerly the dining-room, must have been made into a small drawing-room around 1770 as restoration work during the 1960s accidentally revealed pretty handprinted English wallpaper in the panel frames. Later it became home to a fine collection of guns and swords reflecting the family's military past. Among the items on display are a few bulky blunderbusses, a Kentucky rifle, duelling pistols and a number of flintlocks, later converted to muzzleloaders and used in the siege of Derry in 1689.

The library houses an outstanding collection of books, most of which were acquired by Colonel William Conyngham, while a fascinating medicine chest full of drawers and bottles stands beside the drawing-room door; originally belonging to the Duke of Marlborough, he gave it to his aide-de-camp, the third Viscount Molesworth, after he saved his life during the Battle of Ramillies in 1706.

The large and lofty drawing-room creates a striking contrast to the small rooms of the original house. French Empire sofas, Louis XV tables and an armchair, a Dutch rosewood cabinet and a circular Regency table grace the scene, while family portraits hang on the walls. One is a pretty portrait of Harriet Molesworth by Sir Francis Cotes. The unfortunate Harriet lost her leg while trying to escape a fire at her London home, and an ivory walking stick presented to her by King George III is displayed on a small Chinese cupboard beneath her portrait.

Elsewhere in Springhill are many small rooms, old powder closets and even a secret staircase now permanently concealed. There are curious sloping alcoves for beds in the attics and below, on the first floor, a charming day nursery. One of the two bedrooms open to the public is the blue room where George Lenox Conyngham shot himself in 1816 after spending many months "in a melancholy state of mind". His wife, Olivia, haunts the scene; her ghost is one of the most widely authenticated phantoms in Ulster.

Outside, in the old laundry yard, lies an important costume collection begun in 1964 containing over 2,300 items, including a Court Mantua made in England in 1759 and featuring brocaded Spitalfields silk. The collection is displayed in rotation each year.

Springhill was given as a gift to the National Trust in 1957; included in the transfer was the magnificent 300-year-old beech avenue which sadly had to be replanted in 1984 after the trees developed beech bark disease.

Located near Moneymore on the Coagh Road (B18). NGR: H 869828.

GARDENS

Brook Hall

Arboretum in parkland around Regency house in wonderful setting over the Foyle. A good collection of trees and shrubs, notably rhododendrons, begun in the 1920s by Commander Guilliland and still being developed by his cousin David Guilliland.
1 km (0.6 mile) from roundabout on W side of Foyle Bridge N of Derry.

Downhill

Focus of park is dramatic ruin of Earl Bishop's palace, but demesne also has exquisite neo-classical buildings (Mussenden Temple, Mausoleum, Bishop's Gate), two artificial lakes, extensive woodlands, two enormous Sitka spruce and a small but very attractive gatelodge garden.
1.6 km (1 mile) W of Castlerock on Limavady Coast Road.

The Guy Wilson Daffodil Garden

From the period when daffodil hybridisation first began, Irish breeders have led the world in the number and quality of cultivars raised. As a tribute to these hybridists, a daffodil collection has been established in the grounds of the University of Ulster at Coleraine. The garden is dedicated to the memory of Guy Wilson of Broughshane (1885–1962), one of the country's leading hybridists and the man who did most to develop daffodil breeding in Ireland over the past fifty years.

The collection occupies the site of an old quarry on the south side of the campus at Fortview, close to the Portstewart Road. The setting is attractive with its south-facing lawns, informal paths and irregular-shaped island beds of shrubs interplanted with daffodils. There are around 1,500 old and modern cultivars in the collection, many the creation of Wilson, Richardson, Dunlop, Bloomer and other famous Irish breeders. *1.6 km (1 mile) N of Coleraine on the Portstewart Road at the University of Ulster, Coleraine. NGR: C 847339.*

MUSEUMS/HERITAGE CENTRES

Foyle Valley Railway Centre

This comprehensive railway museum tells the story of the narrow gauge railways in north-west Ireland, with the exhibits housed in a purpose-built centre reminiscent of a Victorian station. Among them are samples of rolling stock from the former County Donegal railway and the Londonderry and Lough Swilly Railway Company, as well as some steam locomotives from the County Donegal Railway. Many railway artefacts are included and some can be operated by visitors. The upper floor has more memorabilia, an electronic railway map, railway models and an audio-visual presentation.
Craigavon Bridge, Derry city.

Garvagh Museum

This museum and heritage centre is set in the walled garden of Garvagh House, the ancestral home of the Canning family for almost 300 years (George Canning became British Prime Minister in 1827). The museum, which claims to be the largest school-based museum in these islands, has artefacts covering most aspects of rural and domestic life in the 19th and early 20th centuries.
20 km (12 miles) S of Coleraine.

Harbour Museum

The former offices of the Derry Harbour Commissioners, built around 1880, have been turned into a splendid maritime museum. The museum recalls the heady days of Derry shipbuilding, which flourished in the 19th century, and in World War II. Then, ships of the countries in the Allied war effort tied up in Derry and their crews brought an exotic foreign influence to the city. The museum is awash with models, maps, drawings and photographs.
Derry city centre, beside Guildhall.

Knockloughrim Windmill

In the 18th and 19th centuries, the Irish countryside was dotted with windmills. Today only two restored windmills are left in Northern Ireland – Ballycopeland on the Ards peninsula, and Knockloughrim Windmill. This latter was built in the 1880s, but only worked for two years before the sails were blown off. Inside the mill display panels and audio-visual presentations detail the history of Knockloughrim village, the windmill itself and wind-power generation.
5km (3 miles) NW of Castledawson, on A6.

Tower Museum

This award-winning museum, opened in 1992, tells the tangled story of Derry from its origins in the 6th century right up to the present day using high technology and modern audio-visual presentation methods. Just inside the city walls, a 16th-century tower house, built originally for the local Gaelic chieftains, the O'Donnells, was reconstructed to house the museum. The many facets of the city's troubled history are impartially told and include the Siege of Derry in 1688–9, events in Ireland leading to partition in the early 1920s and the more recent troubles in Derry,

including the 1969 battle of the Bogside. Derry had a civic museum from 1903 to 1951 and the Tower Museum is an admirable successor.
Derry city centre, entrance from Linenhall Place.

Waterside Workhouse Museum

The harsh conditions of the mid 19th-century workhouse have been recreated with graphic realism in this latest addition to the ranks of Derry's fine museums.
Waterside, Derry city.

LONGFORD

HOUSES

Carrigglas Manor

The blue-grey limestone façade of Carrigglas, with its great oriel windows, battlemented turrets and high-pitched gables, has a mystical, almost dream-like quality as it rises serenely over the surrounding parkland. A finer example of castellated Tudor Revival architecture would be difficult to find. Carrigglas was designed by the Scottish architect Daniel Robertson in 1837 for Thomas Langlois Lefroy, Lord Chief Justice of Ireland, replacing an earlier house belonging to Lord Newcomen who had committed suicide after his bank collapsed. The Lefroy family still live in and maintain the house. With most of its original pictures, artefacts and furniture still intact, the interior exudes an atmosphere of early Victorian living that is unspoiled by later decorative schemes. Passing through a formal entrance hall revealing hard wooden seats for unwanted guests, one arrives in a central chamber dominated by a staircase notable for its cast-iron handrails. This room is lit by a stained-glass window displaying the Lefroy coat of arms – the Lefroys are a family of French Huguenot ancestry. Below the window stands a bust of Thomas – or the Chief, as he was called – modelling as a Roman senator. An enigmatic and colourful character, he had in his youth become an inamorato of Jane Austen and was later immortalised as Darcy in Pride and Prejudice.

Magnificent double doors with Gothic panelling link the three principal reception rooms; at one end lies the drawing-room with its striking compartmented ceiling and cornice of foliage, still coloured the original hues of rose and pale blue. The splendid chimney-piece was a gift from the Countess of Carrara, who sent over a block of white marble with a mason to carve it in situ. The adjacent library has a comfortable appearance; big armchairs, a Siena fireplace, Tudor-Gothic doors and a Gothic bookcase create an air of ease and repose. Despite its large size, the dining-room has quite a warm feel created by the mellow glow of the mahogany table, the old Turkish carpet and the red upholstered dining chairs. A magnificent Chinese painted leather screen stands close to the fireplace, while above the mantel a large portrait of Chief Justice Lefroy commands all aspects of the room.

Upstairs the bedrooms seem endless. One room has a particularly fine silk oriental carpet, an enormous four-poster bed, Irish rosewood table and Staffordshire his-and-hers washing sets. The floral patterned wallpaper is copied from Queen Victoria's bedchamber at Osbourne.

Visitors to Carrigglas must inspect the magnificent double courtyard stable and farmyard complex that was erected before 1790 to the designs of James Gandon, architect of the Custom House and Four Courts. Gandon also designed the main entrance to the park, with their symmetrical flanking lodges.
5 km (3 miles) NE of Longford on the Granard Road. NGR: N 17070.

MUSEUMS/HERITAGE CENTRES

Ardagh

This entire village is an important site and its history, dating back to the church founded here in the 5th century by St Patrick, is well recalled in the Ardagh Heritage Centre. This is one of Ireland's most attractive such centres and details in audio-visual form the ecclesiastical origins of Ardagh, moving on to the plantation of County Longford in the early 17th century. The centre even has a model *seanachie* (traditional storyteller) sitting in front of a turf fire, and displays many details of local life, including the old roll books from the school that once occupied this building.

The Fetherstone family, who rebuilt the village to a Swiss design in the 1860s (it is still one of Ireland's neatest villages), are recalled and Ardagh House, where the Fetherstones lived until 1927, played host over the years to such literary figures as Oliver Goldsmith, Sir Walter Scott and Maria Edgeworth. Its 19th-century courtyard outbuildings have been turned into a museum of rural life, with stables and a herb garden attached.

10 km (6 miles) SE of Longford town.

Corlea Trackway Centre

This new, futuristic interpretative centre built in the middle of the bogs displays the remnants of the prehistoric trackways that were laid through these bogs. In 1984, a trackway made of oak planks was discovered here, quickly followed by other similar wooden roads. Samples of the wood were calculated to date from the 4th millennium BC. In all, over fifty of these prehistoric superhighways were discovered in the area and their history and relevance is well documented here. Visitors can even see the marks of the tools used to cut the wood and 20 metres (65 ft) of trackway is on display.

Nearby is the Newtowncashel Heritage Centre, which had a traditional farmhouse, complete with old utensils and farm equipment.

Corlea: 3 km (2 miles) from Keenagh village, 15 km (9 miles) S of Longford town on R397. Newtowncashel: 5 km (3 miles) SW of Keenagh.

LOUTH

CASTLES

Carlingford Castle

Looking down from a rock above the medieval walled town, this striking fortress stands guard over the harbour and the narrow pass between the town and the lofty mountains of the Cooley Peninsula. Historical references to the castle are sparse, but on architectural grounds it was most likely begun around 1200, probably by Hugh de Lacy. King John stayed here for three days in 1210, and later that century the eastern side of the castle was remodelled.

The original fortification evidently consisted of a many-sided curtain wall enclosing a roughly oval area around the summit of the rock. This survives around the western portion of the castle's courtyard, together with a flanking tower and the remains of a twin-towered gatehouse. Only portions of the northern gatehouse tower survive, but it is evident the gate towers flanked a surprisingly narrow entrance passage. The well-preserved square tower is noteworthy for the way its plan changes to a half-octagon on the upper levels.

The massive cross-wall of the castle was probably added in 1262 when records in a pipe roll show substantial payments being made for stone, timber and lead for building works at Carlingford. At this time, much of the eastern section of the castle was also remodelled to create three-storey apartments and a great hall. A four-storey range was added in the 15th century; this is now ruined but has some interesting fireplaces and arcading.

Carlingford appears to have remained in English hands during the post-medieval period. In 1596 Hugh O'Neill, Earl of Tyrone, tried to take the castle in a surprise attack. It was captured by Sir Henry Tichborne (Royalist) in 1642, surrendered to Lord Inchiquin (Royalist) in 1649 and delivered up to Sir Charles Coote (Cromwellian) the following year. It is likely Coote dismantled the castle, for it plays no further role in Irish history, though the town was used as a hospital station during the Williamite wars. *Carlingford town. NGR: J 188120.*

Castleroche

Still known by its simple Norman-French name of Roche, this impressive castle clings dramatically to the summit of a great rocky outcrop. Striking and powerful, it commands a pass northwards and affords wonderful views over the surrounding country. According to the Close Rolls of 1236, it was raised by Lady Rohesia de Vernon, whose grandfather came to Ireland with Prince John in 1185. There is a tale that she promised herself in marriage to the architect if he completed the job to her satisfaction, but when he came to claim her hand, she had him cast from one of the windows in the west end – still popularly known as the "Murder Window".

Most of the castle was built in the 1230s, though it may have been completed in the following decade. Its peculiar triangular layout, determined by the shape of the rock, comprises a large enceinte enclosure with a twin-towered gatehouse linked to the very considerable Great Hall. A causeway gives access to the entrance across a rock-cut ditch, in the centre of which was a gap with drawbridge protected by a barbican.

The large rectangular hall must have been an impressive building in its heyday. Its main chamber, lit on the south side by three large windows, was so enormous that the basement must have had timber subdividing to support the floor. The east gabled wall survives with some traces of the old roof line and indications of a third storey. A small rectangular building on the north side of the hall is a later addition, while the remains of a free-standing rectangular structure in the ward centre may also be a later feature.

7 km (4.5 miles) NW of Dundalk. NGR: H 996132.

Roodstown Castle

Tower houses became a widespread phenomenon in late medieval Ireland following the collapse of central authority and the resurgence of Gaelic lords. Roodstown is a well preserved, though roofless, example of such a residential tower, with all the typical features – a vaulted ground-floor cellar, a murder-hole inside the main entrance, a well-defended parapet and wall-walk. The windows on the first and second floors have nicely carved 15th-century cusped ogee-headed lights, all with glazing bar holes. The two largest windows, both double lights and one with a transome bar, are in the first-floor hall, which also typically has the largest fireplace. As is usual in such buildings, the third floor – probably the private chamber – was unheated and had only small rectangular windows.

4 km (2.5 miles) E of Ardee on the Stabannon Road. NGR: N 996925.

HOUSES

Beaulieu

On the banks of the River Boyne stands Beaulieu, alias Bewley – a house of considerable charm and enormous architectural importance. It was built in the years of peace and prosperity following the Restoration in 1660, when Irish landowners abandoned their medieval castles and built unfortified luxurious seats. Almost all known examples of these Carolinian country houses have now vanished and only the unchanged splendour and refinement of Beaulieu survives to bear witness to this major turning point in the development of Irish architecture.

The house was built between 1661 and 1667 by Sir William Tichborne, who had been granted possession of the property by Charles II. His father, Sir Henry Tichborne, the prominent military commander in the Civil War, had resided as a tenant in the old castle at Beaulieu since 1650. From the 13th century, ownership of the castle, which stood north-west of the present house, had belonged to the Plunkett family, but in 1639 it was mortgaged and in 1642 was forfeited by the Cromwellian regime in retaliation for William Plunkett's participation in the 1641 rebellion.

Externally the house has remained virtually unaltered since the 1660s, although until the 19th century it was surrounded by a 12-foot-high protective hedge. Beaulieu is a seven-bay two-storeyed building and like many English houses of that time was built in the so-called "artisan mannerist" style, with cantilevered eaves carried on a massive wooden modillion course and a dormered attic in a high-hipped roof surmounted by tall, symmetrical chimney stacks. The rendered walls are of stone, but delicately rubbed orange-pink bricks from Holland have been used for the window surrounds and the string coursing. Any sense of monotony is broken by the grouping of windows on the side façades and by the pushing forward of the two end bays of the front elevation, whose angles are strengthened by stone quoins.

The interior still contains a great deal of its original fittings. Both the dining-room and drawing-room have kept their red pine panelling with bolection mouldings (a form of moulding which projects in front of the face of the frame) and their original ceilings with central ovals surrounded by heavy floral garlands. Most of the subsequent alterations to the interior were undertaken in the early 18th century by Sir Henry Tichborne. His most important addition was the grand staircase with its finely carved balusters and ramps at the newels. Other alterations at this time included a corridor on the first-floor landing and elaborate woodcarvings added to the arches over the doors in the front hall.

This remarkable house has thus remained in the same family for nine generations, covering a period of over 300 years.

Near Drogheda on the banks of the Boyne. NGR: O 128767.

MUSEUMS/HERITAGE CENTRES

Carlingford Visitor Centre

Carlingford town, set enticingly on the Cooley peninsula on the southern shores of Carlingford Lough, has been much restored in recent years. Historic medieval buildings include the imposing ruins of King John's Castle, the Mint and the Tholsel. Taaffe's Castle, a 15th-century square tower, has also been restored. The historical glories of the town are recaptured in the Holy Trinity Cultural and Visitor Centre in a restored church.

25 km (15 miles) NE of Dundalk.

Drogheda Museum

This fine museum, in a former military barracks, has a most impressive collection of material, from prehistoric times right up to the present day, detailing the development of this most historic town. Local industries, some long gone, like shoemaking and brewing, are well documented.

Drogheda town.

Dundalk Museum and Interpretative Centre

In an imaginative project, an old warehouse in central Dundalk, once belonging to the

P.J. Carroll tobacco company, has been transformed into an excellent town museum and interpretative centre, one of the largest and best appointed in the east of Ireland. The ground floor houses the museum, while three upper floors have galleries for exhibitions. It is also the site of Dundalk's library. Visitors to the museum are greeted by the sight of a perfectly preserved Heinkel bubble car, made in Dundalk about 1960. Dundalk has had its share of industrial tragedies, including the closure of the Great Northern Railway works, but has managed to adapt and survive. The story of many of those industries is told here, from cigarette manufacture and shoemaking to brewing and newspapers.
Jocelyn Street, Dundalk town.

Millmount Museum

Drogheda's town museum is a gem among Irish museums, with a large amount of material presented carefully and devoid of high-tech gimmickry. Part of an early 19th-century military complex, the house itself was home to the officers' mess. Among its prize exhibits are three guild banners for weavers, carpenters and brogue-makers, the only such banners left in Ireland. They are augmented by a series of trade banners, including a splendid painting of River Boyne fishermen made in 1867. The basement features a stone collection, representing every county in Ireland, every country in Europe and every continent in the world. Also in the basement is a traditional kitchen, with dresser and settle bed. Old milk cans and butter moulds are complemented by a selection of washing machines, including an 1852 rotary model. Many of the town's old industries, including its iron foundry, brewing, linen-making and shoemaking are featured.

The former Governor's House, across the courtyard, is used for exhibitions, while by climbing the steps to the adjacent Martello tower, visitors can enjoy an unrivalled view of the town and its surroundings.
Drogheda town, on Dublin side of River Boyne road bridge.

MAYO

CASTLES

Rockfleet Castle

Visitors to this relatively small tower house cannot fail to be delighted by the elegant simplicity of its architecture and by the stark beauty of its setting on an inlet of Crew Bay. But the principal attraction of this romantic place is its association with the legendary Grainne ni Mhaille, Grace O'Malley, who lived here after she married Sir Richard Burke (Richard the Iron) in 1566. Few figures in Irish history catch the imagination more than this remarkable woman, known as the "Pirate Queen", for her undisputed control over the west coast in the late 16th century. Her navy routed large Government seaborne expeditions sent against Rockfleet in 1574 and 1579, while in 1588 she captured ships of the dispersed Spanish Armada and mercilessly killed the crews – an exploit which resulted in her being received in great state by Queen Elizabeth I. After the death of her husband in 1583 she remained at Rockfleet with "all her followers and 1,000 head of cows and mares".

The castle has four storeys with a small rectangular corner turret rising above the parapet. The principal apartment must have been in the top floor where there is a fireplace. After the last war the building was restored by the diplomat Sir Owen O'Malley, a direct descendant of Grace, who lived in the nearby late Georgian house. In more recent years it was acquired by a former American ambassador to Ireland.
8 km (5 miles) W of Newport. NGR: L 915954.

HOUSES

Westport House

Westport is the largest and most important country house west of the Shannon and the only house by Richard Castle to remain in the possession of the family that built it. Since the late 18th century, visitors have marvelled at the building's quality and contents and, above all, its magnificent setting on the edge of Clew Bay, though sadly its fine parkland has been seriously mutilated by development in recent decades.

The house is the work of several architects, although the main mass of the building was designed in 1731 by Richard Castle for John Browne, later the first Earl of Altamont. Castle's house incorporated portions of an ancient O'Malley castle that had been acquired and much enlarged by the first Earl's grandfather, Colonel John Browne (1636–1711), a Jacobite who lost his fortune after the Williamite victory at the Boyne. In reduced circumstances, the family moved to Mount Browne outside Westport, but their fortunes prospered again as a result of John Browne's marriage to Anne Gore, sister of the Earl of Arran, in 1729. Two years later the German architect Richard Castle, who later established a highly successful practice in Ireland, began his remodelling of the house. His entrance front remains much as he designed it – a rather austere but attractive nine-bay façade made from beautifully dressed local limestone.

We can see how Westport looked in 1761 from two landscapes by George Moore hanging on the stairs. They show the house in a parkland setting with young plantations, bridges, salmon leaps and the sea coming right up to the house walls. The paintings were commissioned on the completion of John Browne's new park – a massive undertaking that involved not just landscaping and planting trees, but moving the town of Westport from its position around the house to its present location about a mile distant, where a new planned town was created.

Castle's house extended round three sides of an inner court, but between 1776 and 1778 its size was enormously increased when a fourth side was built to the designs of the Cork-born architect Thomas Ivory. This was commissioned by the second Earl of Altamont, whose marriage to an heiress of sugar plantations in Jamaica had made him one of Ireland's richest men. The third Earl employed James Wyatt to complete the interior – Wyatt's original drawings, dated 1781, are on view in the house. More rooms were added at basement level in 1816 when large terraces were built on either side of the house by the second Marquis of Sligo, Howe Peter – remembered for his friendship with George IV and Lord Byron. He brought back to Westport the two columns from the doorway of the Treasury of Atreus at Mycenae when touring Greece in 1812; they remained forgotten in the cellars until discovered by the sixth Marquis who presented them to the British Museum in 1906 on condition that they supply him with the replicas now standing on the south front of the house.

The entrance hall is the only surviving interior by Castle that remains intact. It has a Doric frieze and a magnificent coffered barrel-vaulted ceiling that has been compared to the roof of the temple of Aesculapius at Spoleto. Light pours into the room through a delicately wrought brass lunette above the frieze, though at one time there was also a Venetian window at the west end. The grand staircase of Sicilian marble was designed by George Wilkinson; the cantilevered stairs have undercut treads, while the metalwork balustrade has eagle motifs that were once gilded. The library replaces one that was destroyed by fire in 1826. It is a comfortable room whose walls are lined with bookcases stretching to within two feet of the ceiling; to the right of the door is a secret passage said to have been used to hide arms. On the other side of the hall lies the drawing-room, now inexplicably used as a restaurant. The adjoining long gallery, where there is a collection of family portraits, was decorated by James Wyatt but remodelled by his son Benjamin, who removed all the plaster decorations – a great loss if they resembled the plasterwork in the adjacent dining-room.

Although Wyatt never actually came to Ireland, let alone Westport, the delicate Adam-style plasterwork in the dining-room must rank among the best examples of his work. Both walls and ceilings incorporate medallions of classical figures with garlands, bows, festoons and gilded ears of wheat. The mahogany doors came from the family estates in Jamaica, while the massive sideboards supported by the family eagles were made by Gillow's for the second Marquis. Also on display in this room are Colonel John Browne's dinner service, Waterford glass finger bowls, 18th-century silver dish rings and a potato bowl of bog oak and silver that has belonged to the family since the 17th century. There are more family heirlooms in the small dining-room, most notably the flag of the Mayo Legion which was brought to Ireland by General Humbert when he landed in Killala in 1798 with French troops.

Elsewhere in the house visitors can see the exceptionally beautiful ceiling by Wyatt above the oak staircase and the Chinese room with its handpainted 18th-century wallpaper, which tells the same story as the willow pattern plate.

The house has been opened to the public since the 1960s. It is greatly to be regretted that such an important house has had to develop additional attractions such as the zoo in the walled garden in order to meet the outgoings.

Near Westport. NGR: L 987852.

MUSEUMS/HERITAGE CENTRES

Céide Fields Visitor Centre

The Céide Fields Visitor Centre, looking like a modern pyramid, stands overlooking spectacular cliffs on the north Mayo coast. The story it tells, of the Stone Age landscapes preserved beneath the blanket bogs of this part of Mayo, is equally dramatic. The life of this Stone Age farming community, with its stone-walled fields, homes and megalithic tombs, together with their craft skills and spiritual beliefs, is recreated inside the centre, which is dominated by a 5,000-year-old Scots pine tree. Viewing platforms inside and outside the glass-topped pyramid give striking views over land and sea. Audio-visual presentation.

8 km (5 miles) W of Ballycastle on the Belmullet Road.

Cois Abhainn Folk Museum

This small museum, on the Corraun peninsula near Achill Sound, is in a three-room cottage that dates back 120 years; it has been extensively restored. The kitchen includes an open fireplace complete with utensils and a settle bed, while old photographs recall people and places on the island; tragedies too, including one in 1937 when migrant workers from the island died in a fire in a bothy in Kirkintilloch, Scotland.

3.2 km (2 miles) E of Achill Sound.

Crossmolina Heritage Centre

This intriguing centre, opened in 1992, has a fine collection of vintage farm implements, all dating from the horse-drawn era. Woodcutting is featured, with an original saw pit in operation. Visitors can also see the Mayo spade, or gowl-gob, a two-pronged instrument exclusive to this locality. Regular demonstrations of traditional crafts are given at the centre, which also features restored farm buildings and household utensils.

16 km (10 miles) W of Ballina.

Foxford Woollen Mills Visitor Centre

Over a century ago, the woollen mills were set up by the Sisters of Charity to provide employment in an area that was suffering great economic and social deprivation. The story of these mills, famous for their rugs and other woven products, is told in audio-

visual form in the visitor centre, the Foxford Experience. The trials and tribulations of post-Famine Mayo form a dramatic introduction to the tour of the mills, during which visitors can see Foxford rugs and tweeds being made.
24 km (15 miles) NE of Castlebar.

Kiltimagh

The old railway station has been turned into a museum, with many domestic and farm utensils and artefacts dating from the late 19th and early 20th centuries. It features people with local connections who made good at home or abroad, including Gene Tunney, the world heavyweight boxing champion, and Mike Hogarty, who supervised the first Apollo moon landing. Also a schoolhouse heritage centre and forge.
24 km (15 miles) E of Castlebar.

Knock Folk Museum

The museum details the Apparition of the Virgin Mary at Knock in 1879, which has been drawing pilgrims here ever since. Other sections depict facets of life in rural Ireland: the thatched cottage, traditional furniture and former modes of transport. Another section details items from Gaelic Athletic Association history, while the old-style schoolroom, with wooden desks, inkwells and inspectors' reports from 1865 to 1901, recalls the old teaching era. Fittingly, this detailed view of old times in the West of Ireland concludes with much material on the late Monsignor James Horan, former parish priest of Knock, who did so much to develop this part of the West.
Knock.

Michael Davitt Museum

Michael Davitt (1846–1906) was born, evicted and ultimately buried in Straide; his family eviction experiences helped shape his political convictions. He played a crucial role in pressing for the reform of Ireland's land system, changing tenant farmers into owner occupiers. His life and works are recollected through the extensive collection of documents, photographs, prison and police records, letters, postcards, posters and personal possessions of the man.
15 km (9 miles) NW of Castlebar.

MEATH

CASTLES

Athlumney Castle

Tower houses often provided the nucleus for the unfortified country seats that began to emerge in Ireland from the 17th century. Many remain occupied to the present day, but Athlumney, on the east bank of the Boyne, has long been in ruins. It comprises a mid 15th-century tower house, built by the Dowdall family, which was considerably enlarged around 1630 by a long, narrow gabled mansion with large mullioned windows and a fine oriel window. The tower house has four storeys, with an attic and four projecting corner turrets of different sizes containing the stair, latrines and small chambers. In the south wall of the first floor there is a secret mural chamber reached down narrow stairs from above, created – one assumes – to hide priests, for the Dowdalls remained strong Catholics.

The mansion was burnt in 1649 as "one of ye families of ye Maguires was living in it when Oliver Cromwell took Drogheda and to prevent Oliver from getting any shelter or subsistence there, set ye stately fabric on fire which consumed all ye curious apartments which were said to be very rich and costly".
1.6 km (1 mile) SE of Navan off the Duleek Road. NGR: N 887664.

Donore Castle

The small tower house of Donore may have been built with the premium of £10 that the Government – alarmed by the frequent incursions of Gaelic lords – offered in 1429 to "every liege man" in the Pale who would build "a castle or tower sufficiently embattled or fortified within the next ten years to wit 20 feet in length 16 feet in width and 40 feet in height or more". The inside measurements and height of this simple three-storey rectangular tower certainly meet those requirements. Typically, its lower storeys are vaulted, while it has double-splayed basement loops, a box-machicolation above the ground floor entrance, mural latrine chambers, rounded external corners and a projecting tower at the south-west corner containing the stair.

The little castle came to a very sad end. After it was captured in 1650, the occupants at the time – James, son of MacGeoghegan, and over forty members of his household, including women and children – were all put to death by the Cromwellian general John Reynolds.

13 km (8 miles) SW of Trim on the Kinnegad road, 1 km (0.6 mile) W of Inchamore Bridge. NGR: N 702497.

Trim Castle

Trim Castle is the largest and one of the most important Norman military constructions in Ireland. Its well-deserved reputation as the king of Irish castles rests upon its imposing curtain walls enclosing over three acres, its fine gatehouses and its enormous isolated keep – all of which project a visually striking image of foreboding might and great power.

The first fortification on this site above the banks of the Boyne was a motte erected by Hugh de Lacy in 1172. After this was destroyed by Roderick of Connaught in 1174, de Lacy embarked on building another castle, the nature of which has not yet been established. On the basis of the present limited evidence, it seems likely that the curtain wall and the huge stone keep, which envelopes the stump of the old motte, were begun by de Lacy during the 1170s. Work may still have been proceeding when King John came here in 1210, for the following year, after the Crown had taken control of the castle, the sum of £64 was spent on building work, including "22/- for a large horse ... for strengthening the tower". The keep was probably being completed around this time.

The design of the keep is most unusual, comprising a massive square block with towers projecting from the middle of each face (only three out of the original four remain). On plan it looks like a combination of a square and a Greek cross. The towers have thinner walls than the main core and appear to have been added, not for defensive reasons, but to provide extra rooms and possibly because they looked good. Three of the four projections have ground floors, but the main core of the keep at this level is evidently filled with earth.

The curtain walls at Trim, two-thirds of which still stand, had a perimeter of 500 yards. They must have been completed by 1224 when William Marshall besieged the castle for seven weeks, for it is unlikely the castle could have withstood his army for such a period without the protection of the curtain walls. There appears to have been a barbican on the town side of the west entrance which was further protected by a murder hole, a portcullis, the gate, and a second murder hole through a hole in the passage. It is often claimed that the upper rooms of this gatehouse were used to house the young Prince Hal, later Henry V, who was left at Trim by Richard II in 1399 before his fateful return to England.

An extensive excavation was carried out in the 1970s in the area between the keep and the south curtain wall. This revealed a stone plinth added to the keep, parts of a ditch possibly dug around the keep and a number of ancillary buildings. It is to be hoped that more excavations will be carried out in the keep itself and in the area near the north tower, where it is evident that the Great Hall of the castle once stood.

Trim. NGR: N 202564.

GARDENS

Butterstream

Butterstream does not at first give the impression of being a sizeable garden, but gradually reveals itself through a series of interlinking compartments. Each is devoted to different arrangements of plants, all with wonderfully controlled masses of flower and leaf forms hidden away by clipped hedges and leafy screens.

At one end is a woodland garden where the emphasis is on foliage variations, notably hostas, which are grown in great masses and give a wave-like effect beneath the trees. Nearby is a rose garden with box hedging flanking varieties of old roses that the garden's creator, Jim Reynolds, has collected over the years. The adjacent hot garden is devoted to vibrant colours, such as the golden-yellows of *Hemerocallis* "Golden Chimes" and the brilliant reds of *H.* "Stafford" and by contrast, there is a white garden, with forms of agapanthus, delphiniums, astrantias and campanulas amidst clipped box hedging. Towering above is a round tower providing a look-out over the garden.

The centrepiece is a large herbaceous garden with 30-foot-wide beds and a wide choice of perennials all yielding a good succession of colour from late June to late October. A laburnum-clad pergola leads into the cool atmosphere of an Italian garden, while a large rectangular lawn bordered by shrubs and trees extends to a courtyard flanked by enormous neo-classical pavilions. The surreal effect is completed by terraces, cascades and a pair of canals 150 metres long.

Near Trim on the Kildalkey Road. NGR: N 797572.

MUSEUMS/HERITAGE CENTRES

Francis Ledwidge Centre

The poet Francis Ledwidge was born in Slane in 1887 and was killed in action at Ypres in 1917. The family home, built the year before Ledwidge, one of nine children, was born, has been carefully preserved. The neat cottage has material on the poet and copies of his correspondence include letters to and from his mentor, Lord Dunsany. A newspaper cutting shows his lordship proclaiming the discovery of a new Irish poet (Ledwidge), then aged 22. Seven years later he was killed by a shell on the Western Front and a shell fragment from Ypres is in the display. At the back of the house is a peaceful hillside garden.

0.8 km (0.5 mile) from Slane on the Drogheda Road.

Hill of Tara

The Hill of Tara, with its splendid views stretching far across the Midlands, was once the seat of the High Kings of Ireland, the main centre of political and religious power in pre-Christian Ireland. The hilltop with its closely-cropped grass has little to show these days, apart from the mounds. The layout of the site is well signposted. The early 19th-century church at the approach to the site has been turned into a visitor centre; the highlight is an audio-visual presentation – Tara, Meeting Place of Heroes.

10 km (6 miles) SE of Navan off the Dublin Road.

Newgrange

Several places of interest are grouped on this site, led by the Newgrange passage tomb, built 5,000 years ago and regarded as the world's first solar observatory. At the winter solstice on 21 December, the rays of the sun shine directly down the passageway; during tours, the effect is recreated by electric light.

The nearby great mound of Knowth dates from about 2000 to 2500 BC, has two passage tombs and seventeen satellite tombs. Knowth also has the greatest collection of tomb art ever discovered in Europe. The site has a very modernistic-looking Bru na Boinne Visitor Centre which details the history of the whole site. All tours of Newgrange and Knowth begin here.

Also in this immediate area, it's worth seeing the collection of old farm machinery, the cooper's workshop and the blacksmith's forge at Oengus Lodge.
11 km (7 miles) W of Drogheda.

MONAGHAN

Iniskeen

The birthplace of poet Patrick Kavanagh in 1906, this small, attractive village has several places of interest, primarily the folk museum and the Patrick Kavanagh Rural and Literary Resource Centre. The museum, housed in a former church, has about a dozen sections. Themes covered include the old Great Northern Railway, poitín-making, schooldays, carpentry, shoemaking and blacksmithing, all redolent of rural life in the early years of this century, when the poet was growing up here. The museum also has Kavanagh's death mask. The Kavanagh centre is in a converted church which he attended as a young boy. The centre also has a library and tours of the area are organised. Kavanagh himself is buried in the adjacent graveyard.
14 km (9 miles) W of Dundalk.

Monaghan County Museum

This award-winning museum has two floors devoted to the museum exhibits and a purpose-built art gallery. The museum highlights the development of the area from the time of the first settlers, between 5500 and 2500 BC, right up to the present day.

Sections cover the movement towards independence earlier this century. The highlight of the museum is undoubtedly the 15th-century Cross of Clogher, an oak cross covered with bronze and semi-precious metals, depicting figures of the saints. The old Great Northern Railway, once a vital communications' link, is featured in one section, complete with an old station master's cap, a carriage door key and a chain and whistle, besides many old railway posters. Other sections include linen-making in the town, a craft that had virtually expired here by 1850, and lace-making, particularly at Carrickmacross and Clones.

Also in Monaghan is an exhibition centre in the St Louis Convent, the mother house of the order in Ireland. The centre tells the story of the order from the time it arrived in Ireland in 1895.
Monaghan town.

OFFALY

Birr Castle Gardens

The gardens at Birr extend over 150 acres of an 18th-century "Brownian" demesne park the lake, rivers, woodlands and sweeping open spaces of which are adorned by an outstanding collection of nearly 2,000 species of rare trees and shrubs, many grown from seed collected in the wild. The focus of the layout is a splendid Gothicised castle and the recently restored frame of the "Leviathan", the world's largest 19th-century telescope.

Despite the antiquity of the demesne, the gardens are very much a product of the 20th century, being the creation of the sixth Earl of Rosse from 1918 to his death in 1979. The geography and planting is best appreciated at the River Garden, where some of Birr's most prized plants are found, perhaps none more beautiful than a tender collection of magnolias cushioned by a blue carpet of *Omphalodes cappadocica* in spring. There is a magnificent *Eucryphia x nymansensis* "Nymansay", while other gems include the rare *Carrierea calycina* from western China and the largest known example of a grey poplar. The suspension bridge over the river, built in 1810, is the earliest of its kind in Ireland.

Other delights at Birr include the High Walk where visitors will come across a large specimen of the rare Chinese tree *Ehretia* and a dawn redwood (*Metasequoia glyptostroboides*) – a remarkable deciduous conifer discovered in 1941 and known previously only from fossils millions of years old. This specimen, one of two plants received from Kew, is among the earliest in cultivation.

There is a young arboretum on the Tipperary side of the river and on the opposite bank a restored Victorian fernery with little bridges, jets of water and moss-covered rocks. Beyond lies the Walled Garden containing the famous pair of 30-foot-high box hedges, claimed to be the tallest in the world. The nearby formal garden has a boxwood parterre based on a Bavarian 17th-century design, enclosed by cloisters of pleached hornbeam allées aligned upon statues of the Graces. Prize plants near the old greenhouse include a very old *Magnolia stellata* from Japan and a Japanese bitter orange tree (*Poncirus trifoliata*) whose scented white flowers bloom endlessly in May. Visitors here should also inspect the wonderful tree peony "Anne Rosse"; it was named after the late Dowager Countess of Rosse and is a hybrid between a yellow variety discovered in Tibet and a Chinese Yü introduction with small flowers of dark red.
Birr town. NGR: N 056047.

MUSEUMS/HERITAGE CENTRES

An Dún Transport and Heritage Museum

This museum gives a unique insight into the various methods of transport used in Ireland this century. The older methods of transport are represented by pony and trap and side car exhibits, together with penny-farthing bicycles and pre-World War I bicycles fitted with carbide lamps. Among the motor vehicles are 1920s' lorries and a selection of tractors. There's a model railway and cable car display, complemented by a scale model of an American clipper, a child's late 19th-century doggy cart, old dairy equipment and working oil engines. Cars include a 1930 Baby Austin, converted to a shooting brake, a 1920s' Bullnose Morris Cowley and a more modern, but equally classic, Morris Minor.
11 km (7 miles) SE of Athlone on the Ferbane Road.

Historic Science Centre

This ambitious project plans to tell the story of Ireland's scientific heritage, focussing not just on the remarkable work of the Rosse family from Birr, but on Ireland's many other scientific pioneers. The huge telescope devised by the third Earl of Rosse in the early 1840s, which was for seventy years the largest astronomical telescope in the world, has been restored.

Other aspects being developed include the device made by the fourth Earl of Rosse for measuring the heat of the moon, Victorian photography (a great interest of the third Earl's wife), microscopy (another family interest) and details of the world's first turbine ship, also the handiwork of a family member. Many other achievements of 19th-century Irish scientists are also commemorated. The new centre complements the town's own heritage centre.
Birr Castle, 0.8 km (0.5 miles) W of Birr town.

Tullamore Dew Centre

This centre details the making of Tullamore Dew, as well as the history of the town and its canal.

Tullamore town.

ROSCOMMON

Ballintober Castle

This large "keepless" fortress is often claimed to be the only surviving early medieval castle of an Irish ruler. It was built in the 1290s and has a roughly square plan, with enormous asymmetrical polygonal corner towers and a gateway in the eastern curtain, flanked by comparatively small projecting turrets. However, residential apartments in the upper floors of the towers appear quite sophisticated in their design, indicating that Norman rather than Irish architects were employed. Indeed, the oft-repeated claim that this castle was built by the O'Connors of the Royal House of Connaught is difficult to sustain, especially as Irish chiefs of this period had no use for such fortresses. Furthermore, in the 1333 inquisition of the Earldom of Ulster, a hundred court is recorded at Ballintober. It is likely the builder was William de Burgo, and no doubt the castle's large area was intended to permit an Anglo-Norman settlement within its walls. The northern towers are higher than the others as they were rebuilt and repaired in 1627. Outside the walls extra protection was afforded by a wide water-filled moat.

The castle fell into the hands of the O'Connors in the 14th century and remained in their possession for many centuries, being the chief seat of the O'Connor Don from 1385 until 1652. In 1598 it was surrendered to Red Hugh O'Donnell, who attacked it with cannon, breached its walls and forced Hugh O'Connor Don to recant his allegiance to the Crown. In 1641 it became a centre of Catholic resistance with the result that it was confiscated in 1652. The O'Connors regained possession in 1677 and remained in residence until 1701, when it was abandoned.

17.5 km (11 miles) NW of Roscommon off the Tulsk Road. NGR: M 729748.

Rinnduin Castle

The impressive ruins on the remote Rinnduin Peninsula at Lough Ree have quite a romantic appeal, though they are very overgrown and frustrating to study. The first castle and town was founded here by Geoffrey de Marisco in 1227 as a base during his campaign west of the Shannon. Once the Normans secured a greater foothold in Connaught, Rinnduin assumed an increasingly important position in government military strategy. By the 1270s it was providing a vital link between the royal forts of Roscommon and Athlone, as well as guarding the ships along the Shannon and helping to keep the O'Connor kings of Connaught in check.

The castle is protected by a wide moat, once filled with water, running across the peninsula. This was probably dug in 1227, but the ward wall behind, which has small square loopholes, may not have been completed until 1260. The ward was entered through a rounded-headed archway of cut limestone with slots for a portcullis, outside of which are masonry piers for a bridge that was repaired in 1278.

A town developed under the protection of the castle, defended on the landward side by a substantial towered wall. Only the ruins of the parish church remain, to the east. The town was sacked by the O'Connors in 1236 and 1270. After its final plunder in 1315 it appears not to have recovered.

17.5 km (11 miles) N of Athlone and 4 km (2.5 miles) E of Lecarrow. Access through fields for half a mile to end of peninsula. NGR: N 008539.

Roscommon Castle

Strategically set deep in the plains of Connaught, this great royal fortress was raised as part of a campaign to assert Crown authority west of the Shannon. The first fort was begun in 1269 by Robert de Uffort, but this was demolished by the native Irish under Hugh O'Connor in the 1270s. After this failure, the justiciary embarked on a stronger, more impregnable fortress, built in the early 1280s to the latest military specifications. Similar to Harlech Castle, which it pre-dated by three years, this castle comprised a large quadrangle with projecting D-shaped corner towers and an unusually fine twin-towered gatehouse in the centre of the east wall. A moat with drawbridges surrounded the castle at some distance from the walls, presumably filled from a lake that formerly lay close by.

The castle was stormed in 1308 by a local chief, Donogh O'Kelly, and most of the inhabitants were slain. It remained in Irish hands, though probably largely deserted, until recovered by Sir Henry Sidney from the O'Connors in 1569. Nine years later it was granted to the Governor of Connaught, Sir Nicholas Malby, who built a splendid manor house on the east and north sides of the courtyard, with large mullioned windows inserted into the old walls. This appears to have had gardens on the east side enclosed by high walls with bastions. From 1645 to 1652 the castle was occupied by Confederate Catholics, but was dismantled after surrendering to the Cromwellians. *Near Roscommon town off the Tulsk road. NGR: M 874649.*

HOUSES

Clonalis House

Whatever the great Victorian mansion at Clonalis may lack in architectural beauty, it certainly gains through its historical associations with the O'Connor Dons, descendants of the last High Kings of Ireland whose possession of these lands can be traced back over 1,500 years. The ruins of the old ancestral seat – an attractive late 17th-century gable-ended house incorporating a medieval castle – can still be seen in the demesne. This was abandoned in 1880 after the completion of the present house, a large, rather grim cement-rendered building of two storeys with a basement and dormered attic. Its peculiar mixture of Queen Anne Revival and Victorian Italianate styles is typical of the work of its designer – Frederick Pepys Cockerell, a young and popular English architect who died shortly after building work at Clonalis had begun in 1879.

On the lawn in front of the house stands the inauguration stone of the O'Connors, originally erected at Rathcroghan, the ancient seat of the High Kings of Connaught some 9 miles distant. Entering the building, visitors will be struck by the height of the hall, whose modillion ceiling cornice is supported by graceful arches and Ionic columns of pink marble from Mallow. Over the stairs hangs a banner which was carried by Denis O'Connor Don at the coronation of George V in 1911 – the first Irish-Gaelic family to be so honoured. Family portraits here include Hugh O'Connor, who founded Tucson in Arizona, and Major Maurice of Ballintober who lost his lands under Cromwell, regained them under Charles II and mortgaged them to raise troops for James II.

In the library mahogany bookcases hold over 5,000 books, including the diaries of Charles O'Connor of Belanagare (1710–90), the great historian and antiquary. There are also facsimiles of many early illuminated Irish manuscripts and over 100,000 letters and documents. The Roman Catholic chapel contains a number of relics from penal times, including the altar from a secret chapel located in the outbuildings of the old house and a chalice once used by Bishop O'Rourke to celebrate Mass, which unscrews into separate pieces for easy concealment.

Some of the most interesting items in the house are found in the billiard room, now converted into a small museum. Here visitors can peruse letters and papers from the family archives, including notes written by such famous personalities as

O'Connell, Parnell, Gladstone, Trollope, Napper Tandy, Samuel Johnson and Laurence Stern. However, pride of place in this room is the harp that was once played by Turlough Carolan (1670–1738), the famous blind musician and last of the traditional Irish bards. He often played at Clonalis and once remarked that "when I am among the O'Connor's, the harp has the old sound in it".
10 km (6.5 miles) W of Castlerea on the N60. NGR: M 660813.

Strokestown Park House

Members of the Irish nobility sometimes had rather grand notions, and so it was at Strokestown, where the second Lord Hartland laid out a street wider than the Ringstrasse in Vienna. At one end of this tree-lined mall lies a magnificent Gothic arch that leads to Strokestown Park House, one of Ireland's finest Palladian houses and seat of the Pakenham Mahon family from 1660 to 1979. It now belongs to James Callery who, saving it from almost certain demolition, has carried out a major restoration programme and opened it to the public.

From the front, the house looks enormous with its central block linked by curved quadrants to wings that are prolonged by screen walls with niches and pedimented archways. The main house has seven bays with three storeys over a basement and seems largely to date from 1696 – the date carved on a stone by the front door. The top storey and balustrade were added later probably around 1740 when the architect Richard Castle built the wings for Thomas Mahon, MP for Roscommon for forty-two years. In 1819 Lieutenant General Thomas Mahon carried out some more improvements, such as the addition of the porch and giant pilasters to the front. Except for the gardens, few changes were later carried out at Strokestown and it remained the centre of a vast 30,000-acre estate until the present century.

In contrast to the external grandeur of the house, the interior is quite intimate, with surprisingly small rooms – a product of the early date of much of the building. Early 18th-century wood panelling survives in parts of the house but many rooms were redecorated in Regency times, such as the dining-room which still has its early 19th-century furniture, including a bath-size turf bucket and wonderful pinkish-red damask wallpaper. Regency additions to the house incorporated the study, which also retains its original furnishings, and the smoking-room, which was converted into a laboratory and photographic darkroom by Henry Pakenham-Mahon, an amateur scientist, in the 1890s. The finest Regency addition to the house was the library at the back; originally built as a ballroom with a bowed wall at one end to accommodate musicians, this well-proportioned room has an exuberant and welcoming atmosphere that is remarkable for its unique Chippendale bookcases and for the beauty of its brown-and-gold wallpaper, made especially for these walls in the early 19th century.

The old kitchen in the left wing of the house is approached from the dining-room along a curved corridor, past store rooms for kitchen utensils and sporting equipment. Fitted with spits and ovens for baking, roasting and smoking, this kitchen has its original balustraded gallery which crosses the high-ceilinged room lengthwise – the only example of its kind to survive in Ireland. Once a familiar feature of many Irish 18th-century houses, especially those designed by Richard Castle, these galleries allowed the housekeeper to supervise affairs below – one tradition at Strokestown relates that menus were dropped from the balcony on Monday mornings with the instructions to the cook for the week's meals.

The wing to the right of the central block contains magnificent vaulted stables carried on Tuscan columns; an underground passage linked these stables to the yard on the north side of the house. The estate office was also housed in this wing – a surprising location, for it meant that the tenantry had to come here rather than to an office in the village to pay their rent. The family's relationship with their tenantry during part of the 19th century was not always good. Major Denis Mahon was so unpopular a landlord during the Famine years that he was shot whilst returning from a meeting of the Roscommon Relief Committee in 1847, apparently on suspicion of having chartered unseaworthy ships to transport emigrants from his estate to the shores of America.

16 km (10 miles) W of Longford on the Dublin–Ballina Road. NGR: M 937808.

GARDENS

Strokestown

A 4-acre walled garden close to the house which, until restoration began in 1989, had lost most of its original features and was used to graze sheep. The garden has now been brought back to its Edwardian heyday, complete with a remarkable double herbaceous border, 500 feet long, resplendent in colour throughout the season from May to October. There is also a pergola, a rose garden and a croquet lawn overlooked by a restored summer house. In the centre lies a pool flanked by sentinel yews and in one corner an attractive wildflower garden with grass paths to allow visitors to view the flowers. More modern features include a Venetian window added as a vista stop, the King Harmon gate piers at the entrance and the "Alphabet Walk" with its niches inside a beech hedge.

16 km (10 miles) W of Longford on the Dublin–Ballina Road. NGR: M 937808.

MUSEUMS/HERITAGE CENTRES

Boyle

The small town of Boyle has three outstanding properties. The Cistercian Boyle Abbey, one of the best-preserved in Ireland,was founded in 1161 by monks from Mellifont Abbey. Its substantial ruins include cloisters, church and sacristy – the chancel and the transepts are the oldest part of the church. The gatehouse contains an interpretative centre.

Frybrook House, in Boyle town centre, was built about 1750 as an elegant three-storey Georgian-style house overlooking the river. The drawing-room has some of the finest Georgian decorative plasterwork in Ireland.

King House, off Main Street, was built in the 18th century for the King family and was later a barracks for the Connaught Rangers. The house has now been turned into an interpretative centre, using 3-D displays, audio-visual presentations and special effects to tell the history of Boyle and the King family, besides the turbulent pageantry of Connaught kings and chieftains, among them the O'Connors and the McDermotts.

Boyle town.

Douglas Hyde Centre

Dr Douglas Hyde was Ireland's first President and this permanent exhibition on his life and work is housed in the former church at Portahard, where his father was once rector. Dr Hyde was a prominent scholar and his collection of prose and poetry can be seen here, along with such personal items as his gavel and walking stick. The centre has also the letter nominating him as President of Ireland in 1938. Outside, the Gairdín an Chraoibhín (Garden of the Little Branch) has trees and shrubs that are sacred in Celtic mythology. Douglas Hyde's grave is at the rear of the church.

Frenchpark, 25 km (15 miles) NW of Strokestown on the N5.

SLIGO

CASTLES

Ballinafad Castle

This neat little castle was built as a government military post by Captain St Barbe around 1590 to defend an important pass through the Curlew Mountains, and hence is known as the Castle of the Curlews. It comprises an oblong block of three storeys over a raised basement with stout towers at the corners. There were square rooms in all the towers save the north, where there was a circular timber stair. The door at first-floor level was secured with a drawbar and had an internal grille or gate.

In the early 17th century the castle was garrisoned by a constable and ten warders. In 1642 it was attacked by the insurgent Irish and its defenders were forced to surrender due to lack of water.

Ballinafad village, 9.5 km (6 miles) N of Boyle on the Sligo Road. NGR: G 7808.

Ballymote Castle

Ballymote, begun in 1300, was the last and the mightiest of the Norman castles in Connaught. It was built some distance from an earlier motte by Richard de Burgo, the great Red Earl of Ulster, in order to protect his newly won possessions in Sligo. Almost square in plan with massive round towers at each angle, it is the most symmetrical of all the Irish "keepless" castles and bears an unmistakable resemblance to the inner ward of Beaumaris in Anglesea. There was a formidable double-towered gate in the centre of the north wall; recent excavations revealed that the gate towers, now largely demolished, were protected by a double skin of external walling. A postern gate planned for the centre of the south wall was never completed, probably because of the events of 1317, when the castle was lost to the O'Connors.

Possession of the castle from 1317 until 1584 alternated between the O'Connors and the MacDonaghs. A lack of occupation levels implies that the building was virtually abandoned during these years. In 1584 it was taken by the notorious governor of Connaught, Richard Bingham, and remained an English base until lost to Red Hugh O'Donnell in 1598. It was here that O'Donnell assembled his forces on route to Kinsale in 1601. In 1652 the castle was surrendered by the Taaffes to parliamentary forces, and in 1690 it was captured by the Williamites, who soon afterwards had it dismantled and the moat filled in.

Ballymote village, 24 km (15 miles) S of Sligo town. NGR: G 660154.

HOUSES

Lissadell House

Few houses have such colourful associations as Lissadell – the large and austere Grecian Revival home of the Gore-Booth family – beautifully situated amidst woods and glades on the north shore of Sligo Bay and immortalised by William Butler Yeats in his poem "In Memory of Eva Gore-Booth and Con Markievicz". As a young man Yeats spent many happy days here with Eva, whom he likened to a gazelle, and Constance, the "acknowledged beauty of the county". In later years he fondly remembered the lofty bright rooms of Lissadell with their "great windows open to the south" and the "great sitting room as high as a church and all things in good taste". The old rooms and furnishing remain, their grandeur a little faded now but steeped in remembrance of the many remarkable people who have lived here.

The Gore-Booths stem from an Elizabethan soldier-settler, Sir Paul Gore, ancestor of the Earls of Arran. The Sligo branch first settled at nearby Ardtermon Castle, but in the 18th century moved to a house near the shore at Lissadell. Unfortunately, the damp situation and the danger from high tides was always a problem, so in 1833 Sir Robert Gore-Booth commissioned architect Francis Goodwin to design the present house. The conservative tastes of both patron and architect resulted in the adoption of a chaste neo-classical design – the last time this style was used for a large country house in Ireland. The exterior walls of grey Ballysodare limestone incorporate very little ornament apart from corner pilasters and a strong horizontal frieze, while the treatment of the interior is similarly austere, though relieved by a wonderful sensation of bright light and space pervading the rooms.

In the core of the house lies an enormous apse-ended gallery 65 feet long lit by skylights and a clerestory with tall Doric pilasters along one side and freestanding Ionic columns along the other. It was once the music room and retains its original Gothic chamber organ pumped by bellows in the basement. There is also a walnut-topped grand piano, old masters on the walls and souvenirs collected by Sir Robert Gore-Booth on his many travels abroad. His son Sir Henry Gore was also a great explorer, and in this room stands a model of his yacht Kara on which he rescued his friend Leight Smith from the Arctic ice. It is said that Sir Henry's wife Georgina built the artificial lake at Lissadell in the vain hope that he might stay at home and fish in it, but as the harpoons and whale bones in the billiard room testify, Sir Henry was interested in much larger game.

The library, with its "great windows" in the garden bow, is immortalised by Yeats's poem. The billiard room now displays family memorabilia, including banners presented to Sir Robert Gore-Booth in gratitude for mortgaging the estate during the Famine to help feed the starving thousands of the area – a sacrifice that amounted to a debt of £50,000 over the value of the mortgage and took nearly a century to pay off. The drawing-room has Sir Robert's travelling library of forty-eight leather-bound miniature books, while in the dining-room the pilasters are painted with a remarkable series of life-sized murals. These include the butler – the faithful Kilgallon – who had accompanied Sir Henry to the Arctic and saved his life by shooting the bear that stands stuffed in the front hall. These icon-like murals are the work of Count Casimir Markievicz, the Polish husband of Constance, whom she met at the Paris Art School. Her later exploits are well known: she became involved in the Dublin Lockout of 1913, took part in the 1916 rebellion, was imprisoned and later reprieved from a death sentence, became the first elected female Westminster MP, and later served as Minister of Labour in the first Irish government.

Some of Constance's own artistic efforts line the walls of the grand staircase along with illuminated addresses presented to her brother, Sir Josslyn Gore-Booth, in recognition of his contribution to the co-operative movement. Sir Josslyn was responsible for establishing the creameries still operating in Sligo and Leitrim; at Lissadell he developed the resources of the estate, planting enormous numbers of trees, building a sawmill, an engineering works and a sewing school and greatly expanding the vegetable and flower gardens. As part of this policy, an important daffodil nursery was built up which later gave rise to many famous cultivars.

After 1944 the government assumed responsibility for the administration of the estate and during this time the estate went into sharp decline, resulting in the felling of much fine woodland and the compulsory sale in 1968 of 2,600 acres by the Land Commission, leaving only 400 acres around the house. Lissadell now belongs to Sir Josslyn's grandson and, despite its troubles over recent decades, remains a memorial to a family who for generations contributed selflessly to the well-being of Ireland and its people.

Drumcliffe, 32 km (20 miles) N of Sligo town off the Bundoran Road. NGR: G 6346.

MUSEUMS/HERITAGE CENTRES

Sligo County Museum

Located in the manse of a 19th-century church, this museum has a varied selection of material from Sligo town and county, with the latter's prehistory forming an impressive centrepiece. Other material includes penal crosses, chalices, memorabilia from the War of Independence and documentation from the 19th and early 20th centuries. A special section is devoted to W. B. Yeats, and includes his Nobel Prize, some first editions and a complete collection of his poems, 1889–1936.

In the nearby Yeats Memorial Building, an audio-visual presentation shows the Yeats connection with Sligo. Yeats is buried at Drumcliff Church, and a new visitor centre beside the graveyard includes an audio-visual presentation.

Sligo County Museum/Yeats Memorial Building: Sligo town.
Drumcliff Church: 6.5 km (4 miles) N of Sligo town.

TIPPERARY

CASTLES

Ballynahow Castle

There is something rather attractive about round tower houses, but sadly only a relatively small number were built, mostly in Munster. Perhaps the finest to survive is the impressive early 16th-century tower of the Purcells at Ballynahow. It stands five storeys high with two internal vaults, each covering two storeys; the top storey was formerly covered by a conical timber roof carried on squinch arches. Both the lower floors were dimly lit round chambers that were probably used for storage, though their size was relatively small because of the wall's thickness at this level. The three storeys above were larger and approximated to a rectangular shape, with ogival and segmental headed windows. One of the thicker segments of the wall was cleverly used to contain the entrance porch with its murder hole, the winding stair, the latrines and a number of other mural chambers. A number of small musket holes can be found near some of the principal windows.

5 km (3 miles) W of Thurle, off the Ballycahill Road. NGR: S 082602.

Burntcourt Castle

The magnificent shell of this great 17th-century embattled house derives its peculiar name from being burnt by the Parliamentary army on their march to Cahir in 1650. Cromwell himself mentions stopping at the "stronghouse called Clogheen, belonging to Sir Richard Everard", though there is a tradition that Lady Everard set fire to it prior to his arrival. This gave rise to an old rhyme saying, "It was seven years in building, seven years in living and fifteen days in burning." Sir Richard Everard – a distinguished Catholic Royalist and leading member of the Kilkenny Confederation – was hanged by Ireton in 1651, and his castle, quaintly referred to as "Burnt-Clogheen" in an inquisition of 1693, was never rebuilt.

The stronghouse was erected on lands granted to Sir Richard Everard by Charles I in 1639. A datestone recording the building's completion in 1641 was once placed over one of the doors, but now is inserted in the wall at the entrance to the nearby farmyard. That year Sir Richard and his family left their old ancestral castle at Ballyboy to take up residence at their splendid new home. Known at the time as Clogheen, it was one of the largest private dwellings then built in Ireland and comprised a centre block of two storeys over a raised basement with a gabled attic and four gabled corner towers – the whole building having no less than twenty-six gables. The large number of regularly disposed two-and three-mullioned windows gives the building a quiet, residential air, but its basic design is defensive, notably the use of corner towers, which permits flanking fire along each face of the house. There are pistol loops in the jambs of the back door opening out of the kitchen in the south end, and also in the front entrance on the west side, which has a nicely cut hood moulding with celtic motifs around it, very similar to Monkstown Castle, County Cork.

During the 18th century the artist Anthony Chearnley built a two-storey, five-bay gable-ended house in the bawn and laid out formal gardens outside the bawn wall. A number of engravings, based on drawings by him of Burntcourt, show the ruins as they are now, except that the chimney stacks were then complete.

14 km (8.5 miles) SW of Caher and 6.5 km (4 miles) NE of Ballyporeen. NGR: R 951181.

Cahir Castle

Superbly set on a rocky island in the River Suir, this impressive 15th-century castle – the largest of its period in Ireland – was considered impregnable until the advent of heavy cannon. Described by one Elizabethan commentator as "the bulwark for Munster and a safe retreat for all the agents of Spain and Rome", it fell to Devereux, Earl of Essex, in 1599 after it had been battered for two days with artillery. It surrendered without a fight to Inchiquin in 1647 and again to Cromwell in 1650, but otherwise had a notably undistinguished history, which possibly helps to explain why it survives in such remarkably good condition today.

Making excellent use of the rocky terrain, its layout comprised a series of courts which cleverly served as successive lines of defence, so that each ward or court dominated the one outside. The core of the castle is surrounded by very thick curtain walls, the lowest parts of which belong to the original fortress on the site built by Philip of Worcester in the 13th century. The massive wall-footing across the middle ward marks the south perimeter of this early castle, while the large adjacent building, known as the keep, originally served as the gatehouse, with a passage through the centre flanked by guard chambers. After this was converted into the main residential block of the castle in the 15th century, the gate was moved alongside, possibly with its original arch. The double machicolation over this entrance is largely an 1840s reconstruction, but the adjacent round tower, which served as a prison, may also have 13th-century foundations.

The present castle appears to be largely the work of Seamus Gallda (James the Foreigner), ancestor of the Butlers, Barons of Cahir. After the death of his father, the third Earl of Ormonde, in 1405, James Butler made Cahir his principal seat and embarked on a building programme. By 1599 the castle had reached its present appearance as illustrated in Pacata Hibernia. The only subsequent alterations took place in the 1840s when Richard Butler restored the castle and replaced the picturesque Irish battlements with more solid English ones. The great hall on the east side of the inner ward was also rebuilt at this time though its original form extended much further south; indeed, the main fireplace now lies outside in the open.

The Butlers ceased to occupy the castle in the 18th century and built a house in the town, now the Cahir House Hotel. In the 1860s they erected a mansion, Cahir Park, in the magnificent parkland which adjoins the old castle.

Cahir town. NGR: S 048248.

Carrick-on-Suir Castle

This castle of the Butlers – Earls and later Dukes of Ormonde – stands above the Suir and was acquired in 1515, though the oldest part of the castle is a mid 15th-century walled bawn with a tower house in each of its northern corners. Sometime after 1565 the tenth, or "Black", Earl of Ormonde, who spent many years in the court of his cousin Queen Elizabeth I, added a Tudor manor house of a type common in England but like no other in Ireland. The low U-shaped range of this house forms three sides of a small court attached to the old bawn, whose towers rise behind it. It has two storeys with a gabled attic, rows of mullioned windows and steep brick gables with slender finials. There are few defensive features save for small firing holes either side of the front door.

The house was a favourite haunt of the Great Duke of Ormonde, but afterwards it was deserted by the family although they continued to own it until the present century. Fortunately, it was never allowed to fall into complete ruin and in 1947 was taken over by the State, who subsequently conserved the building. Their most notable achievement was the restoration of the long gallery on the first floor of the front elevation, whose ceiling had largely collapsed. This delightful room, once hung with tapestries, has a magnificent limestone mantel bearing the date 1565, and stucco representations of Queen Elizabeth I flanked by Equity and Justice. The Queen would have felt at home in this room and in the rest of this house, which was probably intended, for she is believed to have promised her favourite cousin "Black Tom" that she would one day honour Carrick with a visit.

Carrick-on-Suir. NGR: S 405216.

Nenagh Castle

The finest cylindrical keep in Ireland – known to generations of Tipperary people as the "Nenagh Round" – was built around 1200 by Theobald Walter, the founder of the great Butler dynasty of Ormonde. It formed the north corner of a pentagonal court with a towered gatehouse on the southern side and strong towers on the north-west and south-east angles. This has now vanished, save for fragments of the gatehouse and east tower, but the keep survives to a height of 100 feet. Its topmost quarter was added about 1860 by the Bishop of Killaloe in emulation of Windsor Castle – the original height to the wall-walk being about 75 feet. There were four storeys, including a basement, with a first-floor entrance giving access to a winding mural stair that was once enclosed by a protecting turret. The second and third floors have narrow loops with large embrasures for crossbowmen, but the top floor is well lit by four windows and was clearly the main chamber.

The Butlers remained at Nenagh until the 14th century, when they moved to Gowran and later purchased Kilkenny Castle in 1391. During the 15th century it was occupied by the O'Briens, but was recovered in 1533 by Sir Piers Ruadh Butler, later Earl of Ormonde. The castle changed hands many times before and during the Cromwellian wars, but after its capture by Ginkel in 1690, the place was dismantled by the Williamites. The Butler link was finally broken in 1703 when the second Duke of Ormonde sold the place to pay debts.

Nenagh. NGR: R 865764.

MUSEUMS/HERITAGE CENTRES

Carrick-on-Suir

This historic town has two interesting sites, Ormonde Castle and the town's heritage centre. The latter, in a former church, has many relics of life in old Carrick – everything from slate and chalk once used in a local school to old grocery bills and old photographs. A stock and apprentices' wage book used by Stephenson Bros. drapery store in the town about 1846 is on display, along with willow baskets made by Joe Shanahan in the town about 1840. The centre also has an extensive collection of church plate.

Carrick-on-Suir.

Cashel

This historic town, dominated by the Rock of Cashel, has several points of interest, not least the Rock itself, with its medieval ecclesiastical buildings dating back to the 12th century. The entrance to the Rock is through the Hall of the Vicars Choral,

where an audio-visual presentation, Strongholds of Faith, is shown. There is also a
small museum in this hall. The most striking feature of the ruins is the cathedral,
much of which dates from the 13th century.

Cashel also has a recently opened heritage centre with a model of the town as it
was in the 1640s. Other features of the town and surroundings are detailed, including
the 8th- and 9th-century Derrynaflan Hoard and the abbeys of County Tipperary.

Cashel Folk Village, nearby, is a museum of rural life with an old-style living
room, pub, butcher's shop (complete with ancient saws) and an old blacksmith's
forge, which has tools and bellows. Also worth seeing is the 18th-century Church of
Ireland cathedral, and in its grounds, the Bolton Library, which has 12,000 books. It
has many examples of early Irish printing, notably from the 17th century. You can
take a tour round the town on the Cashel Heritage Tram.
Cashel.

Fethard Museum

This glorious ragbag of a collection began in an old railway station and has expanded
considerably. The number of exhibits runs to thousands, and includes an
extraordinary range of household items and utensils, including Victorian prams.
Transport of all kinds is a strong theme and one of the recent additions is a horse-
drawn fire engine. Also worth seeing in Fethard are the medieval town walls, very
extensive and sensitively restored.
Fethard, 14.5 km (9 miles) N of Clonmel on the R689.

Lár na Páirce

This fast-moving presentation details the history and development of Gaelic games.
Hurling has been played in Ireland for over 2,000 years and Gaelic football since the
17th century. The Gaelic Games Association (GAA) was formed in nearby Hayes Hotel
in 1884. The Sam Melbourne Collection, formed over many years by a native of Horse
& Jockey in County Tipperary, forms the basis of Lár na Páirce. Among the items
featured are the world's oldest hurley. Certain themes are detailed, including
Protestant connections with the GAA. The first President of Ireland, Douglas Hyde, a
Protestant, supported the GAA and Sam Maguire, who donated the famous football
cup, was also a Protestant. Broadcast coverage of Gaelic games includes videos of
historic games and radio commentaries in Irish and English, including, inevitably, the
most famous GAA commentator of all, Micheál Ó Hehir.
Thurles.

Mining Heritage Centre

The Silvermines area of south Tipperary has seen mining activity for the past 5,000
years. In this ambitious heritage centre visitors will be able to see the old workings
for themselves. If mining history turns you on, you can also explore a smaller mining
museum near Avoca in County Wicklow, where the gold-mining history of that area is
detailed.
Silvermines area of S Tipperary.

Nenagh

The former jail and governor's house at Nenagh have been converted into a heritage
centre. A traditional shop, classroom, forge and dairy have all been recreated, while
the gatehouse, once occupied by condemned prisoners, has vividly recreated cells and
scaffold.
Nenagh.

Roscrea

Damer House in the centre of Roscrea is a well-restored Queen Anne-style town house,
dating from the 1720s, particularly noted for its staircase. Frequent exhibitions are held

here. Beside the house, the garden has been replanted in the 18th-century Georgian style, while at the front of the complex, the 13th-century castle has been restored.
Roscrea.

Tipperary County Museum

This well-run museum in Clonmel has a very representative selection of material on Tipperary life. Pages from 19th-century Clonmel newspapers are accompanied by signage from the local railways and details of some of Clonmel's most famous sons, native and adopted – these include Laurence Sterne, author of *Tristam Shandy*, born in the town in 1713, and Charles Bianconi from Lombardy in Italy, who founded Ireland's first public transport system in Clonmel in 1815. Clonmel also has a transport museum at Richmond Mill, showing the history of motorised transport in Ireland.
Clonmel.

TYRONE

CASTLES

Benburb Castle

The name Benburb, roughly translated as "proud peak", aptly describes the setting of this Plantation bawn, perched on the summit of a limestone cliff towering 200 feet above the River Blackwater. It was built in 1611–14 by Sir Richard Wingfield (later Viscount Powerscourt) who was granted 1,000 acres here from James I. An earlier castle on or close to the site was the "chief seat" of the celebrated Shane O'Neill, before it was burnt in 1566.

The bawn occupies a large irregular quadrangular area enclosed by walls standing almost to full height and generously fitted with musketry loop-holes. No main house was built as Wingfield had no desire to live here, but living accommodation was provided in gabled rectangular flankers incorporated into corners of the bawn. One of these was occupied in 1622 by "Mr Moore, an Englishman, with his wife and family". In the south-east corner of the enclosure is a round stair turret giving access to a postern down the cliff, while the house on the south-west side was built in the late 18th century and remodelled in Victorian times.

The castle was captured in 1641 by Phelim O'Neill, who had all the inmates put to death. In 1646 it was occupied by Owen Roe O'Neill before he defeated the English army at the battle of Benburb. It was dismantled soon afterwards and has remained a ruin ever since.
Benburb town. NGR: H 814520.

Castle Caulfield

Sir Toby Caulfield, later Lord Charlemont, must have had a very strong desire to live like an English gentleman, for he was prepared to build an unfortified English-style mansion in an unsettled area of Ulster during the period 1611–19. Described by Pynnar in 1619 as "the fairest building in the north", it had three storeys in a U-shaped plan – the north-west wing of which has now disappeared. It had fireplaces in projecting breasts and massive chimney stacks capped with octagonal stone shafts, as well as flat-headed mullioned and transomed windows, most of which have been torn out. The gatehouse, with its vaulted passage and guard chambers, probably belong to an earlier O'Donnelly bawn on the site.

During the 1641 Rebellion the house was burnt by Patrick "the Gloomy" O'Donnelly and some of the interior stonework still shows signs of scorching. In the 1660s the house was partially rehabilitated by the Caulfields, who were in residence in 1670 when Archbishop Oliver Plunket was permitted to use the courtyard for

ordinations. It was probably disused by 1700 and was a ruin when John Wesley preached in front of the gates in 1767.
Castlecaulfield village. NGR: H 755626.

Harry Avery's Castle

A curiously enigmatic castle named after and possibly built by Henry Aimbreidh O'Neill, a Gaelic chief celebrated by the Four Masters for his justice, nobility and hospitality who died in 1392. The castle commands wide views over the Mourne Valley and is unusual in being a stone-built stronghold located deep in the heart of pre-Plantation Ulster. It consists of a two-storey rectangular block fronted by a pair of massive D-shaped towers – resembling a gatehouse – projecting from the south face of an artificially scarped knoll, whose sides have been revetted by a wall to form a polygonal enclosure, now ruined to a low level with traces of a latrine tower on the north side. Excavations in 1950 and 1962 confirmed that the keep-like structure functioned more as a tower house than as a true gatehouse, though the only access into the enclosure behind seems to have been up a narrow mural stair and through the hall at first-floor level. Other features include vaults with traces of wickercentring and latrine shafts in one of the towers.

The castle was captured by the English in 1609. Subsequently, it was used as a quarry for building material.
1 km (0.6 mile) SW of Newtownstewart, 16 km (10 miles) SE of Strabane. NGR: H 323852.

MUSEUMS/HERITAGE CENTRES

Benburb Valley Heritage Centre

The Benburb Valley Heritage Centre is in a former linen mill and has a fine collection of linen-making machinery, including an 1899 steam engine. The centre captures well the sights and sounds of an old linen mill, with its warping, weaving, dyeing and beetling.
Benburb town.

Cornmill Heritage Centre

Coalisland was at the heart of the original industrial revolution in the North of Ireland and its history is related in this new centre located in a renovated early 20th-century corn mill. Many facets of the town's industrial history are recorded, including coal mining, developed nearly two centuries ago after coal was discovered in the adjacent district of Congo; the town had a short-lived coal-mining rush. Iron-making was also practised and a canal was dug to nearby Lough Neagh. The audio-visual presentation, in the theatre on the top floor of the centre, uses recorded folk memories.
6.5 km (4 miles) NE of Dungannon.

Tyrone Heritage Centres

Four centres in County Tyrone each have their own not inconsiderable points of interest. In Strabane, Gray's Printing Press shows how the old hot-metal printing worked, with examples of presses and hand-set type. The Castlederg Visitors Centre has a video wall, used to narrate ten stories about the social history and culture of this part of the county. Also on display is a carriage from the Castlederg tramway, which opened in 1884 and was closed after a strike in 1933. The Newtownstewart Gateway Centre and Museum includes the Dunbar collection of Victoriana, militaria, old toys, packaging and photographic equipment. The centre also has a reconstruction of a traditional farmhouse kitchen, complete with half-door. Finally, the Sperrin Heritage Centre tells the story of gold in the Sperrin mountains and has an audio-visual presentation.
Gray's Printing Press: Main Street, Strabane.

Castlederg Centre: 19 km (12 miles) SW of Strabane.
Newtownstewart Centre: 16 km (10 miles) SE of Strabane.
Sperrin Centre: Cranagh, 13 km (8 miles) E of Plumbridge.

Ulster History Park

This 35-acre site tells the story of the settlement of Ireland from the time of the first known settlers, around 8000 BC, to the Plantation period of the 17th century. Based on extensive archaeological and historical research, the park consists of full-scale models of dwelling places and monuments. The Mesolithic camp reconstruction represents the earliest settlement, the huts being based on evidence from excavations at Mount Sandal, near Coleraine. Dwellings in the park range from the raths (circular-shaped houses with thatched roofs from the early Christian era) to a reconstructed Plantation settlement built after the conquest of Gaelic Irish Ulster in the early 17th century.
Cullion, 11 km (7 miles) NE of Omagh on B48.

WATERFORD

HOUSES

Lismore Castle

Everyone who has crossed the bridge over the Blackwater River into the town of Lismore will be familiar with this irresistably romantic castle, whose splendid silvery-grey turrets, towers and battlements rise serenely from a cliff above the wooded banks of this most Rhine-like of rivers. While extensively remodelled in the 19th century, the walls of Lismore incorporate many earlier buildings with a history stretching back over 1,000 years.

Although the name *Lios Mor* means "big fort", the castle site was originally occupied by an important monastery and seat of learning established in the early 7th century. It was still an ecclesiastical centre when Henry II stayed here in 1171, and except for a brief period after 1185 when a castle was built here, it served as the episcopal residence of the local bishop. In 1589 Lismore was acquired by Sir Walter Raleigh, who sold the property in 1602 to another famous adventurer, Richard Boyle, later Earl of Cork. Boyle was a man of extraordinary wealth who had arrived in Ireland as a young man in 1588 with only £27 in capital. He never did anything by halves and having decided to make Lismore his principal seat, proceeded to transform it into a magnificent residence with impressive gabled ranges each side of the courtyard. He also made a fortified garden wall with turrets and an outer gatehouse known as the Riding House.

The principal apartments were opulently decorated with fretwork plaster ceilings and hangings of tapestry, embroidered silk and velvet. Boyle lived in these apartments with his family and it was here in 1626 that his famous son was born – Robert Boyle, father of modern chemistry. Unfortunately, the castle was sacked by the Confederates in 1645 and although the second Earl made it habitable again, neither he nor his successors, who called themselves by their alternative title of Burlington, were interested in Lismore, preferring to live in England.

The castle was acquired by the Cavandish family in 1753. The fifth Duke of Devonshire carried out improvements at Lismore, notably the bridge across the Blackwater in 1775, but it was the sixth Duke, known as the "Bachelor Duke", who was responsible for the castle's present appearance. He began transforming the castle into a fashionable "quasi-feudal ultra-regal fortress" in 1811, engaging the architect William Atkinson to rebuild the castle walls with cut stone shipped over from Derbyshire. The rooms were redesigned with suitably medieval-like Gothic ceilings, the finest undoubtedly in the drawing-room. This room replaced the old dining-room whose "great window" is said to have caused James II almost to faint when he saw the dramatic drop to the river below. It was during this period of building that workmen discovered the 12th-century Lismore Crosier, now in the National Museum, Dublin, and the Book of McCarthy Reagh, popularly known as the Book of Lismore, containing important accounts of the lives of Irish saints.

Lismore was always the Bachelor Duke's favourite residence, but as he grew older his love for the place developed into a passion. In 1850 he engaged his architect Sir Joseph Paxton, the designer of the Crystal Palace, to carry out improvements and additions to the castle on a magnificent scale – so much so, indeed, that the present skyline is largely Paxton's work. At this time J. G. Crace of London, the leading makers of Gothic Revival furniture, were commissioned to transform the ruined chapel of the old Bishop's Palace into a medieval-style banqueting hall. The great architect A. C. Pugin was commissioned to design the room which he left looking rather appropriately like a church. The chimney-piece, which was exhibited at the Medieval Court of the Great Exhibition of 1851, was also designed by Pugin (and Myers), but was originally intended for Horstead Place in Sussex. It was rejected because it was too elaborate and subsequently bought for Lismore.

After the Bachelor Duke's death in 1858 the castle was left more or less as he had redesigned it and has fortunately continued to be loved by his successors who still come here for part of the year.

Lismore town. NGR: X 043987.

GARDENS

Lismore Castle Gardens

Lismore has a splendid surviving example of an early 17th-century garden – notable for its impressive walls, turrets and terracing. Its appeal is perhaps increased by the tradition that Spenser wrote part of his *Faerie Queen* here. Built by Richard Boyle, the Great Earl of Cork, this 3-acre "Upper Garden", as it is known, is entered through an outer gatehouse – the Riding House. The colourful layout now contains herbaceous borders, topiary, lawns, an orchard and a greenhouse designed by Sir Joseph Paxton in 1858. The Victorian pleasure grounds below the walled enclosure have a collection of spring-flowering shrubs, notably camellias, magnolias and rhododendrons. This area also has an ancient yew walk said to have been planted in 1707.

Lismore town. NGR: X 043987.

Mount Congreve

Magnificent garden of 115 acres created by Ambrose Congreve from 1963 onwards. Contains one of the world's largest collection of shrubs and flowering trees, especially notable for its comprehensive collection of rhododendrons, camellias, acers, pieris and magnolias.

Kilmeaden, 5 km (3 miles) W of Waterford city.

MUSEUMS/HERITAGE CENTRES

Duncannon Fort

This 16th-century star-shaped fort is being restored, but it's open to the public. Impressive estuary views.

E shore of Waterford harbour, ferry from Passage East to nearby Ballyhack.

Dungarvan Museum

This small but representative museum depicts the history of Dungarvan, including the building of the adjacent King John's Castle in the 13th century and the arrival of the Augustinians at Abbeyside, also in the 13th century. Many old photographs show such events as fair days in Dungarvan, while old artefacts include a penny-farthing bicycle. The development of the town in the early 19th century is described in detail, but the highlight of the museum is its collection of maritime material: shipwrecks are particularly well documented, notably that of the *Moresby*, lost in Dungarvan Bay on Christmas Eve, 1895.

Also worth seeing near Dungarvan is the Seanachie Inn, where the past has been preserved beneath its thatched roof. Old whiskey jars, mirrors, signs and packets of Van Houten's cocoa, stone floors, even an old spinning wheel help keep the old times alive.

Dungarvan Museum: Dungarvan town.

Seanachie Inn: 5 km (3 miles) S of Dungarvan, just off the Youghal Road.

Lismore

Lismore, set on the banks of the River Blackwater and dominated by the Duke of Devonshire's castle (see above), is one of Ireland's most historic towns, dating back to the foundation of its monastery by St Carthach in the 7th century. In the Lismore Heritage Centre (once the courthouse) the ecclesiastical history of the town is recreated in the audio-visual show, The Lismore Experience. Also in the centre, visitors can see the Book of Lismore, written between the 10th and 13th century, details of the town's historic buildings and material on Robert Boyle (1627–91), who was born in the castle and became the father of modern science in Ireland.

Lismore town.

Reginald's Tower

Believed to date from 1003, the circular tower is the oldest civic building in Ireland and the recently refurbished interior shows many important artefacts and documents relating to the city of Waterford, which dates back to Viking times. These include the city's royal charters, which are most impressive. Other relics include the ceremonial swords of King Henry VIII and King John; Anglo-Norman kings used the place as a residence. The second floor of the tower, where Strongbow and Aoife were reputedly married, features a large limestone fireplace dating from the 15th century. The tower was also used as a mint, which had been established in the city in 1463.

The Quay, Waterford city.

Theatre Royal

Waterford Corporation dates back to 1195, making it one of the oldest in northern Europe. One of the gems of City Hall is the Theatre Royal, one of only three Victorian theatres in Ireland (the others are the Gaiety in Dublin and the Grand Opera House in Belfast). Waterford's theatre dates back to the 18th century, when it was known as the Playhouse. In 1876, it was remodelled; all its Victorian features, including boxes, proscenium arch and decor have been carefully preserved.

The Mall, Waterford city.

Waterford Crystal Visitor Centre

Waterford Crystal is world renowned, one of Ireland's best-regarded craft products. Glass-making started in a major way in the city in 1783 and lasted until 1851 – first-period Waterford is greatly treasured. It was revived after World War II. In the visitor centre, an audio-visual presentation gives the history of glass-making in Ireland from medieval times, through the establishment of the first Waterford Glass factory to present-day production.

Near Waterford, another crystal glass company, Tipperary Crystal, founded by former Waterford workers, also welcomes visitors who can see the original hand-crafted methods still being used.

Waterford Crystal: 2.5 km (1.5 miles) W of Waterford city on the Cork Road.

Tipperary Crystal: Ballynoran, near Carrick-on-Suir, 32 km (20 miles) NW of Waterford city on the Clonmel road.

Waterford Heritage Centre

Between 1986 and 1992, excavations in Waterford yielded an amazing collection of artefacts, over 200,000 in all, from the Viking and medieval period of the city's history. About 180 Viking houses were excavated and most of the objects found, dating back to between the 11th and 13th centuries, were perfectly preserved because of the waterlogged soil. Many examples are on show here, including wine pots, coins, clothing, leather, footwear and jewellery. Waterford's new heritage centre, in a converted old traditional multi-storey warehouse on the quays, is a high-tech presentation of Waterford's history.
Beside Reginald's Tower, The Quay, Waterford city.

WESTMEATH

CASTLES

Athlone Castle

Athlone used to be one of the most formidable medieval fortresses in Ireland, but warfare and substantial rebuilding have left little of the old castle above internal ground level.

The construction of both a bridge and castle at this key river crossing began in 1210, following King John's visit to Ireland, when Bishop Henry de Grey was ordered to begin settling the middle Shannon region between Meath and Connaught. De Grey's stone tower, probably built on an earlier motte of 1199, had to be rebuilt the following year after it collapsed, killing nine of the garrison. It was again repaired in 1251 and in 1273–9 the curtain walls were probably added, flanked by massive D-shaped towers. Most of this structure was still present when drawn by Thomas Phillips in 1685, together with a fine suite of apartments, used by the Lord President of Connaught, overlooking the river.

The castle's strategic position meant that it saw a good deal of military action. In 1691 it suffered the heaviest bombardment in Irish history when the Williamite General Ginkel battered it with over 600 bombs, 12,000 cannon balls and huge quantities of stones. From 1793 to 1815 the whole castle was rebuilt, reduced in height and strengthened for the mounting of heavy cannon in efforts to fortify the Shannon against French invasion. The lower storey of de Grey's polygonal tower is the only part of the medieval fabric to survive.
Athlone town. NGR: N 038413.

HOUSES

Belvedere

A desire to escape from the formality of country house life during the 18th century led to the emergence of small, comfortable holiday retreats known as villas. Undoubtedly the best example of such a building in Ireland is Belvedere – an exquisite house with an unusual elongated plan set in a fine landscape park overlooking Lough Ennell. Belvedere was built around 1742 to a design by Richard Castle, probably as a fishing pavilion, for Robert Rochfort, Lord Belfield. Like other villas of the period, the building was distinguished from ordinary houses of the same size by the exceptionally high quality of its design and construction, most notably its superb joinery and brilliant plasterwork. But the very strange and terrible events that preceded its construction ensured that Belvedere was never really used as a villa, but rather became a country house in its own right.

Belvedere had hardly been completed when a great scandal broke out surrounding its builder, Robert Rochfort, and his wife Mary Molesworth. She was only sixteen when she married Robert in 1736, but at the time the match seemed highly suitable; he was intelligent, handsome and one of the country's richest young men, she was the pretty and well-connected daughter of the third Viscount Molesworth. They settled at Gaulston and all seemed well until 1743 when Robert was informed that his wife had committed adultery with his younger brother Arthur, then living near Gaulston at Belfield. Robert, evidently a hot-tempered and self-centred individual, at once removed to his newly completed house at Belvedere, incarcerated his wife at Gaulston and plotted revenge against his brother, who fled to England. For thirty-one years his wife remained confined at Gaulston with only servants to keep her company. Once in 1756 she managed to escape, but her father refused her entry into his house and within twenty-four hours she was back in Gaulston. Henceforth her movements were further restricted and she was no longer allowed visits by her children. It is said that she used to walk up and down the gallery at Gaulston gazing at the portraits "as if conversing with them". After her husband's death in 1774 she was released by her son, who was horrified to find that she had acquired a "wild, scared, unearthly look, whilst the tones of her voice, which hardly exceeded a whisper, were harsh, agitated and uneven". As for the unfortunate Arthur, he made the mistake of returning to Ireland in 1759 and was sued for adultery by his unrelenting brother, now Earl of Belvedere. Fined £20,000 in damages, he spent the rest of his life in the Marshalsea, the debtors' jail in Dublin.

Lord Belvedere's treatment of his wife makes gripping reading, but it is also an indictment of 18th-century social attitudes. What is so striking is that his behaviour did his reputation no harm at all. At Belvedere he lived an extravagant lifestyle, entertained a great deal and rose through the social ranks to become Master General of the Irish army in 1764.

Although its rooms are now empty, Belvedere remains much as it was in the Earl's time. A solid grey limestone house of two stories with a long front and curved end bows, it is probably the earliest bow-ended house in the country. The Venetian and the bow windows provided light for the drawing-room and dining-room at either end of the house and between them are two small rooms (now united as one), a corridor and a handsome wooden staircase in a projection at the back of the building. Both the end rooms are grand but not large, with unusual chamfered corners and very high-quality joinery – their doors, windows and wainscotting all remain unpainted.

The delicate rococo plasterwork ceilings are the real glory of Belvedere's interior. Framed by rich cornices, these ceilings are notable for their lively quality and freedom of movement. The drawing-room ceiling has scrollwork enclosing medallions of Juno, Minerva and Venus, while that in the dining-room is rather bolder with clusters of fruit and flowers and four puffing cherubs emerging from clouds in the centre. In the hall the plasterwork is in much lower relief and is supposed to represent the night, with an owl, a flaming torch, stars and more swirling clouds. The name of the plasterer is unknown, but it has been noted that the work closely resembles ceilings formerly at Mespil House outside Dublin – these are believed to have been the work of the Frenchman Bartholomew Cramillion who is known to have made the splendid rococo ceiling in the Rotunda Hospital Chapel in 1755.

The small park that Lord Belvedere created around his villa is just as fine as the house itself and was the envy of all visitors, not least John Wesley who in 1767 remarked that "one would scarce think it possible to have such a variety of beauties in so small a compass". One of the attractions was an enormous sham Gothic ruin, which Lord Belvedere in typical fashion built to block out the view of Rochfort House, the home of another of his brothers with whom he had quarrelled. Yet despite his violent and cruel temperament, the Earl was certainly a man of taste and the Gothic arch he had built at the other end of the park is one of the most endearing follies in Ireland.

Following the death of the "Wicked Earl" (as he was later known) in 1774, the house was inherited by his son, the second Earl, who sold Gaulston and continued to live at Belvedere where he added a small wing to the back. Although his father had left him "very embarrassed in his circumstances" he managed to revive the family fortunes sufficiently to build a magnificent town residence – now the home of a famous Dublin school. The property later passed to Charles Brinsely Marley, who laid out the Italianate terraces in front of the house and assembled a remarkable collection of pictures and objets d'art which was given to Cambridge University, forming the core of the Fitzwilliam Museum. The residue of this collection together with the house and estate were left to his cousin, Lieutenant Colonel Howard-Bury, leader of the 1921 Mount Everest expedition. The contents were auctioned by Christie's in 1980 – a catastrophic loss for any such house. However, the interior of Belvedere is so fine that it still retains its soul, empty as the rooms may be.

6.5 km (4 miles) from Mullingar on the Tullamore Road. NGR: N 420477.

Tullynally Castle

During the early 19th century, a craze for building sham castles spread across Ireland with remarkable speed, undoubtedly provoked by a sense of unease in the aftermath of the 1798 rebellion. Security was certainly a factor in Johnson's 1801–6 remodelling of Tullynally, otherwise known as Pakenham Hall, where practical defensive features such as a portcullis entrance were included in addition to romantic-looking battlements and turrets. Later enlargements during the 1820s and 1830s were also fashioned in the castle style and made Tullynally into one of the largest castellated houses in Ireland – so vast, indeed, that it has been compared to a small fortified town.

Masonry walls 10 feet thick are all that remain of the castle that originally stood here in 1655 when Tullynally was purchased by Henry Pakenham, ancestor of the Earls of Longford. By the 1730s this stronghold had been transformed into a grand two-storey house surrounded by extensive formal gardens with canals. Traces of panelling and a few chimney pieces still survive from this building, which was remodelled in 1780 as a five-bay three-storey classical block to the designs of Graham Myers, the architect of Trinity College. It was this building which Francis Johnson, the outstanding architect of his generation in Ireland, was commissioned in 1801 to Gothicise for the second Earl of Longford. Johnson designed battlements and label mouldings over the windows, but as work progressed it was felt this treatment was too tame, so more dramatic features were added, notably round corner turrets and a portcullis entrance, transforming the house with characteristic Irish nomenclature from Pakenham Hall House to Pakenham Hall Castle.

Additions to Johnson's work were made in the early 1820s when James Shiel added a bow on the east garden front and redesigned the entrance hall. More substantial additions followed between 1839 and 1846 when Richard Morrison, that other stalwart of the Irish architectural scene, was employed by the Dowager Countess to bring the house up to improved Victorian standards of convenience. Under Morrison's direction the main house and Johnson's stable court were linked by two parallel wings both of which were elaborately castellated and faced externally with grey limestone. Following the fashion recently made popular by the great Scottish architect William Burn, one of the new wings contained a private apartment for the family, while the other on the east side of the courtyard contained larger and more exactly differentiated servants' quarters with elaborate laundries and a splendid kitchen. After 1860 the castle was modernised with all the latest equipment for supplying water, heat and lighting. Except for a water tower erected in the stable court by the Dublin architect J. Rawson Carroll in the 1860s, these modifications did not involve altering the fabric of the building, which has remained remarkably unchanged to the present day.

Visitors entering the castle will first arrive in the great hall – an enormous room 40 feet square and 30 feet high with no gallery to take away from its impressive sense of space. A central-heating system was designed for this room by Richard Lovell Edgeworth, who earlier in 1794 had fitted up the first semaphore telegraph system in Ireland between Edgeworthstown and Pakenham Hall, a distance of 12 miles. In a letter written in 1807 his daughter Maria Edgeworth, a frequent visitor to Pakenham Hall, wrote that "the immense hall is so well-warmed by hot air that the children play in it from morning to night. Lord L. seemed to take great pleasure in repeating twenty times that he was to thank Mr. Edgeworth for this." Edgeworth's heating system was, in fact, so effective that when Shiel remodelled the hall in 1820 he replaced one of the two fireplaces with a built-in organ that visitors can still see. James Shiel was also responsible for the Gothic vaulting of the ceiling, the Gothic niches containing the family crests, the high wood panelling around the base of the walls and the massive cast-iron Gothic fireplace. Other features of the room include a number of attractive early 19th-century drawings of the castle, a collection of old weapons, family portraits and an Irish elk's head dug up out of a bog, once a familiar feature of Irish country house halls.

The drawing-room is a pleasant room, with canvases of sea battles, a Chinese cabinet hand-painted by an Irishman and a dinner service donated to Admiral Sir Thomas Pakenham by grateful German merchants rescued from pirates. The adjacent library, which also has magnificent views over rolling parkland, is a spacious and comfortable room; oak bookcases tower from floor to ceiling and a delightful alcove stands in one corner. Over the mantelpiece is a portrait of the second Earl's brother, Sir Edward Pakenham, a Peninsular War general who later lost his life at the Battle of New Orleans in the War of 1812. The distinguished military past of the Pakenhams has been replaced this century by an equally distinguished literary tradition. Family members include the present Earl of Longford (who has written numerous books including the lives of Nixon and de Valera), his wife Elizabeth (who has written important biographies of the Duke of Wellington and Queen Victoria), their son Thomas Pakenham (author of highly acclaimed accounts of the 1798 rebellion, the South African War and the colonial struggle for Africa), his sister Antonia Fraser (another distinguished biographer) and novelist Rachel Billington.

One of the most fascinating features of Tullynally Castle is surely the rooms below stairs. Visitors can tour the splendid kitchen with its great ovens, a great pestle and mortar, an early ice chest and a dresser with gleaming brassware. Sadly, because this kitchen remained in continuous use, its huge 1875 range was replaced by an Aga in the 1940s. Other rooms of special interest include the Victorian laundries, which remain largely as they were after being remodelled between 1863 and 1864. Here the inquisitive will find a wash house with lead-lined sinks and a giant mangle with a heavy roller used for sheets, an ironing room and a drying room fitted up with vertical racks on rails that could be pulled in and out of a heated chamber. Some of the drying, however, had to be done in an open-air drying yard beyond the stables; this was approached by a sunken passage allowing the laundry maids (who were apt to be pretty) to carry the washing to the yard without having to meet any of the grooms on the way.

1.6 km (1 mile) from Castlepollard, 19 km (12 miles) N of Mullingar. NGR: N 445705.

GARDENS

Belvedere

One of the finest examples of a planned landscape in Ireland, Belvedere occupies 110 acres of rolling topography commanding wonderful views of Lough Ennel. The park's cleverly contrived "naturalistic" layout survives largely intact from the 1740s, when it was created as a setting for a villa designed by Richard Castle. It contains a number of romantic follies, all of which epitomise the mid 18th-century taste for Elysian allusions. These include the Gothic Arch, designed by Thomas Wright of Durham, an

octagonal gazebo and the remarkable Jealous Wall – an enormous sham ruin with pointed windows built to blot out views of a neighbouring house. The Walled Garden, which is a Victorian addition, contains many colourful borders and includes some plants brought back by Lieutenant Colonel Howard-Bury from his Himalayan expeditions. The terraces and enormous rockery flanking the house, added in the 1880s, provide a fine platform for viewing this memorable landscape.
6.5 km (4 miles) from Mullingar on the Tullamore Road. NGR: N 420477.

MUSEUMS/HERITAGE CENTRES

Athlone Castle

Athlone is at the very centre of Ireland and at the heart of much Irish history, particularly with the sieges of 1690 and 1691. The town's strategically important location is reflected in the castle (see above). Today, it contains an exhibition centre and a museum. The exhibition centre details the history of Athlone and the castle, while an audio-visual presentation recreates the great sieges. Athlone's military history is highlighted, as is the role of the modern-day Irish Army in United Nations peacekeeping. The flora and fauna of the Shannon are also detailed, while Athlone's most famous son, John Count McCormack, forms a main highlight of the centre. McCormack, who became a world-renowned tenor, was born in a house just across the bridge in 1884 and died in Dublin in 1945. Among the items on show is his own gramophone, while his artistry is recalled splendidly in an audio-visual presentation. The folk museum in the castle has local craft artefacts, old household and dairy equipment, and a reconstructed hearth.
Athlone town.

Locke's Distillery

Locke's is one of the venerable names in Irish whiskey distilling, dating back to the mid 18th century. The distillery ceased production in 1954 and closed in 1957. Fortunately a new generation of Locke's whiskey has returned to the market and thanks to local community effort in Kilbeggan the old distillery has been preserved as a museum. Much of the equipment once used at the distillery is still in place, including the brewing vats, the millstones and the mash tuns. At each stage, the complicated details of the distillation process are explained.
Kilbeggan, 32 km (20 miles) E of Athlone town on the N6.

WEXFORD

CASTLES

Enniscorthy Castle

The town of Enniscorthy developed around this much rebuilt and restored 13th-century castle standing on a rock at the head of the Slaney's navigable tideway.

The original building was probably built by Gerald de Prendergast during the 1230s, and like both Ferns and Carlow, comprised a rectangular keep of four storeys strengthened at the corners by communicating three-quarter drum towers. In 1253 it passed through marriage to the Rochford family, and by the 15th century was held by the MacMurrough Kavanaghs. By the 1530s the castle was evidently in Crown possession and serving as the Seneschal's residence. It was leased to Edmund Spenser for three days in 1581 and five years later was acquired by Sir Henry Wallop. It was captured by Cromwellian troops in 1649 and was used as a prison during the 1798 Rebellion.

During the early 19th century the castle suffered a restoration by the Earl of Plymouth, and yet another at the end of the century by a local MP who enlarged it and used it as a residence. The building now houses the county museum.
Wexford town. NGR: S 971399.

Ferns Castle

The much-ruined castle at Ferns is the largest of a distinctive group of 13th-century Hiberno-Norman keeps that comprise rectangular blocks with cylindrical corner towers. Known as "towered" or "four-towered" keeps, they evolved independently in the South Leinster region at least a century before any comparable castles were built in England. Considering the great size of the Ferns keep it is perhaps surprising that we have no historical reference for the date of its building, but it was probably begun around 1222 by Earl William Marshall the younger. Architectural details, however, suggest that it was not completed until the mid 13th century, when it was held by William de Valance.

In its heyday the castle must have been particularly imposing. The three storeys of the main block were divided into vast apartments, the upper floors of which were lit by rather splendid trefoil-pointed windows, mostly grouped in pairs beneath pointed and camber-headed embrasures. There are similar windows in the beautiful circular chapel on the second floor of the largely complete south-east tower. This room, often cited as the most perfect chapel to be found in any Irish castle, is particularly noteworthy for its moulded rib-vaulting and supporting corbels in the shape of capitals. Of the other corner towers, one has vanished, only fragments remain of another, while about half survives of the south-west tower, which has a cellar hollowed out of solid rock, said to have been used to keep Kathleen, daughter of William Marshall, to prevent her eloping. Outside the walls a ditch was partly exposed during archaeological excavations carried out in the 1970s.

The castle evidently ceased being a residence in the early 14th century, for the ditch appears to have been filled by about 1310, while the building was in a bad state of repair by 1324. It was captured by the O'Tooles in 1331, recovered by Bishop Charnell shortly afterwards, and seems to have stayed in the hands of the Bishopric of Ferns until the 1370s when it was taken by the MacMurroughs. Lord Grey captured the place during the 1536 revolt, but the MacMurroughs managed to remain until 1551, when it was taken over for the Crown by John Travers. The Mastersons held the castle from 1583 until 1649, when it was surrendered to Cromwellian soldiers. It is likely these troops were responsible for demolishing much of its structure.
Ferns village. NGR: T 017501.

Rathmacknee Castle

Many Irish castles have lost their parapets during the course of time, but those at Rathmacknee are fully intact and are a superb example of the picturesque multi-stepped crenellations so characteristic of late medieval Irish architecture. Other features of the castle have survived equally well, and although now lacking its roof and floors, it may be considered one of the most complete examples of a tower house in South Leinster.

The tower occupies a corner of a well-preserved five-sided bawn that has a boldly projecting machicolation above the entrance. In plan the tower is a simple rectangle with one small projection – a prolongation in the east wall to accommodate latrines. There is a mural stair linking all five storeys, each having one apartment with closets or chambers in the thickness of the wall. The two lower storeys are beneath vaulting, while the timber floors had cross-beams that were tenoned directly into the wall-beams rather than laid directly upon them – an unusual practice that allowed the depth of the floor to be reduced.

It is probable that the castle was built by John Rossiter, Seneschal of the Liberties of Wexford, in 1451, whose family had lived in this area since the 12th century.

Though staunch Catholics, they survived the Reformation purges, but ultimately forfeited their lands in the 1650s. The castle remained occupied until the 1760s.
12 km (7.5 miles) SW of Wexford town, off a minor road W of the main Kilmore Road. NGR: T 037143.

Slade Castle

The picturesque little harbour of Slade is dominated by the brown rubble walls and striking merlons of this castle, formerly home of the Laffans, possibly merchants here in late medieval times. The building comprises a tower house built in the late 15th or early 16th century, and an attached two-storey hall of slightly later date.

The tower, standing 56 feet high and gracefully tapered, contains a mural stair in the south-east angle and barrel vaults over the second and fifth floors; above the latter rises a turret accommodating the stair head, a small apartment and the base of what was once a tall chimney stack. The rooms were all very small, including the main chamber on the third floor, which had a latrine, fireplace, cupboard recess and two windows. No doubt the two-storey house was later added to provide more living space. It has its own entrance on the south side, leading via a lobby up a straight mural staircase to three fair-sized rooms on the first floor. A low-pitched slated roof once covered these rooms rising from the wall-walk behind the attractive many-stepped battlemented parapet, though on the east side the roof was at a higher level to accommodate an extra storey. The three ground-floor rooms strangely cannot be entered from the living quarters above and may have been intended as a warehouse on the quay.

The castle was forfeited by the Laffan family in the aftermath of the 1641 Rebellion, though the Laffan heir was only a young boy who could not possibly have been implicated in the war. The building appears to have been used and extended in the late 18th century as part of an extensive salt works adjoining the site.
Located at the E end of Hook Head, 9.5 km (6 miles) SW of Fethard-on-Sea. NGR: X 747986.

GARDENS

John F. Kennedy Arboretum

This enormous arboretum covers 623 acres on the hill slopes overlooking the Kennedy ancestral home at Dunganstown. Planting began in 1964 and the collection now contains 4,500 species of trees and shrubs. The layout reflects the underlying function of the arboretum as a research institution – around 150 acres are divided into 250 forest plots, each devoted to a particular tree, while the remaining area of 310 acres is laid out in botanical sequence with three examples of every species represented. The collections of maples, poplars, cherries and eucalyptus are impressive, as is the rocky Alpine Garden, covering about one acre, with a colourful planting of over 320 varieties of dwarf and slow-growing conifers. There is a Phenological Garden, which explores the relationship between climate and biological phenomena, a display of waterside plants by a small lake and an Ericaceous Garden, which in addition to heathers, pieris and other peat-loving plants, has more than 500 rhododendron species and hybrids. The arboretum is administered by Coillte Teoranta – the Irish Forestry Board.
11 km (7 miles) S of New Ross. NGR: S 729193.

Johnstown Castle

A gleaming silver-grey early 19th-century castle, built for the Grogan-Morgan family, is the focus of a marvellously picturesque demesne with lakes, woodlands and many good trees and shrubs. The lake opposite the castle has Gothic towers rising from its waters and a terrace lined with statues on the opposite bank. The variety of mixed planting here includes lovely examples of *Cryptomeria japonica* "Elegans", enormous

redwoods and some of the largest specimens of Monterey cypress in Ireland. There are fine magnolias in the Woodland Garden, while the old Walled Garden has flower borders with a long hothouse sheltering a colourful display of plants. Other attractions include a cemetery with wrought-iron gates, the site of the sunken Italian Garden and two other lakes. The farm buildings house the Irish Agricultural Museum where old horticultural implements are on display.
Murntown, 5 km (3 miles) SW of Wexford. NGR: T 020170.

MUSEUMS/HERITAGE CENTRES

Ballyhack Castle

This Crusader castle was built about 1450 by the Knights Hospitaller of St John and has been partially restored. On the eastern shore of Waterford harbour, it looks over to Passage East – the two villages are connected by car ferry. The castle is one of about 3,500 tower houses built in Ireland between the 14th and 17th centuries and Ballyhack is a particularly fine example. The first-floor vaulted chamber is being developed to show the history of the Normans in Ireland. The original castle had six storeys. Among the features still existing are some of the original fireplaces, a chapel and dressing rooms, together with a cell in which prisoners were kept – the only entrance was through a narrow grill-covered opening high above the cell.
13 km (8 miles) E of Waterford city (via Passage East and car ferry).

Ballymore Historic Features

This "walkabout" open-air museum has an intriguing range of interesting places, including a Norman motte, an ancient church, graveyard and holy well. The Donovan family have lived here for the past 300 years and describe this as a family museum.

The large hayloft in the 18th-century farmyard buildings has been converted into an indoor museum and it has a very eclectic mixture that includes lace, embroidery, costumes, children's clothes, toys, a late 19th-century wedding dress and old farm accounts and records, as well as some 1798 exhibits. The museum has lots of old weapons and sporting gear. There's a new painting gallery beside the museum. In the adjoining former dairy, old dairy equipment and household items are on show, along with horse-drawn farm equipment.
Ballymore, Camolin, 9.5 km (6 miles) SW of Gorey.

Berkeley Costume and Toy Museum

A collection of toys and costumes, nearly all made in Ireland between about 1740 and 1925. Exhibits also include toy carriages and embroidered textiles. One of the most interesting pieces is a dress made in Kilkenny about 1760. The 18th-century costumes in particular are remarkably extravagant in their use of materials, colours and embroidery. Altogether there are hundreds of exhibits in the 18th-century house, owned by the Bernstorff family. Children can go for a ride in the Victorian goat carriage in the garden.
6.5 km (4 miles) NE of New Ross, off the Enniscorthy Road.

Dunbrody Abbey

Substantial ruins still exist of this Cistercian foundation, dating from around 1200 and founded by monks from St Mary's Abbey in Dublin. The site has a small museum and a full-sized hedge maze, one of two in Ireland.
Near Campile, 13 km (8 miles) S of New Ross.

Enniscorthy Museum

Wexford's county museum has an incredible collection packed into three floors of this late 16th-century castle. A stone plaque at the entrance to the castle marks the first flight between Britain and Ireland, which landed near Enniscorthy on 22 April 1912. The ground floor includes a brougham carriage that once belonged to Moira O'Neill, the Glens of Antrim poetess, a late 18th-century sedan chair and a jaunting car. Upstairs rooms include an ecclesiastical collection, a section on the 1916–23 fight for independence and, appropriately for Enniscorthy, a section on the 1798 uprising. Vinegar Hill, the last battle site of that rising, can be seen from the castle windows. There is also a police room with memorabilia from police forces all over the world. On the second floor are models of ships and old farming implements, plus detail on the nearby Carley's Bridge Potteries, founded in 1654.

The 1798 theme is continued in Enniscorthy at the National 1798 Visitor Centre, which uses modern audio-visual and other technology to tell the story of the 1798 uprising.

The Fr Murphy Centre at Boolavogue is a recreation of the homestead of this principal figure in that uprising. The centre also contains traditional music archives. Enniscorthy Museum and Visitor Centre: Enniscorthy town.

Fr Murphy Centre: near Ferns, 13 km (8 miles) NE of Enniscorthy town.

Hook Lighthouse

This lighthouse is reckoned to be the oldest in Europe – it was demanned some time ago.

At the southern end of the Hook Peninsula, SW of Wexford town.

Irish Agricultural Museum

This museum, set in the wonderful grounds of Johnstown Castle, displays and details the old rural way of life. In the transport section, old carts, pony traps and tractors are on view, while many of the old rural crafts are brought to life in displays that include harness-making, basketmaking, a carpenter's workshop and a blacksmith's forge. Farmhouse interiors are reconstructed in detail and the museum has a good collection of Irish furniture. Among the recently added sections is the large permanent exhibition on the potato and the great mid 19th-century Famine.

8 km (5 miles) SW of Wexford town, off the Rosslare Road.

Irish National Heritage Park

This open-air museum has fourteen separate sites in a magnificent rural setting beside the Slaney estuary, complete with winding paths, streams, ponds and an abundance of wildlife. The full-scale reconstructions of homesteads and places of ritual and worship are archaeologically authentic. The tour begins with the Stone Age (7000 BC–2000 BC) and includes a Neolithic farmstead. The Bronze Age reconstruction (2000 BC–500 BC) includes a stone circle, while the Celtic/early Christian era (500 BC–AD 1169) includes examples of Ogham, the earliest Irish form of writing. The displays end with the early Norman period (1169–90) when the Anglo-Norman invaders arrived in Ireland: the site includes an almost Moorish-looking reconstruction of an early Norman castle.

5 km (3 miles) W of Wexford, off the main Dublin Road.

Kilmore Quay Maritime Museum

The *Guillemot II*, an old lightship, stands guard at the top of the harbour in Kilmore Quay while work goes on all around her, turning the harbour into one of Ireland's main fishing ports and creating a marina. The ship was built in Leith, near Edinburgh in Scotland, after World War I with German reparations, to replace an earlier vessel sunk during that war. The interior of the ship gives an excellent idea of shipboard life in the old days, complete with captain's cabin, crew's quarters and cramped kitchen.

More than that, it has been packed with maritime artefacts, everything from a 200-year-old compass and binnacle to a whale's backbone. The history of the Irish Navy from 1922 onwards is detailed and so too is the story of Irish Shipping, until it

was scuppered in 1982. About 1,000 shipwrecks lie off the south-east coast and many of them are detailed here, while another section is full of figureheads. This fascinating shipborne museum is complemented by the maritime artefacts in James Kehoe's pub on Kilmore Quay's main street of thatched cottages. The lounge bar of the Hotel Rosslare, on the cliffs above Rosslare Harbour, also has interesting sea items.
24 km (15 miles) SW of Wexford town.

New Ross

This small and largely unspoiled town has three sites of interest. The Dunbrody is an exact replica of a mid 19th-century Famine ship. Dunmain House dates from the 17th century and is a fascinating warren of old rooms, towers and memorabilia. At Dunganstown, the John F. Kennedy homestead is preserved just as it was 150 years ago and as it was during Kennedy's visit in 1963. Forebears of the Boston Kennedys lived here before emigrating to the US from New Ross.
New Ross.
Dunganstown: 5 km (3 miles) S of New Ross.

Tacumshane Windmill

In the 18th and 19th centuries, the Irish countryside was dotted with windmills and their sails powered the millstones that ground the grain. Of two restored windmills that can be seen in the Republic, the thatched-roof windmill at Tacumshane, near Lady's Island Lake, is probably considered the most attractive. This small windmill, dominated by its large sails, was built in 1846 and was restored to its present state in the 1950s.
17.5 km (11 miles) SE of Wexford, near Lady's Island Lake.

WICKLOW

HOUSES

Russborough

Irish country houses are generally distinguished by their architecture rather than their contents, but Russborough is a striking exception to this rule. Not only does this magnificent Palladian mansion boast lavish plasterwork, splendid chimney-pieces and superb joinery, but it also contains the world-famous Beit collection of pictures, furniture and objets d'art. It can justifiably be said that Russborough, with its superb landscape setting, is indeed a temple of the arts – a place of rare quality and beauty.

The house was commissioned by Joseph Lesson, later the first Earl of Milltown, after inheriting the wealth of his father, an opulent Dublin brewer. Completion of the building, which began in 1741, took over ten years so that its designer, Richard Castle, never lived to see the final stages that were carried out by his associate Francis Bindon. The house is built of local silver-grey granite with wonderfully crisp detail and has an entrance front that extends to 700 feet, the longest in Ireland. The centre block of seven bays and two stories is relatively small, but is extended via colonnaded quadrant wings to seven-bay, two-storey pavilions.

Fortune has smiled kindly upon Russborough for it has remained free of subsequent alterations, with most of Castle's original features surviving intact. Ascending the broad flight of granite steps guarded by a pair of carved lions, the visitor enters the front hall – a well-proportioned room with a floor of polished oak and an ornate but severe compartmental ceiling with Doric frieze quite similar to the one Castle designed for Leinster House. The monumental chimney-piece is of black Kilkenny marble, much favoured by Castle for entrance halls. Five doors with magnificently carved architraves of West Indian mahogany lead to the major reception rooms: the saloon, the drawing-room, the dining-room, the tapestry room and the grand staircase.

Undoubtedly the finest room in the house is the saloon, which occupies the three central bays of the north front. It has a coved ceiling with rococo plasterwork incorporating flowers, garlands, swags and putti, which on stylistic grounds can be attributed to the Francini brothers of Italy. The walls are covered with Genoese velvet dating from around 1840, an ideal background for paintings which include the principal Dutch and Flemish pictures in the Beit collection. The room also has Louis XVI furniture and a pair of Japanese lacquer cabinets from Harewood House. A striking feature of the room is the inlaid sprung mahogany floor with a central star in satinwood. This was covered with a green baize drugget when the house was occupied by rebels during the 1798 rebellion. The potential of the drugget for making four fine flags was considered but rejected by the rebels, lest "their brogues might ruin his lordship's floor". The rebels, in fact, did virtually no damage to the house during their stay, although the government forces who occupied the building afterwards were considerably less sympathetic. It is said that the troops only left in 1801 after a furious Lord Milltown challenged Lord Tyrawley to a duel "with underbusses and slugs in a sawpit".

Flanking the saloon is the music room and the library, both framed by ebullient rococo ceilings that were probably also the work of the Francini brothers. The coffered and richly decorated barrel-vaulted ceiling of the tapestry room is by a less experienced artist, though the room is no less impressive than the others and contains an English state bed made in London in 1795 and two Soho tapestries of Moghul subjects by Vanderbank. Infused with a restless energy the plasterwork in the adjacent drawing-room spills onto the walls, where fantastic plaster frames surround the four oval marine scenes by Vernet representing morning, noon, evening and night. Although part of the patrimony of the house, these pictures were sold in 1926 and only after a determined search were recovered forty-three years later by Sir Alfred Beit.

The dining-room has a monumental Irish chimney-piece of mottled grey Sicilian marble and the walls are ornamented by a series of six Murillo paintings acquired by Alfred Beit from Lord Dudley in 1895. Five of these pictures had been purchased in 1867 at the Salamanca sale in Paris, while the sixth was later acquired by Dudley from the Vatican Museum in exchange for a Fra Angelico and a Bonifazio. No one who visits Russborough is likely to forget the staircase with its extraordinary riot of exuberant plasterwork; there is nothing quite like it anywhere else in the British Isles. In later years the decorator Mr Sibthorpe is reported to have remarked that it represented "the ravings of a maniac", adding that he was "afraid the madman was Irish".

Russborough passed out of the family in 1931 but fortunately most of its famous art collection remained in Ireland when it was bequeathed to the National Gallery of Ireland in 1902 – a bequest so important that a new wing was built to contain it. Russborough was not devoid of art treasures for long, however; the property was acquired by Sir Alfred Beit in 1951 as the setting for one of the world's most outstanding private art collections, dominated by Dutch, Flemish and Spanish masterpieces. The house and its collection have now been given to a foundation and are open to the public, while the Beits have moved into one of the wings. It is extremely sad that the Beits' remarkable generosity to the Irish people was rewarded in 1986 by a robbery of some of the finest pictures in the house.

4 km (2.5 miles) SW of Blessington. NGR: N 957100.

GARDENS

Avondale

Former home of Charles Stewart Parnell. Planting in the arboretum was begun in 1777 by Samuel Hayes and taken over by the State in 1903 as a Forestry School –

Augustine Henry was closely involved with planting from 1913. Avondale has many rare and fine trees.
2.5 km (1.5 miles) S of Rathdrum.

Hunter's Hotel Gardens

This is one of Ireland's oldest coaching inns, now in the fifth generation of the same family, and boasts a small but charming garden bordering the River Vartry. It contains a neat knot garden, cordylines, rose beds and colourful herbaceous borders, amidst plush lawns and box hedging. An excellent place to relax with tea and scones after a busy day touring the area.
Newrath Bridge near Rathnew, off N11 at the bridge in Ashford.

Kilruddery

Perhaps the most complete example of a late 17th-century formal garden to survive in the British Isles. It was created in the 1680s by the fourth Earl of Meath and later extended in the 1720s and the 1840s. The central features are two parallel water canals extending from the house down a large rectangular lawn and aligned upon a lime avenue. A circular pond lies beyond the canals and to one side is a *patte d'oie* – an arrangement of radiating hedges known as the "angles" – composed of lime, hornbeam and beech with an enclosing hedge of yew and statuary at the diagonal intersections. On the opposite side the canals are flanked by a beech woodland known as the Wilderness, divided by symmetrical walks with statuary placed at focal points. Nearby stands a circular pond surrounded by a beech hedge and a mini amphitheatre of tiered grass seats used for amateur theatricals. Mid 19th-century additions include a parterre, an ornamental dairy and a domed conservatory.
1.6 km (1 mile) S of Bray on the Greystones–Delgany Road. NGR: O 207160.

Mount Usher

Over 4,000 species are represented in this exquisite garden, including many outstanding specimens, all incorporated into an authentically wild "Robinsonian" layout, covering only 20 acres. A sense of space and fluidity is provided by the Vartry River which flows through the central axis of the garden, while grassy vistas help to relieve any sense of being hemmed in by the many trees and shrubs.

Visitors arrive through a courtyard housing a number of craft shops and enter an area known as the Orchard, bordered by a fine beech hedge. A path uphill passes a small pavilion dedicated to the Walpole family, who owned the garden from its inception in the 1860s to its sale in 1980. From here the Maple Walk draws the visitor down towards the river – the focal point of the garden – where bold, effective plantings frame the water's margins. The river views are particularly striking in autumn, when the water reflects the rich colours of liquidambars, fothergillas, acers and a host of other plants. From the croquet lawn with its magnificent American Eastern hemlock, visitors taking the Azalea Walk can admire a 50-foot-high *Pinus montezumae*. Rhododendrons, davidias, azaras and a quantity of *Eucryphia glutinosa* line the Azalea Walk, while at the far end stands a grove of spectacular eucalyptus trees, some over 130 feet tall. Across the river the imposing Palm Walk is lined with Chusan palms and nearby, the main eucryphia collection features clumps of the special hybrids *E. x nymansensis* "Mount Usher", the result of a cross between *E. glutinosa* and *E. cordifolia*. The Lime Walk to the north has an excellent collection of ornamental southern beeches and beyond the house in the area known as the Island, there are some fine acers, magnolias and a lily pond with ornamental rushes. The Riviera, a long narrow strip bordering the river, also has some fine plants including a splendid *Pinus montezumae*. Before leaving the garden, visitors often admire the fine specimen of a Japanese banana tree against the garden wall.
Ashford, on the main Dublin–Wexford Road. NGR: T 258977.

Powerscourt

This is a garden on a spectacular scale, lavishly endowed with an extensive range of antique statuary, magnificent wrought ironwork, broad sweeping terraces, elaborate parterres, some of the most remarkable trees in Ireland and above all, a superb setting beneath the shadow of the Great Sugar Loaf.

The focus of the garden is a Palladian mansion built in the 1730s and recently rebuilt as a shopping centre after destruction by fire in 1974. The steep slopes below are cut into an amphitheatre of grass terraces leading down to the Triton Pool – all transformed into an Italian Garden during the mid 19th century with the addition of a stone terrace nearest the house, sunken parterres and a magnificent central perron with flanking stairways. The design incorporates features brought back from the continent, including statues of the Fontainebleau Diana, winged figures of Fame and Victory and a pair of Italian bronze figures of Eolas from the Palais Royale in Paris. By the pool, above a 1730s grotto, stand bronze-painted winged pegasi, the heraldic supporters of the Wingfield coat of arms and, in the pool, a jet over 100 feet high. The adjacent Walled Garden has some magnificent iron gates, including the famous Perspective Gates from Bamberg Cathedral in Bavaria (c. 1770).

The Wingfields, Viscounts Powerscourt, were enthusiastic planters of trees and the many outstanding specimens are best viewed by purchasing the late Alan Mitchell's tree trail at the entrance. Visitors normally start by walking to the Pepperpot Tower across the terrace and on through the Tower Valley, where numerous fine conifers can be inspected, including a big-coned pine (*Pinus coulteri*) which, at 56 feet, is the tallest in the British Isles. Below the valley lies the Japanese Garden, a pleasant area laid out on reclaimed bogland in 1908 with many *Trachycarpus fortunei* palms, magnolias, maples, cherries and viburnums. A path by the lake brings visitors past an extraordinary specimen of a Monterey cypress planted in 1898 and on, by a large pets' cemetery, to the Dolphin Pond with its surrounding lawns and exotic plantings. From here fine wrought-iron English Gates lead onto a herbaceous border down the inner Walled Garden, claimed to be the longest in Ireland, though the quality of its planting is not matched by its grand pretensions. A line of Wellingtonias running alongside the Walled Garden is, however, a magnificent sight and much more worthy of the grandeur of Powerscourt.
Near Enniskerry, 17.5 km (11 miles) S of Dublin. NGR: O 212164.

MUSEUMS/HERITAGE CENTRES

Arklow Maritime Museum

This "unvarnished" collection uses no modern display techniques whatsoever, which helps enhance its authenticity. Arklow has a very fine fishing and maritime tradition – early this century it had eighty schooners, brigs and brigantines, a tradition continued in the present day by Arklow Shipping, which has the largest Irish-flagged fleet. There's a model of Sir Francis Chichester's *Gypsy Moth III*, built in the Arklow yard of John Tyrrell & Sons. The museum also recalls the great hardships of World War II (the "Emergency" in Ireland) and a mine from this period stands at the entrance to the museum. Arklow was the first place in Ireland to have a lifeboat station, in 1826, and that proud tradition is also recalled. This delightful miscellany of material includes everything from old navigational instruments to a uniform worn by a merchant navy officer and a shoe worn by a woman passenger on the ill-fated Lusitania.
St Mary's Road, Arklow town.

Avondale House

This house, of 18th-century design, was the birthplace and family home of Charles Stewart Parnell, the great 19th-century nationalist leader and uncrowned "king" of Ireland. The large hall opens into the reception and dining-rooms, both of which are

filled with Parnell memorabilia. Much of the house has now been restored to its decor of around 1850. An audio-visual presentation on the life and times of Parnell precedes the tour of the house. The surrounding forest estate extends to over 500 acres and is a fine testimony to Ireland's natural heritage of trees, plants and animals. The oldest trees were planted by Samuel Hayes, who built the house over two centuries ago.
2.5 km (1.5 miles) S of Rathdrum.

Bray Heritage Centre

Located in an old courthouse built in 1841, this centre tells the story of Bray and its rise to prominence as a seaside resort. The arrival of the railway in the town in 1853 was the key element for change and there's plenty of detail about William Dargan (1799–1867), the railway pioneer, accompanied by a fine model of Bray railway station and old photographs. The building of the seafront esplanade from 1859 onwards is detailed, along with some of Bray's now-vanished buildings, including the Turkish Baths on the seafront.
Lower Main Street, Bray.

Coolakay House Agricultural Museum

This collection of agricultural implements and equipment is exhibited in a large shed divided into three sections and attached to Coolakay House. Items of old farming equipment include an early Ferguson tractor, a 1936 threshing machine, made in Aberdeen in Scotland, which travelled from farm to farm during the harvest, and an old combine harvester. Smaller items include a drill grubber, made by Pierces of Wexford, old hay rakes and ancient ploughs. The museum has a couple of tub traps and an old side cart.
4 km (3 miles) SW of Enniskerry, 17.5 km (10.5 miles) S of Dublin.

Glendalough Visitor Centre

This low-key, unobtrusive centre is a useful introduction to the whole Glendalough site, one of Ireland's most notable monastic locations, set in a new national park that will eventually extend to 12,141 acres. The centre has an audio-visual presentation – Ireland of the Monasteries, an introduction not only to Glendalough but to the arrival of Christianity in Ireland and the spread of the Irish religious influence to Britain and mainland Europe. The centrepiece is a large model of the site as it probably looked about 1080. Outside, the well-preserved ruins include a cathedral, St Kevin's Church and a round tower, 33 metres (100 feet) high and one of the best preserved in Ireland.
51 km (32 miles) SW of Dublin. Turn off the Dublin–Wexford N11 at Kilmacanogue and take the R755.

Wicklow's Historic Gaol

More harsh conditions have been vividly brought to life, this time in the reconstructed town gaol in the centre of Wicklow town. The Rising of 1798, as it affected County Wicklow, is depicted and so too is the history of the deportation of convicts to Australia during penal times.
Wicklow town.

CHAPTER THREE

ANIMALS

INTRODUCTION

This section is an introduction to forty of Ireland's best-known "wild" animals. The term "wild" is used loosely to distinguish them from domestic animals like livestock and pets. Most of the animals are mammals (i.e. they suckle their young) but others have been included despite their lower status on the evolutionary scale. These are Ireland's three amphibians – the Frog, Toad and Newt – and her only species of Lizard.

In the case of the cetacea (Porpoises, Dolphins and Whales) it has been possible to deal with familiar representatives of the family only (there are about twenty recorded from Irish waters but most of those are irregular or rare visitors). Ireland's seven species of Bat have been included, as investigation has shown most of them to be more widespread than was formerly thought. Britain has fifteen bats, to Ireland's seven, illustrating well the fact that, proportionally, Ireland is less well endowed than her neighbouring island. In overall terms Ireland's total species tally (both of flora and of fauna) is about one third less than that of Britain. The impoverishment has been attributed to the geographic location of Ireland with respect to Europe (from which the species migrated at the end of the Ice Age).

BACKGROUND

Many of the animals that are now found in Ireland in a wild state are descendants of the first waves of north-westerly spreading fauna – from before the first arrival of humankind in Ireland. Others are the progeny of creatures introduced accidentally or intentionally by man over the past nine millenia.

Before Ireland became insular in form (a thousand or so years before the coming of man), it was part of the land mass of present-day Europe. Unfathomable quantities of water having been solidified in the form of glaciers, Ice Age animals roamed freely over the dry land. Fossils indicate that Reindeer, Lemmings, Lynx, Giant Irish deer and before that even Mammoths roamed the tundra on what is now Ireland. With the advent of warmer conditions following the end of the Ice Age, the Mammoth and the Giant deer became extinct. The others which were not able to survive in the temperate conditions retired northwards with the retreating Arctic circle.

By the time man settled in Ireland these Arctic species were long gone but he found a post-glacial environment densely populated with a varied indigenous fauna. The land was thickly wooded with pine, hazel and birch and contained Wolves, Brown bear, and Wild boar. Other more familiar creatures like Red deer, Foxes, Badgers, Stoats, Pine martens and Otters were undoubtedly in Ireland from this time too. But a range of mammals including Moles, Voles and a number of amphibians and reptiles did not get there before low-lying tracts of land were engulfed by the rising sea level – a product of the melting ice. Although the land surface itself recovered to a height many feet higher than it had been under the weight of the ice, it never again provided the means whereby animals from Europe could gain access to Ireland overland. Some of the first settlers must have brought animals with them but being primarily hunter/gatherers they favoured a nomadic-style life, roaming the land and leaving behind only isolated signs of their effect on it.

It was not until some 3,000 years had elapsed that the first farmers found their way to Ireland. The bogs were swelling imperceptibly out of the vegetation-clogged wetlands and the landscape was a rich green canopy of hardwood trees like oak, ash and elm. These early agriculturalists made clearings in the forest and set up semi-permanent enclosures to protect their livestock from wild animals – particularly wolves. They husbanded primitive cattle, goats, sheep, pigs and eventually horses, and made an abiding impact on their terrain. Extensive grazing had been created for stock prior to the advent of Christianity. Though much still remained as wilderness, a network of monastic settlements was established throughout the land from which early Irishmen cultivated the countryside. The colourful poetry and other writings of these Christian Celts not only indicate the wide variety of animals that cohabited the country then, but also speak of the empathy which existed between these people and their wildlife.

The Normans, who were hunting enthusiasts, maintained wild habitats and introduced the Rabbit and the Fallow deer for this purpose. Inadvertent introductions from this period included the House mouse and the Black rat. The latter (now almost non-existent in Ireland) was once abundant and carried the infamous plague, or "Black Death", in its fleas. This disease decimated the population of Ireland in the 14th century. The larger, more robust and more resilient Brown rat has since displaced its black relative and, though notorious for its capacity to spread disease, is generally regarded as being less harmful.

Up until the Middle Ages landscape modification by man had been occurring to fluctuating degrees, though undoubtedly less significantly than in Britain and elsewhere in Europe. Retarded technological development and relatively low population tended to render these changes impermanent, permitting wildlife to survive both in abundance and in diversity. As a consequence of the Tudor and subsequent plantations, however, dramatic changes occurred which resulted in the virtual total eradication of Ireland's woodlands by 1800. Other once wild habitats like bogs, fens and mountains have since been utterly man-modified as well. Countless small, now-obscure creatures must have gone as a result of these changes – now lost to Ireland's native ecology. Gone too are the Bear, the Wolf, the Wild boar, the Red squirrel (since reintroduced) and almost exterminated were the Pine marten and the Red deer. It is perhaps only through adaptation that some of these more "habitat specific" animals managed to survive at all.

Despite the fact that some animals were brought to Ireland by man and others were exterminated by him, more than half the number considered here are thought to be native – long-term survivors. These include the Lizard, the Newt, the Bats and a number of the larger mammals. A few – the Stoat, the Otter and the native Hare – are regarded as Irish endemics (i.e. races unique to Ireland) and there were probably others. These species can be (due to factors like colour difference, size, etc.) readily distinguished from their British or European counterparts. The Irish Stoat for instance is smaller and darker than the animal from Britain, having evolved in separation. The Irish Otter is still common and widespread in suitable habitat, in contrast to the decline which had been recorded throughout Britain and Europe. Recent research into Ireland's seven Bat species has shown them to be more widespread and locally common than was formerly thought. The European stronghold for the Leisler's and the Daubenton's bats may be in Ireland and this country has thus a special responsibility for their continued survival and that of the Lesser horseshoe bat, which also has a particularly western distribution.

An entire group of animals – the *cetacea* (Porpoises, Dolphins, Whales) – are less well known than their terrestrial relatives. In fact, until relatively recently it was not known that many species from the smallest, the Porpoise, to the largest, the Blue whale, passed close to Ireland's western Atlantic seaboard on their seasonal migrations. During the course of commercial whaling activities, carried out in the early years of the 20th century off Ireland's western coast, half a dozen of the larger species were sadly exploited, including the Blue, Fin, Humpback, Sei, Right and Sperm whales.

Thankfully these activities were wound up before they were permanently destructive. *Cetacea* of many species are still to be seen off Irish coasts and the sightings of some, like Killer whales off Cape Clear Island, have shown that these leviathans are still regular visitors to Irish inshore waters.

ANIMAL AWARENESS

Most of the animals here are nocturnal, which means that good views are usually restricted to glimpses in car headlights or in the beam of a torch. It is possible to see many of them in the half-light of dawn or dusk. The best views are often quite unexpected and the would-be animal watcher who goes out after dark will often return home unrewarded. Certain animals like Pine martens, Bats and Badgers are more strictly nocturnal than others and may only occasionally be seen in daylight. Others, like Stoats, Foxes and Otters, are regularly seen during the day, while Hares, Rabbits and similar grazers are decidedly diurnal. However, some (like Deer), being understandably wary of people, are difficult to view well.

Many of the best views of Ireland's wild fauna are unfortunately at the side of the road where they have been killed by road traffic. Badgers, Foxes, Stoats, Hedgehogs, Rabbits and some rodents are the most common victims, but Hares, Otters and Deer are occasionally killed too. It is unlikely that the continued survival of any species could be thus threatened, but a lot of this unnecessary carnage could be avoided by more careful driving. Hibernation is used by some of Ireland's animals, notably the Bats and Hedgehog, but also Frogs, Lizards and Newts. Animals in this state should not be disturbed as this renders them extremely vulnerable. Once awakened they may not be able to return rapidly to their torpid state and may die from shock. Bats are particularly vulnerable – it has been suggested that they use up most of their latent energy (stored as body fat) on being disturbed more than once. Stones in the garden may provide winter homes for Newts – often a fair distance from their summer ponds. If these stones are overturned to reveal their torpid troglodytes they should be carefully replaced.

The presence of wild animals can be readily detected from "tell-tale" signs using the senses – debris from feeding, footprints or other tracks in soft ground or snow, droppings of animal waste matter, scenting points and animals sounds all are useful indicators. Many of these are subtle and will go undetected unless the senses are alert. The musky smell of a Fox's scenting post is highly recognisable to a "tuned" nose but usually goes unnoticed even by country folk. Squirrels leave half-eaten cones at the bottom of conifer trees and Deer make clear-cut gnaw marks on their bark; once recognised, the marks made by Badgers foraging for worms are never forgotten, and the "spraining" mounds of Otters make a similar indelible impression.

The "chittering" sounds made by Otters can be heard a long way off while the weird howling and barking of mating Foxes is equally audible. One of the most far-carrying country sounds is the piercing whistle of the Sika stag during the rut. The animal has usually "hightailed" it though, by the time the animal watcher has got to the spot from which the sound came. In contrast, the Pigmy shrew utters a succession of barely audible squeaks but it is an exasperating little animal for it can run around the observer's feet in the grass and remain quite invisible. The most accomplished squeakers, though, are the Bats. Each has its own sonar/echo-location system, distinguishable (to the expert) by its frequency and pitch. Even normally silent Common frogs emit subdued croaking during the breeding season which is distinguishable from the nocturnal rattling of Natterjacks.

Otters leave wide, slightly webbed footprints in soft mud which can easily be distinguished from those of Mink. Hares have large padded forefeet and long hindfeet which make recognisable prints in open ground; Rabbits' prints are like scaled-down versions. The long claws on Badgers' feet make clear marks in the ground at the sett

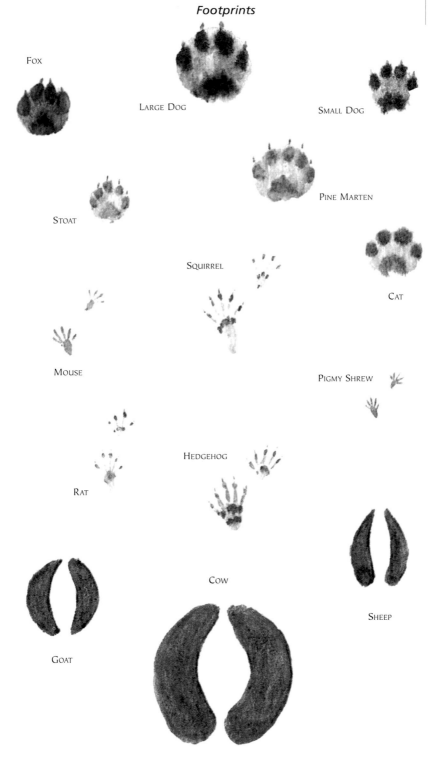

Fox

Large Dog

Small Dog

Pine Marten

Stoat

Squirrel

Cat

Mouse

Pigmy Shrew

Rat

Hedgehog

Cow

Sheep

Goat

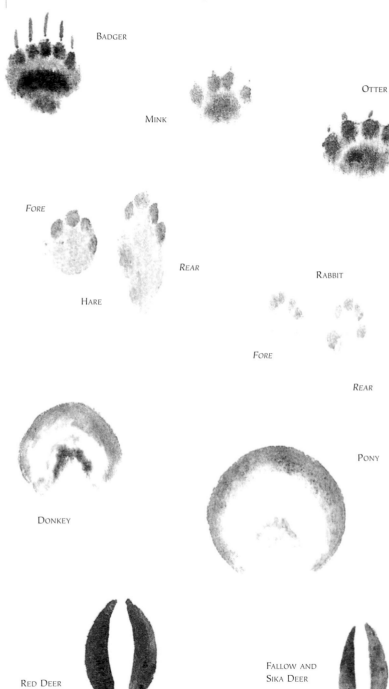

Footprints

BADGER

MINK

OTTER

FORE

REAR

HARE

RABBIT

FORE

REAR

DONKEY

PONY

RED DEER

FALLOW AND
SIKA DEER

Mating Pair

Frog

Natterjack Toad

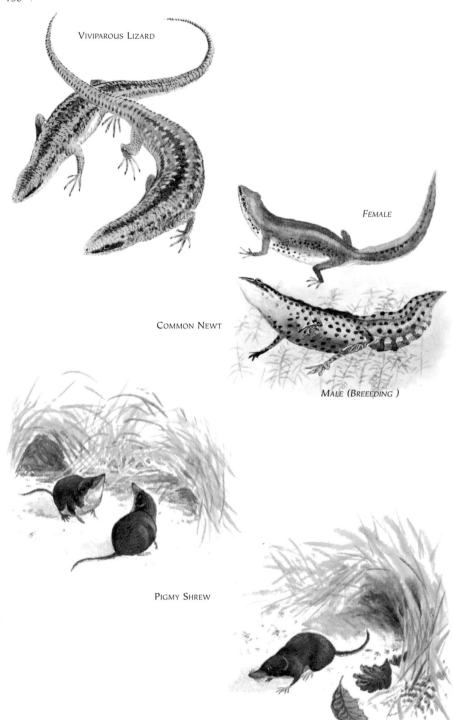

VIVIPAROUS LIZARD

FEMALE

COMMON NEWT

MALE (BREEEDING)

PIGMY SHREW

HEDGEHOG

LESSER HORSESHOE

DAUBENTON'S

LEISLER'S

WHISKERED

NATTERER'S

LONG – EARED

PIPISTRELLE

IRISH HARE

BROWN HARE

RABBIT

HARE
(*REAR VIEW*)

RABBIT
(*REAR VIEW*)

GREY SQUIRREL

RED SQUIRREL

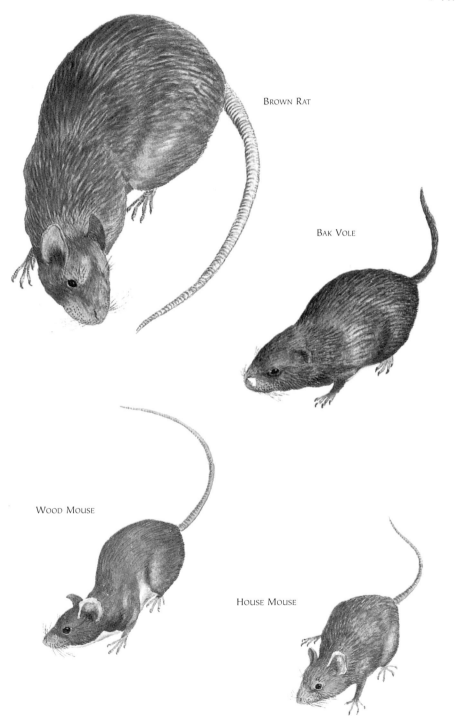

BROWN RAT

BAK VOLE

WOOD MOUSE

HOUSE MOUSE

DOLPHINS

DOLPHINS

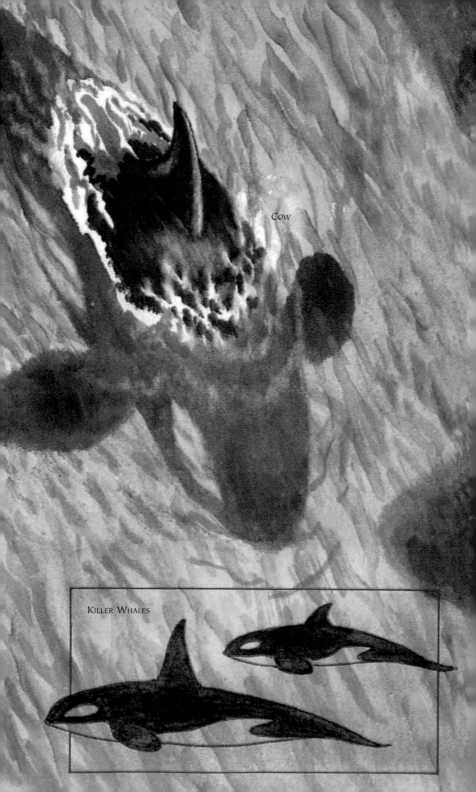

Cow

Killer Whales

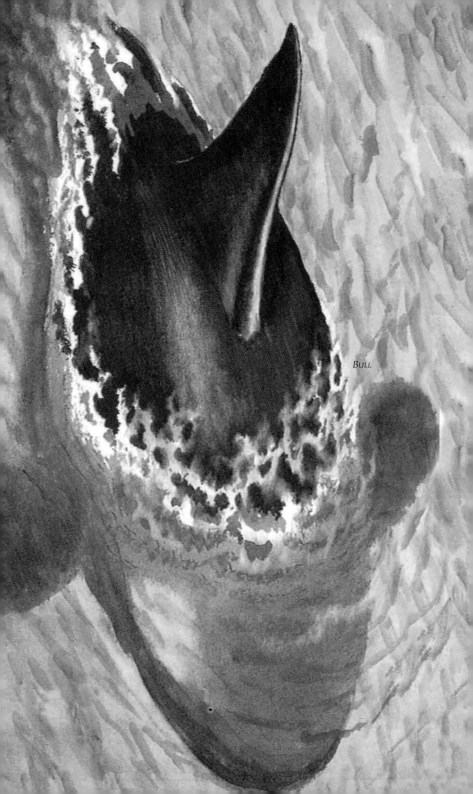

Bull

FOX

BADGER

IRISH STOAT

PINE MARTEN

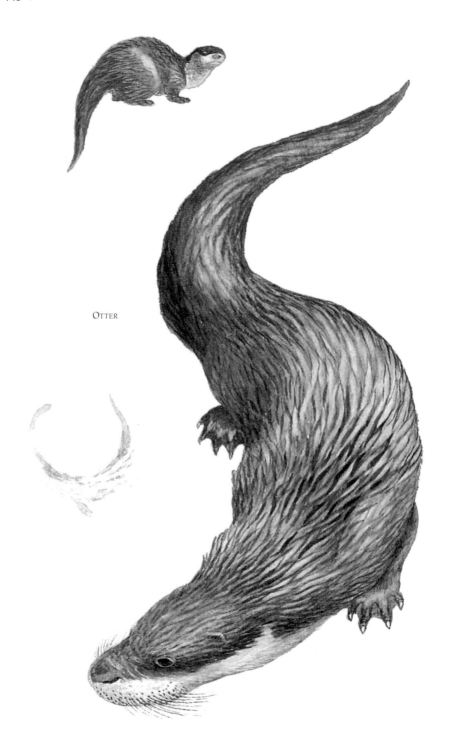

Otter

MINK

Bull

Cow

Grey Seals

Calf

Bull

Cow

COMMON SEALS

Calf

RED DEER

STAG

HIND

CALF

BUCK

FALLOW DEER

DOE

SIKA DEER

BUCK

DOE

FERAL GOAT

MALE

FEMALE

CONNEMARA PONY

or where the animals have been digging for food. Martens and Mink have disproportionately large paw marks, rounded and similar to a cats', but no claw marks show in cat prints since their claws are retractible. Dog prints are likewise distinguishable from those of the Fox, which show the impression of fine hairs. In the cases of the smaller rodents, the footprints are quite similar to one another. Size is the best distinguishing factor. The Pigmy shrew, the smallest of all, shows five toes in the prints of the forefeet – one toe more than those of the other small mammals. One should exercise care when identifying the footprints of larger mammals. Though Horse and Donkey prints are clear, those of other livestock like the Cow, Pig and Goat are not always obviously different from those of the Deer.

Common Frog • *Rana temporaria* • *Loscán*

Though not thought to be native the frog is now a very common and widespread amphibian, being found from the most low-lying to the highest places, wherever there are freshwater ponds. The remarkable life cycle of the frog begins in late winter when masses of them congregate in ponds, ditches and the like having overwintered in hibernation. Here nuptials and mating occur *en masse*, the smaller males sitting "piggy back" on the females and fertilising the eggs as they are laid. The spring-time metamorphosis of spawn to tadpole to froglet to frog is a spectacle that has instilled wonderment in countless generations of children and forms the centrepiece of many a school nature table. Frog food is mainly small and invertebrate like snails, slugs and insects. Frogs vary considerably in colour from yellow-brown to green and even grey and are capable of changing their colour to suit their environment.

Natterjack Toad • *Bufo calamita* • *Cnádán*

The Natterjack has been regarded as a remnant from the end of the Ice Age or, perhaps more likely, a relatively recent introduction. Its few colonies are confined to dune "slacks" (marshy ponds in sandy places near the sea) in County Kerry. In the sanctuary of these habitats the toads emerge from hibernation, and croaking noisily at dusk, carry out their reproductive cycle which is similar to that of the frog. The spawn lies in the water in strings rather than in massive globules. The toad tadpoles take a month or more to develop into little toads and take four or five years to grow into adults capable of reproduction.

Natterjack toads look like smallish dark frogs with shorter, unwebbed hindfeet. They are generally dull greenish in colour with a clearly defined yellow line down the middle of the back from the head. The skin has an irregular surface of lumps and bumps and, being mucus covered, may look quite shiny. The large eyes protrude from the head like those of the frog. Unlike the frog the toad does not hop but scurries on all fours along the ground. In places where it is common it may be seen occasionally in the open in daylight but is much more active at night.

Viviparous Lizard • *Lacerta vivepara* • *Earc luachra*

This, Ireland's only lizard, is found in all sorts of dry habitats but favours sandy or rocky places, particularly near the sea. It is well known inland though, being found even on the raised bogs of the midlands. Insects and other invertebrates that can be caught are the lizard's food. Like other animals that are found against backgrounds of variable pattern, its subtle tones and markings render it inconspicuous in its habitat. It is generally yellowish brown with irregular blackish markings along the length of its body but it can look greyish or greenish in different situations. The length of the male averages about 13 cm (5 inches) and the larger female may measure as much as 20 cm (8 inches). The skin is beautifully segmented with scales. The young are produced live (hence the name) and not from eggs as is normal with reptiles. They range in number from two to ten or more and though able to fend for themselves within minutes of birth they often fall prey to Kestrels and other predators. On being grabbed by the tail the lizard can escape by detaching itself from its tail.

Common Newt • *Triturus vulgaris* • *Earc sléibhe*

Only one species of newt is found in Ireland (there are three in Britain) which sh‍
simplify identification. However, being amphibians, newts spend the summer in fr‍
water and hibernate in winter, usually beneath stones. In this state they have been
mistaken for lizards but they do not have the hard shiny and scaly skin of the latter.
They are also smaller and have a vertically flattened tail which is "finned" along its
length on both sides. Their size is up to 10 cm (4 inches).

The female is light brownish, paler underneath, and the larger male is greyish,
profusely spotted with black. In spring when the pair have taken up residence in a
pond, disused well or other freshwater habitat, the male develops a bright orange
belly flush with blue and red markings on the tail. A long wavy crest along the back is
used to full effect in an elaborate underwater courtship display.

Eggs are laid individually in a folded pondweed leaf; these hatch out into tadpoles
complete with gills for underwater breathing. This phase lasts well into autumn when,
with the adults, they leave the water to begin the terrestrial phase of their life cycle.

Pigmy Shrew • *Sorex minutus* • *Dallóg fhraoigh*

It is difficult to realise just how small this little creature is until it is picked up in the
hand. The body would fit comfortably into a tablespoon (5 cm/2 inches) with a
further 3.5 cm (1.5 inches) of tail. It weighs only a few grammes – a third of the
weight of a House mouse. Apart from being much smaller than a mouse it is a
different shape as well, with a disproportionately long, thickly whiskered nose. The
eyes are tiny compared with those of the mouse, as are the ears, which are more to
the sides of the head and almost concealed in the fur. The tail is lightly furred along
its length. The colour of the fur is usually dark brown above, light greyish beneath,
but it may be quite greyish brown in some cases. It often has a velvety sheen.

Pigmy shrews are living dynamos. They have to scurry around, feeding constantly
just to stay alive. They feed energetically for an hour or so, then rest for a while
before resuming the pattern, which goes on more or less ceaselessly throughout the
lifetime of this miniscule mammal – usually only a year or a little longer. The food is
almost entirely insect or insect-like, for example, spiders and woodlice. The elongated
nose with extra-long, sensitive whiskers is the main tool with which the Pigmy shrew
seeks out its prey. Those which fail to keep up with this hectically demanding lifestyle
simply die off. It is not unusual, especially in winter, to find a shrew dead on a path
or other open place, where it has simply succumbed to the conditions. They are
prolific breeders, to counteract a high mortality rate. Half a dozen or more offspring
are produced in the spring litter which may be repeated one or more times during the
summer. The young stay with the female until weaned and then go off to establish
their own territories.

Habitats of different kinds are occupied by these creatures but particularly grassy
and weedy places. Nettle beds, bramble patches and even bogland hold them. Often
their presence can be detected by almost imperceptible squeaking noises emitted
constantly as they go about their business. The squeaking often becomes frenetic
when two shrews meet – there may be a heated exchange before each goes off on its
way. One of the best places to look for them is at the seashore at night. Here they
may be found foraging for sandhoppers amongst seaweed and other material along
the high-tide line.

Hedgehog • *Erinaceus europaeus* • *Gráinneog*

The Hedgehog is a creature that everyone can describe. Its spine-covered dumpy
body, pointed face and rather innocent demeanour make it a favourite animal
character for children everywhere. It is unique among Irish animals in having a spiny
jacket – a vital defensive shield for such a slow-moving and otherwise vulnerable
creature. The true value of this defence can best be seen when it is under attack. By
bringing its back legs up to its head the little animal rolls into a spiny ball like an

sea-urchin which can repel dogs, foxes and other predatory animals –
...ng man.

...n hibernation the Hedgehog, or "little ugly fellow" as it is humorously described
...its Irish name, rolls into a tight ball in its winter nest. This is usually a bundle of
...ied leaves and mosses in an undisturbed nook in a garden, behind a shed or under
...a log pile. The Hedgehog retires to this cosy retreat at the onset of winter, having
fattened up on food for weeks beforehand. Its body temperature drops as does its
breathing and heartbeat and there it remains in a torpid state for weeks. The
Hedgehog may be aroused from its deep sleep at intervals when there are significant
fluctuations in the outside temperature. During these periods it leaves the nest and
goes foraging for food to replenish its dwindling body-fat reserves. Despite the
obvious advantages of hibernation it has been estimated that only one out of two
Hedgehogs that doze off in this state are alive to see the following spring.

Throughout the summer months the Hedgehog is nocturnal, spending the day in
the nest and going looking for food after dark. This comprises worms and other small
invertebrates but a wide range of foods are taken including birds' eggs and berries –
they can even be encouraged to take milk left out overnight in a saucer. Mating
occurs in the spring and four or five young are born in the summer.

Due to high mortality (particularly on the roads) only two or three may survive to
the winter. Should the first litter be lost another may be produced before the end of
the summer. There is much folklore associated with the Hedgehog, from its supposed
ability to carry away apples impaled on its spines to its alleged ability to drink from
cows' udders at night. It has, however, some surprising talents like tree climbing and
being able to catch and kill a rat. Despite its small size, about 23 cm (9 inches), the
adult animal weighs more than 1 kg (2.2 lbs).

Lesser-horseshoe Bat • *Rhinolophus hipposideros* • *Crú-ialtóg bheag*

This little bat occupies a westerly range throughout the British Isles – in Ireland most
are found west of the Shannon and in Munster. Throughout its range it is local and is
regarded as something of an endangered species. In summer it occupies roof-spaces
with large open attics – particularly those of castles and undisturbed buildings in
rural areas. In winter it moves to caves, mine shafts and souterrains. Here it can be
seen hibernating, hanging by its feet from the roof with its wings wrapped tightly
round its body Dracula-style! Most underground passages hold only a few but in
some places dozens are found. They are very vulnerable during hibernation and may
not survive repeated disturbance.

At close range identification is easy due to the horseshoe-shaped face-leaf (which
is, in fact, part of the echo-location equipment of the animal). There is no "tragus"
(central lobe inside the ear) as in other bats. The body is the size of a golf ball and
furry, brownish above and light brownish below. The flight dimensions are: wing span
25 cm (10 inches); width 7 cm (2.75 inches).

Leisler's Bat • *Nyctalus leisleri* • *Ialtóg Leisler*

Though no more than a small/medium bat by European standards, the Leisler's is the
largest found in Ireland. It is about three times the weight of the Lesser-horseshoe
and its flight dimensions are: wingspan 33 cm (13 inches); width 10 cm (4 inches). It
is a thickly furred, dark brown bat with a conventional-looking mammal face, lacking
a nose-leaf. The ears are large and broad and contain a club-shaped element or
"tragus". The size, head shape and particularly the ear structure make identification
of this bat straightforward. Leisler's bats roost in dense groups in the attics of
buildings and hibernate in holes in trees or crevices in undisturbed ruins or other
buildings. Some colonies are large, such as one of a thousand in West Cork. As with
the former species, Ireland has a special responsibility for this bat. It is likely that
Ireland is their European stronghold.

Whiskered Bat • *Myotis mystacinus* • *Ialtóg ghiobach*

This bat is widespread throughout Ireland but is nowhere particularly common. This regional scarcity is reflected in the small numbers found in the roosts. It tends to be solitary, clinging to the wall or inside a crevice for the winter hibernation. In summer it occurs in small numbers (less than a dozen) in the corners at the end of roof trusses in attics. In appearance it is more furry than its close relations. The hind toe extends about half the distance from the foot to the point of the tail; the "tragus" in the ear is pointed but only half the length of the ear. The flight dimensions are: wingspan 23 cm (9 inches); width 7.5 cm (3 inches).

Daubenton's Bat • *Myotis daubentoni* • *Ialtóg Dhaubenton*

Although this has been nicknamed the "water bat" other bats are often found hawking for insects at dusk along river banks or over lakes. This bat is widespread and fairly common in Ireland in suitable habitat. In winter Daubenton's bats hibernate usually in ones and twos, in crevices in the upper walls and roofs of caves. In summer the roosts are in the attics of buildings but like those of the former, numbers are small. From close up this bat is distinguishable by its long hindtoe and by a fringe of fine hairs along the edge of the tail skin. The "tragus" in the ear is not as pointed as that of the others of this group. Flight dimensions are: wingspan 23 cm (9 inches); width 8 cm (3.75 inches).

Natterer's Bat • *Myotis nattereri* • *Ialtóg Natterer*

This is a widespread and locally common Irish bat. In some roosts 500–600 may be found together in the attics of buildings. During winter they hibernate in caves or other dark passages but are difficult to locate as they favour long, narrow cracks and crevices. The upper fur is greyish brown, sharply contrasting with the white underfur. The "tragus" in the ear is long and pointed – more than half the ear length. The best feature is the tail skin. This has a curved edge with a fringe of bristles along the edge. Flight dimensions are: wing span 28 cm (11 inches); width 9 cm (3.5 inches).

Pipistrelle • *Pipistrellus pipistrellus* • *Ialtóg fheascrach*

This tiny bat with a most lyrical name competes with the Pigmy shrew for the distinction of being Ireland's smallest mammal. They both weigh about 5 grams and have approximately the same body bulk.

The Pipistrelle is a widespread and common bat in Ireland being found wherever there is suitable habitat. It roosts in or around roof spaces, soffit and fascia boards or around window frames and sills in older buildings. It is even found occasionally in electricity boxes and outdoor lamp casings. In winter the Pipistrelle usually hibernates alone, in cracks in the walls of older buildings like churches and in a variety of other nooks and crannies. A single young is born after a delayed implantation period and it can fly within a few weeks of birth. The body fur of this little bat is brown but it is often quite reddish brown. The underbody fur is light brownish. The face is blackish and prominent. The ears are also dark, longer than broad and have a blunt (though narrow) "tragus" inside. The flight dimensions are: wing span 21.5 cm (8.5 inches); width 6 cm (2.5 inches).

Long-eared Bat • *Plecotus auritus* • *Ialtóg chluasach*

The ears of this bat are almost as long as its body but they are usually extended only in flight. When roosting or in hibernation the ears are folded down beneath the wings giving them a strange "ram's-horn" appearance. Roosting usually takes place in attics, roof beams and similar roof spaces. The bats huddle together in groups of up to thirty or forty. Hibernation often occurs in old buildings but also in dark caverns beneath the ground. There are two Long-eared bats in Britain – the Grey long-eared and the Brown long-eared – but only the latter is found in Ireland. The fur is brownish, paler beneath. The young are, however, greyish. This bat is common and widespread throughout Ireland and is thought to migrate in some instances. The flight dimensions are: wingspan 25 cm (10 inches); width 7.5 cm (3 inches).

Irish Hare • *Lepus timidus hibernicus* • *Giorria*

The Irish hare is a race of the Arctic hare – quite distinct from the Brown hare (*Lepus capensis*) of Britain and as such a living link with the Ice Age fauna of 10,000 years ago. The Brown hare is found in the north of Ireland, having been introduced for coursing on a number of occasions, but it is not common or widespread and is no longer found on many of the release areas. Hares can run at 65 km.p.h. (40 m.p.h.) and more, and nothing (save greyhounds) can catch them. Their eyesight is unremarkable, though due to the prominence of the eyes on the head they have a very wide field of view. They rely more on their sense of smell and hearing for warning against predators.

The differences in the appearance of the Irish hare and the Brown hare are fairly obvious. The former is slightly smaller and stockier than the latter, with shorter ears (not longer than the length of the head). The tail is all white – not just on the underside as in the Brown hare. Both have warm brown-coloured fur but that of the Irish hare may be almost foxy coloured in the summer. The Irish hare becomes paler and greyer in winter and is often whitish on the underparts and legs. In some cases it can be predominantly white, suggesting its Arctic ancestry.

The native animal is common and widespread wherever suitable habitat exists. This varies from dune systems, machair and raised and blanket bogland, to open flat areas like airports, golf courses and large fields. They are found from sea level to the tops of mountains in many places. Their food is vegetable matter of all kinds, particularly grasses and the shoots of plants and shrubs, but they will venture on to the shore to seek out sea lettuce among the wrack. They are not averse to sampling horticultural produce.

In late winter and early spring hares indulge in strange pre-nuptial behaviour. The males chase each other around in the open and indulge in brief "boxing" matches. Herds of dozens together can be seen at this time. The young are produced in a "form" – a neat dry hollow in open ground which is the hare's temporary home. One to three leverets are produced per litter and there may be up to three in the course of a season.

Rabbit • *Oryctolagus cuniculus* • *Coinín*

Like so many of Ireland's wild animals the ubiquitous rabbit gives the impression of being a native species. In fact, although it is not, it has been in Ireland for at least 750 years and has as legitimate a claim to be regarded as "native" as other long-standing residents. The Normans introduced them to Ireland and established warrens throughout the country where colonies could be maintained as a food source.

Rabbit colonies are found normally in sandy, dry situations. Uncultivated places like sand dunes, eskers and other "waste" grounds are favoured. Being highly adaptable animals they are often found at the sandy bottoms of hedgerows or the dry banks of field boundaries. The warren is a labyrinth of tunnels which in certain circumstances cover acres of ground.

Up to half-a-dozen young are produced per litter and there are usually several litters in the year. Indeed, the adage "breeding like rabbits" is well founded and population surplus is a feature of the species. It is so prolific that it is regarded as an agricultural pest often causing widespread damage to crops. Vegetable matter of a wide range forms the diet but they are particularly fond of grasses. They will freely avail themselves of horticultural produce when accessible. Efforts to control the burgeoning populations have generally been clumsy and ineffectual and in the case of myxomatosis unnecessarily cruel. It is likely that effective control would have occurred naturally had their natural predators like Buzzards been permitted to survive in Ireland on a widespread basis.

The Rabbit is immediately recognisable by its white "puff-ball" tail which is jerked ostentatiously by the fleeing animal. The fur colour is generally grey-brown though there is considerable variation (from almost white to almost black). The overall length of the animal is about 41 cm (16 inches) but it is only about half the weight of the hare – about 1.5 kg (3.3 lb). The ears are long and often held upright but they are shorter and lack the blackish tops of the Irish hare. The legs are much shorter besides, giving it a more dumpy, less leggy look when sitting. Rabbits run away with a bounding, jinking dash, seeking the nearest cover.

Grey Squirrel • *Sciurus carolinensis* • *Iora glas*

The Grey squirrel is non-native. It was introduced into County Longford in the early years of the present century and has since spread to a few other counties in the midlands and the north. Like most North American animals it is more robust and aggressive than its European counterpart and often out-competes it wherever it is found. However, Grey squirrels prefer hardwoods – particularly mature trees in demesnes and the like – while the Red squirrel is most abundant in softwood plantations.

As with the Red squirrel the Grey constructs dreys – characteristically in the smaller branches and not usually in a major fork in the tree – and leafy twigs are used, unlike the bare ones used by the Red. Three or four young are produced in two litters in early spring and mid-summer and the young stay in the drey until the autumn. Grey squirrels feed on a variety of nuts and seeds from trees. The berries and fruits of shrubs and trees supplement the diet as do fungi and birds' eggs (and nestlings) in season. Despite its opportunistic behaviour the Grey does less damage to conifer plantations than does the Red.

The Grey is much larger – about 50 cm (18 inches) – than the Red and is almost twice as heavy – up to 0.75 kg (2lb). It is generally grey above but the fur is suffused with yellowish-brown in the summer, particularly on the face and back. The tail is less furry but longer than that of the Red and is silvery edged. The underbody fur is white. The facial appearance is more "rat-like" and less "cute" than that of the Red. The ears are quite round-ended and not pointed and tufted as in the native species.

It is less "nippy" than the Red squirrel but it is nonetheless very agile, running up and down tree trunks with equal ease. When sitting upright to eat it often twitches its long tail in a nervous fashion. It moves easily over the ground in a series of fluid hops and will forage for scraps in litter bins and car parks.

Red Squirrel • *Sciurus vulgaris* • *Iora rua*

This delightful animal is quite widespread in Ireland today though it is locally more common in some places than others. It is scarce in the midlands and in parts of the north where the more aggressive Grey relative is more abundant. Attractive as it is to the eye, the Red squirrel is despised by the forester. Not only does it chew the cones but it nibbles the shoots and strips the bark of a variety of conifers. Large numbers are shot as pests in plantations where control is necessary. Besides the above, the principal food items are nuts, berries and seeds of a range of trees and shrubs depending on the habitat. In hazel scrub, for instance, Red squirrels feed on hazelnuts and hoards can be found where reserve nuts are stockpiled for winter emergencies.

Squirrels make dreys or nests which are no more than untidy bundles of twigs, lined with finer material, high in a tree. These may be specially constructed or they may be adapted birds' nests. One is utilised as the family home in which an average of three young are produced each spring or summer.

The adult is only the size of a rat but due to its luxuriant brick-red fur and its bushy tail it looks larger. It is reddest in the breeding season but with the onset of winter the fur becomes thicker and greyer. Some are even dark brown. In all coats the underfur is whitish or creamy. The bushy tail may be, in some individuals, creamy coloured also.

Due to its shyness, most of the views to be had are fleeting as it demonstrates its agility, flitting nimbly from one tree to another. Occasionally the patient observer will be rewarded with a view of one of Ireland's prettiest creatures as it sits upright on its "hunkers", perhaps nibbling delicately, with its thickly furred tail curled up its back. In such a view its large dark eyes, pale eye-rings and tuft-tipped ears are obvious.

Though the Red squirrel is native to Ireland it is thought to have become extinct in the 18th century as a result of the final woodland clearances and of the market for exported squirrel skins. It is believed that the squirrels found in Ireland today are the progeny of a series of introductions from Britain which occurred throughout the 19th century.

Brown Rat • *Rattus norvegicus* • *Francach donn*

By all accounts the ubiquitous and despised Brown rat is a relatively recent member of Ireland's fauna. Until about 250 years ago the rat of this country (itself a non-native species) was the Black rat (*Rattus rattus*). The latter appears to have been out-competed by the former to such an extent that it is now almost unknown in Ireland.

Brown rats are now so well established that they are found throughout the country – mainly in association with man. They are most common in and around granaries, sewage infrastructure, old warehouses and in rubbish dumps. They often occur in pest proportions and their reputation for being carriers of disease is completely justified (though not bubonic plague: that was carried by the flea on the Black rat). Efforts at eradication tend to be only partially successful and often depend on the destruction of their habitats. Brown rats breed throughout the year but mainly in the summer months. The loss of a litter merely means the production of another later in the year. Litters of up to a dozen offspring are commonplace.

They will consume cereals, fruit and offal with enthusiasm but can survive on pickings from rubbish tips and even on materials apparently devoid of food value, like chipboard. They will kill and eat small mammals (including their own young), and birds and their eggs are taken when found. They are well known for their aggressiveness on being cornered.

The Brown rat needs little description being, as the name states, brown or greyish brown with flesh-coloured and hairless feet, ears and tail. Adults are usually about 22.5 cm.(9 inches) long but with a tail the same length again. Stories of "rats as big as cats" are exaggerated but on occasions particularly large examples have been noticed. A black or melanistic form of the Brown rat is well known in Ireland and is often mistakenly taken for *Rattus rattus*. The latter is, however, smaller, slimmer and has a proportionately longer tail. Nowadays it is found only occasionally at docks where it has come ashore from foreign ships.

Bank Vole • *Clethrionomys glareolus* • *Vól bruaigh*

This little rodent is a newcomer to the Irish scene, though how it arrived in Ireland is still a mystery. It was first noticed in 1964 in County Kerry and was subsequently found to be quite widespread in the south-west (counties Limerick, Kerry, Cork and Clare). It has been suggested that it arrived around 1950, probably as an unsuspected stowaway on shipping docked in Limerick port.

Part of the reason for the successful spread of this animal is that it favours scrubby habitat of which there is an abundance in Ireland. It also inhabits verdant ground cover amongst bramble patches and hedgerows. It forages for soft vegetable matter like the fruits and leaves of a variety of plants and its largely vegetarian diet is supplemented by invertebrates.

More like a miniature rat than a mouse, the Bank vole has an even blunter-looking face than its larger relative. The ears and tail (which is only half the length of the body) are entirely fur covered. The fur is reddish brown in general but is more greyish on the flanks and shades to pale greyish on the underparts. Despite its superficial resemblance to a rat, the Bank vole is easily handled and quite harmless.

Several litters comprising up to half a dozen young are born to a pair of voles in an average year over the spring and summer. Within a month or so the young can reproduce themselves. It is easy to see how they can have "population explosions" in countries where they are common.

Bank voles are both nocturnal and diurnal. They can be seen scurrying about in the undergrowth in broad daylight. They are good climbers and will run over fallen trees or other obstructions with ease. Their average size is 15 cm (6 inches), including the tail.

In Britain, Bank voles are prey to a number of large birds of prey, most of which are not found in Ireland. It seems likely, therefore, in the absence of these links in the food chain, that the Bank vole will become a widespread and common rodent throughout Ireland in time.

Wood Mouse • *Apodemus sylvaticus* • *Luch fhéir*

Known also as the Field mouse and the Long-tailed field mouse, this "wild" mouse has been in Ireland much longer than its "domestic" relative, the House mouse. Wood mice will be found wherever suitable habitat can be found – hedgerows, scrubland, woodland and overgrown gardens. They will occasionally come into houses in the autumn but much less so than the House mouse.

A nest made of dried grass is constructed in a dry place, often in a hole in the ground. Breeding occurs throughout the summer and several litters are reared, with up to half a dozen young per litter. The food consists of a range of nuts, seeds, fruits and other vegetable matter and small invertebrates are taken as a supplement.

The Wood mouse is easily distinguished from the House mouse by its warm brown, not greyish, coat. The underparts are white and there is a tan-coloured "birthmark" on the chest. It is slightly larger and has a finer, more flexible tail than the latter. The dark eyes and flesh-coloured ears are prominent. All in all it is a more attractive little animal than the House mouse. Its overall length is about 17.5 cm (7 inches) of which the tail is about half.

House Mouse • *Mus musculus* • *Luch thi*

Nowadays no warehouse, farm complex, old building or ruin would be complete without its mice in residence. They are abundant too in granaries and fields with stored hay or cereals. With the first cold weather of the winter House mice enter houses they do not normally occupy and wreak havoc for a period until they can be arrested – dead or alive. They are notorious disease carriers and can eat their way into apparently "mouse-proof" drawers, cupboards and boxes. Highly communal, House mice construct nests of any available material in which six or more litters of up to six young are reared throughout the year.

The animal itself is unmistakable, with its greyish upperparts and silvery underparts, though variations do occur including a sandy brown type – on the Bull Island, Dublin. The eyes and ears are less prominent than those of the Wood mouse and the tail in the adult is generally stouter than that of the latter. The overall length is 16 cm (6.5 inches) including tail.

Dolphins • *Delphinidae* • *Deilf*

Many people are unaware of the fact that dolphins are found in Irish inshore waters as wild animals as distinct from those found in marinas and aquaria. In the summer and autumn dolphins of a number of different species may be found off the south and west coasts in particular. They are feeding schools which follow the shoals of fish, crustacea and other marine animals brought inshore by the Gulf Stream. Their presence is usually detected by the synchronised roll of their shiny backs as they break the surface of the sea to expel and inhale air. Occasionally they breach the surface spontaneously when they are accompanying a ship in a series of playful leaps. On these occasions their distinctive "beaks" and swept-back dorsal fins distinguish them from porpoises. They do not breed in Irish waters, preferring to rear their young elsewhere.

The Common dolphin (*Delphinus delphis*) is the species most likely to be encountered, being found regularly in schools of up to a hundred or more. It is generally steel-grey on the upper body and white underneath. There are large, oblong, ochre-coloured patches on either side of the body and wavy blackish lines along the sides extend up to the face. Usually about 2 metres (6.5 feet) in length, it weighs up to 75 kg (165 lb).

The other dolphin likely to be encountered in Irish waters is the Bottle-nosed Dolphin (*Tursiops truncatus*). Like the Common dolphin it occurs in schools but in numbers rarely more than a dozen. It is generally less abundant and apparently less widespread than the former. It is much larger than the Common dolphin, up to 3.5 metres (12 feet), and is generally greyish brown with white throat and belly. The name "Bottle-nosed" is derived from the strange snout or beak which is longer and more pronounced than that of the commoner animal. The Bottle-nosed is the species most commonly tamed in aquaria, where it is taught to perform incredible tricks and to demonstrate its startling intelligence.

Other dolphins occur irregularly in Irish waters.

Porpoise • *Phocoena phocoena* • *Muc mhara*

This is the commonest cetacean to be found in Irish waters. It occurs mainly in late summer and autumn but it may be encountered at any time of the year. It is commonest in schools of a few individuals together but it has been seen in dozens and occasionally in hundreds. Like the others of their kind, Porpoises pursue migrating shoals of fish, crustaceans and cuttlefish found in the Gulf Stream along Ireland's southern and western seaboard. They are less frequent in the Irish Sea and along the northern coasts. Porpoises are often accompanied by seabirds like gannets, shearwaters and petrels.

The Porpoise is smaller and stockier than the dolphins, averaging about 1.5 metres (5 feet) and 50 kg (110 lb) in weight. It does not have the "beak" so characteristic of the latter group; instead the dome-shaped head is blunt-fronted like those of some whales. The dorsal fin is smaller and triangular in shape. The colour of the animal is steel-black above with a pale under-belly. There is a grey patch (which varies in shape and size) on the sides near the head. Another diagnostic feature of the Porpoise is that, although it rolls over to the front as it comes up for air, it does not jump clear of the water surface as the dolphins occasionally do.

Porpoises are found mainly offshore and venture inshore only when the feeding is particularly good. At certain vantage points on the south and west coasts they can be watched at close proximity on occasions (for example, Cape Clear Island in County Cork). Occasionally they become isolated in harbours, estuaries and even along some of Ireland's larger rivers. They are sometimes stranded as a result of these wanderings, and "beached" animals are not rare. The reasons for strandings among cetacea in general are not fully understood, given the sophistication of their navigational equipment.

The Porpoise is the smallest whale to be found in Irish waters but there have been more than twenty other species recorded including the largest of all animals, the Blue whale. Most of them are irregular visitors in small numbers but some, like the Killer whale, are regular off the western coast.

Killer Whale • *Orcinus orca* • *Cráin dhubh*

The Killer whale is arguably the most spectacular animal to be found in or around Ireland. The male has true whale proportions, being up to 9 metres (30 feet) long with a 2-metre (6-foot) dorsal fin giving the animal an unmistakable and decidedly sinister shape in the water. The female is only about half this size and the dorsal fin is much shorter and curved back, dolphin-style. Both are very strongly patterned;

black above, white below, the white extending onto the sides in a wavy patch. There is another oval-shaped white patch above the eye on both sides of the head. These patches and the dorsal fins show clearly as the animals break the water's surface.

Killer whales are sometimes seen alone but they often turn up in small groups (which may be family groups, often containing bulls, cows and calves) which hunt as a pack. They prey on seals, porpoises, dolphins and large fish including salmon. Despite their bloodthirsty reputation they can be tamed like dolphins and exhibit the same gentleness and intelligence in aquarium conditions. They are popularly featured giving "piggy-back" rides to fearless handlers.

In the wild, Killer whales are found mainly in the seas above the Arctic circle. They do not reach maturity until they are about ten years old and they reproduce at a very slow rate – only one calf is born over a period of a few years. In autumn family packs follow migrating salmon to warmer waters and it is at this time that most are seen in Irish waters – they are annual visitors off the south and west coasts of Ireland.

These whales communicate with each other underwater with a series of squeaks and other noises which facilitate navigation in inshore waters bringing them occasionally into estuaries and inlets. Despite the sophistication of their sonar equipment the odd one (as with other whales) becomes stranded in shallow water. In 1977 a Killer whale nicknamed "Dopey Dick" thrilled citizens of Derry by showing itself for a few days on the River Foyle before making its escape out to sea again.

Fox • *Vulpes vulpes* • *Sionnach*

Since Neolithic times (5,500 years ago) the red Fox has been under non-stop attack by man in Ireland, for it has always conflicted with the interest of farmers. While other predators like the Wolf have succumbed to the onslaught, the Fox has survived and even proliferated. This is as much a testimony to the inherent cunning of the creature as to its adaptability.

It has gained a bad reputation for its plundering raids on poultry and game birds which occur whenever the opportunity arises. But few are wanton killers. The majority shun the farmyard, preferring to hunt in the open countryside. They are carnivores and will take a wide range of living prey like Rabbits, other small mammals and birds. But they are scavengers too and will take carrion and human refuse. Berries and fungi are also eaten.

There are few more attractive-looking animals than the Fox. When the luxuriant winter coat is donned, this otherwise slim and rather angular dog fills out to become indeed the *madra rua* ("red dog") of the Irish countryside. The underside and much of the face is white while the backs of the large triangular ears and the forelegs are black. The brush or tail is thickly furred, cylindrical in shape and white tipped. It is usually held horizontally as the Fox ambles on its rounds.

Foxes are highly territorial, the dog performing circuits of his patch nightly and defining his boundary by scenting strategic points with his unmistakable musk. The den is usually a hole in the ground beneath rocks or tree roots where the brood of three or four cubs is raised in spring. Although blind at first the cubs can look after themselves within a couple of weeks. Foxes are generally nocturnal but can often be seen during the day as well. They will "rest up" in a thorny patch and may be suddenly surprised by a passer-by. Fox cubs have been tamed as pets but often they remain shy in captivity.

Badger • *Meles meles* • *Broc*

Though their closest relations are other carnivores like the Otter and the Marten, the Badger is for all the world Ireland's bear. It has a similar shape and a low centre of gravity and frequently adopts bear-like attitudes.

Its favourite food is earthworms and other invertebrates but a variety of berries, fruits and nuts are also taken. Small mammals and other animals are also occasionally killed and eaten.

Adults are usually less than a metre (3 feet) in length but are very heavy for their size (as anyone who has lifted a dead one off the road will agree). They can weigh 23 kg (50 lb) in exceptional cases. The striking black-and-white head pattern and greyish body fur give the Badger a singular appearance. The underbody is blackish as are the large paws. The Badger's claws are more than an inch long and are used to great effect by the burrowing and foraging animal. They leave an unmistakable print in soft ground.

Badgers are nocturnal though they may be seen at dawn and dusk going to and from the sett. This is an underground tunnel usually opening out into a network of tunnels which may be occupied by several Badgers. The entrance is often in woodland and reasonably adjacent to agricultural land where earthworms and other food can be sought. Characteristically there is a communal latrine near to the sett entrance and old bedding material (dried grasses, leaves and moss) is deposited outside too. These are good indicators of an occupied sett.

Young Badgers, from one to five per litter, are produced in early spring and nurtured by the adults for about two months. Some young may overwinter with the adults in their sett.

The Irish name *Broc* is used universally as a term of endearment for the Badger and it is affectionately regarded in story and folklore. It is ironic that so much abuse has been levelled at this harmless animal as well. Badger baiting – a barbaric activity in which a captive Badger is pitted against a series of dogs – still occurs in parts of the country despite public outcry.

Irish Stoat • *Mustela erminea hibernica* • *Easóg*

This is the "mighty midget" of Irish mammals. Not only can it kill animals much larger than itself but it can lift and drag them away as well. Neither Rabbit nor Rat has the defence to withstand attack by this savage little carnivore. Were it much larger it would probably present a threat to man himself. There are, in fact, stories of people having been attacked both in Ireland and elsewhere.

The prey is dispatched with clinical efficiency, the Stoat inflicting a lethal bite on the nape of the victim's neck. Much has been written about the manner in which they stalk their prey; the strange ritualistic dancing which seems to hypnotise the hapless Rabbit has been well documented.

The gambolling has been noticed in a less sinister context. Stoats with their young sometimes indulge in high jinks, perhaps as instruction to the young. It nevertheless looks like mere fun and games. The young, which may number anything from a pair to a dozen, are produced in a single litter in spring or summer. They stay with the adults as a family unit until the autumn at least after which they seek out their own territories.

The Irish Stoat is a distinct, endemic race. It is smaller and slightly darker than the British Stoat. It is deep reddish brown above with a noticeable black tip to the tail. The underbody is creamy white but it is irregularly demarcated from the upperparts, not neatly so as in the British race. The average overall length is about 38 cm (15 inches), a third of which is tail. Males are larger and much heavier than the females. The body is long, narrow and sausage-shaped. The legs look unusually short but the paws are proportionately large and leave a distinctive mark in soft ground. The head is small with shining nose and beady eyes and the ears are noticeably rounded.

Stoats are remarkably inquisitive animals and many people will recount an experience of being watched or encircled by one in apparent curiosity. They will run along or in and out of stone walls with breathtaking agility and often show a reluctance to depart even on close approach.

There are no Weasels in Ireland though the Stoat is often called Weasel, perhaps as a corruption of the similar-sounding Irish name Uasal.

Pine Marten • *Martes martes* • *Cat crainn*

This, arguably the most beautiful of Ireland's wild animals, is a relation of the Stoat, but, as the Irish name suggests, looks more like a Cat. Usually only a fleeting glimpse is to be had of this shy creature for it is rarely seen in daylight. Like most carnivores the Pine marten is nocturnal and hunts a wide variety of small mammals and birds and even insects. The diet is supplemented with berries, fruits and birds' eggs, in season.

The name Pine marten is suggestive of its traditional habitat in conifer trees, and although it still occupies this habitat in the Scottish Highlands it has had to adapt to alternatives in Ireland. It is found here in the recent conifer plantations and in some semi-natural deciduous woods. In the west of the country (where it is well established) it has adapted to life on the open limestone and hazel scrub, notably in the Burren area.

The adult male is over 60 cm (2 feet) long, about a third of which is tail. The smaller female is only about two-thirds of the weight of the male. Both are richly clad in soft fur, which though generally dark brown can vary considerably in colour. In spring it is warm brown while after the winter moult it can look dark chocolate or nearly black. The large paws (with prominent claws) are blackish as is the facial fur. Bright beady eyes and black shiny nose stand out in the face which is more foxy looking than that of the Stoat or the Mink. The ears are large, parabolic in shape and creamy edged. There is a large creamy yellow patch on the chin and throat which can look almost orange in some animals.

Pine martens make their nests in undisturbed places such as a hollow tree, a hole in a dry rocky place or the abandoned nest of a large bird or a squirrel. The nest is lined with dry grass for comfort. Normally two litters of four or five young are reared each summer. The young stay with the adults until the autumn when they leave to establish their own territories.

Despite the fact that their skins were exported in quantity in the Middle Ages (the fur being especially high quality) and that its woodland habitat was more or less completely removed in the 17th and 18th centuries, the Pine marten has survived and is once again on the increase. It is more widespread and common than the rare daylight sightings would suggest.

Otter • *Lutra lutra* • *Dobhrán*

An alternative Irish name for this fine animal is *Madra uisce* or "water dog" – a name somewhat suggestive of its appearance and playful character. The Otter spends most of its life in and around water – both fresh and salt – though it is probably best known as a river or lake dweller. In the west of Ireland it is found quite commonly along undisturbed rocky shores and on inshore islands.

Ireland has a special responsibility for the survival of the Otter. It is decreasing over most of its range and is completely absent from most of Britain – in Ireland it is still widespread and abundant. The Irish Otter is an endemic race, having been distinguished over 150 years ago. Evidence of its pedigree goes back much further, though, having featured in the illuminations and poetry of the early Christians in Ireland.

Despite this, not many people are familiar with Otters. Their nocturnal habits and extreme shyness render them elusive to all but the most patient. Those who have been lucky to catch a glimpse of this mammal may have been struck by its size – up to 1.5 metres (5 feet) including tail – and its strange long-bodied, short-legged appearance. The tail is an extension of the elongated body and the long head is curiously flattened on top.

On the river bank or shore the Otter shuffles along steadily, a hump-backed brown beast with whitish face and underbody. In the water, however, it is transformed into a sleek streamlined creature which performs marvellous underwater gyrations in pursuit of its main quarry – fish. In freshwater, eels and frogs are especially favoured and along the shore any available fish or crustacean is eaten. Young mammals and waterbirds supplement their diet.

Otters' homes are called "holts", tunnelled holes in the ground, often under large boulders. Holts are used in daytime as resting places but also for breeding. The two or three Otter cubs are born usually in the spring and stay in the security of the holt for about two months, after which time they are able to fend for themselves. There are few more charming sights in nature than that of an Otter family having fun at the water's edge. Otters are extremely playful and they frolic about uttering their cheerful chittering calls when circumstances afford them sufficient security.

In the past Otters have been subjected to persecution for a variety of reasons including their alleged threat to fish stocks, their valuable pelts, or simply for "sport". Thankfully, most of this persecution has now ceased.

Mink • *Mustela vison* • *Minc Mheiriceánach*

It is difficult to warm to this little animal, a released species. It is a native of North America which, having escaped (or been released) from fur farms over the past few decades, has gained a worse reputation than other importees like the Grey squirrel. It has yet to be proved that Mink out-compete other carnivores like the Stoat and the Otter but they certainly intrude aggressively in the Irish environment. Favouring wetland habitats they are known to catch a wide variety of small animals like rodents, fish and amphibians. They also raid the nests of waterbirds, taking eggs, young and even adult birds when accessible. Birds of the rail family are particularly vulnerable. They are voracious plunderers and the remains of their feasts in a reed-bed or along a river bank are indicators of their presence.

The majority of Mink seen wild in Ireland are black or brownish black in colour with a white patch on the throat, but there is considerable variation and recently sighted examples may be greyish or even white. The fur is thick and soft, particularly on the tail, and when it is swimming the top of the tail shows above the water, distinguishing it immediately from the Otter. It is also a much smaller animal than the Otter or the Pine marten (with which it has also been confused). It rarely exceeds 46 cm (18 inches), a third of which is tail, and it weighs under 1 kg (2.2 lb).

Little is known of the breeding habits of the animal in its feral state but presumably they correspond with those of similar carnivores. Judging from the animal's rapid proliferation it must produce several offspring per litter and enjoy a healthy survival rate.

Though still local west of the Shannon, Mink must be considered widespread and fairly common in Ireland, having spread from their initial points of escape (and release) in the 1960s. Extensive trapping has failed to reduce their numbers significantly and it is likely that they will increase uncontrollably and regrettably.

Grey Seal • *Halichoerus grypus* • *Rón glas*

Also known as the Atlantic seal, its range corresponds roughly with the north-western seaboard of the Atlantic. In Ireland it ranges along all the coasts but its main habitats and breeding areas lie on the western, northern and parts of the southern coasts. It is much more local on the east coast where it is largely replaced by the Common seal. Grey seals are in general "commoner" than Common seals, preferring rocky, wave-pounded coasts to the calmer inshore waters favoured by the latter animal.

Breeding occurs on rocky islets and uninhabited islands in the autumn, a year after the bulls have established territories and mated with the cows. A single pup is born to the cow, and this is nurtured throughout the winter by the female. For the first month the pup remains on the land only. Grey seal pups are among the most attractive of all young animals, with their beautiful silky white fur, large appealing eyes and general attitude of helplessness.

The bull Grey seal is generally dark grey above, paler beneath and irregularly blotched with black. Colour and pattern varies though, and they may look very dark all over in certain circumstances. The cows are generally paler, particularly underneath. Bulls are massive, up to 3 metres (9 feet) or more in length and weighing 227 kg (500 lb). The cows are a couple of feet shorter and only half the weight. A wide variety of marine food is eaten, ranging from crustaceans like crabs and lobsters to shellfish and squid. Fish of many species are eaten as they are caught including, in season, salmon.

Conflict between fishermen and seals is not new but it has been intensifying in recent years. Large numbers of Grey seals from the northern and western colonies in both Ireland and Scotland have been held responsible for significantly reducing fish stocks and damaging nets. This has resulted in legal and illegal "culling" to try to control numbers. Conservationists (and others) hold that overfishing in conjunction with improved technology are the main culprits, not the seals.

Whatever the case, Ireland has a special responsibility towards the continuing existence of Grey seal colonies in view of the fact that half the European population of the species is found here.

Common Seal • *Phoca vitulina* • *Rón beag*

Like so many creatures with "common" in their name, the Common seal is badly named. It is indeed common on parts of the north, east and west coasts of Ireland but it is replaced by the Grey seal over much of the western and northern coastline. The Harbour seal – a name by which it is also known – is probably more appropriate, for it is an inshore animal frequenting inlets, estuaries and unpolluted harbours.

There is considerable variation in the colour and pattern of this seal's silky coat. That of the adults is usually predominantly greyish or greyish brown on the upperparts. The underparts are paler – silvery or creamy on the belly. It is heavily mottled with irregular blackish markings. The young are dusky grey-brown mottled darker, quite unlike the creamy white pups of the Grey seal.

Common seals vary also in size. Old bulls may be over 2 metres (6 feet) long and weigh 250 kg (550 lb), while females are generally about 1.5 metres (5 feet) and weigh 150 kg (330 lb). Though smaller and lighter than the Grey seal, this is not always easy to assess "in the field", particularly when the animal is alone. The best distinguishing features are the shape of the head and nostrils (if they can be seen). The head is quite dog-like, with raised forehead or brow. The nostrils are noticeably angled.

Breeding occurs in early summer and usually takes place on a low-lying sandy islet or spit at low tide, where the seals habitually haul up. They adopt distinctive banana-shaped postures with head and tail flippers lifted clear of the ground. The new-born pup is able to swim within hours and is weaned for a month after birth. The family group remains together till the winter when the pups become more solitary and fend for themselves.

Common seals eat a variety of marine food including fish (mainly inshore and estuarine species), shellfish and crustaceans. They are non-specific and to some extent opportunist feeders as well and squid, octopus and other marine creatures are taken when available. In general, Common seals are tolerated by fishermen and have not earned a bad reputation for poaching salmon.

Irish seals are essentially saltwater animals but the Common seal may be seen occasionally in brackish water or sometimes even on larger rivers, miles from the sea.

Red Deer • *Cervus elaphus* • *Fia rua*

It is probably only as a result of conservation efforts that this magnificent animal is still found wild in Ireland, for it has suffered the ravages of habitat destruction and persecution for centuries. Formerly a creature of the forests, it has adapted to life above the tree line and the last herds are found in the mountain moorlands of Donegal and Kerry. It is thought that the only truly native Red deer remaining are found in Kerry; those found elsewhere have been affected by introduction and hybridisation with Sika deer.

Red deer are herbivores, relishing rough grasses, mosses and other mountain herbs. These are supplemented by woodland plants in winter when the deer come down to the shelter of the trees.

Access to the best grazing is dependent on the hierarchical system of the herd. The dominant male and his harem gain this privilege, thus ensuring the continued strength of the strain. Intense sparring during the rutting season is characteristic of Red deer. Deep gutteral roaring heralds the start of the rut and acts as a warning to potential rivals.

The hind reaches calf-bearing age at four, and a single offspring is produced in spring. It is nurtured for almost a year and the young stay with the hinds for about two years. The males leave the groups of females and young for the winter after losing their antlers and do not rejoin them again until the following spring.

The male Red deer is as large as a pony – 1.4 metres (4.5 feet) high at the shoulder – and may weigh over 200 kg (440 1b). The antlers, which are mere spikes in the young males, are majestic, multi-forked branches in the adult stags. The hinds are more slightly built than the stags and have a less threatening demeanour. Both males and females have warm red-brown coats, an oval-shaped, buff-coloured rump patch and dark tails in summer. In winter the coat colour becomes darker and greyer. Red deer fawns have real "Bambi" looks, with their long gangly legs, rust-coloured, white-spotted back and gentle expression.

Due to the extinction of their natural predators, the Wolf and the Golden eagle (which preyed on fawns), Red deer numbers have to be controlled by man. In the past, his influence had been steadily depleting stocks. Nowadays, culling is officially restricted, though poaching remains a depleting factor.

Fallow Deer • *Dama dama* • *Fia buí*

The Normans, who established hunts in Ireland from the 13th century onwards, introduced the Fallow into their parks. Until about a hundred years ago they were restricted to the large demesnes which existed throughout the country but with the break-up of this regime many Fallow are now found in small unrestricted herds. The best known, though, is still that in Dublin's Phoenix Park. They graze on a variety of grasses and herbs.

As in other deer there is a definite herd structure, dominated by a male. During the rut, which takes place in the autumn, the male delineates his territory by marking young trees with urine and with scent from facial glands. A harem of females is then gathered by the male who declares his intentions with deep grunting noises. Rival bucks are repelled with vigorous and prolonged sparring. Mating with the harem occurs once nuptial rights have been established.

The female gives birth to a single calf in the summer months which is tended away from the herd in a quiet spot until it is strong enough to join and keep up with the others.

The Fallow is much the same size as the Sika – about 1 metre (3 feet) high at the shoulder – but is altogether a finer animal. It is less stocky with proportionately longer legs. The adult stag weighs around 100 kg (250 lb), the female is much lighter. Though the colour of the coat varies considerably (from very pale to very dark) it is usually deep fawn above, whitish below and on the legs. The upperparts are heavily spotted with white and there is a white rump patch which is bordered with and bisected (on the tail) by black. In the winter the coat becomes darker and greyer and most of the white spots disappear. The most distinctive feature is the antler spread of the males, which, unlike that of Ireland's other deer, are flattened out like hands at the extremities. Only the stags develop this elegant headgear.

The sight of a herd of Fallow in a parkland setting with old and spreading hardwoods is more typical of the large estates and managed woodlands of England than of Ireland, though they will probably continue to be a feature of modern Irish forest parks.

In recent years Fallow have been farmed in Ireland for the venison market. Whether or not it will become as important a source of meat as it has become elsewhere in Europe is yet to be seen.

Sika Deer • *Cervus nippon* • *Fia Seapánach*

This deer is a recent introduction from its country of origin, Japan. The first herd to be established was at Powerscourt, County Wicklow in the middle of the 19th century. They have since spread to wooded areas in Leinster and are now also found in parts of Munster and the border counties. In places they are common and widespread as in Wicklow and they have continued to hybridise with Red deer (difficult to imagine in view of the size and other differences between the two species, but nevertheless true). Their propensity to mate with wild Red deer has given rise to the belief that, apart from in parts of Kerry, Ireland's native strain is no longer to be found anywhere in the country.

In Ireland the Sika is found mainly in the coniferous plantations and feeds mainly on a variety of grasses in the "ride lines" and other clearings. Tree shoots are also eaten and the Sika has gained a bad reputation with foresters for its habit of chewing the bark of pines and spruces to sample the mineral-rich inner bark.

Though it is roughly the same size and weight as the Fallow, the Sika is more reminiscent of a diminutive Red than a Fallow. It is a stockier animal, having little of the graceful proportions of the other species. The stag's antlers are branched like those of the Red but lack the majestic appearance of the latter. Some hybrids, however, have impressive spreads. The coat is warm brown in summer and is liberally covered with creamy spots. In winter the coat is dark brown. In all seasons the rump patch and tail are white – obviously different from that of the Fallow and Red. In addition there is a small whitish patch on the back of the hind legs which is helpful in long-distance identification.   As with other deer, the mating season is in late autumn, the stag rounding up his harem of hinds in the usual fashion. His call is a loud, piercing whistle often followed by a grunt – quite different from other deer. About half a dozen hinds are serviced by the stag during the rut. The calf is born in early summer and stays with the hind for a year after which it either remains with the females or joins up with the stags, depending on its sex.   Many Sika are shot annually in an effort to control their numbers and to maintain the virility of the strain. In recent years deer shooting on a commercial basis is thought to be seriously depleting the overall numbers.

Feral Goat • *Capra hircus* • *Fia ghabhar*

The origins of Ireland's scattered herds of Feral goats are now obscure. Some may have ancient pedigree but other are doubtless descendants of animals released into the wild over the past few decades.

Despite their domestic influences Feral goats adopt a hierarchical structure typical of wild ungulates, with a dozen or more individuals per herd dominated by an old male. This is obvious when the herd is approached and the old male takes up an aggressive posture in front of the herd. These old males are formidable animals which may be over 45 kg (100 lb) in weight and have large swept-back horns. These horns may be more than 46 cm (18 inches) long and coiled upwards and outwards. Females are much smaller and lighter and have smaller, straighter horns.

The colour of the coat is very variable but is usually white or a combination of black, brown and white. The texture is thick and shaggy and may be so rough on the adults as to make them quite inconspicuous against a background of lichen-covered rocks.

Unlike the male deer, which have head-to-head sparring bouts with their antlers entangled, Feral goats indulge in "head-bashing". Each combatant rears up on its hind legs to head-butt the other violently and with an audible thump – quite a spectacle in the wild. Mating takes place in late autumn and the kids are born in the early spring – approximately five months' gestation period.

Goats are well known for their capacity to eat almost anything growing and Feral goats show the same characteristic. Plants shunned by other browsers are avidly consumed by these animals. Indeed a herd of goats will totally inhibit the natural regeneration of trees and shrubs. Brambles, ivy, gorse and heather are eaten as readily as are thistles, nettles and a wide range of more conventional fodder.

Feral goats are denizens of the wilder mountainous regions of Ireland. Most of the herds still found here occupy this kind of habitat in Ireland's coastal counties. They are also found in the rocky plateau of the Burren. These herds were formerly more widespread but target practice with high-powered rifles has reduced their numbers in recent years.

The herd of goats is to most people an acceptable and interesting feature of the wilder Irish landscape. The bearded, twisted-horned old males give character to these places, now devoid of other wild ungulates.

Connemara Pony • *Equus caballus* • *Capaillín chonamara*

The Connemara pony is a living symbol of Ireland's ancient past for it is believed that it is a descendant of animals brought to the country by the Celts. As such it cannot be considered "native" and since the early years of the 20th century (when it was first bred under controlled conditions) it hardly merits the term "feral". The ponies have, however, traditionally run wild in the Connemara countryside and have developed many of the characteristics of the semi-wild or feral horses found in other parts of the world like those of the Camargue in the south of France.

Though it has retained much of the spiritedness of the "free-range" animal, the Connemara has other characteristics which have made it much sought after both in Ireland and abroad. It is a sturdy, compact animal and, having good bone structure and relatively short legs, has been found to be ideal for work in awkward circumstances. Its sure-footedness has made it ideal for work in uneven, rocky terrain. In the past it was much utilised in mining and quarrying activities. Because of this versatility and its acclaimed good-naturedness it has also become a valuable animal in equestrian activities. Its smallish size and reliability have rendered it highly usable by children; it is also widely used by adults in show-jumping and hunting.

Since the 1920s, when the Connemara Breeders Society was established, a register of pure bred mares has been kept. The idea has been to try to propagate for future generations the type of animal which typified the breed. Important criteria were that the ponies should have free and easy movement, compact deep-set bodies, good bone and an ideal height of 13 to 14 hands – approximately 1.4 metres (4.5 feet).The colour of the animal was once typically dun but interbreeding with Arab and Spanish stock has generated varieties of a number of different colours including bay, brown, black, grey and occasionally chestnut. The commonest colour is now grey.

Though presently kept in many Irish counties, the main stock of these ponies is still found in Connemara. They have been exported to many countries throughout the world and there are now Connemara Pony Societies in the UK, USA, Scandinavia, Australia and elsewhere.

CHAPTER FOUR

BIRDS

A total of 123 birds are covered in this section – these are birds that could be considered to be "widespread" in Ireland. This does not mean that they are abundant or common, as this depends on the density of distribution. One or two birds have been omitted which could be considered as fairly widespread and one or two have been included which are not yet widespread but look like becoming so.

The birds here have been grouped together, generally in threes, fours or fives, under a particular heading. This may be because they are of the same family, are related to one another, or simply have something in common. In some the connection may seem a little contrived but it has been necessary, for the sake of compactness, to group them as such. Each is given an English, scientific and Irish name in that order.

The description of each species is brief, concentrating on the important features for identification. Everyday phrases (such as "dumpy looking") are used instead of more formal terminology and the size of the birds, where mentioned, is given as either small, medium or large (small means up to Blackbird size; medium, up to Woodpigeon size; large, greater than this).

The term "immature" refers to any sub-adult bird – that is, any bird which has not yet reached maturity and acquired the plumage of the adult bird. "Juvenile" refers to the first-year state only, during which the chick or young bird wears plumage which it will lose at its first moult.

BIRDWATCHING

Birdwatching is good fun. It's a leisure activity for all the family – age doesn't matter. You don't need expensive equipment, your God-given faculties will do! After a while it may be necessary to buy a pair of binoculars but good binoculars can now be obtained quite cheaply. The type you look for are 8 x 40 or equivalent, and there are many good makes.

You can birdwatch anywhere. The back garden, the local wood, the estuary, the coast and the mountains all support birds. It may be possible to see a dozen different kinds in the garden but you may see fifty at an estuary or on the coast.

Take time to identify the different kinds (species) and watch how they live. Birds have feeding grounds, roosting grounds and breeding areas and many also migrate to warmer countries for the winter. If you write down the ones you see in summer and compare those seen in winter it becomes obvious that some of our birds leave in winter but others come here from other countries too.

It adds to the enjoyment of a country walk or a picnic if you take notice of the birds that you see on the way. It's a good idea to take notes and make sketches as well, as this helps to tune the senses. Birdwatching teaches you to look and listen and, perhaps more importantly, to be aware of your surroundings. It is by being aware that you can learn to understand nature and how we, as people, relate to it.

So there's more to birdwatching than meets the eye!

DIVER-TYPE BIRDS

Red-throated Diver • *Gavia stellata* • *Lóma rua*

The Red-throated Diver breeds mainly in northern Europe and has a fine plumage with brick-red throat at this time. As a widespread winter visitor to inshore coastal waters it is usually seen in Ireland in its rather drab winter plumage – grey, finely speckled white above; white below and on the face. Though distinctly smaller than the Great-northern Diver, this species is nevertheless quite large. It has a recognizable profile when sitting on the water, with a slightly up-tilted bill position.

Great-northern Diver • *Gavia immer* • *Lóma mór*

The Great-northern Diver is, as the name suggests, mainly an Arctic breeder. It occurs as a widespread winter visitor to inshore coastal waters. Only in breeding plumage does it have the fine black-and-white plumage with barred neck band and back patches. In winter plumage, when it is most common in Ireland, it is, like the Red-throated Diver, quite drab, dark grey above and whitish below and on the face. The head and bill are large and rather angular looking and noticeable from even long range.

Great-crested Grebe • *Podiceps cristatus* • *Foitheach mór*

The Great-crested Grebe both breeds and winters in Ireland. The breeding habitat is usually in a lake and the majority spend the winter on estuaries or other inshore waters at the coast. A medium-sized bird with a long neck, this grebe has a strikingly beautiful summer plumage. Both male and female have unusual and elaborate head plumage used in nuptial display. In winter the plumage is dark grey above, white below, on the front of the neck, face and above the eye – a "ghostly" looking bird. In the rather laboured flight the wings show clear white patches.

Little Grebe • *Tachybaptus ruficollis* • *Spáigaire tonn*

The Little Grebe, or Dabchick, is very small and dumpy in shape. It is brownish overall with rust-coloured cheeks in summer and yellow bill-gape. In winter it is greyer and paler. It is a widespread breeder in ponds and small lakes with aquatic vegetation. The Little Grebe is hyperactive, diving constantly from the water surface for food. Both this and the Great-crested Grebe have the endearing habit of carrying their chicks "piggy-back" fashion on the water near the nest. Dabchicks make an unusual "whinnying" sound at the breeding site.

OCEAN-GOING BIRDS

Fulmar • *Fulmarus glacialis* • *Fulmaire*

The Fulmar is much more "seagull-like" than the others in this group and is often mistaken for one. The wings are grey as in the gulls but so is the back and tail (white in the gulls). The thick yellow bill and deep-set, dark eyes in the heavy white head look different from those of the gulls. The shearing and stiff-winged flight is more like that of the shearwaters than the gulls. The nest is usually on a sea cliff and colonies are found all around the Irish coast in suitable habitats.

Gannet • *Sula bassana* • *Gainéad*

One of Ireland's most obvious sea birds; larger than the biggest gulls, with brilliant white plumage and black wing tips. Only the adult is white – the juvenile is dark grey with fine white speckling, and gets progressively whiter until full plumage in its third year. Gannets may be seen fishing anywhere around Irish coasts but there are only a few breeding colonies, on islands on the south and west coasts.

Manx Shearwater • *Puffinus puffinus* • *Cánóg dhubh*

The Manx Shearwater is much smaller than the Gannet, with a striking pattern of black above and white below. It has a most recognizable flight. Lines of shearwaters glide close to the waves, showing at one minute black uppersides and at the next, white undersides. They nest in colonies in holes in the ground on cliff tops or similar locations and approach the nests under cover of darkness. As birds of the open sea, Manx Shearwaters are unusual inshore during the winter.

Storm Petrel • *Hydrobates pelagicus* • *Guairdeall*

The Storm Petrel is not often seen in Ireland, though countless thousands of them breed in nest-hole colonies in locations along the western seaboard. As with the Manx Shearwater, it comes to the nest at night-time only. It is a tiny bird (about the size of a House Martin) which, having a white rump, is sometimes mistaken for a petrel. The plumage is sooty black relieved only by the noticeable white rump. During and after storms it may sometimes be seen on inshore coastal waters.

LONG-NECKED BIRDS

Cormorant • *Phalacrocorax carbo* • *Broigheall*

The Cormorant is a large, long-necked diving bird, often incorrectly called a "diver". It feeds by plunging from the water surface and catching fish, which it swallows on the surface. It is well known for its habit of stretching out it wings to dry while standing at its roost. The plumage is glossy black and in summer the adult has white patches on the face and flanks. The immature birds are much browner than the adults and are pale on the entire underparts. Cormorants nest in colonies on rocky coastal islands and headlands and also in trees alongside some inland lakes.

Shag • *Phalacrocorax aristotelis* • *Seaga*

The Shag is a smaller version of the Cormorant but is strictly coastal. In habits and general behaviour it resembles the larger bird. Its plumage is blackish but has a distinctly greenish sheen and lacks the white patches on face and flanks. The breeding bird sports a tufted crest and bright yellow bill-gape. The immature bird is, like the immature cormorant, pale on the face and the underparts and dark brown on the upperparts. Shags nest colonially, often amongst other seabirds on rocky islets and cliffs.

Grey Heron • *Ardea cinerea* • *Corr riasc*

The Grey Heron needs little description, being so well known as to be a favourite subject of Irish folklore. Its singular appearance, both on the ground and in the air, has long drawn the attention of even the least observant of people. It is one of Ireland's largest birds, with a slow, ponderous flight. The legs protrude beyond the tail of the flying Heron but the long neck is tucked back, giving a "blunt-fronted" look. The plumage is basically grey above and white below but there is a distinctive black streak above and behind the eye extending to a long plume. Long plumes are found also on the neck, breast and back of the adult. The young bird is duller and less strikingly marked than the adult. Herons nest in colonies in the tops of high trees, and sometimes nearer the ground on islands in lakes.

SWANS

Mute Swan • *Cygnus olor* • *Eala bhalbh*

The Mute Swan needs little description, its beauty having captivated man for centuries. The puffed-out back feathers and gracefully curved neck are well-known features of this bird. The bill is orange and has a black knob at the base. In flight the wings make a tuneful "wheezing" sound but, as its name suggests, it is more or less vocally silent. The nest is a massive affair, often in an inaccessible spot in a reedbed or along a river. The cygnets are greyish and have an endearing appearance. The adults are less "innocent", with aggressive tendencies, sometimes feeding on young birds as well as their more staple diet of aquatic plants.

Whooper Swan • *Cygnus cygnus* • *Eala ghlórach*

The Whooper Swan is as large as the Mute Swan but has a less graceful form. A distant flock can look stiff-necked and somewhat angular compared with Mutes. Flocks of Whoopers make, however, the most tuneful sounds, adding atmosphere to stark winter wetlands. The bill is bright yellow with a black tip and the head and bill combined have a wedge-shaped appearance. The young are greyish with pinkish, black-tipped bills. Whooper Swans often feed on riverside callows and other low-lying ground near wetlands, and can look like grazing sheep from a distance. They are fairly widespread visitors to Ireland's larger inland wetlands.

Bewick's Swan • *Cygnus columbianus* • *Eala Bhewick*

The Bewick's Swan is like a smaller version of the Whooper Swan. Like the larger bird, the bill is yellow and black but there is less yellow than black. The head shape too is more rounded and less wedge-shaped than that of the Whooper Swan. The young are dull grey with pinkish, dark-tipped bills. The calls of the Bewick's Swan are similar to those of the Whooper but less musical. Wild swans often feed in fields and when Bewicks are intermixed with Whoopers they may be difficult to distinguish. Less widespread than the Whoopers, Bewicks are nonetheless regular winter visitors to many of the larger Irish wetlands.

GEESE

White-fronted Goose • *Anser albifrons* • *Gé bháneadanach*

The Greenland White-fronted Goose is smaller than the Greylag. It is much browner and darker and gets its name from the small white patch on the forehead (though this is absent in the young birds). The best distinguishing features from a distance are the heavy black blotches on the under parts of the adult. In flight it shows less grey on the wings than does the Greylag and the call is a more high pitched yelping. The White-fronted Goose is now mainly confined to the Wexford Wildfowl Reserve, though scattered flocks overwinter elsewhere.

Greylag Goose • *Anser anser* • *Gé glas*

The largest of the geese is the Greylag, so called because of the large, pale grey patches on the wings. The overall colour is grey-brown, with a large white area beneath the tail and a smaller one on the rump visible in flight. The large orange bill and pink legs are good identification features and are visible from a long way off. When disturbed or in flight, the Greylag makes loud confused honking calls and sounds very like the farmyard goose. The favoured habitats are extensive callows and reclaimed scrubland.

Barnacle Goose • *Branta leucopsis* • *Gé ghiúrainn*

Almost all of Ireland's wintering Barnacle Geese are found in islands on the west and north coasts, to which they migrate from Arctic Greenland each year. The most striking of geese to be seen in Ireland, its grey and black-and-white patterns of plumage make identification straightforward. In flight, extensive grey patches show on the wings and the flock calls with a noisy yelping. The main habitat is on low, grassy islands but flocks also commute to coastal fields on the mainland.

Brent Goose • *Branta bernicla* • *Cadhan*

The Brent Goose is the smallest of Ireland's geese, being not much larger than a Mallard Duck. The pale-bellied form (the form occurring in Ireland) is greyish on the belly and flanks. Brent Geese have small white markings on the sides of the neck and the bill is very small. The young have pale edges to some of the feathers on the back. Flocks of Brents call with a low "gurgling" noise both on the ground and in the air.

They feed on eel grass and other marine plants on coastal mudflats, their primary habitat.

DABBLING DUCKS

Shelduck • Tadorna tadorna • Seil-lacha

The Shelduck is Ireland's largest duck – the size of a small goose. It is surprisingly common and widespread as a winter visitor to muddy estuaries and inlets. It is also a widespread breeder in Ireland. The Shelduck is strikingly beautiful, with its black-and-white plumage, orange breast band, under-tail patch and dark green head. The sexes are alike, though the male is larger and has a conspicuous knob on top of the bright red bill.

Wigeon • Anas penelope • Rualacha

The Wigeon is an abundant winter visitor from northern Europe to Ireland. Flocks are to be found in grassy places alongside lakes, estuaries and some large rivers. On the ground, Wigeon can be quite inconspicuous despite their fine plumage but in the air they are very obvious. The males have large white wing patches and they call continuously with a far-carrying whistle "whee-oo". The female is dull and brownish.

Teal • Anas crecca • Praslacha ghlaseiteach

The Teal is Ireland's smallest duck, being little bigger than a Moorhen. In winter it is more widespread and abundant than it appears. The drake is a beautiful but subtly marked bird with rust-coloured and shiny green head, spotted breast and finely marked grey body. As with most other ducks, the female is dull and brownish. Teal call from the water with a curious ringing note when anxious. Some Teal stay and breed in Irish wetlands but they are not common breeders.

Mallard • Anas platyrhynchos • Mallard

The Mallard is the common "wild duck" of the ponds and ditches. A large duck, the male is a fine bird with greyish body, bright orange legs, yellowish bill and curly black feathers above the tail. The female is dowdy brown with a pale eyestripe. Both sexes have a blue-green patch on the wing, edged on both sides with white. The Mallard nests in a wide variety of situations near water.

Shoveler • Anas clypeata • Spadalghob

The Shoveler is roughly the same size as the Wigeon but very different in appearance. The drake is a striking bird, showing a lot of white but with a blackish head, huge bill and obvious rust-coloured sides. The female is dull brownish. Both male and female have conspicuous light blue wing patches, obvious in flight. The Shoveler is a widespread but thinly distributed winter visitor, mainly to freshwater wetlands but also to some estuaries. Very few breed in Ireland.

DIVING DUCKS

Pochard • Aythya ferina • Poiseard

The Pochard is quite widespread as a winter visitor to Irish lakes – it is even abundant in some places. Unlike the Tufted Duck, it only rarely breeds in Ireland. The male Pochard is greyish with black breast and rear end. The head is deep rust-coloured. The female is much duller. In flight, both sexes show pale grey wing bars and the flight is rapid and direct like that of the Tufted Duck, to which it is similar in size and shape.

Tufted Duck • *Aythya fuligula* • *Lacha bhadánach*

The Tufted Duck is a widespread and, in some places, abundant winter visitor. Although smallish in size, the pied plumage of the males makes them easily recognizable from a distance. Only the male has the tuft on the back of the head; the female is dull chocolate brown. In flight, a clear white bar shows on the wings of both sexes. Tufted Ducks stay to nest on islets on a few of Ireland's larger lakes.

Eider • *Somateria mollissima* • *Éadar lacha*

Ireland's largest diving duck, the Eider is exclusively coastal, favouring rocky areas where it can dive for its favourite foods. The male is unmistakable – a predominantly white sea-duck with a black patch on the sides and other less noticeable black and coloured marks. The female is heavily barred and brownish. Both sexes have a most striking wedge-shaped bill and head. Eiders make strange human-sounding notes when they are displaying.

Goldeneye • *Bucephala clangula* • *Orshúileach*

The Goldeneye is a widespread but thinly distributed winter visitor from northern Europe. The plumage of the male is striking, with predominantly white body and contrasting glossy black head, with a white spot near the base of the bill. The female is dull brownish with a pale neck band. In flight, the Goldeneye is particularly noticeable due to the large white wing patches and the curious ringing noise made by the wings.

Red-breasted Merganser • *Mergus serrator* • *Síolta rua*

The Red-breasted Merganser is a widespread resident in Irish inshore coastal waters and larger lakes. Mergansers have particularly streamlined bodies, enabling swift movement underwater. The male is beautifully marked black, white and greyish. The female is greyish brown with red-brown head. Both sexes have very thin red bills. In the air Mergansers fly swiftly and show large white wing patches rather like those of the Goldeneye.

HAWK-LIKE BIRDS

Sparrowhawk • *Accipiter nisus* • *Spioróg*

The Sparrowhawk is Ireland's most widespread bird of prey. It hunts by flying fast and low and by ambushing its prey. The wings are short and rounded for quick acceleration and to facilitate hunting in confined areas. The tail is noticeably long. The male Sparrowhawk is blue-grey above, barred reddish below; the female is grey-brown above and barred dark below.

Kestrel • *Falco tinnunculus* • *Pocaire gaoithe*

The Kestrel is Ireland's most common and widespread falcon, hunting mainly in open country. It hovers as if suspended by an invisible thread, eyes fixed on the ground below, and swoops down to capture its prey. The male is light red-brown on the back, heavily spotted with black; the head and tail are light blue-grey. The underparts are creamy, spotted with black. The female is larger and duller coloured and is barred rather than spotted.

Peregrine • *Falco peregrinus* • *Fabhcún gorm*

This is Ireland's largest and most dynamic falcon. The main prey in the wild are medium-sized birds like pigeons. The Peregrine is heavily built but retains the falcon flight profile. The male is slate-grey above, whitish barred with black below. There are very noticeable black facial marks contrasting with the white cheeks. The larger female is similar but the young bird is browner above and streaked, not barred, below.

Merlin • *Falco columbarius* • *Meirliún*

The Merlin is Ireland's smallest falcon but is a highly mobile and effective hunter, being usually found in wild moorland. In winter it often hunts in coastal habitats. The male Merlin is only the size of a Blackbird. It is slate-grey above, whitish streaked reddish below. The female and immature birds are brownish above, whitish streaked dark below. The flight profile is like that of a scaled-down Peregrine.

Cuckoo • *Cuculus canorus* • *Cuach*

The Cuckoo is a rather mysterious bird, being much more often heard than seen. It is a summer visitor from winter quarters in Africa. Cuckoos like open country, where they search for the nests of potential foster parents for their offspring. The adult Cuckoo is grey above, white barred with black below and has a long barred tail. The young are rich brown and heavily barred all over. Cuckoos look particularly hawk-like in flight.

GAME BIRDS

Red Grouse • *Lagopus lagopus* • *Cearc fhraoigh*

The Red Grouse is a bird of moorland and bog, where its staple foods, the shoots and berries of heathers and associated plants, are found. The Irish Red Grouse is a medium-sized but very dumpy bird. The male is heavily mottled red-brown, causing it to blend into its heathery surroundings. A bright red wattle is noticeable over the eye. The female is overall paler. On being flushed, grouse appear very dark except for whitish underwing patches. They call with human-sounding notes often described as sounding like the words "go-back".

Pheasant • *Phasianus colchicus* • *Piasún*

The Pheasant is an introduced bird which has been in Ireland for centuries. The largest of Ireland's game birds, it is so familiar as to require little description. The cinnamon-coloured plumage of the male is heavily spotted with black and the extraordinarily long tail is barred along its length. The female is duller but is also heavily barred and lacks the long tail of the male.

Snipe • *Gallinago gallinago* • *Naoscach*

The Snipe is similar to the Woodcock but smaller and camouflaged more for hiding in marshy vegetation than on the woodland floor. The rich brownish plumage is broken up with straw-like streaks. The very long bill is used for probing in soft mud for food. When the marshes are frozen in cold weather, Snipe seek food at springs or even on dry, rough ground. The Snipe's name is descriptive of its sharp call – a typical wetland sound.

Woodcock • *Scolopax rusticola* • *Creabhar*

Although the Woodcock breeds in Ireland it is more widespread as a winter visitor. It is not easy to get a good look at this bird for it either sits perfectly camouflaged on the ground amongst dead vegetation or else flies away rapidly through the trees. It is medium-sized and very dumpy in shape with broad, rounded wings and short tail. The bill is very long and straight – ideal for probing in soft ground for food. The rust-coloured plumage is heavily barred and the sexes are alike. Breeding Woodcocks are territorial and the male flies around his "beat" at dusk.

GROUND AND WATER HENS

Corncrake • *Crex crex* • *Traonach*

The Corncrake is sadly decreasing throughout western Europe due to a number of factors. It is now much less widespread than formerly but still breeds in parts of the west of Ireland. It is a medium-sized, brownish bird with rust-coloured wing patches and barred flanks. Corncrakes are rarely seen and identification using the call is reliable. This is a raucous shout – "aic-aic" – uttered from the cover of a rough meadow or similar location.

Water Rail • *Rallus aquaticus* • *Rallóg uisce*

The Water Rail is another secretive bird, much more often heard than seen. The calls are strange and varied, the most familiar being a piglet-like squealing. It is slightly smaller and slimmer than the Corncrake and more attractively marked. The upper parts are red-brown, streaked darker; the face and underparts are slate-grey and there is black-and-white barring on the flanks. In flight the reddish pink legs often dangle. The bill is also reddish and is long and slightly downcurved. Although resident in Ireland, Water Rails also turn up at coastal islands on migration.

Moorhen • *Gallinula chloropus* • *Cearc uisce*

The Moorhen, known also as the "Waterhen", is a common and widespread resident, inhabiting wetland locations throughout Ireland. It is a medium-sized, sooty bird with long greenish legs and bright red, yellow-tipped bill. There is white marking along the edges of the flanks and a clear white patch beneath the tail. This is jerked up and down and the head is nodded as it walks or swims. The calls are a series of shrill squawks, mostly uttered from cover.

Coot • *Fulica atra* • *Cearc cheannann*

The Coot favours permanent wetlands like larger ponds and lakes. It is larger than the Moorhen, with a bulkier body, and, like the Moorhen, nods its head whilst swimming. Overall blackish in colour, it has a distinctive white bill and shield on the forehead. Coots dive from the water surface for underwater food. On being disturbed they scuttle along the surface of the water in a half-hearted attempt at flight. The Coot calls its own name – a resonant "coot" – revealing its presence even from the midst of reeds.

LARGE WADERS

Curlew • *Numenius arquata* • *Crotach*

The largest of the waders is the Curlew – a well-known Irish bird which not only arrives in winter hordes but also breeds in suitable Irish localities. It is a leggy, light brown bird, heavily streaked and flecked and with a downcurved bill 2.5 cm (6 inches) long, with which it probes for food. In flight, the rump and finely barred tail are white. The wild call from which the name is derived is a familiar sound of wetland pasture and bog, the Curlew's breeding habitats. Curlews feed on agricultural land as well as mudflats.

Bar-tailed Godwit • *Limosa lapponica* • *Guilbneach stríocearrach*

The Bar-tailed Godwit is like the Curlew in many respects. It too is a bird of the open mudflats (though not exclusively so) where it probes for invertebrate food using its long, slightly upturned bill. In winter plumage it resembles the Curlew both on the ground and in flight but it is much less vocal than the larger bird. A widespread winter visitor to Ireland from the Arctic, it is unusual to see it in its brick-red summer plumage in this country.

Black-tailed Godwit • *Limosa limosa* • *Guilbneach earrdhubh*

The Black-tailed Godwit is also a winter visitor and passage migrant to Ireland from breeding grounds in Continental Europe. It is similar to the Bar-tailed Godwit on the ground, though the bill and legs are slightly longer, but in flight it has a striking white wing bar and rump and, as the name implies, a black tail. This godwit is not restricted to coastal habitats, but occurs inland in marshy habitats also. In summer plumage (scarce in Ireland) the Black-tailed Godwit is like the Bar-tailed, reddish in colour, though with black bars on the flanks.

Oystercatcher • *Haematopus ostralegus* • *Roilleach*

The Oystercatcher is a large black-and-white shore bird. It is striking both on the ground and in the air. A broad white bar shows on the wings in flight. In all plumages the bill is bright orange and very noticeable. The legs are pink. The end of the thick bill is quite blunt and used to hammer open the shellfish on which the Oystercatcher feeds. The call is a clear pipe, a familiar sound of the shoreline. The masses of Oystercatchers on Irish shores in winter are mainly visitors from elsewhere in Europe, though many breed in Ireland also.

MEDIUM-SIZED WADERS

Redshank • *Tringa totanus* • *Cosdeargán*

The Redshank is one of Ireland's commonest and most widespread shorebirds. The majority are winter visitors or migrants from elsewhere in Northern Europe, though they breed in Ireland as well. On the ground the Redshank is a nondescript brownish bird, paler on the underparts but with long, bright orange-red legs. In flight the wings show clear white trailing edges – a very noticeable fieldmark. The call is a clear whistle, "tiu-oo-oo".

Greenshank • *Tringa nebularia* • *Ladhrán glas*

The Greenshank is slightly larger than the Redshank, with a slightly upturned, not straight, bill. The long legs are grey-green, not orange-red. The overall plumage is greyer, especially in winter plumage. In flight the Greenshank lacks the pale wing edges of the Redshank, and a long white wedge shows on the rump. The flight call is a clear whistle, "tu-tu-tu", quite different from the Redshank's. It is a widespread though thinly distributed migrant and winter visitor.

Lapwing • *Vanellus vanellus* • *Pilibín*

The Lapwing is one of Ireland's most familiar waders. The majority are winter visitors, but many also breed in Ireland. The Lapwing looks black and white from a distance but in fact the upperparts have a greenish gloss, visible from close range. A remarkable upward-pointing plume is visible on the head, though this is absent in the young birds. In the air the wings are noticeably rounded and the flight is buoyant. The call is thin and nasal.

Golden Plover • *Pluvialis apricaria* • *Feadóg bhuí*

The Golden Plover is another well-known winter visitor to Ireland. It is also a scarce breeding bird. Two races occur here – Northern and Southern. The Southern race is distinguished from the Northern race by incomplete blackish underparts and face. In winter the races are identical – golden brown above and on the breast, paler below. The call is a rather sad-sounding note.

Grey Plover • *Pluvialis squatarola* • *Feadóg ghlas*

The Grey Plover does not breed in Ireland, being a winter visitor from northern Europe to Irish coastal mudflats. In summer it is similar to the Northern Golden

Plover but with silver, not gold-flecked, upperparts. In winter it looks like a silvery counterpart of the Golden Plover, except in flight, when the clear white rump and wing bar and unusual black "armpits" can be seen. The call note recalls that of the Golden Plover but is somewhat extended.

SMALLER WADERS

Turnstone ● *Arenaria interpres* ● *Piardálái trá*

The Turnstone is a well-known winter visitor from the Arctic to rocky and seaweedy shores. In winter the dull, mottled greys and browns of the plumage merge with the background and Turnstones can be difficult to see well. In summer plumage they are more conspicuous. In flight they are conspicuous in all plumages. The wing pattern is composed of clear black-and-white bars. The flight call is a series of stuttered notes quite unlike any of the other small waders.

Knot ● *Calidris canutus* ● *Cnota*

The Knot is another Arctic species which comes to Ireland for the winter months. It occurs mainly on coastal mudflats. At the regular resorts Knots are very gregarious, forming flocks that can be difficult to locate against a background of grey mud. Close up, the Knot can be seen to be a dull grey bird, paler on the underparts. Even in flight it shows no clear-cut identification features. In summer plumage (which is unusual in Ireland) it is transformed into a predominantly brick-red wader.

Dunlin ● *Calidris alpina* ● *Breacóg*

The sparrow-sized Dunlin is an abundant and widespread migrant and winter visitor and breeds in a few places. In winter plumage it is greyish above, whitish below and the bill and legs are black. The bill is quite long and slightly downcurved. The flight pattern has a dark band running up the tail and rump and a thin white wing bar. In summer plumage it is rust-brown above and there is a black belly patch. The call is a thin, buzzing trill.

Sanderling ● *Calidris alba* ● *Luathrán*

In winter plumage the Sanderling is an even paler bird than the Dunlin – silvery grey above, white below and on the head. In flight the pattern is also Dunlin-like but more striking. The flight call is a clear "whit-whit", noticeably different from the Dunlin's. In summer plumage the Sanderling is rich brown on the upperparts and on the breast and clear white on most of the underparts. They are widespread migrants and winter visitors.

Ringed Plover ● *Charadrius hiaticula* ● *Feadóg chladaigh*

The Ringed Plover has an unmistakable plumage pattern. The upperparts are brown, the underparts white, but there is a neat black breast band and black facial markings. The legs and bill are orange, the latter with a black tip. In flight it has a wing pattern similar to that of the Dunlin. The flight call is a more tuneful "prrip". Ringed Plovers are widespread migrants and winter visitors and breed in Ireland as well.

LARGER GULLS

Herring Gull ● *Larus argentatus* ● *Faoileán scadán*

The Herring Gull is perhaps Ireland's commonest and most widespread gull, being found almost anywhere where food is available. The majority of nesting colonies are on coastal cliffs and islands but it has taken to nesting on city buildings and elsewhere. The plumage of the adult is mainly white with grey wings and back. The wing tips are black with white spots. The legs are pink; the bill is yellow with a red spot on the lower half. Juvenile Herring Gulls are grey-brown, heavily mottled darker and the bill is all dark. The immature birds have paler plumage and dark-tipped bills. Herring Gulls call with a well-known high-pitched yelping.

Great Black-backed Gull • *Larus marinus* • *Droimneach mór*

The Great Black-backed Gull is easily recognized by its white body, black back and wings and large size. Like the Herring Gull, the legs are pink and the bill, which is larger and more vicious-looking than that of the Herring Gull, is also yellow with a red spot on the lower half. The young bird follows the same plumage development of the other gulls but is recognizable in any plumage by its large size, heavy build and massive bill. Great Black-backs nest in coastal localities often amongst colonies of other gulls. The call of the Great Black-backed Gull is deeper than that of the Herring or Lesser Black-backed Gulls.

Lesser Black-backed Gull • *Larus fuscus* • *Droimneach beag*

The Lesser Black-backed Gull is identical to the Herring Gull in size and shape but has dusky grey wings and back (intermediate in shade between the Herring Gull and the Great Black-backed Gull). The legs of this species are yellow, not pink as in the other large gulls. It is difficult to distinguish between young Lesser Black-backs and young Herring Gulls, especially in the juvenile plumage. Lesser Black-backs are largely migratory and are not usually found in Ireland in winter. The colonies that nest here do so mainly on islets on the larger lakes and, although there are many colonies, it is nowhere particularly numerous.

SMALLER GULLS

Black-headed Gull • *Larus ridibundus* • *Faoileán ceanndhubh*

The Black-headed Gull in fact has a dark brown head – and this only in summer plumage. In winter plumage only a blackish spot remains, behind the eye. The best identification feature, however, is the white front to the wings which is an obvious feature in all plumages. Even the young, which are mottled brown above and have a black tip to the tail, show the white forewing. The bill and legs of the adult are red; those of the immature bird are yellowish, the bill having a black tip. The calls are unpleasant, raucous notes and are somewhat like those of the terns. The colony is usually located on a low islet or marshy place and the nests are placed very close together.

Common Gull • *Larus canus* • *Faoileán bán*

The Common Gull is badly named, for it is by no means Ireland's commonest gull. It nests in colonies on some inland lakes. In appearance it resembles a smaller version of the Herring Gull, having white body, grey back and wings with black tips. The wing tips are noticeably marked with white and the legs and bill are greyish green, not pink and yellow as in the larger bird. The immature bird is mottled grey-brown above and the tail has a thick black terminal band. In flight the front of the immature bird's wings are noticeably darker than the rear. The call is a pleasant mewing.

Kittiwake • *Rissa tridactyla* • *Saidhbhéar*

The Kittiwake could be described as a coastal counterpart of the Common Gull, being similar in size and general shape. The back and wings are grey, the latter with black "dipped-in ink" tips. The bill is dull yellow and the legs are black. There are clear black markings on the upperparts of the immature bird: on the back of the neck, on the tip of the tail and diagonally across the wings. Kittiwakes nest in colonies on sea cliffs and stacks all around Irish coasts, and often associate with other seabirds like

Auks and Fulmars. The name is derived from the call at the nesting site, which is unmistakably "kittiwake".

TERNS

Common Tern • *Sterna hirundo* • *Geabhróg*

The Common Tern is grey on the back and wings and white over the remainder of the plumage except for a striking black cap on the head. The bill and short legs are red, the former with a black tip. The call is usually uttered on the wing and is a harsh "k-reeagh". The young birds are mottled with black and brown on the upperparts, have a partial black cap on the head and lack the deeply forked tail of the adults. Common Terns nest in colonies along coastal sandspits and coastal or lake islets.

Arctic Tern • *Sterna paradisaea* • *Geabhróg artach*

The Arctic Tern resembles the Common Tern in many ways. The differences are subtle, the most obvious being a greyish tinge on the underparts, highlighting the white cheeks; the deeper red bill lacking the black tip; the shorter red legs. Despite these differences, identification is difficult, especially when they are breeding together in large mixed colonies. The young are almost identical to young Common Terns.

Sandwich Tern • *Sterna sandvicensis* • *Geabhróg dhúscothach*

The Sandwich Tern is the largest of Ireland's terns and is more gull-like than the others. In bulk it is equivalent to the smaller gulls. The tail is less noticeably forked than either the Common or the Arctic Terns. From a distance it looks overall whitish, the back and wings being the palest grey. The black cap on the head is shaggy at the rear. The bill is long, black and yellow-tipped and the short legs are also black. The young are, as in the other terns, mottled on the upperparts. The call is a loud, grating "kro-ick".

Little Tern • *Sterna albifrons* • *Geabhróg bhídeach*

The Little Tern is much smaller than the others described. The main features are a white forehead in summer plumage, short yellow legs and black-tipped bill, and a thin rasping call. The tail is only slightly forked and the flight is noticeably light and dainty. The young have striking diagonal wing markings but are smaller than other species for which they might be mistaken. The nesting colonies are restricted to a small number of beaches on Irish coasts.

PENGUIN-LIKE BIRDS

Guillemot • *Uria aalge* • *Foracha*

The Guillemot is the largest of this group and is found in many colonies around Irish coasts. The noise of these colonies has to be heard to be believed – the cumulative effect sounds like weird gargling. The bird itself is warm brown on the upperparts, head and neck, white below and on the edge of the wings. The bill is black and dagger-shaped, the legs blackish also. In winter the Guillemot becomes duller on the upperparts and the face turns whitish.

Razorbill • *Alca torda* • *Crosán*

The Razorbill is similar to the Guillemot in size and shape but sits less upright. Razorbills usually breed in association with Guillemots on the sea cliffs. They are black rather than dark brown on the upperparts, head and neck and there are intricate fine white lines on the bill, which is deeper and less dagger-shaped than that of the Guillemot. In winter plumage they become whitish on the face like the Guillemot.

Black Guillemot • *Cepphus grylle* • *Foracha dhubh*

The Black Guillemot is smaller and less gregarious than the larger bird. It favours piers, harbours and rocky locations close to the edge of the sea. In summer plumage the Black Guillemot is indeed black but with large white wing patches. The legs and feet are strikingly red. The inside of the bill is also red but the bill itself is black. In winter plumage it looks totally different. After the moult it becomes ghostly white, finely marked with black.

Puffin • *Fratercula arctica* • *Puifín*

The Puffin is perhaps the best-known auk. Its dumpy upright stance, black-and-white plumage and remarkable multi-coloured bill have brought it to the attention of many. It is noticeably smaller than either the Razorbill or the Guillemot and is more stocky in appearance. Besides being coloured with red, blue, white and yellow, the bill is very deep and parrot-like. The winter plumage is much duller. Puffins also nest colonially, but in burrows in the turf at the cliff top rather than on the cliff face itself.

PIGEONS AND DOVES

Rock Dove • *Columba livia* • *Colm aille*

The Rock Dove is smaller than the Woodpigeon and lacks the white markings on the neck and wings but there is an obvious white rump patch visible in flight. Two black bars show on the wings both on the ground and in the air and there are glossy green and purple sheens on the head and breast. In the wild form, Rock Doves are found along Ireland's rocky coasts. The "feral" or street Pigeon, so familiar in Irish towns and cities, is descended from Rock Doves that have escaped or have been released from captivity.

Stock Dove • *Columba oenas* • *Colm gorm*

The Stock Dove favours agricultural land. It is similar in appearance to the Rock Dove, though slightly smaller and neater. In flight the upperparts show none of the striking white markings of the Rock Dove or the Woodpigeon, though there is a dark trailing edge on the wings and tail. The head and breast have glossy sheens like those of the Rock Dove. Although less approachable than the other Pigeons, Stock Doves often accompany Woodpigeons feeding in the fields.

Woodpigeon • *Columba palumbus* • *Colm coile*

The Woodpigeon is the largest, most common and widespread of Ireland's pigeons. They roost in woods and large flocks feed together on seeds along roadsides, in fields, etc. The Woodpigeon has a strange gliding nuptial flight and often makes loud smacking noises with the wings. The plumage is greyish with a pink tinge on the breast and greenish tinge on the neck. There is a large white neck marking and clear white patches on the wings. The tail, which has a dark terminal band, is often fanned out in flight. As with the other Pigeons, the feet are pinkish.

Collared Dove • *Streptopelia decaocto* • *Fearán baicdhubh*

Since its first appearance in 1959, the Collared Dove has become a widespread and common resident. It is found in a wide variety of habitats but it is usually near human habitations. Although it is smaller in body than the other members of the family it has a longer tail than the others. The overall plumage is pale sandy and there are whitish sides to the tail. The undertail region is strikingly black and white, visible in flight. There is a fine black half-collar on the neck from which the name is derived.

SMALL GROUND BIRDS

Skylark • *Alauda arvensis* • *Fuiseog stairiceach*

The Skylark is Ireland's only widespread and common lark. It is well known for its remarkable display song in which it ascends vertically into the sky, singing all the while. Larger and more robust than the pipits, it is nevertheless similarly marked with heavily streaked brownish plumage and white outer tail feathers. Skylarks feed on both insects and seeds and gather in flocks in stubble fields in the winter.

Meadow Pipit • *Anthus pratensis* • *Riabhóg mhóna*

The Meadow Pipit is a common and widespread ground bird, somewhat like the Skylark, with brownish, heavily streaked plumage and white outer tail feathers. It is, however, a more delicate bird, with thinner bill, and lacks the crest on the head. Meadow Pipits call with a distinctive squeak, a very familiar open-country call.

Rock Pipit • *Anthus spinoletta* • *Riabhóg chladaigh*

The Rock Pipit is an exclusively coastal relative of the Meadow Pipit. It is larger, darker and less noticeably streaked. The outer tail feathers are paler than the others but not white. The bill and legs are blackish, not pinkish as in the Meadow Pipit. The call, too, is a bolder squeak than that of the smaller bird.

Grey Wagtail • *Motacilla cinerea* • *Glasóg liath*

The Grey Wagtail is a bird of watery habitats, particularly running streams and rivers. The back is blue-grey, the wings and tail blackish, the latter with white outer feathers. There are clear black-and-white head markings – more noticeable in the male. The underparts are lemon-yellow, deeper under the tail. In winter the summer finery of the male is dulled and both sexes are alike. The call note has a metallic, ringing quality.

Pied Wagtail • *Motacilla alba* • *Glasóg shraide*

The Pied Wagtail is a widespread species as much at home in the country as it is in the town. It is distinctively patterned with a noticeably long black-and-white tail which is constantly wagged up and down. The female is greyish on the back and the juvenile is dull and less clearly marked. The call is a clear "chissick".

SWALLOW-TYPE BIRDS

Swallow • *Hirundo rustica* • *Fáinleog*

The Swallow is a familiar and widespread summer visitor. It is glossy blue-black on the upperparts, creamy on the underparts with brick-red head patches. There is a row of white spots on the tail which become obvious when the tail is opened and closed. This is deeply forked with very long outer streamers in the adult but not in the young bird. The flock calls with pleasant twittering.

House Martin • *Delichon urbica* • *Gabhlán binne*

The House Martin is similar to the Swallow in its glossy black upperparts. The underparts and a neat rump patch are white, however. The notched tail lacks the Swallow's long streamers. The call is a tuneless "tirrup" – quite different from that of the Swallow. House Martins land on the ground during the breeding season and may be seen collecting mud to construct their unique cup-shaped nests.

Sand Martin • *Riparia riparia* • *Gabhlán gainimh*

The Sand Martin is slightly smaller than the House Martin and is warm brown above and white below with a distinct brown breast band. The tail is only slightly forked. The call is similar to that of the House Martin but is quieter. Like the House Martin, this species nests colonially but in holes in banks rather than on buildings. They arrive in Ireland in spring before the other members of the family – often before the end of March.

Swift • *Apus apus* • *Gabhlán gaoithe*

The Swift is often taken for a member of the Swallow family but in fact is only a rather distant relative. It is a longer bird, with longer narrower wings and notched tail. Although it is dark brown, the Swift normally appears black. Swifts are so totally designed for life on the wing that they can even roost in the air. The call is a high-pitched rasping or screaming. They arrive later and leave earlier than the others in this group.

SMALL BROWN BIRDS

Spotted Flycatcher • *Muscicapa striata* • *Cuilire liath*

The Spotted Flycatcher is a summer visitor to Ireland from African winter grounds but it is rather locally distributed. Insects are caught from a branch or other vantage perch, the Flycatcher flying out quickly and returning to the perch again with the prey. The plumage is grey-brown above, white below with faint marking on the brownish breast. The call is a clear "tick" and is heard frequently when the young are about.

Treecreeper • *Certhia familiaris* • *Snag*

The Treecreeper is often misnamed "woodpecker" in Ireland due to its manner of feeding – by climbing up the trunks of trees in search of insects in the bark. It is a small, delicate bird with thin curved bill designed more for probing than "pecking". The longish tail feathers are stiff and prop the bird against the tree as it climbs. The plumage is streaked brownish above and whitish below. It has a mouse-like appearance as it moves jerkily up and around a tree. The call is a thin and indistinct squeak.

Dunnock • *Prunella modularis* • *Donnóg*

The Dunnock, commonly misnamed the Hedge Sparrow (for it is not a sparrow), is a secretive and inconspicuous little bird. It is aptly named dun-ock or og (meaning "little dark one") as it is dark brown, streaked darker on the back and tinged with grey on the head and underparts. The call is a monotonous "jeep" and the song is an undistinguished little refrain.

Wren • *Troglodytes troglodytes* • *Dreolín*

The tiny Wren is one of Ireland's most familiar and certainly one of its commonest and most widespread birds. This energetic little bird with typical cocked-up tail and low buzzing flight needs little description. The plumage is heavily barred on the sides and tail and there is a warm, rusty tinge on the rump and tail. The song is incredibly loud for such a small bird and the call is a sharp "chick".

THRUSHES

Song Thrush • *Turdus philomelos* • *Smólach*

The Song Thrush is perhaps Ireland's tiniest song bird. Its plumage is warm brown above, pale below, heavily speckled with black. The spots run into one another in dark blotches and streaks. The underwings are noticeably honey-coloured, sometimes visible in flight, and the call is a distinct "tsip". Song Thrushes are familiar garden birds, feeding on worms and grubs and using favoured stones as "anvils" for breaking open snails.

Redwing • *Turdus iliacus* • *Deargán sneachta*

The Redwing is the northern counterpart of the Song Thrush. The brown upperparts are darker and less warm in tone. The pale underparts are much more heavily streaked and marked with black. There is a clear yellowish eyestripe. A deep rusty patch is visible on the flanks and is further revealed as an underwing patch by the Redwing in flight. The call is a thin "ts-eer". They are abundant and widespread winter visitors, mainly from Iceland.

Mistle Thrush • *Turdus viscivorus* • *Liatráisc*

The Mistle Thrush, so named for its liking of mistletoe berries, is larger than the Song Thrush and generally greyer and paler. It is spotted with black on the underparts, the spots being more distinct and less suffused. The tail is also longer and has pale tips to the outer feathers, noticeable in flight, as are the shining white underwings. The call is a harsh rattling but the song is melodious and fluty.

Fieldfare • *Turdus pilaris* • *Sacán*

The Fieldfare is about the size of the Mistle Thrush and is similarly proportioned. It is, however, a darker bird on the back, wings and tail. The head and rump are noticeably grey. The underparts are tinged yellowish, heavily speckled and blotched with black. In flight the underwings are shining white like those of the Mistle Thrush. The flight call is a distinctive "chack, chack". Large flocks are found in stubbles and other fields during the winter. Fieldfares are abundant and widespread winter visitors from Scandinavia.

GARDEN AND RIVER BIRDS

Blackbird • *Turdus merula* • *Lon dubh*

The male Blackbird's matt-black plumage and striking orange-yellow bill are so distinctive that it requires no further description. The brownish female is sometimes mistaken for a Thrush because of its pale and speckled throat but the differences are obvious from close range. The male Blackbird is one of Ireland's best song birds. Its song is deeper, with less repetition, than that of the Song Thrush, but is nonetheless similar. The alarm call is an excited squawk.

Starling • *Sturnus vulgaris* • *Druid*

The Starling is as much at home in close proximity to man as it is in open countryside, and its adaptability to circumstances is one of its outstanding characteristics. Starlings have a wide variety of call notes and as great mimics they often impersonate both animate and inanimate sounds. The plumage is glossy black with fine pale speckling in summer. In winter it is more heavily specked and the young bird is brown rather than shiny black.

Dipper • *Cinclus cinclus* • *Gabha dubh*

The Dipper is about the size of a Starling but "dumpier" in shape. The dark brown and blackish plumage is relieved only by the white throat and breast patch. A rusty band borders the white patch but is by no means easy to see in the field. It is named for its curious and nervous dipping as it stands on a stone in flowing water. The call, which is often uttered as the bird flies with whirring wings close to the water surface, is a ringing "zit". The young bird is dull greyish and lacks the adult's white bib.

Kingfisher • *Alcedo atthis* • *Cruidín*

The Kingfisher is even smaller than the Dipper but has the plumage of an escaped exotic bird. There are various shades of green and blue on the upperparts. The underparts are orange and there are white and orange patches on the head. The bill is long and heavy for the size of the bird and the small feet are bright red. In flight, which is rapid and direct, the Kingfisher looks like an electric blue flash due to the bright turquoise feathers on the back and rump.

SMALL "PERKY" BIRDS

Robin • *Erithacus rubecula* • *Spideog*

The Robin is a most familiar garden bird. It needs little description, for its warm brown upperparts and orange-red face and breast are well known. The young bird can be confusing, as it lacks the red breast and is heavily marked with pale speckles. Robins are gardeners' constant companions, sometimes hopping about within arm's reach looking for grubs and insects as they are uncovered. The call is a pronounced "tick" and the song, which may be sung at any time of the year by the highly territorial male, is a recognizable and pleasant warbling.

Stonechat • *Saxicola torquata* • *Caislin cloch*

The Stonechat is an ostentatious little bird which is often to be seen perched on a post or wire fence, or on a sprig of gorse, and particularly in rough ground near the sea. The Stonechat characteristically flicks its wings and tail and calls with short "chipping" notes, from which the name is derived. The male in summer is a bright little bird with black head, wings and tail and white markings on the wings and rump. The breast is orange. In winter the plumage is duller and the female looks duller throughout the year.

Wheatear • *Oenanthe oenanthe* • *Clochrán*

The Wheatear prefers to perch on walls and fences rather than on bushes. It is a summer visitor to Ireland from wintering quarters in Africa and is to be found most commonly at the coast in spring and autumn. The bird itself is at once recognizable by its white rump and black-tipped tail – a striking feature in flight. The wings are blackish and there is a black mark on the cheeks of the male. The male's upperparts are light grey and the whitish underparts are tinged yellowish on the breast. In autumn the plumage is duller, more closely resembling the brown-beaked females and juveniles. The call is a sharp "chack" and the song is a pleasant jangling.

WARBLER TYPES

Willow Warbler • *Phylloscopus trochilus* • *Ceolaire sailí*

The Willow Warbler is a common and widespread summer visitor to Ireland. It is found mainly in scrubby habitats but on migration it can be found in all kinds of cover. It is an inconspicuous little greenish bird, paler below and with a yellowish tinge on the breast of the young bird. The call is a distinctive "lui" and the song is a pleasant cascading warble.

Chiffchaff • *Phylloscopus collybita* • *Tuif-teaf*

The Chiffchaff is, like the Willow Warbler, a widespread summer visitor. Very like the Willow Warbler, it does, however, tend to be tinged more brown and less yellow. Other differences, like blackish rather than pinkish legs, are less reliable identifiers. The call is similar but the song is completely different. The name is derived from the unmistakable "chiff-chaff", sung from the treetops in summer.

Goldcrest • *Regulus regulus* • *Cíorbhuí*

The Goldcrest is closely related to the warblers and is Ireland's smallest bird. The plumage is greenish and whitish beneath and there are black and white marks on the wings. Both sexes show a flash of colour on the top of the head – orange in the male, yellow in the female. The call is a thin mouse-like squeak and the song is simply an extended version of the same.

Sedge Warbler • *Acrocephalus schoenobaenus* • *Ceolaire cibe*

The Sedge Warbler is a common and widespread summer visitor to Ireland, favouring marshy vegetation. The upperparts are heavily streaked, there is a distinct pale eyestripe and a rusty tinge on the rump. The call is a harsh single note and the song is a loud, varied warbling with harsh sequences.

Whitethroat • *Sylvia communis* • *Gilphíb*

The Whitethroat is a widespread summer visitor, but is nowhere particularly common. Its preferred habitat in Ireland is amongst gorse, brambles or similar vegetation in rough ground situations. The song is a jumbled chattering and the usual call is a low "churr". The male is grey on the head and white on the throat – the underparts are tinged pinkish and the back is tinged brown, rusty on the wings. The female is less colourful.

TITS

Long-tailed Tit • *Aegithalos caudatus* • *Meantán earrfhada*

The Long-Tailed Tit is the smallest of the family in body but has the longest tail. It differs too in colour, being mainly pinkish and black above, greyish white below. There are distinctive double blackish head stripes. The main habitat is scrubland and woods in general. It is less a garden bird than the others of the family. Long-tailed Tits feed in nomadic groups on a wide variety of insects and often join other small birds in the winter. The calls are varied and are reminiscent of those of the Treecreeper.

Coal Tit • *Parus ater* • *Meantán dubh*

The Coal Tit is similar in size and shape to the Blue Tit but is quite different in appearance. The plumage is mainly grey and brown rather than blue and green, and the head is black with whitish cheeks and nape patch. The Coal Tit calls with a whistled "tui" and a variety of other short notes. It is one of the commonest birds of Ireland's conifer plantations, where it feeds on insect life in the canopy.

Blue Tit • *Parus caeruleus* • *Meantán gorm*

The Blue Tit is the familiar "blue-bonnet" of the garden which feeds acrobatically on suspended food. It will feed on a wide variety of food, from insects to nuts. The Blue Tit is very small and compact and has a clearly marked head, yellowish underparts and green and bluish upperparts. The call is nasal and buzzing, quite different in quality from the others in the family.

Great Tit • *Parus major* • *Meantán mór*

The Great Tit is the largest of the family – roughly sparrow-sized. Like the Coal Tit, it has a black head with bright white cheeks but lacks the white nape patch. Like the Blue Tit, it is green and blue above and yellow below but there is a thick black band running from the chin to beneath the tail. In general it is a striking and beautiful bird. The calls are similar to those of the Coal Tit but the "seek-er, seek-er" song is unmistakable. It joins other small birds in winter foraging flocks.

FAMILIAR CROWS

Magpie • *Pica pica* • *Snag breac*
The Magpie must be one of Ireland's best-known birds, due largely to its pied plumage. A clever opportunist, it has learned to exploit food sources of all kinds, including the eggs and chicks of other birds. The Magpie's striking appearance and its legendary thieving habits have endeared the bird to many. The black tail and wing feathers have a green and blue sheen respectively.

Jackdaw • *Corvus monedula* • *Cág*
The Jackdaw is Ireland's smallest crow. It is well known for its rather mischievous appearance and sinister white eye. It is mainly sooty black, though the sides of the head are greyish. The Jackdaw struts rather than walks, and the call is a resonant "chack". Like the Starling, the Jackdaw has "streetwise" habits and coexists comfortably with man.

Rook • *Corvus frugilegus* • *Rúcach*
The Rook is a large crow with a more agreeable personality than some of the others. It feeds in the fields but is not above foraging on the shore or feeding on carrion at the roadside. It is very recognizable in breeding season, with its pale featherless patch at the base of the bill and rather shaggy black plumage. The young bird lacks the bare face patch and can look like an all-black Hooded Crow. Rooks call with a monotonous cawing, making the rookery a noisy and raucous woodland.

Hooded Crow • *Corvus corone* • *Feannóg*
The Hooded Crow is less associated with man than the others of this group. Although it does take eggs and young birds it does a valuable job in cleaning up carrion from the roadsides and elsewhere throughout the countryside. The Hooded Crow is so-called because of its clearly demarcated black head. The wings and tail are also black but the body is grey. The call is a rather drawn-out "gw-a-ak".

LESS FAMILIAR CROWS

Raven • *Corvus corax* • *Fiach dubh*
The Raven is a massive bird, being substantially larger and heavier than the Rook or the Hooded Crow. On the ground the most obvious features are the outsize, powerful-looking bill and the shaggy-looking throat. In the air Ravens have longer wings and tails than the other crows, the wings showing "fingered" ends and the tail being quite diamond-shaped. During the breeding season Ravens perform spectacular rolling and tumbling exercises in flight and call with a variety of strange notes near the nest site. The usual call is a resonant "pruck" or similar croak.

Jay • *Garrulus glandarius* • *Scréachóg*
The Jay is about the size of a Jackdaw but much more attractively coloured. Brownish pink is the general colour but there are black-and-white patches on the wings, and the tail and rump are respectively blackish and white. A "kingfisher-blue" patch is evident at the bend of the wing and there is a black mark on the face at the base of the bill. Jays are excitable birds and when uttering their squawking calls they raise and lower a rough crest on the top of the head. They rarely afford a good view and are most usually seen flying in or around a wood.

RED-THROATED DIVER

Sum.

Win.

FULMER

Win.

Sum.

GREAT-NORTHERN DIVER

Win.

DABCHICK

Sum.

Ad.

Juv.

GANNET

STORM PETREL

Sum.

Win.

GREAT-CRESTED GREBE

MANX SHEARWATER

CORMORANT

IMM.

AD.

MUTE SWAN

SHAG

AD.

IMM.

WHOOPER SWAN

GREY HERON

AD.

IMM.

BEWICK'S SWAN

SHELDUCK

F

M

WHITE-FRONTED
GOOSE

SHELDUCK

M

F

GREYLAG GOOSE

TEAL

F

M

BARNACLE GOOSE

MALLARD

F

M

BRENT GOOSE

SHOVELER

F

M

POCHARD

SPARROWHAWK

KESTREL

TUFTED DUCK

PEREGRINE

EIDER

JUV.

GOLDENEYE

MERLIN

CUCKOO

RED-BREASTED
MERGANSER

F

M

RED GROUSE

CORNCRAKE

M

F

PHEASANT

WATER RAIL

SNIPE

MOORHEN

WOODCOCK

COOT

199

REDSHANK

CURLEW

WIN.

BAR-TAILED
GODWIT

GREENSHANK

WIN.

BLACK-TAILED
GODWIT

LAPWING

WIN.

GOLDEN PLOVER

SUM.

WIN.

OYSTERCATCHER

GREY PLOVER   SUM.

200

WIN.

TURNSTONE

SUM.

AD.

HERRING GULL

IMM.

WIN.

KNOT

WIN.

AD.

DUNLIN

SUM.

IMM.

GREAT BLACK-BACKED GULL

SANDERLING

AD.

RINGED PLOVER

IMM.

LESSER BLACK-BACKED GULL

Juv.

Sum.

Win. BLACK-HEADED GULL

COMMON TERN

Juv.

ARTIC TERN

COMMON GULL

SANDWICH TERN

Juv.

KITTIWAKE

LITTLE TERN

GUILLEMOT

SUM.

ROCK DOVE

RAZORBILL

SUM.

STOCK DOVE

SUM.

BLACK GUILLEMOT

WOOD PIGEON

PUFFIN

SUM.

COLLARED DOVE

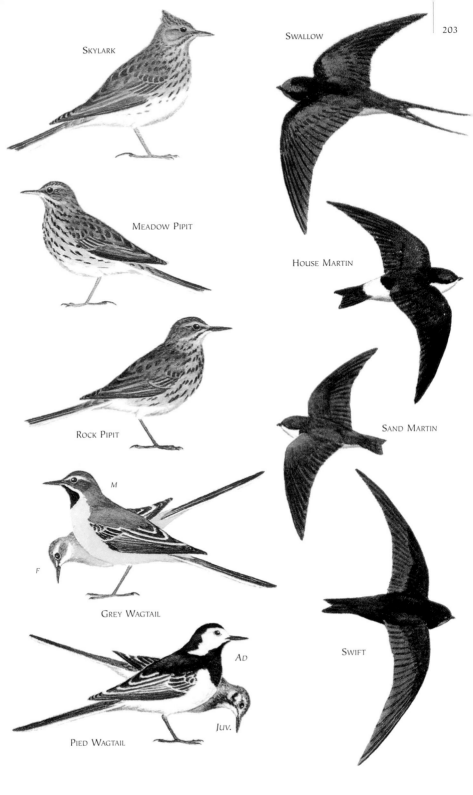

SKYLARK

SWALLOW

203

MEADOW PIPIT

HOUSE MARTIN

ROCK PIPIT

SAND MARTIN

M

F

GREY WAGTAIL

SWIFT

AD

JUV.

PIED WAGTAIL

SPOTTED FLYCATCHER

SONG THRUSH

TREE CREEPER

REDWING

MISTLE THRUSH

DUNNOCK

WREN

FIELDFARE

BLACKBIRD

JUV.

ROBIN

AD.

STARLING

F

STONECHAT

M

DIPPER

F

WHEATEAR

KINGFISHER

M

WILLOW WARBLER

LONG TAILED TIT

CHIFFCHAFF

COAL TIT

M

GOLDCREST

F

SEDGE
WARBLER

BLUE TIT

GREAT TIT

F

M

WHITETHROAT

MAGPIE

RAVEN

JACKDAW

JAY

ROOK

AD.

JUV.

CHOUGH

HOODED CROW

CHAFFINCH

M

F

GOLDINCH

GREENFINCH

SISKIN

BULLFINCH

M

F

M

F

HOUSE SPARROW

LINNET

M

F

REDPOLL

M

YELLOWHAMMER

F

M

REED BUNTING

F

Chough • *Pyrrhocorax pyrrhocorax* • *Cág cosdearg*

The Chough could be regarded as one of Ireland's speciality birds, as it is more abundant and widespread here than elsewhere in western Europe. It is nevertheless restricted to wilder coastal areas, especially in the west. It is slightly larger than the Jackdaw, more elegant in shape and with glossier black plumage. The bill and legs are bright red, the former with a slight downward curve. In flight the Chough has broad "finger-ended" wings and, like the Raven, performs marvellous tumbling aerobatics during the breeding season. The name "chough" (as in "rough") is derived from the wild and evocative call "keeow" which has a far-carrying quality.

FINCHES

Chaffinch • *Fringilla coelebs* • *Rí rua*

The Chaffinch is a familiar garden bird. The white wing and outer tail markings are features of both sexes, particularly in flight. On the ground the male can be seen to be an attractively coloured finch with blue cap, green and brown on the back and with brick-coloured cheeks and underparts. The female is duller. The call is a distinctive "pink" and the song is a pleasant jangling.

Greenfinch • *Carduelis chloris* • *Glasán darach*

The Greenfinch is even stockier than the bullfinch, with a very stout pinkish bill which will deal with almost any kind of seed. Both sexes are alike in having greenish plumage and bright yellow flashes on the wings and at the sides of the tail. The young birds have duller plumage, but have the stout beak and general appearance of the adults.

Goldfinch • *Carduelis carduelis* • *Lasair choille*

The Goldfinch is a most attractive finch with its black, white and sandy plumage, red face and bright yellow wing flashes. The beautiful plumage of both sexes and the pleasant liquid notes of the song are well known. It is more of an open country bird than the other finches, and will feed avidly on the seeds of thistles and other weeds.

Siskin • *Carduelis spinus* • *Siscín*

The Siskin is somewhat like a miniature Greenfinch, being predominantly greenish, but it is more tit-like in behaviour. The male is clearly marked, with black on the chin, top of the head and streaks on the back. There are yellow flashes on the wings and tail. The female is a duller version of the male. Siskins call with lively twitterings as they move from treetop to treetop, feeding on the cones of a variety of trees.

Bullfinch • *Pyrrhula pyrrhula* • *Corcrán coille*

The male Bullfinch is blue-grey above, soft pink below and on the cheeks. There is a black cap on the head and the wings and tail are also black. The female's plumage is much duller but both sexes show a clear white wing bar and rump in flight. Bullfinches call with a soft "beoo". With their stout bill they are well equipped to deal with seeds of all kinds.

FINCH-TYPE BIRDS

House Sparrow • *Passer domesticus* • *Gealbhan binne*

The House Sparrow is familiar to everyone. So well does it coexist with man that it is rarely to be found far from buildings. Sparrows have seed-eating bills like the finches but will eat almost any household scrap. The male is quite well marked, with grey and rust-brown head, brown back and black throat. The female is a rather nondescript grey-brown.

Linnet • *Carduelis cannabina* • *Gleoiseach*

The Linnet is a little finch associated most commonly with rough and uncultivated ground. At the breeding site the male sings with an extended and pleasant song. The male in breeding plumage has a red smudge on the breast and forehead; the remainder of the head is greyish and the back is brown. The female is duller. In winter, males and females are alike but both show distinctive pale flashes on the edges of the wings and tail.

Redpoll • *Carduelis flammea* • *Deargéadan*

The Redpoll is rather like a small, slim Linnet. In breeding plumage the male has reddish markings on the head and breast. The female is duller, more obviously streaked, and lacks the red smudge on the breast. Both have a black chin mark and clear pale wing bars. Redpolls are highly active feeders. The flock calls with a variety of twittering notes, including a buzzing trill. They are recognizable, even at a distance, by their tiny size and cleft tail.

Yellowhammer • *Emberiza citrinella* • *Buióg*

The Yellowhammer is a most attractive member of this family. It is a slim bird with yellow head and breast and red-brown, heavily streaked back. The rump is particularly rust-coloured and noticeable in flight, as are the white outer feathers. The female is a duller version of the male. The usual call is a loud "chick" and the song sounds like "a little bit of bread and no ch-e-e-e-se". The main habitats are gorse-covered commonages and some hedgerows.

Reed Bunting • *Emberiza schoeniclus* • *Gealóg ghiolcaí*

The Reed Bunting is similar in size to the Yellowhammer, with streaked back and white outer tail feathers, but the male has a black head and throat and whitish underparts. The female is quite different, being generally brown, but is richly streaked with black. The call is a thin "tiu" and the song is an unremarkable little jangling. The main habitat is in reedbeds or marshy ground but it is also found in scrub, sometimes well away from water.

CHAPTER FIVE

TREES & SHRUBS

INTRODUCTION

This section describes and illustrates sixty-four of the common species of the countryside, as well as providing some hints to identifying a further thirty or forty other closely related species which are rarer. Included are plants found naturally in Ireland (called natives) as well as many that have been introduced from other countries that have sometimes gone wild. The species are arranged in families, placed in botanical order, next to their closest relatives. The most primitive families come first and the most advanced families, in evolutionary terms, come last. English, Irish and scientific (Latin) names are given for each species where possible. Unfortunately, some of the rarest species have neither Irish names nor commonly used English names.

GYMNOSPERMS – THE CONIFERS

PINACEAE – THE PINE FAMILY

Noble Fir • *Abies procera* • *Giúis*

This handsome tree grows up to about 50 metres (165 feet) in Ireland and is used in forestry in western areas where it has proved to be quite resistant to strong winds and harsh weather. It is also widely planted in parks and large gardens. It is originally native to the US in Oregon and Washington. It has a pyramidal shape, with smooth bark when young which becomes rough and fissured when mature, rather variable in colour from pale grey to purplish. Its needles are 1.5 to 3.5 cm long, about 1.5 mm wide, bluish grey in colour and very densely arranged at the top and sides of the shoots. When they drop they leave a flat circular scar on the smooth twigs. The Noble fir has large erect cones up to 30 cm and 9 cm across, purplish brown when mature. This species makes an attractive Christmas tree and holds onto its needles even when dead, unlike those of the more frequently used *Picea*. Evergreen; flowers in May.

Sitka Spruce • *Picea sitchensis* • *Sprús sitceach*

The Sitka spruce is the most popular and widely planted forestry tree in Ireland. It is native to the western seaboard of North America from Alaska to California. It grows up to 60 metres (200 feet) tall, and is a conical tree with grey bark peeling in small scales. Its branches are stiff and slightly upturned, except the side shoots which droop somewhat. Its needles are 15 to 30 mm long, have a slate-grey or bluish tint, are striped underneath with two white bands and end with a sharp point. When they drop off they leave a small raised peg behind, an easy way to recognise a *Picea*. *Picea* has pegs, in *Abies* they are absent. Its cones are 6 to 10 cm long, pendulous, pale brown in colour, with thin papery scales which have crinkly toothed edges – *Abies* has ascending cones.

Sitka spruce grows well in wet, peaty soils and in high rainfall areas. Its growth can be very rapid – more than one metre (3.3 feet) per annum. Its timber is used for telegraph poles, fencing, chipboard and hardboard manufacture and in house building. It is the major tree used for cellulose in paper milling. Evergreen; flowers in May.

European Larch • *Larix decidua* • *Learóg*

This deciduous conifer native to the Alps is quite widely planted in Ireland for forestry, in parks and large gardens, on roadsides and in shelter belts. It is a tall, conical and fast-growing tree up to 35 metres (115 feet). Its needles are mainly in spiral clusters on short woody spurs off the branches. The needles are soft, 12 to 30 mm long, pale green and turning yellowish in autumn before falling. The tips of the shoots hang down and give the tree a vaguely weeping look. The male cones begin whitish but become yellow as they shed their pollen. Female cones are usually rosy-red when young and 20 to 40 mm long by 20 to 30 mm wide when ripe. Many trees retain the old dead cones on their branches for several years.

Another closely related species widely planted is the Japanese larch, *Larix kaempferi*, and there is also an intermediate hybrid between the two, *Larix x eurolepis*. The Japanese larch is much broader leaved than the European larch and a darker grey-green, not weeping. Its smaller cones have the upper edge of the cone-scales rolled back, and the whole tree is more densely branched. Larch timber is strong and one of the most durable conifer woods. It is widely used for fences, gates, estate repair work and for fishing boats. Deciduous; flowers from March to April.

Scots Pine • *Pinus sylvestris* • *Péine albanach*

The Scots pine is pyramidal when young but becomes a fine and tall flat-topped tree when mature. Its fissured and flaking chocolate-reddish bark is an easily spotted characteristic of the species even at some distance. Its needles are in pairs, grey-green in colour and stiffly twisted, 4 to 8 cm long. Its male cones are very small and massed together in clusters at the start of the new year's growth. The female cones are also small, 3 to 4 mm long only, dark red, in groups of two to five at the ends of stronger shoots. The female cones take two seasons to mature and eventually reach a length of 3 to 7 cm. When the cones dry out in drier spells the seeds are shed.

The Scots pine was common in Ireland 7,000 to 9,000 years ago when the climate was drier. It died out in about AD 300 when the Atlantic climatic influences made Ireland a wetter and warmer place. It was reintroduced in about 1700 and is now commonly planted and well established in most counties. The nearest native stands of the Scots pine are in the Highlands of Scotland. In many Irish bogs remnant stumps of large pine forests long submerged have been revealed where the peat has been cut away. Scots pine also occurs in Europe eastwards to Siberia. Its timber was much used for railway sleepers and telegraph poles. Evergreen; flowers from May to June.

Lodgepole Pine • *Pinus contorta* • *Péine contórtach*

The lodgepole pine is common in commercial forestry in Ireland and can attain a height of more than 25 metres (80 feet) as a tall and rather narrow tree. It has a fissured and reddish bark often patterned with small, squarish plates. Its needles are in pairs, somewhat twisted, arranged very densely, especially on the younger vigorous shoots, which vary in colour from deep green to yellowish green, and in length from 4 to 7 cm. The ripe female cones are 2 to 6 cm long and occur in whorls of two to five, and are oval to conical in shape.

Lodgepole pine is not particularly well suited to limestone soils, but has been used as an effective pioneer tree for bogs, coastal sands and dry sandy soils. It is native to western North America from Alaska to California and into the Rocky Mountains. Although the species varies considerably throughout its natural range, its coastal form is the variety generally planted in Ireland. Evergreen; flowers from May to June.

Monterey Pine • *Pinus radiata* • *Péine*

The Monterey pine is native only to a few small areas of California. In Ireland there are probably many times the number of trees than survive in their natural habitat. It is a rapidly growing tree which reaches up to 35 metres (115 feet) tall in the British Isles and so is quite commonly planted for forestry and in parks. Growth rates of up

214

NOBLE FIR

SCOTS PINE

SITKA SPRUCE

LODGEPOLE PINE

EUROPEAN LARCH

MONTEREY PINE

JUNIPER

IRISH ELM,
WYCH ELM

YEW

ENGLISH ELM

LONDON PLANE

BOG-MYRTLE

Beech

Pedunculate Oak, English Oak

Spanish Chestnut, Sweet Chestnut

Silver Birch

Sessile Oak, Common Oak

Downy Birch

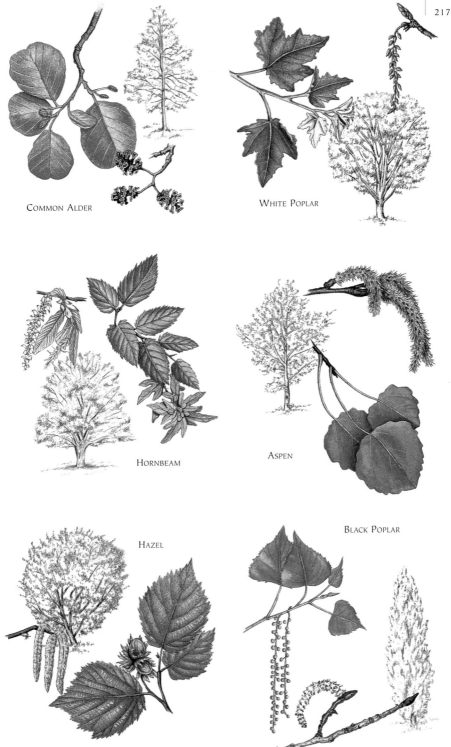

COMMON ALDER

WHITE POPLAR

HORNBEAM

ASPEN

HAZEL

BLACK POPLAR

GOAT WILLOW

CRACK WILLOW,
WITHY

WHITE WILLOW

SALLY, RUSTY WILLOW

OSIER

EARED WILLOW

RHODODENDRON

BLACKBERRY,
BRAMBLE

STRAWBERRY-TREE

DOG ROSE

ESCALLONIA

SLOE,
BLACKTHORN

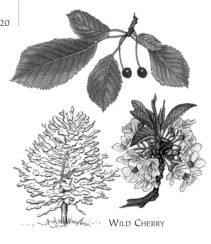

WILD CHERRY

BIRD CHERRY

WILD PLUM

PORTUGUESE LAUREL

DWARF CHERRY

CHERRY LAUREL

CRAB-APPLE

COTONEASTER

ROWAN,
MOUNTAIN ASH

HAWTHORN

IRISH WHITEBEAM

BROOM

222

GORSE,
FURZE, WHIN

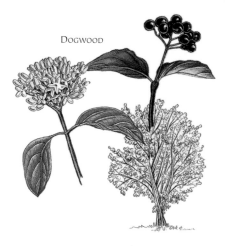

DOGWOOD

MOUNTAIN GORSE,
WESTERN GORSE

SPINDLE-TREE

FUCHSIA

HOLLY

BUCKTHORN

IVY

HORSE-CHESTNUT

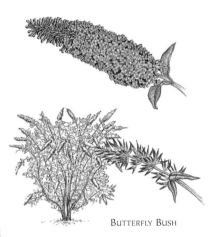

BUTTERFLY BUSH

SYCAMORE

ASH

224

WILD PRIVET

ELDER

GUELDER-ROSE

SNOWBERRY

to 2.5 metres (8 feet) per annum have been recorded. However, it is not completely hardy and can be damaged by hard frosts.

It has grey-brown and deeply fissured bark and a conical shape to its crown. Its branches are at first drooping but turn upwards at their ends as they elongate. The bright green needles are in threes, very slender, straight and reach 10 cm or more in length. The male cones are small and bright yellow in spring. The female cones vary in size, 7 to 20 cm in length and 6 to 10 cm across, light glossy reddish brown in colour, oval and very asymmetrical at the base. The cones tend to be retained on the branches long after they have ripened and shed their seeds. Evergreen; flowers in April.

A wide range of other fine species are cultivated in Ireland, especially in large gardens, parks and demesnes. These are mainly from Europe, North America and Asia, although some species occur native to Central and South America. Worldwide, over ninety species of pine are known.

CUPRESSACEAE – THE CYPRESS FAMILY

Juniper • *Juniperus communis* • *Aiteal*

The juniper can be either an upright or a prostrate bushy shrub. It has red-brown flaking bark and short, stiff and prickly needle-like leaves, 0.5 to 2 cm long, blue-green in colour, arranged in a whorl of three around the shoot. Male and female flowers occur in cones but grow on separate trees. The male cones are small and rather inconspicuous. The female cones also begin very small but swell to form green berry-like fruits that turn blue-black on ripening, eventually reaching a size of 6 to 9 mm long.

Two subspecies of the juniper occur in Ireland: subsp. *communis* can be either upright or prostrate, with sharply pointed leaves, growing on limestone soils; subsp. *alpina* is always prostrate and has broader incurved, blunter leaves and grows mainly on acid soils. It is commonest in Connemara. Although a wide range of exotic junipers are grown in gardens, in the wild it is not common except in rocky places, on mountains and lake shores in the west and north-west of Ireland, especially in Kerry, Clare, Donegal and Connemara.

A native of Ireland, in the past its foliage was used for kindling. It has a fragrant smell when burnt. Juniper oil is an important constituent of gin and a peppery spice may be obtained from its seeds. Evergreen; flowers in May.

TAXACEAE – THE YEW FAMILY

Yew • *Taxus baccata* • *Iúr*

Almost every old churchyard in Ireland has a yew tree. Even in pre-Christian Ireland the yew was associated with religious sites. Yew wood has long been prized for its durability and is decorative for cabinet-making. The oldest human tool ever found in Europe is a spear made of yew wood lodged in the ribs of a straight-tusked palaeolithic elephant in Lower Saxony. The best bows were also made of yew wood.

Yew grows to be a large spreading tree or shrub up to 25 metres (80 feet) tall with reddish peeling or flaking bark. Its leaves are dark green on top with two pale stripes underneath. They are flat, long and narrow, 10 to 40 mm in length, and although they are attached almost spirally to their shoots they appear to be in a row on each side of the shoot. Yew fruits consist of a seed about 6 mm in length surrounded by a scarlet cup-shaped fleshy coat called an aril. Although the seeds themselves are known to be poisonous, the aril is not.

A native of Ireland, the yew is rare in the wild and occurs mainly in woods and rocky places and cliffs in the west (especially the Burren and Kerry) and in the north. Evergreen; flowers in March.

ANGIOSPERMS – THE FLOWERING PLANTS

PLATANACEAE – THE PLANE FAMILY

London Plane • *Platanus x hebrida* • *Plána Londan*

The London plane is a frequent street tree in Ireland. It is easily recognised by its peeling bark which is ideal for the city environment. By the time the bark is dirty and grimy with pollution it is dropped as large flakes like peeling scabs. It is also easy to prune without killing the tree, which then sprouts freely again.

Its leaves are like those of the maple, similar to the sycamore but spikier. It can also be distinguished from maples by its alternate leaves and by its enlarged leaf-stalk bases. Maples have opposite leaves. Its flowers occur usually in two globular heads which hang on long stalks. The fruits develop in the winter and are spiky, globular and rather woody. Deciduous; flowers from June to July.

ULMACEAE – THE ELM FAMILY

Elms have long been important street, timber and hedgerow trees. Today, their populations have been devastated by Dutch elm disease, which spread like wildfire through the countryside wiping out every mature tree in most districts. The disease is caused by a fungus and is spread from tree to tree by a beetle. The fungus blocks the sap vessels of the tree, first killing individual branches and then the whole tree.

Nowadays, most elms found are multi-stemmed scrubby trees that have arisen as suckers sprouted from the bases of diseased trees. The identification of elm species is not easy, even for experts. The identification of suckers can be almost impossible.

Elm flowers are small, in dense reddish-brown clusters and open before the leaves in spring. Their fruits are composed of a single seed, completely surrounded by a leafy green wing, with a deep notch at the top.

English Elm • *Ulmus procera* • *Leamhán gallda*

The English elm grows to be a tall, massive and very erect tree. It has leaves up to 8 cm long, smaller than the next species, rough on their upper surface and longer leaf-stalks (4 to 6 mm) than the wych elm.

Ulmus minor (or *U. carpinifolia*), the small-leaved elm (Leamhán mion), is an introduction to Ireland. It is less frequently seen than the next species. It has leaf-stalks 6 to 12 mm long, hairless or nearly hairless twigs (the other species have hairy twigs) and smooth upper surfaces to its leaves.

The timber of the elm is one of the most prized. It is very resistant to splitting and therefore ideal for furniture (and coffins). It is slow to rot in water when kept wet and thus the first water pipes from the Middle Ages onwards were made from elm. Indeed, many of the fine and ancient elms in Dublin, now gone, were planted first for this purpose and only survived because lead pipes became popular instead, only to be killed by disease recently. Deciduous; flowers from March to April.

Irish Elm, Wych Elm • *Ulmus glabra* • *Leamhán sléibhe*

The wych elm is a large tree with spreading branches. It has been commonly planted in most areas but is rare as a native, except in remoter parts of the north-west and west where pockets of trees unaffected by disease still occur. Leaves are large (10 to 12 cm long), undivided and roughly toothed along their edge, broadly oval and pointed with very asymmetrical bases and rough upper surfaces. Deciduous; flowers from March to April.

MYRICACEAE – THE MYRTLE FAMILY

Bog Myrtle • *Myrica gale* • *Roideóg*

Bog myrtle is the most characteristic bushy species of Irish bogs and is also found on some lake shores. A native, it is common in most of the west although it becomes rarer towards the east. It is a small bushy species which obtained its name from the myrtle-like aroma given off by its shoots when crushed. It was formerly used as a source of candle wax which gave off a delicious perfume as it burned. As a rustic bedding in the Middle Ages, it was a useful species to keep away fleas and was used to flavour beer before hops became the norm. An old tradition in Ireland says that the bog myrtle was once a great tree but was condemned to the bogs as a scruffy little shrub because it had been used to make the cross for Christ's crucifixion.

It grows to a height of about 1 metre (3.3 feet), is deciduous and has hairless, long (6 cm) and narrow (2 cm), dark green, slightly glossy leaves. Its flowers are borne in catkins appearing in early spring before the leaves open. Male and female flowers occur on separate catkins; the male catkins are about 15 mm long and the female ones shorter, up to 6 mm. Deciduous; flowers from April to May.

FAGACEAE – THE BEECH FAMILY

Beech • *Fagus sylvatica* • *Feá*

Beech is not native in Ireland although magnificent native beech woods occur as close as south-east England. Nevertheless, pollen fossils of beech have been found near Gort, County Galway, dating from a warm period many thousands of years earlier, suggesting that it once was a native tree. Not being as frequent here, beech timber never gained the importance in Ireland that it had in England where it was widely used, especially for furniture.

Beech can grow to a height of up to 40 metres (130 feet) and has a characteristic smooth silvery grey bark. Its leaves are alternate, short-stalked, oval and entire, up to 10 cm long and 6 cm broad. They open a brilliant green with a fringe of silvery, silky hairs along their edges. In autumn they turn to attractive shades of yellow and red before falling. The long, narrow, brown, dormant winter buds are borne on fine slender twigs. The small male flowers appear in short catkins and the small female flowers in clusters of twos and threes. When ripe, the fruits occur as paired triangular-shaped nuts surrounded by a spiny husk or woody sheath that grows up from the base of the female flowers and then splits into four lobes to release the nuts. Deciduous; flowers from April to May.

Spanish Chestnut, Sweet Chestnut • *Castanea sativa* • *Castán*

The sweet chestnut is native to south-west Asia. It was probably introduced to southern Europe and North Africa by the Greeks and to the British Isles by the Romans as a food source. Its nuts are still widely collected and used in Europe; in Corsica they are a staple food. Their kernels are dried and ground into a flour. Sadly, in Ireland the nuts do not often reach a very worthwhile size. The nuts can be boiled or roasted. The sweet chestnut has been widely planted in Ireland, especially in large gardens, parks and estate woodlands. It occasionally seeds itself.

It can grow to be an enormous and ancient tree, up to 30 metres (100 feet) tall with a trunk of huge girth. Its bark is covered by deep and regular fissures which weave their way around the trunk in a spiral. Its large leaves (up to 20 cm long) are dark green and glossy, narrow (about 7 cm across), tongue-shaped with holly-like points at the end of each vein. When young the leaves have a yellow "fur" underneath which later disappears. In summer, the tree produces creamy white male and female flowers in long catkin-like spikes. When the fruits ripen they are globular and very spiky to touch and contain one, two or three brown nuts, pointed at one end. Deciduous; flowers from June to July.

OAKS

Before the face of Ireland was changed by human settlement and agriculture, oak woods were the dominant vegetation and probably covered most of the land, everywhere except on bogs, high mountain slopes and in some coastal habitats. There are two native oaks in Ireland as well as a range of cultivated species found mainly in parks and larger gardens. The best known of these exotics is the holm or evergreen oak, *Quercus ilex*, native to the Mediterranean region.

Oak timber is still the most widely used and prized temperate hardwood. It has been used for furniture and ship building. Charcoal from oak timber was used for iron smelting and a multitude of other purposes. The finest whiskey is matured in oak barrels while oak bark was used for leather tanning. Oak leaves make tolerably good wine. Roasted acorns can be used as a coffee substitute and leprechauns even use acorns to make the pipes they smoke.

English Oak, Pedunculate Oak • *Quercus robur* • *Dair ghallda*

A native of Ireland, the pedunculate oak, *Q. robur*, is found on the better Irish soils but only a few midland woods survive. It grows up to be a tall tree, ultimately somewhat taller than the common oak. It has pale grey bark marked with narrow vertical fissures. Its leaves are similar in shape to the sessile oak but are generally smaller (up to 10 cm long); furthermore, they lack a stalk, are hairless underneath and have two small upturned lobes, called auricles, at the leaf-base. The male flowers are in bunches of very slender catkins 2 to 5 cm long and the female flowers are small and at the ends of the shoots. The acorns have a long stalk usually between 4 and 8 cm long, a useful characteristic to distinguish them from *Q. petraea*. Deciduous; flowers in May.

Sessile Oak • *Quercus petraea* • *Dair ghaelach*

The native common oak, *Q. petraea*, covered the upland, western and northern parts of Ireland, even on the poorer soils. It was and is less common in the midlands and in lowland areas. The best remaining oak woods are those in Killarney, County Kerry.

It is a tree up to 40 metres (130 feet) tall with grey bark marked with narrow, shallow fissures. Its leaves are more or less oval but with five to nine deep rounded lobes on each side, about 12 cm long and 7 cm wide with a leaf-stalk of about 2.5 cm. Its leaves are quite leathery, glossy green above and have rather a pale grey-green and hairy underside. Its male flowers are in catkins 5 to 8 cm long while the female flowers are small and borne at the ends of the shoots. The acorns (fruits) are about 3 cm long and may or may not have very short stalks. Deciduous; flowers in May.

BETULACEAE – THE BIRCH FAMILY

There are two native birches in Ireland. Both are attractive, elegant and slender trees. They are "colonist" trees, being often amongst the first trees to become established in a new site. The two Irish species are not always easy to distinguish, even for an expert. They often cross to produce hybrids which may be intermediate in morphology between the two. Birch has had many uses in the past in Ireland. In prehistoric times the trees were laid down to make trackways through marshy ground and their bark used to waterproof floors. The timber is not much used now but can make attractive veneers and has been employed for cotton reels, herring barrels, plywood, clogs and even modern aeroplane propellers. Birch twigs are also flexible and strong, ideal for use in corporal punishment!

Silver Birch • *Betula pendula* • *Beith gheal*

The silver birch is a tall, slender and attractive tree up to 30 metres (100 feet) with silvery white peeling bark. Its delicate branches are gently drooping at their tips. Young shoots are hairless and covered with slightly raised pale green resin-filled glands. The leaves are 2.5 to 7 cm long, oval to somewhat triangular in shape with long points and edged with sharp double teeth. The catkins appear at the same time as the leaves. The male catkins are 30 to 60 mm long and occur at the ends of the branches while the female ones are 15 to 35 mm and are produced along the shoots.

Widely planted in gardens, hedges and estate woods, the silver birch is also used as a street tree in Ireland. It appears as a rare native tree in parts of the midlands and south, beside lakes, in scrubby woods, bogs and on sandy soils, and occurs throughout Europe except in the drier and warmer parts of the south. Deciduous; flowers from April to May.

Downy Birch • *Betula pubescens* • *Beith chlúmhach*

This is a slender small tree or shrub up to about 25 metres (80 feet). It has brown, grey or rarely off-white peeling bark and spreading branches which do not droop at their tips. Young shoots are usually covered in soft down and are without resin glands, although, in the west, some trees can be found which are more or less hairless and which have brown resin glands and so may seem similar to the silver birch. Its leaves are up to 55 mm long, oval to triangular but more rounded than the previous species and with a shorter point. Their edges have irregular teeth. The catkins are similar to those of the silver birch but have scales that are spreading or curved upwards. Both species have seeds with broad membrane-like wings. Deciduous; flowers from April to May.

Common Alder • *Alnus glutinosa* • *Fearnóg*

The common alder is a smallish, often rather inconspicuous and overlooked tree. It is very widespread in Europe, Asia and North Africa and common throughout Ireland in damp and moist habitats. It often grows on stream, river and lake shores and banks, thriving in boggy soils and in moist woodlands.

As a timber tree it is little used now. In Britain it was used to make clogs as its timber is a poor conductor of heat. Its wood is useful and long-lasting in moist situation; indeed much of the city of Venice rests on alder piles.

Its leaves are dark green, round or broadly oval with bluntly toothed edges, 4 to 7 cm across. Separate male and female catkins are produced in early spring. The long male catkins are dark purple in colour and drooping in clusters generally of three to five. The female cones open later and are short and ovoid, dark brown and woody when ripe. These female catkins persist on the tree after the leaves have dropped, which themselves can stay on the tree until winter. The alder is not a very remarkable tree and in Ireland was often regarded as unlucky. Nevertheless, it has a quiet, self-assured dignity and grows well even in the most apparently unfavourable situations.

A close relative, although not a native, the grey alder, *Alnus incana* (*Fearnóg liath*), is occasionally planted and gone wild in a few areas. It has toothed and pointed leaves that are paler underneath than those of *A. glutinosa*. Deciduous; flowers in March.

Hornbeam • *Carpinus betulus* • *Crann sleamhain*

The hornbeam is native to the south-eastern counties of Britain but has been widely planted in Ireland, especially in estate woodlands. It is a popular species for high-class hedges. In a few areas it has seeded itself in the wild. It gains its name from its timber which is as hard as horn and was formerly used for many of the toughest tasks for which wood was required, such as cogs, pulleys and wood screws, skittles, mallets and brush backs. It is sometimes called "iron-wood". In England, some ancient hornbeam coppice woodlands still survive but in Ireland its role has probably been purely an ornamental one.

Hornbeam most frequently grows as a shrub, but when it becomes a tree it has a distinctive fluted trunk and smooth grey bark. Its leaves are oval in shape, toothed and pointed about 8 cms long by 5 cm broad, and more or less hairless. Flowers occur in catkins: the male catkins are 3 cm long and the female catkins up to 7 cm long with conspicuous long green bracts (which turn brown before falling) at the base of which are the small nuts. Deciduous; flowers from April to May.

Hazel • *Corylus avellana* • *Coll*

One of the most widespread woodland plants in Ireland is the hazel. It is typically a bushy multi-stemmed shrub between 1 to 6 metres (3 to 20 feet) tall in oak and ash woods but may rarely become a small tree. It was widely used for coppice to provide slender sticks for many purposes: fences, fuel, hurdles, hoops for barrels (before these were replaced by metal bands). Their nuts are excellent to eat, although there is no commercial production of them in Ireland that I know of. The hazel has always been a special tree in Ireland, used to ward off evil spirits and fairies. A hazelnut carried in the pocket was said to keep away lumbago and rheumatism.

Hazel leaves are alternately arranged, rather wrinkled, about 10 cm long, oval to almost round with a pointed tip and jaggedly double-toothed edge, light green and softly hairy. The twigs are also hairy and covered with reddish, slightly sticky (glandular) hairs. Male catkins are about 8 cm long, bright yellow and hanging down like lambs' tails but in clusters of up to four. The female catkins are much smaller, like tiny buds 5 mm long from which the bright red styles protrude. The fruits ripen as brown hard-shelled nuts about 1.5 cm long contained in a shaggy leaf-like cup.

A native of Ireland, hazel occurs commonly in hedgerows and woodlands and sometimes as dense thickets where it can be the dominant species, such as in the hazel scrubs of the Burren in County Clare. Deciduous; flowers from February to March.

SALICACEAE – THE WILLOW FAMILY

Aspen • *Populus tremula* • *Crann creathach*

On a breezy day the aspen is an easy tree to identify. Its leaf-stalks are flattened in an unusual way, from side to side, allowing the leaves to "shake like an aspen" and to rustle noisily in the wind. The aspen can grow to be a tree of up to 20 metres (65 feet) tall with smooth grey bark, but it often occurs as a suckering shrub in hedgerows. A native of Ireland, it is commonest in the west and north of the country in hedgerows and rocky and wild areas, generally on the poorest soils. It is much less frequent in the east and south and where it occurs it has usually been planted.

Its twigs are dull greyish brown and more or less hairless. The leaves are alternate, 1.5 to 8 cm long and 3 to 5 cm across, ranging from broadly oval to almost circular, roughly and irregularly toothed, quite pale green in colour and lighter underneath. The leaves on young suckers may vary more in shape and tend to be hairy and more regularly toothed. Catkins are 5 to 8 cm long and male and female ones occur on separate trees. The male catkins have reddish purple anthers and the female catkins have pink stigmas. The timber of the aspen is used for making matches and wooden matchboxes as it is light and easy to work.

Populus x canescens, the grey poplar (*Poibleog lia*), is a hybrid between the white poplar, *P. alba*, and the aspen. It is quite commonly planted and well established in many sites, especially in woods and hedges. It differs from the aspen by having more deeply divided leaves and lots of grey hairs on the leaf undersides. It spreads easily by suckers. Deciduous; flowers from February to March.

Black Poplar • *Populus nigra* • *Poibleog dhubh*

The black poplar may be a native Irish tree, although a rare one. It has been found especially in the midlands, predominantly in hedgerows in wet farmland near deep water-filled ditches, particularly along the River Shannon. It is a tall tree growing up to 35 metres (115 feet) with rough fissured dark grey bark. Its twigs are a shiny orange-brown, smooth and more or less hairless. The leaves are triangular oval, 5 to 10 cm long with toothed edges, bright glossy green on top and paler beneath. The leaf-stalks are flattened from side to side, like those of the aspen but less markedly so. Male and female flowers (in catkins) occur on separate trees. The male catkins have distinctive crimson anthers and the female catkins have green stigmas. The catkins open 3 to 5 cm long and gradually elongate as they ripen.

The most familiar and commonly planted variety in Ireland is the Lombardy poplar, *P. nigra var. italica*. It is tall, upright and narrow. Lombardy poplars are often planted in long avenues, a use for which they are particularly badly suited as they are fragile and mature quickly but then may become dangerous. Deciduous; flowers from March to April.

White Poplar • *Populus alba* • *Poibleog gheal*

The white poplar is a distinctive, attractive and strong-growing spreading tree usually 15 to 20 metres (50 to 65 feet) and rarely up to 40 metres (130 feet). It prefers moist soft ground but often leans as a result. Numerous suckers usually grow around well-established trees which can become quite a nuisance for gardeners. It is native to central and south-east Europe and extends eastwards to central Asia.

It has grey or blackish bark, often fissured lower down and smooth further up the trunk. Its young shoots and twigs are densely covered in white hairs. The leaves of the white poplar are very distinctive and striking even from a distance: shaped like maple leaves, 3 to 10 centimetres long and wide, dark green on top and densely covered with pure white hairs underneath. Most if not all the Irish trees are female. Their catkins are 3 to 5 cm long, brown and hairy, with greenish stigmas. Deciduous; flowers from February to March.

WILLOWS

There are more than a dozen willows found in the wild in Ireland, although not all are natives. They vary from small shrubs to several large trees. Most thrive in the wettest soils, in bogs, ditches and river banks but many of the common species will grow almost anywhere and are easy to cultivate, rooting easily from cuttings, no matter which way up they are planted. All willows have catkins with male or female flowers without petals or sepals. Another characteristic they share is the single scale that surrounds each bud, most noticeable in winter.

The identification of different willow species is not easy, especially as most cross freely with each other to form hybrids which may be intermediate between their parents in morphology. Hybrids between *Salix cinerea*, *S. aurita* and *S. caprea* are very common.

Crack Willow, Withy • *Salix fragilis* • *Saileach bhriosc*

Introduced into Ireland, this is a very fast-growing tree that can grow to a height of 25 metres (80 feet). It gains its name by having brittle twigs and branches that can easily be broken off with a "crack". Its twigs are generally yellow-brown in colour. When planted at the water's edge, a tangled mass of conspicuous red vein-like roots often grows into the water. It is often pollarded to sprout a mass of slender shoots ideal for basketmaking. It is commonly planted and occurs on river and stream banks, ditches and many wet habitats on marshy soils.

Its leaves are about five times as long as broad, lanceolate, with a finely toothed edge, often rather blue-green underneath usually 7 to 10 cm long, having silky hairs when young and then becoming hairless. Its catkins are long and drooping and appear at much the same time as the leaves. The male catkins are 2.5 to 6 cm long and the females 3 to 7 cm. Its stipules are long and narrow. Deciduous; flowers from April to May.

Eared Willow • *Salix aurita* • *Crann sníofa*

The eared willow is a shrub from 1 to 3 metres (3–10 feet) in height with many spreading branches. Its leaves are dull grey-green in colour and very wrinkled on their upper surface, grey and hairy underneath, one and a half to three times as long as broad, 2 to 3 cm long, and vary in shape from oblong to oval. Catkins are ovoid in shape, erect, 2 to 3 cm long, appearing before the leaves. Stipules are large, leafy and toothed.

A native of Ireland, this is a common shrub, especially of mountain and moorland, occurring on stream banks, field margins and by ditches and in damp scrubby woods. Deciduous; flowers from March to April.

Goat Willow • *Salix caprea* • *Sailchearnach*

This is a large shrub or small tree growing up to 10 metres (32 feet) tall, and occasionally more. Its leaves are dark green, hairless and relatively smooth above but wrinkled and covered with grey down underneath, oval to oblong or almost round, shortly pointed, up to 13 cm long, and about one and a half times as long as broad. Stipules are small and ear-shaped. Its catkins are 15 to 25 mm long and appear before the leaves. It is one of the most easily recognised willows in Ireland with its large and broad leaves.

This species was cut on Palm Sunday in Ireland, and a staff of this willow carried on a journey was said to be lucky. It is native and a common species through the country, occurring on damp and rough ground, in woods and hedges, and not only in wet habitats. Deciduous; flowers from March to April.

Osier • *Salix viminalis* • *Saileánach*

This very vigorous shrub or tree, 3 to 6 metres (10 to 20 feet) tall, is often pollarded and cropped to give a head of long, straight flexible twigs used for basketmaking. Introduced to Ireland, it is widely planted and many of the mature trees seen are a relict of cultivation. Basketmaking was one of the most widespread rural crafts and Connemara and Lough Neagh were famed for the quality of their baskets.

Its leaves are long, up to 20 cm in length, eight to twenty times as long as broad, hairless above but covered with silvery, silky hairs beneath. Leaf edges are enrolled and slightly wavy. Its twigs are often yellowish brown. Catkins are 12 to 30 mm long, erect, appearing before the leaves. Stipules are very narrow.

The osier is common in all parts of Ireland. It is a conspicuous tree, occurring on riversides, banks and ditches. Deciduous; flowers from April to May.

Sally, Rusty Willow • *Salix cinerea* • *Saileach rua*

The sally is a robust shrub or small tree up to 10 metres (32 feet) tall. Its twigs are downy when young and become hairless as they mature. The leaves are rather variable in shape, oval to lanceolate, two to three and a half times as long as broad, slightly downy on top (but not wrinkled like the eared willow), blue-green below with variously coloured hairs. Leaf edges are inrolled and toothed. Ear-shaped stipules are usually present but are quite small. Catkins are 20 to 30 mm long and appear before the leaves.

A native to Ireland, two subspecies of this occur: subsp. *oleifolia*, the rusty willow, and subsp. *cinerea*, the grey willow. However, they are difficult to distinguish, though the former tends to have rusty red hairs under the leaves while the latter has grey hairs.

This is probably the commonest Irish willow, occurring in hedges, field margins, by ditches, streamside and river banks and in scrubby woodlands. Deciduous; flowers from March to April.

White Willow • *Salix alba* • *Saileach bhán*

The white willow is a beautiful pyramid-shaped tree up to 25 metres (80 feet) tall with grey-green foliage. It is similar to the withy except that it has branches that are more erect, and also lacks the fragile twigs and shorter, less drooping catkins. This species is also often pollarded. A distinct variety, var. *caerulea*, is the cricket bat willow with more blue-green coloured leaves and upright branches, and another, var. *vitellina*, is highly decorative with bright yellow or orange twigs. White willow bark was widely used for tanning leather.

The leaves of the white willow are lanceolate, narrower than those of the crack willow, about ten times as long as broad, 5 to 10 cm long, and are covered with white silky hairs on both the upper and lower surfaces. An introduced species, this tree is common throughout Ireland in hedges, river and stream banks and in a wide range of wet soil habitats. Deciduous; flowers from April to May.

ERICACEAE – THE HEATH AND HEATHER FAMILY

Rhododendron • *Rhododendron ponticum* • *Ródaideandrón, Róslabhras*

A large range of rhododendron species and hybrids are grown in Irish gardens. They grow best in acid (lime-free) soils and occur in a wide range of colours.

Most garden rhododendrons are native to the Himalayas. However, *R. ponticum* comes from Turkey and from a small area in Spain. During at least one warm period in the Ice Age, *R. ponticum* was found naturally in Ireland, but when the ice returned the species was pushed south and left to survive only in these two widely separated localities. It returned during the 19th century when it was planted in woodland demesnes to provide cover for pheasants. It certainly liked Ireland's woodlands and wet boggy mountainsides and so quickly spread by seed and vegetatively to colonise many wild habitats that it is now regarded as a beautiful but dangerous weed.

R. ponticum can grow to 3 metres (10 feet) tall and is an evergreen shrub. Its leaves are dark green, oblong and about 12 by 6 cm in size. The numerous large (about 5 cm across) purple flowers are clustered together in heads at the ends of the shoots. Evergreen; flowers from May to June.

Strawberry Tree • *Arbutus unedo* • *Caithne*

The strawberry tree is a large shrub or medium-sized evergreen tree native to the Mediterranean coast of Europe, Brittany and Ireland. It is found rarely in Cork and Kerry and by Lough Gill in Sligo, but its Irish stronghold is around Killarney in County Kerry.

It is generally found on dry soil between rocks, in woodland margins and on islands and lake shores where most specimens are probably extremely ancient. It is also a popular garden plant usually grown as a bushy shrub. It has alternate oval leaves which are slightly toothed, 5 to 8 cm long, leathery and hairless. When mature, the tree has a reddish bark that is papery and flakey. Its flowers are white and like those of lily-of-the-valley, sometimes tinged with green or pink, in drooping clusters. These are followed by fruits that are a rich red colour, rough-skinned and round. They look very like strawberries, attractive looking and edible when ripe. However, the species name "unedo" implies that eating one fruit would be more than enough. Fruit and flower clusters hang on the tree together in early winter, as the previous year's fruit matures just as the present year's flowers bloom.

During the Middle Ages in Ireland it is said to have been a popular tree with charcoal burners and may have been exterminated from many areas with woodland clearance. The Irish name, *Caithne*, occurs occasionally, especially in the west.

The strawberry tree is one of Ireland's few native evergreens and is a most interesting plant. It is not native to Britain. The English botanist, John Parkinson, referred to it in his *Theatrum Botanicum*, published in 1640, reporting it remarkable that this tree grew in Ireland "of its own accord". Thomas Molyneux recorded in 1696, presumably with displeasure, that these trees, which did not grow in any "neighbouring kingdoms", were being cut up for fuel. There is one theory that the strawberry tree was first brought to Ireland from southern Europe by early monks, but this is thought to be unlikely. The tree is referred to in Brehon laws of the 8th century together with elder, blackthorn and some others.

The strawberry tree is more interesting than beautiful. It grows taller in Ireland than it does on the continent, and looks straggly and awkward out of the fruiting season, though the reddish bark is handsome. It is cultivated in large gardens for its striking fruit, and looks decorative at Christmas time if surrounded by more compact shrubs. There is a bushier variety "Croomei", with deep pink flowers. Evergreen; flowers from September to October.

GROSSULARIACEAE – THE CURRANT FAMILY

Escallonia • *Escallonia rubra var. macrantha*

This common evergreen shrub is often grown as a hedge. It can reach a height of more than 3 metres (10 feet) but never becomes a tree. Native to Chile, it was introduced to the British Isles in 1846. It is quite tolerant of salt and is therefore frequent in mild coastal areas.

Its leaves are alternate, oval in shape, glossy green on top and sticky with tiny glands underneath. The leaves have toothed edges and are about 8 cm long and 5 cm broad. The flowers occur throughout the summer and have five rosy red petals about 1.5 cm long and broad, arranged in long (about 10 cm) heads at the ends of the branches. Evergreen; flowers from June to September.

There are three other hedge plants common in Ireland that might be confused with this and are worthy of note. Privet, *Ligustrum ovalifolium* is the first. "Hedge", *Lonicera nitida*, from China, with small roundish dark green leaves about 1 cm long, is a rather dull shrub but makes a useful and neat hedge. Another, *Griselinia littoralis*, is a very fast-growing species from New Zealand. It has large oval to round leaves about 11 cm long by 7 cm broad, markedly yellowish green in colour.

ROSACEAE – THE ROSE FAMILY

Blackberry, Bramble • *Rubus fruticosus* • Dris

Blackberries are deciduous or semi-evergreen shrubs with prickly and woody scrambling stems. New shoots are produced from the base each year which lengthen and strengthen during their first year, then flower, fruit and die in their second year. After that the dead branches provide a useful skeleton through which the next year's shoots can grow, creating a dense and often impenetrable jungle. Like the shoots, blackberry leaves are prickly and are divided into three to five leaflets, very variable in shape and size. Their flowers are 20 to 30 mm broad, white or pink. The familiar fruits, made up of lots of separate fleshy segments each containing a single seed, change from green to red and finally ripen to purplish black.

A native, blackberry bushes occur abundantly in Ireland. They have the ability to produce seeds without having to be pollinated and so each bush is genetically isolated and any chance change in the genes can give rise to a new micro-species. Over 2,000 such micro-species have been named and described, making the group a nightmare for botanists. Deciduous/semi-evergreen; flowers from June to August.

Dog Rose • *Rosa canina* • *Feirdhris*

Roses are probably the world's most popular garden plants and there are about a dozen wild roses native to Ireland. Most occur in hedges, scrubs and thickets. All are upright or straggling shrubs with prickly stems and leaves divided into five to nine toothed leaflets. They have large flowers and leafy green sepals behind the petals, each sepal with five teeth. In the centre of the flowers are numerous stamens and the female parts are sunk into the area at the base of the petals, which swells and becomes fleshy in fruit.

The dog rose is the commonest Irish species. The flowers are exquisite and decorate hedges throughout Ireland in midsummer. It has upright and arching stems with thick, curving prickles and hairless leaflets. Its large flowers are scented and usually pink (sometimes white), occurring singly or in small groups. Its fruits are scarlet oval.

The most frequent other species are as follows. *R. arvensis*, the field rose, has very long stems with fewer prickles and pure white flowers. It is commonest in the midlands and south-east but rare elsewhere. *R. pimpinellifolia*, the Scotch or burnet rose, is very bushy and squat, seldom up to 1 metre (3.2 feet) tall, with numerous prickles on the stems and small flowers. It is generally found in sand dunes and rocky places near the sea. *R. tomentosa*, the harsh downy-rose, has straight or almost straight prickles, rather bright flowers and leaves smelling strongly of resin. It is widely distributed but nowhere abundant.

Rose fruits (hips) are worth collecting to make syrup or wine. Their flesh is full of vitamin C. They must not be confused with the red berries of hawthorn which are indigestible. The hips contain lots of seeds covered in tiny, rather nasty, hairs which must be strained out through a very fine jelly bag. Evergreen; flowers from June to July.

Sloe or Blackthorn • *Prunus spinosa* • *Draighean*

This is a dense shrub up to 6 metres (20 feet) tall with almost black branches. Many short side shoots are produced which become thorns. Leaves are oval, 1 to 4 cm long, slightly hairy when young but more or less hairless when mature, and faintly toothed. Blackthorn flowers early in the spring, before the leaves have opened. Flowers are pure white, almost without stalks, and 1 to 2 cm across singly or in pairs. The fruits are blue-black and resemble miniature plums, about 1.5 cm across, but never become sweet and tasty.

Native to Ireland, blackthorn is a common tree in hedges and woods. It sometimes forms almost pure and extremely dense scrub. It is not very tolerant of deep shade and tends to die out when overtopped by larger trees.

Blackthorn was traditionally made into strong sticks or tough shillelaghs; sometimes these were buried with corpses. The leaves were considered a cure for indigestion. Its fruits can be used for making wine or as a flavouring for gin. Sloe gin is made by filling a bottle with sloes, adding some sugar, topping up with gin and leaving for as long as possible before drinking. In the old days it was picked before Hallowe'en and considered unwholesome afterwards. Deciduous; flowers from March to May.

Wild Cherry • *Prunus avium* • *Crann siliní fiáin*

This attractive tree up to about 25 metres (80 feet) has smooth reddish brown peeling bark when mature. Younger plants have greyer bark. It produces some suckers from the base but less freely than do many other wild Irish cherries. Its leaves are oblong or oval with a toothed edge and a longish point, light dull green and hairless on top and sparsely hairy below, about 12 cm long and 5 cm broad. When young, the leaves are often slightly drooping at their tips. In autumn they can turn a rich red before dropping. Its flowers are white, usually shallowly cup-shaped and about 20 mm across, in small clusters on long slender stalks 1.5 to 4.5 cm long. Its fruits are round, about 1 cm in diameter, dark red, and normally bitter to taste.

The wild cherry is widespread in Ireland, mainly in old hedges and woodlands.

Elsewhere it occurs throughout Europe, North Africa and western Asia. Cherry wood was much used for cabinet-making, musical instruments and smoking pipes, as it is hard and dark reddish brown, similar to some tropical hardwoods such as mahogany. Wild cherries can be used in cooking but tend to have less flesh per fruit than their cultivated cousins and need more sugar. It is usually necessary to pick them before they are completely ripe as they are quickly cleared by the birds. They can also be used for cherry brandy or wine. Deciduous; flowers from April to May.

Wild Plum • *Prunus domestica* • *Baláiste*

The wild plum is a large tree or shrub up to 12 metres (40 feet) tall rather similar to *P. spinosa*, the blackthorn, but with brown bark and less spiny branches. Its leaves are 3 to 8 cm long, oval or somewhat elongated and, unlike the previous species, rather hairy. It has large white flowers which appear at about the same time as the leaves. *P. domestica* is an introduced species and is well distributed in the wild in Ireland, especially in the east and the midlands. The greengage and damson are cultivated varieties (subsp. *insititia*) derived from the wild plum. Wild plums are larger than sloes and are certainly better to eat but they are still rather bitter. They become sweeter after they have suffered a few frosts and can then be used in cooking or for wine.

Several hundred cultivated varieties of the plum are grown in gardens and orchards (subsp. *domestica*) and have larger fruit which can be yellow, red, purple, green or blue-black in colour. Deciduous; flowers from April to May.

Dwarf Cherry • *Prunus cerasus* • *Crann silíní searbha*

This species usually grows as a densely suckering shrub, but as a tree can reach a height of up to about 8 metres (25 feet). It is similar to *P. avium*, differing principally by having saucer-shaped flowers in smaller clusters of usually two to four, on shorter stalks than those of the previous species. Its leaves are also hairless and do not droop at their tips when young. Its fruits are bright red and always bitter to taste.

Garden, sour and morello cherries are all varieties of *P. cerasus* and many wild Irish trees are probably derived from these, sown in the wild by birds. The dwarf cherry is widely distributed in Ireland, mainly in hedges. It is frequent in some areas but in others quite rare. Its original wild origins are somewhat uncertain but it probably came from south-western Asia, perhaps arising as a hybrid cross between the wild cherry and another European or Asian species. Deciduous; flowers from April to May.

Bird Cherry • *Prunus padus* • *Donnroisc*

This is a shrub or tree up to about 15 metres (50 feet) tall but usually rather less, whose brown peeling bark has a strong unpleasant smell. Its leaves are 60 to 100 mm long, from oval to lanceolate in shape and with finely toothed edges, and are hairless or with white hair tufts along the leaf midrib underneath. The arrangement of the flowers in long, usually hanging or drooping heads (called racemes) makes this species easy to recognise. Flowers are 15 mm across, white and with a scent of almonds. Fruits are small, 6 to 8 mm, almost round and shiny black in colour.

The native bird cherry is quite rare in Ireland although widely distributed. It is located frequently in parts of the north-west, growing in woods and thickets, especially on damp soils in rocky places. Outside Ireland it occurs throughout Europe and is found across Asia to the Himalayas. It is widely planted for ornament and a number of cultivated forms are grown, one with semi-double flowers and another with purple leaves and pale pink flowers. Deciduous; flowers from May to June.

Portuguese Laurel • *Prunus lusitanica* • *Labhras portaingéalach*

This can be a tree up to 17 metres (55 feet), but is more commonly a bushy shrub up to 6 metres (20 feet), with dark green, hairless, glossy leaves, about 5 cm broad and 12 cm long, oval in shape with toothed edges and short points and short reddish stalks. Its flowers are in long heads (called racemes) 10 to 25 cm long, scattered along the shoots or occasionally at their ends. Flowers are white and about 1 cm across. The fruits are very dark purple and about 8 mm in length.

It is commonly planted in woods, especially in old demesnes, and in shrubberies. Portuguese laurel is native to Spain, Portugal and the islands of the Canaries, Madeira and the Azores where it forms interesting and ancient laurel woods. Evergreen; flowers from May to June.

Cherry Laurel • *Prunus laurocerasus* • *Labhras silíní*

This is a large and spreading fast-growing shrub or small tree up to 7 metres (23 feet). Its leaves are oblong, up to 20 cm long, dark green and glossy, pointed but with a hardly toothed edge. When bruised, the leaves have a bitter almond fragrance, derived from a chemical close to cyanide. Indeed, the leaves are deadly poisonous. The white flowers are borne in upright heads (called racemes) like the previous species but are smaller, about 8 mm across. Fruits are similar to those of *P. lusitanica*, small, turning from red to dark purple.

The cherry laurel is very commonly planted in gardens, woods, estate woodlands and shrubberies. It quite frequently self-seeds and grows wild in many parts, especially in the southern half of Ireland. Although it is native to eastern Europe and Asia Minor it has been widely cultivated in gardens in the British Isles for several centuries. Evergreen; flowers from April to June.

Crab Apple • *Malus sylvestris* • *Crann fia-úll*

This small tree or large shrub up to 10 metres (32 feet) tall has a grey-brown scaly and fissured bark when mature and reddish brown twigs that are often spiny. Its leaves are oval and toothed, hairless when mature and up to 4 cm long. Its flowers are pink and white, 2 to 3 cm across. Its fruits are the familiar crab apples, yellowish green, sometimes flushed with red, only 2 or 3 cm broad and looking like typical but miniature apples.

The native crab apple is widely distributed in Ireland, in hedges, woodlands and scrub, and is quite common in many districts. It occurs throughout Europe and reaches into south-western Asia. Its fruits are best in September or October and are used not raw as they are very bitter, but for making jelly (crab apple jelly sets quickly and easily), wine, cider and for a vinegar called verjuice that is used as one would lemon juice. Crab apple wood is good for carving, having a very even texture and an attractive rosy brown colour. It was formerly used for making printing blocks and the heads of golf clubs. Deciduous; flowers in May.

The cultivated apple is *Malus domestica*. It can be distinguished from the crab apple by its persistently hairy leaves and its flower stalks (pedicles) covered with woolly hairs. Although not native to Ireland, it is quite widely established in the wild, mainly in and around larger towns and cities, growing from pips in discarded apple cores.

Rowan, Mountain Ash • *Sorbus aucuparia* • *Caorthann*

Also called quicken tree, this is a slim and attractive tree with smooth grey bark, up to 20 metres (65 feet) but usually less. Its leaves are divided into about fifteen longish narrow leaflets with sharply toothed edges. Each leaflet is about 5 cm long and altogether a leaf is about 15 cm in length. The white or cream flowers are numerous and about 8 mm across and produced in dense heads. The clustered spherical fruits are scarlet, about 1 cm across, containing several seeds in the orange flesh.

A native of Ireland, the mountain ash is quite common throughout the country, growing in light soil by mountain streams and valleys, in woods and many rocky habitats. Although it grows at higher altitudes than any other Irish tree it is also a common ornamental tree in gardens and for street planting and occurs as a diverse range of cultivated varieties with variously coloured fruits and leaves. It is also found throughout Europe and into Asia Minor.

The rowan is widely featured in old Irish legends and traditions, and was an important tree in pre-Christian times, being held sacred by the Druids. It was supposed to have magic and protective qualities and was used as a talisman against evil and witchcraft. The rowan was used to prevent fires from being bewitched on May 1st, and on the same day a branch would be tied to the churn to prevent the milk from being stolen.

Its fruits, mixed with crab apples, are useful for wine and jelly. Rowan jelly is excellent with many meats. Deciduous; flowers from May to June.

Irish Whitebeam • *Sorbus hibernica* • *Bíoma bán*

The Irish whitebeam is a shrub or small tree up to about 6 metres (20 feet) high. It is found only in Ireland and is widely distributed in the west, midlands and east of the country, but rare in the north and south. It has oval, undivided leaves, very regularly toothed except at their base. It is hairless above and covered with white hairs underneath when the leaves first open. The hairs gradually turn to pale grey as the leaf matures. Its flowers are 12 to 15 mm across in dense heads and are followed in autumn by red fruits.

The Irish whitebeam is an attractive tree found in woods, hedges, rocky places and scrubs on limestone soils. Its berries are edible and best to use when they start to soften after several late autumn frosts. Deciduous; flowers from May to June.

Several other native whitebeams are found, each one broadly similar to the Irish whitebeam and rather difficult to distinguish from it. However, *Sorbus aria* is most widespread in County Galway and has a more markedly white underside to its leaves. *Sorbus rupicola* has leaf edges which are not toothed in their lowest third; it is rather rarely seen, only in the west and north. *Sorbus devoniensis*, a species with orange-brown fruits, is found only in the south-east and *Sorbus anglica*, a red-fruited species with rather divided leaves, is known only from around Killarney.

Cotoneaster • *Cotoneaster integrifolius (C. microphyllus)* • *Cotóinéastar mionduilleach*

A range of cotoneaster species is commonly grown in Ireland in gardens. They are native to much of Europe, except Ireland, as well as northern Asia and North Africa. All are shrubs with small, waxy, mostly evergreen leaves. One of the commonest that escapes into the wild is *C. integrifolius*, an Asian species, more generally known as *C. microphyllus*. It is a small shrub with prostrate or ascending branches up to 1 metre (3 feet) long. Its small, oblong, shiny evergreen leaves are 5 to 9 mm long. Its white flowers occur singly and are 8 to 10 mm across with five petals. The fruits are red and globular, 5 to 8 mm across.

This cotoneaster is widely distributed in Ireland, especially in the west, having become established mainly in rocky or gravelly habitats from bird-distributed seeds. Another species that is also seen both in gardens and the wild in Ireland is *C. horizontalis*, from China. It is deciduous and a more robust shrub with generally larger leaves and a characteristic herring-bone arrangement to its branches. Its flowers are in ones or twos but are otherwise similar to *C. integrifolius*. Evergreen; flowers from May to June.

Hawthorn • *Crataegus monogyna* • *Sceach gheal*

A bushy shrub or small tree up to about 15 metres (50 feet) tall with hairless twigs liberally covered with sharp spines up to 15 mm long. Its leaves are roughly triangular, 15 to 45 mm long but deeply divided into three to seven pointed lobes. The flowers are in clusters with five white (or more rarely pale pink) petals 8 to 15 mm across; they have pink or purple anthers. Its fruits are about 10 mm across, vary in colour from bright to dark red and contain a single seed.

Also called whitethorn or may tree, the native hawthorn is one of Ireland's most abundant shrubs occurring in woods, especially on their margins, in scrubs and in practically every rural hedge. For several centuries hawthorn has commonly been planted for hedges. If trimmed when young it quickly becomes a dense stock-proof barrier. Hedge-laying is an old country craft that is now, sadly, almost gone – this old rhyme may be a reason: "Here lies Giles Thorn, honest hedger and ditcher/Who was born poor, and never grew richer."

It has always been an important tree in Ireland, with great mystic and sacred connections. It grows by most holy wells, and rags are tied on it as offerings. Many people are terrified of digging up or cutting down a solitary thorn tree, perhaps because hawthorns are linked with sacred places, graves, hidden treasure, trysting places. Some say that the crown of thorns was a hawthorn. In any case, the flowering thorn tree symbolised the end of winter to many primitive peoples; this may have given it a sacred value from pagan times onward. The flowers have a sweet but stale smell and were considered unlucky to bring indoors because they were said to smell of the great plague of London or to be suggestive of sex.

The young spring leaves of hawthorn are edible and eaten by children as "bread-and-cheese". Its wood is too irregular to be much use but it is durable and tough. The red berries (haws) are indigestible and there is a tradition in Ireland that they cause jaundice. However, they can be used for making jelly or wine in the autumn. Deciduous; flowers from May to June.

FABACEAE (OR LEGUMINOSAE) – THE PEA FAMILY

Broom • *Cytisus scoparius* • *Giolcach sléibhe*

The broom grows as a shrub up to about 2 metres (6.5 feet) tall, has large, bright, lemon-yellow pea-like flowers and green branchlets. Its leaves are divided into three oval leaflets and arranged alternately on the five-angled shoots. However, the leaves are soon lost as the branchlets mature. Its flowers are about 2 cm long and its seed capsules are black, with brown hairs along the edges, and 2.5 to 4 cm in length.

Native to Ireland, it occurs in dry heathy places, open woods, on dry banks and roadsides and is widespread throughout the country but rarely common. It occurs through Europe, growing on light lime-free soils only. The broom obtained its name from the former use of its branches for making brushes. A rare prostrate form with silky leaves is found on a few coastal cliffs and is worth looking out for. A wide range of European species and cultivated varieties are grown in Irish gardens. Evergreen; flowers from May to June.

Gorse, Furze or Whin • *Ulex europaeus* • *Aiteann gallda*

When gorse is in flower, kissing is in fashion – so goes the old expression. The two species of gorse in Ireland flower at different times, one in spring, *U. europaeus*, and the other, *U. gallii*, in autumn, so there is rarely a week of the year when some flowers cannot be found.

The native *U. europaeus* is a very spiny and bushy shrub with blue-green branchlets and leaves reduced to small scales or thorns. It can grow to more than 2 metres (6.5 feet) tall. It is found throughout Ireland, especially in the east on lime-free soils in rough pastures, heaths and rocky places, but not in woodlands. In the west and on higher mountain slopes it is replaced by the next species. In some areas it was planted to form hedges.

Gorse was formerly used for fuel and was a good fodder source for stock once its spines had been crushed, usually with large stone rollers or wooden mallets. Gorse flower wine is, I am told, worth trying. Its flowers are golden yellow, sweetly scented and from 15 to 20 mm long, surrounded by a short hairy brown calyx. The seeds develop in a small pea-pod-like black capsule that when mature is similar in length to the flowers. During dry summer days one can often hear the cracking open of pods as they explode to disperse the seeds. It is widespread throughout western Europe and North Africa and introduced to many other parts of the world. Evergreen; flowers from April to June.

Ulex europaeus "strictus", a variety with erect branches and soft, flexible spines, was first discovered as a once-off chance freak plant in Northern Ireland in the 19th century. It is now a frequently grown garden plant.

Mountain Gorse, Western Gorse • *Ulex gallii* • *Aiteann gaelach*

The native mountain gorse is also a bushy shrub but is a smaller, darker green species than the previous one, less hairy and with smaller, deeper yellow flowers. It can also be distinguished by having only faintly furrowed spines whereas those of *U. europaeus* are deeply furrowed. Its seed pods are burst open in spring. It occurs distributed along the Atlantic coastal fringes of Europe, from Spain to Scotland. Evergreen; flowers from August to October.

ONAGRACEAE – THE WILLOWHERB FAMILY

Fuchsia • *Fuchsia magellanica* • *Fiúise*

Many people find it hard to believe that fuchsia is not a native plant in Ireland. It comes from Chile and Argentina but has long been used here in gardens and as a hedge plant. It is easy to grow from cuttings, tolerates strong winds and will grow well even in quite boggy or peaty soils, making it ideal for western Ireland.

Fuchsia forms a bushy and spreading shrub up to 3 metres (10 feet) tall, but never a tree. Its bark is a light yellowish brown and peeling. Its leaves are opposite, oval and toothed, about 2.5 to 6 cm long, with short stalks. Its distinctive drooping flowers are produced singly along the stems and consist of four bright red sepals arising from the end of a swollen tube and four deep purple petals from which protrude the eight long stamens. In autumn the fruits are black, fleshy, almost spherical berries 1.5 to 2 cm long.

The commonest variety found is var. *riccartonii*, which originally arose as a garden variety. It has fat spherical buds which pop when squeezed. A rarer variety, *magellanica* proper, has longer and thinner buds. Fuchsia does not tolerate too much frost and so is rarest in the midlands, east and north. Deciduous; flowers from July to September.

CORNACEAE – THE DOGWOOD FAMILY

Dogwood • *Cornus sanguinea* • *Conbhaiscne*

C. sanguinea grows to be a shrub up to 4 metres (13 feet) tall but is usually somewhat smaller. Its leaves are rather unpleasant smelling, arranged opposite each other on the shoots, oval to elliptical in shape, 4 to 10 cm long, covered on top and underneath with short, flattened, soft hairs. The leaves turn purple-red in autumn before they are dropped and new shoots also turn dark red then. Dogwood flowers are whitish with four petals, clustered together in dense, more or less flat-topped, heads. The fruits are dark purple to black and berry-like, 5 to 8 mm across.

The dogwood is rather rare in Ireland as a native and confined to limestone soils in woods, scrub and rocky places mainly in the midlands. It also occurs occasionally as a garden escape. Its fruits can be made into jam and have been used to flavour liqueurs in parts of Europe. Deciduous; flowers from June to July.

A closely related but non-native species, *C. sericea*, the red osier dogwood from eastern North America, is established quite widely in Ireland often on water margins, as an escape from gardens, parks and demesnes. It is also a deciduous shrub but spreads freely by numerous suckering shoots. It has white or creamy coloured flowers which are smaller than those of *C. sanguinea*.

CELASTRACEAE – THE SPINDLE-TREE FAMILY

Spindle-tree • *Euonymus europaeus* • *Feoras*

Worldwide there are over 175 species of *Euonymus*, widely distributed across Europe and Asia, most of them shrubs. The ubiquitous and dull, variegated evergreen shrub, *E. japonicus*, is well known and all too commonly grown as a hedging plant.

The only wild Irish spindle-tree is a small easily overlooked deciduous shrubby tree with smooth grey bark and shortly stalked, opposite, oval to lanceolate leaves, slightly toothed on their edges, and four-angled green twigs. The latter characteristic is the easiest way of identifying the species, winter or summer. It is an unremarkable species except when in fruit. The fruits are orange-red in colour and surrounded by a rose-pink fleshy sheath called an aril. In autumn, a spindle-tree well laden with fruits can be a most striking sight. Its flowers are small, inconspicuous and greenish, occuring in the axils of the leaves.

A native, *E. europaeus* is widespread, especially in the centre and parts of the west, but rarer in the east and north. It is commonest in woods, hedgerows and thickets and frequent in rocky places and lake shores, particularly on limestone soils.

Spindle-trees produce a durable white timber, formerly used for making spindles, viola bows, skewers and toothpicks. The whole plant is poisonous though. Deciduous; flowers from May to June.

AQUIFOLIACEA – THE HOLLY FAMILY

Holly • *Ilex aquifolium* • *Cuileann*

The native holly is a densely branched small tree or shrub that is widespread in Europe and North Africa. In Ireland, it is widespread in woodlands, especially oak woods, as an undergrowth tree and in hedges.

The slow-growing holly produces very hard and durable wood and is used for such purposes as tool handles. It makes an excellent fuel wood. As a winter decoration its use goes back in Ireland to pre-Christian times. The tree was regarded as "gentle" in Ireland and beloved of the fairies. Sprigs brought into the house were useful to ward off evil spirits which were especially wary of the scarlet fruits.

The berries are unpleasant tasting but apparently not poisonous. The leaves are alternate, hard, bright or dark green on their upper surfaces and with spiny buckled edges. The small white flowers are noticeably fragrant. Male and female flowers are produced on separate trees and so holly berries are only to be found on the females. The berries can last all winter until the following summer, unless cleared by birds, especially fieldfares in February, or if cut off by humans for Christmas. Evergreen; flowers from May to June.

RHAMNACEAE – THE BUCKTHORN FAMILY

Buckthorn *Rhamnus catharticus Paide bréan*

The native buckthorn is not a common plant in Ireland although in a few areas, particularly in the north and west, it is locally common. It grows on limestone soils as a shrub or small tree 4 to 6 metres (13 to 20 feet) tall, occurring in woods, scrub, river banks and rocky lake shores. It is a rather unremarkable tree without any easily recognisable features. Its branches are often rather spiny and arise in opposite pairs almost at right angles to the main stem. Its leaves are usually alternate, undivided, 3 to 6 mm long, oval or slightly elongated with a toothed edge. Its flowers are very small with four green petals. The fruits are black, berry-like and inedible. Deciduous; flowers from May to June.

A close relation, *Frangula alnus*, the alder buckthorn (*Draighean fearna*), is a much rarer native deciduous small tree or shrub of rocky or boggy habitats. Although it has been recorded in about half the Irish counties, it is nowhere common. It is similar in leaf to the buckthorn but it has five petals, is not spiny and its fruits are red, gradually turning black.

HIPPOCASTANACEAE – THE CHESTNUT FAMILY

Horse Chestnut • *Aesculus hippocastanum* • *Crann cnó capaill*

It is ironic that one of the most familiar Irish trees is not a native tree and indeed is rare and even endangered in the wild. The horse chestnut is native to parts of the Balkans, found in Greece, Albania and in a single site in Bulgaria. It has been grown in Ireland as an ornamental tree for over 200 years and although it is still commonly planted it has self-seeded and spread into wild habitats in woods and hedges throughout Ireland.

The horse chestnut grows to be a magnificent, large, spreading tree with broad leaves divided into five to seven leaflets. Its bark varies in colour from reddish brown to dark grey-brown. Its twigs and branches are robust and in winter bear large, sticky brown buds. In spring the tree produces large upright branched heads (panicles) of white flowers with five petals speckled with pink or yellow spots. In September the globular and spiny fruit capsules are produced containing one or two dark brown (chestnut-coloured!) fruits or "conkers".

The tree is little used except as an ornamental and for its conkers. Its timber is soft and pithy. The common name is said to be derived from the former use of its fruits having been ground up for horse feed, although as they contain copious amounts of the chemical saponin (a useful soap substitute) they cannot be very tasty, even for horses. Deciduous; flowers in May.

ACERACEAE – THE MAPLE FAMILY

Sycamore • *Acer pseudoplatanus* • *Seiceamar*

Although the sycamore is one of the most familiar Irish trees, it is not native, having been introduced to the British Isles in the 15th or 16th century. It grows to be a large and occasionally a magnificent tree with greyish bark. More often it is a small weedy tree of waste places, woods, hedges and gardens. Although native to the European mountains, it is completely happy in the Irish climate and indeed makes an excellent shelter-belt tree for coastal situations.

Sycamore produces a valuable pale creamy coloured wood. Sycamore wood table-tops maintain a smooth white surface despite constant scrubbing; it was also used for rolling pins, wooden spoons, the sides and backs of violins and is also a popular wood for carving.

The leaves are typically maple-shaped, 9 to 12 cm across, with five pointed lobes and a coarsely toothed edge. The flowers are small and greenish and occur in drooping heads; they are a useful source of early spring nectar for honey bees. The seeds are always popular with children as mini "helicopters", having two divergent membranous wings on each side of the two-jointed fruit. Deciduous; flowers from May to June.

A close relative, *A. campestre*, the field maple, also an introduction, is occasionally planted in hedges in the east. It has much smaller leaves.

ARALIACEAE – THE IVY FAMILY

Ivy • *Hedera helix* • *Eidhneán*

Although not strictly a tree or shrub, this native climber is included because it can become very woody, with stems up to 25 cm (10 inches) in diameter and sometimes climbing to more than 30 metres (100 feet) in height. It is unusual in that it produces its flowers in autumn, when they are often hungrily visited for their nectar by flies and wasps as the only flowers left at that time.

The stems of ivy are densely covered with clinging roots. The small flowers in rounded heads have five yellow-green petals, 3 to 4 mm long, and are followed by round black berries 6 to 8 mm in size. Ivy leaves are a glossy dark green, hairless and easily recognised by their characteristic five lobes, spread out somewhat like the fingers of a hand. The leaves of flowering branches are without lobes and more oval in shape. Ivy only flowers in the sun towards the top of whatever it is climbing on.

Ivy is common in woodlands, hedgerows, rocks, walls or creeping along the ground in shady woods or hedgebanks. Evergreen; flowers from October to November.

BUDDLEJACEAE - THE BUDDLEIA FAMILY

Butterfly bush • *Buddleia davidii* • *Tor an fhéileacáin*

This large shrub is a relative newcomer to Ireland. It is native to China where it was discovered by Augustine Henry, a famous Irish plants and forestry pioneer who first collected many important Chinese plants. Until the middle of this century buddleia was grown only in gardens, but over the last few decades it began an explosive invasion of many urban habitats throughout the country. Now it is one of the commonest weeds of Ireland's larger towns and cities, especially Dublin. Spreading easily by seed, it is an important food plant for butterflies which are attracted to the nectar-rich flowers.

B. davidii grows up to 4 metres (13 feet) tall and has long (10 to 20 cm) lanceolate leaves, green on top, white and felty underneath. The flowers are lilac-mauve, small and tubular with an orange eye, borne in massed conical heads. Fruits are small, dry, brown capsules.

Several different attractive colour varieties of B. davidii are grown in gardens, from white to purple, as well as some other related species. Deciduous; flowers from June to September.

OCEACEAE – THE ASH FAMILY

Ash • *Fraxinus excelsior* • *Fuinseóg*

A tall native tree up to 40 metres (130 feet) with grey bark, smooth when young but becoming grooved with interwoven fissures when older. Ash twigs are thick and grey with large conspicuous black buds in winter. The leaves are opposite and divided into nine to fifteen jaggedly toothed, long (about 7 cm), narrow leaflets. The flowers are tiny, purple and without petals or sepals and appear in dense clusters well before the leaves in spring. Male and female flowers often occur on separate branches. The fruits (called keys) are long and slim, 25 to 50 mm long, with a single membranous wing, ideal to catch the wind for easy distribution. They are produced in dense dangling clusters.

Ash is a common and often abundant tree of the Irish countryside, in woods and hedges. It grows best on deep, moist, lime-rich soils but is not very fussy about its habitat. It provides one of the most important native timbers, pale brown in colour, lightweight and flexible but very tough. It has been used for carts, furniture, ladders, table-tops and a range of sports implements such as tennis rackets and hurley sticks ("the clash of the ash") as it is fine grained and smooth to the hand. Ash wood is also good for fuel and even burns well when fresh and green. It is an altogether useful species and even its fruits can be eaten, if picked very young, boiled and pickled in vinegar. Deciduous; flowers from April to May.

Wild Privet • *Ligustrum vulgare* • *Pribhéad*

This is a semi-evergreen shrub that can grow up to about 4 metres (13 feet) tall, with young shoots that are densely covered by short hairs. It has opposite, shortly stalked, untoothed leaves, oblong to lanceolate in shape, pointed at their ends and 3 to 6 cm long. Its flowers are white, 4 to 5 mm in diameter with a long tube. The flowers are followed by shining black fruits 6 to 8 mm long. Wild privet is very rare in Ireland and only occurs naturally on a few cliffs and rocky habitats in four counties, as well as throughout Europe and North Africa. However, in Ireland it is also widespread as a planted species in hedges and gardens, mainly grown from cuttings. Its seeds germinate very slowly. Semi-evergreen; flowers from June to July

It could be easily confused with a closely related species, *L. ovalifolium*, the Japanese or garden privet, which is now more widely planted for hedges than its wild relative. Japanese privet can be distinguished by being more reliably evergreen, with broader leaves and hairless shoots. Variegated or yellow-leaved colour variants of the Japanese privet are also widely cultivated but are rather less strong-growing than the typical form.

CAPRIFOLIACEAE – THE ELDER FAMILY

Elder • *Sambucus nigra* • *Trom*

The elder is a tree or shrub up to 10 metres (33 feet) tall. It is easily recognisable by its grey to light brown corky and grooved bark. Second-year shoots are covered by numerous raised spots called lenticels. It often produces new shoots straight from the base which is just as well as it is a rather brittle tree whose branches collapse quite frequently. Its leaves are opposite and divided into five to nine leaflets resembling those of an ash. Each leaflet is 5 to 15 cm long and has a strong unpleasant smell. Its flowers are white and fragrant, very small and with five petals. They occur in dense flat-topped heads 10 to 25 cm across; they have pale yellow anthers. The fruits are black and berry-like when ripe and contain three seeds each. They are very juicy and succulent and full of dark red flesh that is ideal for wine making. When the soft pith is removed from the centre of young shoots, these can be cut and grooved to make quite satisfactory home-made flutes.

It was a custom in rural Ireland to scoop up clay from under an elder bush to soothe an aching tooth. Both the flowers and the fruit are used to make drinks; the flowers make a refreshing summer soft drink and the fruit a traditional wine. The fruit must not be muddled up with the very similar berries of the much smaller Danewort (Sambucus ebulus) which are poisonous.

The elder is native in Ireland but also widely planted. It is often associated with disturbed soils and is a frequent tree of waste grounds in town and cities, preferring soils rich in nitrogen that often accompany human settlements. It also occurs commonly in woods and hedges. Deciduous; flowers from June to July.

Guelder-rose • *Viburnum opulus* • *Caoir chon*

Guelder-rose is a deciduous shrub 2 to 4 metres (6 to 13 feet) tall that is widespread in Europe, Asia and just reaches North Africa. A native of Ireland, it occurs in woods, scrub and hedges and is frequent, particularly on moist soils.

Its leaves are 4 to 8 cm long with three or five pointed lobes and an irregularly toothed edge, turning reddish in autumn. It produces flat rather loose heads of white flowers some 5 to 10 cm across. The outer flowers are sterile, 15 to 20 mm across with large showy petals, there only to attract insects for pollination. The inner flowers are fertile and about half the size. Geoffrey Grigson in The Englishman's Flora suggests that the flowers have a fragrance of "crisply fried well-peppered trout" which is something I will take his word for. In autumn the flowers are followed by crimson berries that are not very popular with birds as they contain lots of bitter valerianic acid but can be used to make a tasty and tangy jelly if you add lots of sugar. Deciduous; flowers from June to July.

The snowball tree is a well-known garden plant that is a variant of this species. It only has sterile flowers which are clustered together in a globular head. Another close relative, V. *lanata*, the wayfaring tree, is an introduction and is occasionally planted in hedges in the east. It can be distinguished by its oval leaves and flower heads which only have fertile flowers.

Snowberry • *Symphoricarpos albus* • *Póirín sneachta*

This is a small, twiggy shrub widely planted in hedges and thence spreading by suckers, rarely by seed. It is a useful garden plant which thrives in shade and will tolerate very low temperatures and frost. It is native to North America.

Snowberry has small oval leaves and pinky white small tubular flowers in terminal heads. Its fruits are globular, 1 to 1.5 cm across, white marble-like and very conspicuous in winter especially when the leaves have dropped. The fruits are variously described as "edible" to "poisonous" in different reference books, so I would not chance eating them myself! Deciduous; flowers from June to September.

Chapter Six

WILD FLOWERS

INTRODUCTION

There is a new and thriving interest being taken in Irish wild flowers, perhaps because of the fashion for conservation.

This section will help people of different ages and stages to know more. In it there are descriptions of eighty plants – some of them are well-known favourites whilst others are unusual and especially rewarding. There are plants in Cork and Kerry that have their main home in south-west Europe (Wild London Pride and Greater Butterwort to name two) and these have been included. In the Burren in County Clare, plants like Spring Gentian and Mountain Avens, usually associated with high mountains, grow nearly down to sea level; these are described in the Spring and Early Summer sections.

The story of Irish plant discovery is fascinating. One can imagine the thrill felt by the keen amateur botanist, the Reverend Richard Heaton, when he found such numbers of gentians growing between Gort and Galway; this was before 1650. And in 1700 Edward Lhuyd, a Welshman of avid curiosity, was well rewarded after an exhausting journey. He was the first to discover in Ireland not only, among other plants, St Dabeoc's Heath (usually at home in south-west Europe), but also the pretty, yellow-flowered Shrubby Cinquefoil, rare in Britain, which he found growing on the banks of Lough Corrib.

Irish wild flowers are lavish in certain districts. In the north of Ireland, the shores near Giant's Causeway and the banks of Lough Neagh and Lough Erne are outstanding, as are, down the west coast, the slopes of Ben Bulben, the Roundstone district and the Burren. Further south, good hunting grounds are the lake shores of Killarney and the coast near Derrynane. But this leaves out too much; there are many prodigal areas.

To find wild flowers one must be energetic. Somebody once complained to me that "to see the flowers in the Burren you have to get out of the car!" You do indeed, and walk over the rocky pastures and limestone pavements. Some plants will grow obligingly on road verges. Many more will be on lake shores, sea cliffs and dunes, in marshes, on rock ledges, at the edge of woods, on moors – all well away from roads and even from footpaths.

This guide avoids arranging the flowers into families, as is so often done. They can be hard for the non-botanist to follow: how many people would think of looking up Wood Anemone in the Buttercup family, for instance? It is simpler to divide plants into seasons of flowering, and this is what has been done. The three sections are for plants flowering in spring, early summer and late summer. This is not a foolproof arrangement. A cold season will make every plant flower late, and plants growing on the north side of a hill will bloom later than plants on the south side. If the plant you look for is not in the section you expect, look in the adjoining one.

Plants are arranged alphabetically within the sections and are given their English, their botanical and where possible their Irish names. They are described in simple, unscientific language. Many of them have points of interest; they may have been used as cures or to ward off evil spirits – old wives' tales mostly, but fascinating. The cures must not be taken seriously; many plant treatments are extremely dangerous.

The world distribution of plants given in these texts is taken mainly from Clapham, Tutin and Warburg's *Flora of the British Isles*.

SPRING

Bilberry • *Vaccinium myrtillus* • *Fraochán*

Bilberry, or Fraughan, is a small deciduous shrub. The bell-shaped flowers are green, usually tinged with pink. The leaves are oval, slightly toothed and a bright green colour. The fruit is purplish black and edible. It is a twiggy plant, a member of the heath family. Bilberry grows on acid soil all over the country on heaths, moors and in open woods, and is a far more common plant than *Vaccinium vitis-idaea* (Cowberry) and *Vaccinium oxycoccos* (Cranberry). It is pollinated by bees. The flowers come out in April and May.

In the past bilberry twigs were cut to make into brooms. The berries are sweet and have traditionally been made into jam. Fraughan picking was an activity in many places every July, sometimes on a regular "Fraughan Sunday", when children were taken to help gather the fruit.

Bilberry grows on heaths and high ground in Britain, and on the mountains of Europe and northern Asia.

Bogbean • *Menyanthes trifoliata* • *Bearnán lachan*

Bogbean, or Buckbean, is an aquatic perennial of the Gentian family. The flowers grow in the form of a spike; they are a pretty pinkish white colour and have white hairs in a fringe. The leaflets grow in threes on a long stalk and the leaves and flowers are held well above the surface of the water. The plant grows in shallow ponds and lakesides as well as marshes and fens all over Ireland. Country people considered Bogbean a blood purifier, and used it as a remedy for boils. The flowers open in April and May.

Bogbean grows in Europe, northern and central Asia, Greenland and North America.

Common Wild Violet • *Viola riviniana*

Common Wild Violet is a low perennial. The petals are violet with a short cream-coloured or whitish spur. The leaves are round to heart-shaped; some of them grow on long stalks in a central non-flowering rosette. This familiar plant grows on banks and in pastures throughout Ireland as well as on sand dunes and in woods. The flowers bloom in March and April and again in July and August.

Common Wild Violet is common all over Britain and western Europe, and is found in Morocco and Madeira.

Cowslip • *Primula veris*

Cowslip is one of Ireland's best-known wild perennials. The bright yellow flowers grow in a cluster and droop. The fresh green leaves are in a rosette; they narrow suddenly at the base to a short stalk. The plant grows in large drifts in rough pastures where there have been cows in the past, and where the soil is limy. Many pastures have been ploughed up lately and re-seeded and cowslips have become scarcer. However there are still some to be seen. The plant is mainly one of the midlands and is rare in the north and the extreme south. In the past it was traditional to make wine out of cowslip flowers. The flowers are out in April and May.

Caleb Threlkeld mentioned Cowslip in his *Synopsis Stirpium Hibernicarum*, published in 1726 – "The Cowslips are Friends to the Nerves," he wrote.

Cowslip grows in Britain, except for some counties of Scotland, and in temperate Europe and Asia.

Cuckoo Flower • *Cardamine pratensis* • *Biolar Griagháin*

Cuckoo Flower, sometimes called Lady's Smock, is a medium-sized perennial. The flowers grow loosely together at the top of the stem; they are a pale lilac colour with yellow anthers. The upper leaflets are narrow; the lower ones, coming from the base on long stalks, are rounder. This elegant spring plant grows in wet meadow and marshes in many places. It is sometimes grown as a garden plant. The flowers appear in April and May.

Cuckoo Flower grows in similar conditions in Britain. In Europe a related form grows in drier country.

Early Purple Orchid • *Orchis mascula*

Early Purple Orchid, or Blue Butcher, is a short- to medium-sized perennial, a widespread member of the orchid family. The flowers are a deep purple, or more rarely pinkish mauve or white. The leaves are long and blotched. It is to be seen all over the country near wood and on open pastures, and is especially attractive growing, as it does, in west Clare, where it flowers in late May among the Gentians, wild Geraniums and Mountain Avens; the other plants soften the Orchid's starkness. The flowers are at their best in April and May.

Early Purple Orchid grows all over Europe, in North Africa and in northern and western Asia.

Heartsease • *Viola arvensis*

Heartsease, or Field Pansy, is a small delicate annual. The flowers are a cream colour with a yellow and orange tinge. The leaves vary from oval to narrow. It is an exquisite flower and appears, though infrequently, in ploughed land all over Ireland, but is not a serious weed. The flowers start blooming in April and can continue until the autumn.

Heartsease is common throughout most of Europe, western Asia, North Africa and Madeira.

Irish Orchid • *Neotinea maculata*

Irish Orchid, or Dense-flowered Orchid, is a short perennial. The flowers are a greenish white or a dull pinkish purple, barely open and crammed together. The leaves of the purple-flowered flowers have purple spots. The plant grows in rocky or sandy places mainly in the Burren district of Clare, and extends, usually on stony soils, to north Galway and east Mayo. A few outlying colonies have recently been found in Roscommon, Offaly and Cork.

Though not obviously attractive, Irish Orchid is an interesting plant. It does not grow in Britain and is a native mainly of the Mediterranean region. It was not found in Ireland until 1864 when it was discovered by Miss F.M. More at Castle Taylor in Galway. Strangely, this southern plant grows in the same area as the Spring Gentian and Mountain Avens. Flowering time is May.

Irish Orchid is unknown in Britain but has recently been found in the Isle of Man. It grows in southern Europe, Madeira, the Canaries and North Africa.

Irish Spurge • *Euphorbia hyberna* • *Bainne caoin*

Irish Spurge is a medium-sized perennial, often growing in clumps. The flowers are puzzling to the amateur, but the effect is of a yellowish green, leafy group on about five stalks. The stalks join together in a group of five leaves. Below this is a single stem with leaves, large, oblong and slightly downy, growing alternately down it. The plant grows on lime-free soils in damp places and at the edge of woods. It grows prolifically in Cork and Kerry, and more rarely in south-east Galway and east Donegal.

It is poisonous and, crushed, was and still is used by poachers to kill fish. Country people used to rub it on warts as a cure. It is in bloom in May.

Irish Spurge is a plant that needs a mild winter, and is rare in Britain. It is found, but only sparsely, in Cornwall, Devon and Somerset. It mainly grows in south-west Europe.

Kingcup • *Caltha palustris* • *Lus buí bealtaine*

Kingcup, or Marsh Marigold, is a short- to medium-sized perennial of the buttercup family. The flowers consist of five bright yellow sepals. The leaves grow on long stalks and are thick, scallop-edged and kidney-shaped. It grows in marshes, fens, lakesides and even in open fields in wet clay soils; it is larger and more luxuriant in the shade. The plant is common all over Ireland. There is a double-flowered variety "Plena" used for water gardens. The flowers are open from March until June.

Kingcup grows in Britain, in temperate and Arctic Europe, temperate and Arctic Asia and North America.

Large Bitter Cress • *Cardamine amara*

Large Bitter Cress is a medium-sized to fairly tall perennial. It resembles Cuckoo Flower in many ways. The flowers of Large Bitter Cress are smaller, however, and grow in a broader cluster; they are nearly always white whereas those of Cuckoo Flower are lilac-coloured. The anthers are different also; instead of being yellow like Cuckoo Flower they are a vivid violet colour. The leaflets are oval and like watercress. The plant grows in wet places, riversides and damp woods, mainly on peat. It is rare in Ireland and only found in the northern counties, chiefly around Lough Neagh. The flowers bloom from April to June.

Large Bitter Cress grows throughout Europe to Asia Minor, often in damp alder woods.

Lesser Celandine • *Ranunculus ficaria*

Lesser Celandine, or Pilewort, is a small perennial of the buttercup family. It frequently forms flat, matted clumps. The flowers have eight narrow petals; at first they are bright yellow and later they fade to white. The leaves are dark, thick, heart-shaped and on long stalks. The plant grows wild all over Ireland on damp shady banks and at the edge of woods. There is a variety which reproduces by little bulbs formed at the base of the leaves. The flowers appear from March to May.

Lesser Celandine grows throughout Europe and western Asia. It has been introduced into North America.

Primrose • *Primula vulgaris*

Primrose – the name means "first rose" – is a small, favourite perennial. The pale yellow flowers are solitary on long fragile stalks. The leaves are bright green, crinkled, and narrowed gradually at the base without a definite stalk. In most of Europe it is a woodland plant, but the damp air of Ireland lets it grow in pastures and on sand dunes as well as in shady banks. It is especially fine and prolific round Murlough Bay in Antrim. Flowering time is from March to May.

Primrose grows all over western Europe, the Balkans, the Crimea and North Africa. In eastern Europe, instead of being pale yellow the flowers are often a dull pink.

Seaside Pansy • *Viola tricolor subsp. curtisii*

Seaside Pansy is a very small perennial, a subspecies of tricolor Pansy. The flowers are bright yellow or violet, or sometimes a combination of the two. The stems and leaves are thin and delicate. It grows in attractive groups on dunes round the coast of Ireland, and is also occasionally found on lake shores, specifically by Lough Erne, Castlewellan Lake and Lough Neagh. The flowers open in late April and bloom for several months afterwards.

Seaside Pansy grows round the coast of Britain and on the shores of the Baltic.

Spring Gentian • *Gentiana verna*

Spring Gentian is a very small perennial. The flowers have five petals and are a vivid blue. The leaves grow mainly in a rosette. The rootstock throws up several flowering stems, making the flowers grow close together. As Spring Gentian is a mountain plant over much of Europe it is exciting to find it at a low altitude in west Clare, on short turf over limestone. It is the most famous flower of the Burren, and is also found in Galway and parts of Mayo.

The plant was first recorded here in 1650. It had been found growing between Gort and Galway by Richard Heaton, a Yorkshire-born parson and a keen botanist. It is cultivated in gardens in the form "Angulosa". Flowering time is from April to June.

Spring Gentian grows in Britain only in Teesdale, in the north Pennines, where there is grass on limestone, and in central and southern Europe as far as the Caucasus, mainly on the higher mountains.

Thrift • *Armeria maritima* • *Nóinín an chladaigh*

Thrift, or Sea Pink, is a small, cushion-like perennial. The round-headed flowers are a bright pink. The leaves grow up from the base and are narrow yet fleshy; there are many of them and with the compact flower heads they form a dense hummock. The plant grows in great quantities on rocks and cliffs round the coast of Ireland, and occasionally on mountains. The Irish name, when translated, is "Daisy of the Sea Shore".

It makes a pretty garden plant for border edgings: it is cultivated in the forms "Alba" (white), "Merlin" (pink) and "Vindictive" (a strong red). The flowers first appear in March and plants are often still flowering in September.

Thrift is a common plant round the British coast; it is found on the coast of Europe from Norway to northern Spain.

Wild Cherry • *Prunus avium* • *Crann silín*

Wild Cherry, or Gean, is a medium-sized to large deciduous tree. The flowers are white and grow in loose clusters. The leaves are pointed, oval and stalked. The fruit is bitter, and a deep red colour. The plant is one of Ireland's most handsome and ornamental native trees, with fine spreading branches and a shiny reddish brown bark. It grows, though not prolifically, on good soil in all counties of Ireland except for Longford and north-east Galway. The flowers bloom in March and April.

Wild Cherry is found in most of Europe, in mountainous North Africa and in western Asia.

Wood Anemone • *Anemone nemorosa* • *Nead cailleach*

Wood Anemone is a small fragile perennial. The flowers consist of seven white sepals which close up in the evening; there is an occasional blue form, *caerulea*. The leaves are deeply cut; they grow on long stalks coming from the main stem in groups of three. The plant is poisonous. It grows charmingly in drifts at the edge of deciduous woods where the soil is not too acid. It is mainly found in the north of Ireland, and less often in other parts of the country. The naturalist, Robert Lloyd Praeger, mentions a blue form growing in abundance in the Ow river valley above Aughrim, Wicklow. The plant is frequently used for wild gardens, sometimes in the blue form "Robinsoniana". Flowers come out from March to May.

Wood Anemone grows all through the temperate zone of central Europe and western Asia.

Wood Sorrel • *Oxalis acetosella* • *Samhadh coille*

Wood Sorrel is a small creeping perennial. The flowers have five white petals with lilac veins. The leaflets, grown in threes, are heart-shaped; they sometimes fold up. Both flowers and leaves have long fragile stalks. The plant grows in and at the edge of woods throughout Ireland; in the west it can be found on shady banks or among bracken. It is sometimes planted to naturalise in a shady part of the garden but must be treated with caution; it can become a rampant weed. The flowers are out in April and May.

Wood Sorrel grows throughout western Europe and north and central Asia to Sakhalin and Japan.

EARLY SUMMER

Bitter Vetch • *Lathyrus montanus* • *Carra mhilis*

Bitter Vetch is a perennial of the pea family; it is sometimes called Heath Pea. The flowers are a rosy purple; the narrow leaflets grow in pairs. It is remarkable that Bitter Vetch, unlike most other peas and vetches, has no tendrils. It is a common plant on acid soil, at the edge of woods and in scrubland. It grows in many districts of Ireland, but is not found in Meath or Longford; it is easily found by the lower Lake of Killarney. The flowers are in bloom from May to July.

Bitter Vetch grows in Britain, except for East Anglia, and in much of western and central Europe.

Bird's-foot Trefoil • *Lotus corniculatus* • *Crúibín cait*

Bird's-foot Trefoil, or Bacon and Eggs, is a small, brightly coloured perennial. Like Bitter Vetch it belongs to the pea family. The flowers are a strong yellow with red streaks and tips. The leaflets grow in fives; as the lower two leaflets slope back the upper ones appear to be in threes, hence the name Trefoil. The pods are long and they join together in the shape of a bird's foot. The plant grows on grass and in rough pastures all over the country; it is widespread and decorative and has many local names. The flowers bloom between May and September.

Bird's-foot Trefoil is one of the most universal wild flowers. It grows over most of Europe, Asia and parts of Africa, and is found on mountains in the tropics.

Bladder Campion • *Silene vulgaris* • *Cuirean coilleach*

Bladder Campion, or White Bottle, is a fragile-looking medium perennial; it is shiny and greyish green. The flowers are usually a pure white, occasionally pink, with five deeply cleft petals. Sepals join to form an inflated calyx, which resembles a bladder; this is purple or yellowish. Bees are attracted to the plant, which grows in many part of Ireland beside hedges and roadside verges, usually on lime. The flowers open in May and can continue until August and September.

Bladder Campion grows in Britain, though not often in the north of the country, and in Europe, Asia and North America.

Bloody Cranesbill • *Geranium sanguineum*

Bloody Cranesbill is a small, spreading perennial. The flowers are large and of a brilliant crimson purple, very occasionally pink or white; the petals are slightly notched. The leaves are deeply cut. This is one of the most beautiful of wild Geraniums and looks especially dazzling in late May when it flowers among Gentians and Mountain Avens. A good place to see this is the Burren in west Clare. It grows on limestone in west Clare, the Aran Islands, by Lough Corrib and in Donegal, also in County Dublin on cliffs at Howth and Killiney. Flowering time is from May to August.

Bloody Cranesbill grows, but rather rarely, over most of Britain except for the south-east. It is found in Europe from Scandinavia east to the Urals and the Caucasus.

Bugle • *Ajuga reptans*

Bugle is a small perennial. The flowers are a dark blue, and occasionally white or pink; they grow in a spike. The leaves are shiny, oval and a strong green; in some plants they are bronze coloured. Rooting runners are sent out in all directions. Bugle is found in damp shady meadows and the edge of woods and is common over Ireland in such places. It is cultivated in gardens in various forms. The related and rare Pyramidal or Limestone Bugle (*Ajuga pyramidalis*) has paler blue flowers, and is only found in rocky ground in west Clare and around Galway Bay. Bugle has flowers from May to July.

The plant grows throughout Britain and much of Europe, south-west Asia, Algeria and Tunisia.

Burnet Rose • *Rosa pimpinellifolia* • *Rós*

Burnet Rose, or Scotch Rose, is a small deciduous shrub; it forms so many suckers that it becomes a bushy patch. The flowers are a cream colour, and occasionally pink. The leaflets are small with roundish toothed edges. The stems are immensely prickly. The fruit is unmistakable, large and black. It likes to grow on sand dunes and between rocks and limestone pavements. In Ireland, Burnet Rose is mainly a seaside plant and it is found round the coast. Occasionally it hybridises with Dog Rose. The Scotch Roses of gardens are derived from Burnet Rose. It is in flower from May to July.

Burnet Rose grows over most of Britain, but is rare in the south-east. It is widespread in Europe and temperate Asia as far as Manchuria and north-west China.

Charlock • *Sinapis arvensis* • *Praeseach bhuidhe*

Charlock, or Wild Mustard, is a tall annual. The flowers are a bright yellow. The leaves are hairy and coarsely toothed; the lower ones are stalked and large, the upper unstalked and narrow. It is a tiresome weed of cultivated land and used to be rampant where no selective weedkillers are used, but is now less common. Charlock is supposed to have been used as a food in Famine times. The flowers bloom in May, June and July.

Charlock grows throughout Europe, south-west Asia and Siberia. It has been introduced in North and South America, South Africa, Australia and New Zealand.

Common Butterwort • *Pinguicula vulgaris* • *Liath uisce*

Common Butterwort is a small graceful perennial. The flowers are violet coloured with a white throat. The leaves are distinctive. They are a pale yellow-green and form a basal rosette; they are covered with glandular hairs, and these secrete fluid while the leaves roll up at the edges so as to trap and digest insects. The whole plant is a little sticky. It grows in bogs and wet places and is found mainly in the north and west of Ireland. It is less common in the rest of the country and is not found in Cork.

This is one of Ireland's few insectivorous plants. Country people believe, or did believe, that Common Butterwort caused a fatal disease in sheep, possibly dropsy. The flowers appear in May and June.

Common Butterwort grows in the north and midlands of Britain and in mountainous districts of southern Europe. It is also found in northern Asia and North America as far as British Columbia.

Field Scabious • *Knautia arvensis*

Field Scabious, also called Gypsy Rose or Pincushion Flower, is a medium to tall perennial of the Teazel family. The flowers are on long stalks and are a bluish mauve; they form flat cushiony heads. The leaves are variable and deeply lobed. The stalks are a little hairy. The plant grows over the east, centre and south of the country, nearly always on limestone, on dry grass, road verges and dry banks. It is less common in the north and west. It is visited by butterflies and bees. The Scabious of gardens, used for herbaceous borders, are derived not from this species but from, mainly, *Scabiosa caucasica* or *columbaria* or *atropurpurea*. The name Scabious comes from a Latin word meaning itch; the English herbalist Culpeper recommended the use of this plant to cure skin disorders. Flowering starts in June and continues until September.

Field Scabious grows over Britain and northern Europe, the Caucasus and western Siberia.

Greater Butterwort • *Pinguicula grandiflora*

Greater Butterwort, or Bog Violet, is a larger plant than Common Butterwort; even so it is a small perennial. The flower makes many botanists consider it to be the most beautiful of the Irish flora; it is a rich violet colour. Like Common Butterwort this plant is insectivorous, the sticky, yellowish leaves rolling inwards to trap and digest insects.

Similarly it grows in bogs, damp clearings in woods, wet heaths and rocks. Unlike Common Butterwort it only grows in a limited area: Cork and Kerry, where it is prolific, and Limerick and Clare, where it is rare. It can be cultivated in an Alpine house or as a garden plant in acid, boggy soil.

As well as being beautiful Greater Butterwort is interesting. James Drummond, a Scot, curator of Cork's botanic garden, was the first to discover it in Ireland; he found it in wet country in Cork in 1809. The flowers appear in May and June.

Greater Butterwort is considered a plant mainly of south-western Europe and, except for an introduction in Cornwall, does not grow in Britain. It grows on the Jura, the French Alps, the Pyrenees and the mountains of northern Spain.

Hoary Rockrose • *Helianthemum canum*

Hoary Rockrose is a very small shrub. The flowers have five petals and are a pale yellow. The small narrow leaves are greenish grey above and white beneath. The stems creep and make the plant form a small mat. This pretty little plant makes tiny spreading clumps in the bare limestone pavements of west Clare, where it is prolific. It is found also on Inishmore.

Hoary Rockrose was first reported in Ireland in 1806 by the enthusiastic plant hunter James Mackay, Curator of Dublin's Trinity College Botanic Garden. The plant should not be confused with the larger-flowered Common Rockrose, *Helianthemum chamaecistus*, common in Britain but in Ireland only found in one place near Ballintra, in Donegal. The name *Helianthemum* is derived from the Greek word for sunflower. The flowers are in bloom in May and June.

Hoary Rockrose is rare in Britain. It grows on limestone pastures in Wales, Yorkshire and parts of Cumbria. It is found, given the right conditions, in Europe, including Sicily and Macedonia, in the Caucasus, and in Morocco and Algeria.

Kerry Lily • *Simethis planifolia*

Kerry Lily is a small perennial. The flowers grow in a loose cluster and have six petals, white with purple veins. The leaves are narrow, greyish and grass-like; they grow up from the base and curl slightly. It is one of the rare plants of the British Isles, and in Ireland only grows in a small area of rocky ground near Derrynane, Kerry. The flowers appear in June and July.

Kerry Lily is mainly a southern European plant and was not discovered in Ireland until the mid 19th century. In 1848 the *London Journal of Botany* reports it as growing wild near Derrynane in ground which has "never been turned up". The discoverer was the Reverend Thaddeus O'Mahony, Professor of Irish at Trinity College, Dublin, and a keen naturalist.

Kerry Lily only grows in one place in Britain, where it was almost certainly introduced. It is found in western and southern France and many Mediterranean countries including Morocco, Algeria and Tunisia.

Kidney Saxifrage • *Saxifraga hirsuta*

Kidney Saxifrage is a small perennial related to London Pride. The loosely clustered flowers are white or a very pale pink. The leaves are hairy and a handsome kidney shape; they are scalloped, bright green and grow on long stalks. The plant is not widespread and is found in rocky, damp shade and by mountain streams, always in Cork and Kerry. The Killarney woods are good hunting grounds. The flowers bloom from May to July.

Kidney Saxifrage is not found in Britain but is native in the Pyrenees and northern Spain.

Kidney Vetch • *Anthyllis vulneraria*

Kidney Vetch, or Lady's Fingers, is a medium-sized perennial. The flowers are usually yellow but near the sea they are sometimes white, crimson or purple; the flowerheads often grow in pairs. The leaves are narrow and pinnate. The whole plant is slightly downy. It grows near rocks and on dry pastures, especially near the coast. The name vulneraria was given to show that wounds were sometimes treated with this plant. Flowering time is from June to August.

Kidney Vetch grows on sandy soils and near the sea in Britain. It spreads through Europe to the Caucasus and grows in North Africa.

London Pride • *Saxifraga spathularis* • *Cabáiste mhadra rua*

London Pride, or Wild London Pride, also called St Patrick's Cabbage and Fox's Cabbage, is a small- to medium-sized perennial. It is more widespread than Kidney Saxifrage. The flowers are held up in a loose cluster above graceful stalks; they are pink and white with crimson spots. The leaves grow in a basal rosette; they narrow towards the base. The stems are reddish and the plant gives a reddish impression. This is one of Ireland's most elegant native plants, and is confusingly variable. It can easily be found among mainly acid rocks in Cork and Kerry, and less prolifically northward to Donegal, also in the Galtees, Waterford and Wicklow. The plant grows luxuriantly in the shade, especially in the woods round Killarney. The London Pride of gardens is a hybrid between this plant and *Saxifraga umbrosa* which grows only in the Pyrenees.

In 1696 the Dublin physician Thomas Molyneux recorded this saxifrage; he had found it growing over a mountain in Kerry. The flowers open from May to July.

Wild London Pride is not native to Britain. It grows in northern Spain and in the mountains of northern Portugal.

Marsh Pea • *Lathyrus palustris*

Marsh Pea is a tall climbing perennial. The flowers are a lilac blue. The leaflets are narrow and grow in pairs; the leaves end in branched tendrils. The plant is rare and grows in boggy meadows and fens. It was once growing freely round Lough Neagh, but may not be found there now. Look for it round Lough Erne and the Westmeath lakes. The flowers appear in June.

Marsh Pea is a northern plant. It occurs in the east of England, in Europe to northern Norway, Arctic Russia and Siberia, and east to Japan. It is also found in eastern North America.

Milkwort • *Polygala vulgaris* • *Glúineach*

Milkwort, or Common Milkwort, is a small perennial. The flowers are blue, or mauve, or even white with blue tips; they grow up in a spike. The leaves are narrow. It is common on dry grass and sandhills on calcareous soils all over the country. The name of the plant *Polygala* is from the Greek and means "much milk"; it was believed to be good for the milk yield. In Ireland the juice of Milkwort was one of those used to cure warts. Common Milkwort can easily be confused with Heath Milkwort (*Polygala serpyllifolia*), a plant with shorter spikes and darker flowers, which grows in acid soil. The flowers are in bloom from May to August.

Common Milkwort grows widely in Europe, west Asia and North Africa.

Mountain Avens • *Dryas octopetala* • *Leaithín*

Mountain Avens is a spreading undershrub. The flowers are pure white and have about eight petals. The leaves are shaped like oak leaves and are dark green above and white beneath. The fruit is long and feathery. The plant is rare and only grows in rocky places, usually on high ground; in west Clare, however, its main home in Ireland, it comes down almost to sea level. It is occasionally found on limestone through Galway, Leitrim and Sligo, and very sparsely, on Slieve League in Donegal and Binevenagh in Antrim. The flowers are in bloom in May and June.

Mountain Avens is beautiful enough to be a sought-after rock plant for gardens. The name *Dryas* was given it because of the striking, oak-like leaves; a Dryad was the nymph of oak woods in the ancient world. Like Spring Gentian, it was found by the Reverend Richard Heaton shortly before 1650; he compared the feathery fruit to that of the Wild Clematis.

Mountain Avens is rare in Britain, locally found on high ground in northern Wales and Teesdale; it grows down to sea level in northern Scotland. It grows in Arctic Europe, and on the higher mountains further south.

Ox-eye Daisy • *Leucanthemum vulgare* • *Nóinín mór*

Ox-eye Daisy has many names – Moon Daisy, Dog Daisy and Marguerite. In Scotland, where the daisy is called Gowan, Ox-eye Daisy is known as Horse-gowan. It is a medium-sized perennial. The flowers consist of a bright yellow disc of florets surrounded by many white rays. The leaves are sparse and toothed. The stems, like the leaves, are slightly downy. It is rampant on verges and on fertile pastures all over the country. Flowers start blooming in May and continue for the rest of the summer.

Ox-eye Daisy is native to Britain. It has been introduced in North America and New Zealand.

Ragged Robin • *Lychnis floscuculi*

Ragged Robin is a medium to tall perennial. The red flower petals are deeply cleft, giving a ragged look. The upper leaves are sparse and narrow, the lower ones rounder. The stem, reddish looking and slightly downy, is sticky towards the top. The calyx is red and bloated with purple veins. The plant grows in many marshes and fens and is conspicuous. Butterflies visit the flowers which produce honey. The flowers appear in June and July.

Ragged Robin is common in Europe, and has been introduced in North America.

Rose Campion • *Silene dioica* • *Coireán coilleach*

Rose Campion, or Red Campion, is a tall perennial. The flowers are bright pink and form loose clusters; the petals are cleft. The oval leaves are downy; they grow stalkless, opposite each other on the stems which are also downy. The calyxes are swollen and reddish. This colourful plant grows in good soil in wood clearings, hedge banks and sea cliffs. It is widespread in the north-east of Ireland but much more uncommon in the rest of the country. The flowers appear in May; bloom continues until October.

Rose Campion grows in Britain, Europe, North Africa and western Asia.

Scarlet Pimpernel • *Anagallis arvensis* • *Rinn-rúisc*

Scarlet Pimpernel, also called Shepherd's Weatherglass and Poor Man's Weatherglass, is a small annual. The scarlet flowers have five petals. The leaves are oval, have no stalks and grow opposite each other. There is a prostrate stem which throws up flowering shoots. The plant grows in dry conditions in disturbed ground, sand dunes and ploughed fields, and is very common in the south of Ireland, less so in the north. The name Weatherglass is aptly given to this pretty flower, as the petals close when the sun goes in; they close regularly in mid-afternoon also. Flowering starts in May and continues until the autumn.

Scarlet Pimpernel grows in most non-tropical countries.

Sea Campion • *Silene vulgaris subsp. maritima*

Sea Campion is a subspecies of Bladder Campion and is a smaller perennial. The flowers of Sea Campion are often solitary whereas those of Bladder Campion form a loose cluster. The petals differ also – those of Sea Campion are broader. Sea Campion's leaves are narrower; many of them are non-flowering and these form a kind of mat. The swollen calyxes of Sea Campion have broader mouths. Sea Campion is a plant of the seaside and of rocky coasts. It grows all round the coasts of Ireland and is one of the many beautiful plants flourishing near the Glens of Antrim. It is grown in gardens in the double white form "Flore pleno". The flowers appear from June to August.

Sea Campion grows round the coast of Britain and round Europe's Atlantic coast.

Sea Rocket • *Cakile maritima*

Sea Rocket is a slightly bushy, medium-sized annual. The flowers are lilac to white and have four petals; they form a relaxed cluster of four to six blooms. The leaves are unmistakably shiny, fleshy, and deeply lobed. The stem is prostrate, with a tap root that goes down a long way for water, for this is a plant that grows on sand and shingle above the drift line. It is found round the Irish coast, more commonly in the north and east. The name *Cakile* is said to derive from an Arabic word for the plant, or one similar. Flowers bloom from June to August.

Sea Rocket grows round the Atlantic coasts of Europe.

Shrubby Cinquefoil • *Potentilla fruticosa*

Shrubby Cinquefoil is a small deciduous shrub, and one rare in the British Isles. The five-petalled flowers are yellow and grow in loose clusters. The leaflets, greyish and slightly downy, usually grow in fives. The bark peels every third year or so. The shrub is grown in gardens, as are many hybrids with related species. In the wild it is best known as growing in cold countries and at high altitudes. In Ireland it only thrives on stony or rocky ground likely to flood, as the roots need to be damp. It is still found by turloughs and lakes in north Clare and on the eastern shore of Lough Corrib. The flowers of this decorative plant bloom from early June until August.

Shrubby Cinquefoil was first discovered in Ireland in 1700 by Edward Lhuyd, Assistant Keeper of the Ashmolean Museum, Oxford, who was on a plant-hunting expedition in the west of the country. He recorded it as growing on the shores of Lough Corrib between limestone rocks.

In Britain, Shrubby Cinquefoil grows on Helvellyn, in Upper Teesdale and, rarely, in the Lake District. It is a native of the Baltic countries, Greenland, Labrador and Alaska, and of many mountain ranges in the northern hemisphere.

Wall Pepper • *Sedum acre*

Wall Pepper, or Biting Stonecrop, is a small evergreen perennial. The flowers are star-like with five petals and are a bright yellow. The leaves are small, thick, fleshy and have a peppery taste. The creeping stems make the plant form an attractive, yellow-flowered mat. It grows on mortared walls, poor soil, shingle, railway embankments and limestone generally and is very common in Ireland. There is a garden form "Aureum".

Roger Phillips in his book *Wild Flowers of Britain* claims that in Suffolk and Dorset this plant used to be known as "Welcome home husband, though never so drunk." The flowers appear in June and July.

Wall Pepper grows all over Europe, western Asia and North Africa. It is naturalised in North America.

Water Avens • *Geum rivale* • *Machall uisce*

Water Avens, or Billy's Button, is a small- to medium-sized perennial. The flowers are nodding and grow on long stalks, they are bell-shaped and a soft red colour. The few leaves are lobed and toothed. The plant is downy. This delicate-coloured and unusual plant grows, though not prolifically, in damp places near woods and streams in many parts of Ireland; it is more widespread in the north of the country than the south. It is related to Wood Avens. A few varieties of Water Avens are grown in gardens. Flowering time is May and June.

Water Avens is widespread in Britain, though not in the south-east, and in most of Europe and much of North America.

Welsh Poppy • *Meconopsis cambrica*

Welsh Poppy is a medium-sized perennial. The flowers are large and an attractive mid-yellow colour. The leaves are deeply divided. The whole plant is slightly downy. It grows in wet rocky places and shady banks, and is uncommon except as a garden escape. There are cultivated double forms of this lovely plant in yellow and orange. The flowers bloom in June and July.

Welsh Poppy is native to Wales and to the west of England, also to western France, Portugal and northern Spain.

Wild Thyme • *Thymus praecox or Thymus drucei*

Wild Thyme is a very small undershrub. The flowers are a purplish rose colour. The tiny leaves are hard and sometimes hairy. The plant forms an aromatic tuft or mat. It grows in sunny dry places, usually, but not always, near the coast; it is not found in Tyrone or Carlow. There are cultivated varieties for the garden: "Albus" with white flowers, the shell-pink "Connie Hall", the crimson "Coccineus" and others. Flowering time is from June to August.

It is native to western Europe from Norway to north-west Spain.

Yellow Flag • *Iris pseudacorus* • *Seilistrom*

Yellow Flag is a tall handsome perennial. The flowers are a strong yellow colour. The leaves are stiff and sword-like. It grows by fresh water, river and lakesides, marshes and ditches; sometimes it takes over large parts of wet fields. This can be a wonderful sight in June. In the old days leaves of this plant were sometimes used for thatching and bedding. Country people traditionally placed flowers of Yellow Flag outside their houses as a decoration for the Corpus Christi festival. Caleb Threlkeld called the plant Yellow Water Flower de Luce. There are cultivated varieties of this Iris, "Bastardii", with pale yellow flowers, a deeper yellow "Golden Queen" and "Variegata" with yellow striped foliage. The flowers are in bloom from June to August.

Yellow Flag grows in the same conditions in Britain and in Europe, North Africa and western Asia.

Yellow Pimpernel • *Lysimachia nemorum*

Yellow Pimpernel (another name is Woodland Loosestrife) is a small creeping perennial. The flowers are five-petalled, wide open and a clear yellow. The leaves are oval and grow opposite each other. It must not be confused with the related Creeping Jenny (*Lysimachia nummularia*) which has cup-shaped and larger flowers. Yellow pimpernel is common in Ireland on damp mountain pastures and in woods with damp soils. Flowering time is from May to September.

It is native to the damper parts of Britain and is found throughout Europe.

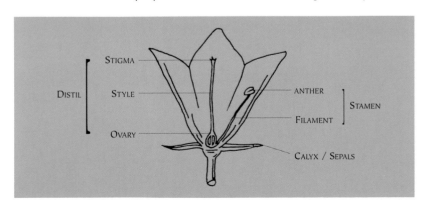

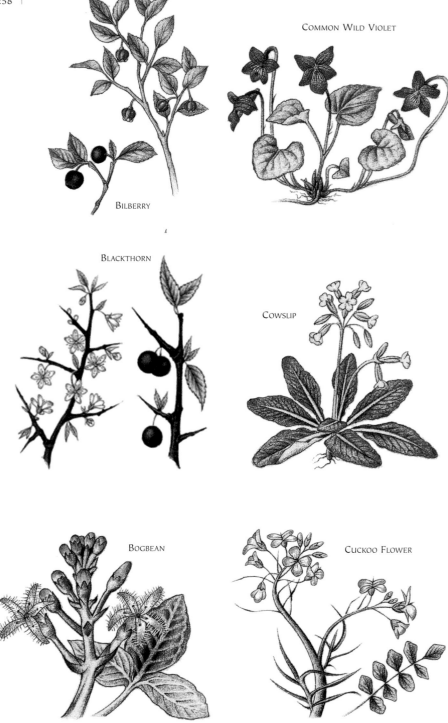

COMMON WILD VIOLET

BILBERRY

BLACKTHORN

COWSLIP

BOGBEAN

CUCKOO FLOWER

EARLY PURPLE ORCHAID

IRISH SPURGE

HEARTSEASE

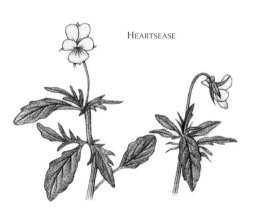

KINGCUP

IRISH ORCHID

LARGE BITTER CRESS

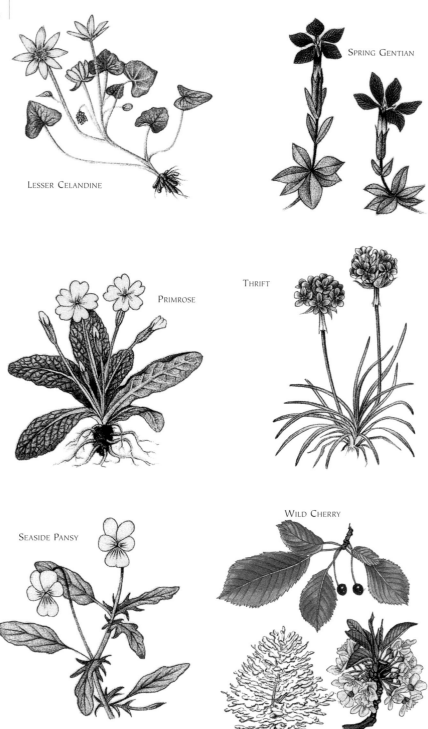

LESSER CELANDINE

SPRING GENTIAN

PRIMROSE

THRIFT

SEASIDE PANSY

WILD CHERRY

WOOD ANEMONE

BIRD'S-FOOT TREFOIL

WOOD SORREL

BLADDER CAMPION

BLOODY CRANESBIL

BITTER VETCH

BUGLE

COMMON
BUTTERWORT

BURNT ROSE

DOG ROSE

CHARLOCK

ELDER

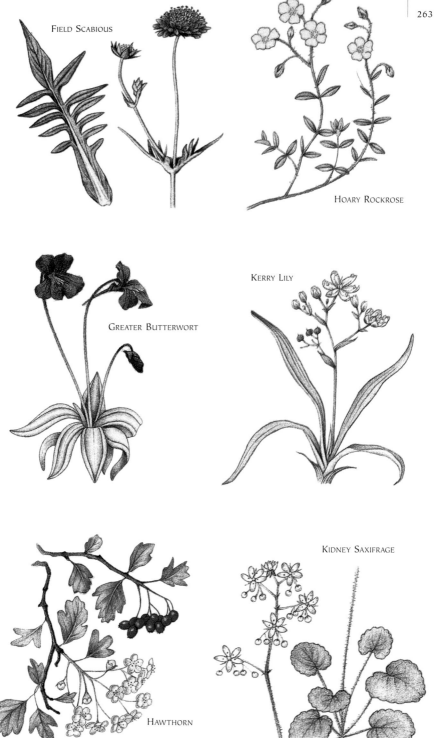

FIELD SCABIOUS

HOARY ROCKROSE

GREATER BUTTERWORT

KERRY LILY

KIDNEY SAXIFRAGE

HAWTHORN

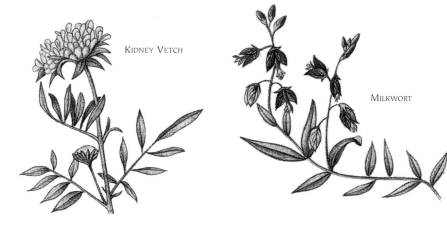

KIDNEY VETCH

MILKWORT

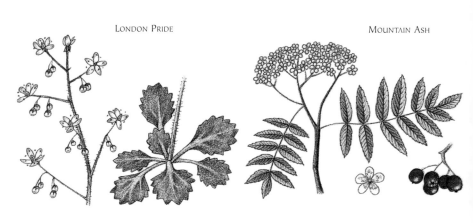

LONDON PRIDE

MOUNTAIN ASH

MOUNTAIN AVENS

MARSH PEA

Ox-Eye Daisy

Scarlet Pimpernel

Ragged robin

Sea Campion

Rose Campion

Sea Rocket

SHRUBBY
CINQUEFOIL

WELSH POPPY

WALL PEPPER

WILD THYME

WATER AVENS

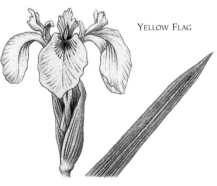

YELLOW FLAG

YELLOW PIMPERNEL

FOXGLOVE

CHAMOMILE

GRASS PARNASSUS

GREATER SPEARWORT

COMMON MALLOW

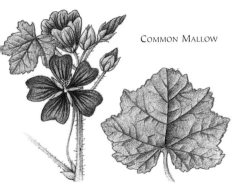

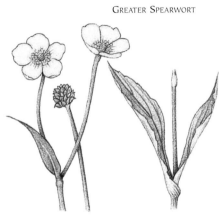

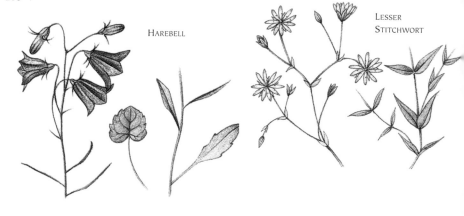

HAREBELL

LESSER
STITCHWORT

MEADOW CRANESBILL

HERB BENNET

MEADOW VETCHLING

LAX-FLOWERED
SEA LAVENDER

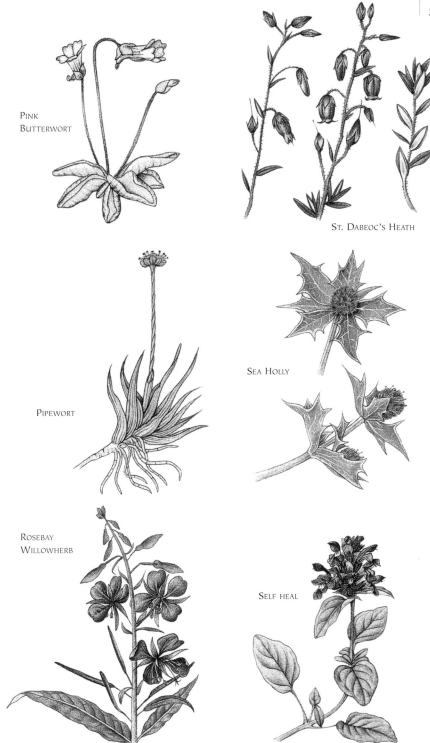

PINK
BUTTERWORT

ST. DABEOC'S HEATH

PIPEWORT

SEA HOLLY

ROSEBAY
WILLOWHERB

SELF HEAL

TRAVELLER'S JOY

WATER LOBELIA

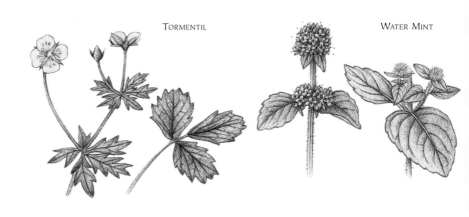

TORMENTIL

WATER MINT

WATER GERMANDER

WOOD SAGE

STRAWBERRY TREE
FLOWERING SEASON

STRAWBERRY TREE
FRUITING SEASON

LATE SUMMER

Chamomile • *Chamaemelum nobile* • *Comán meall milis*

Chamomile is a creeping, small- to medium-sized perennial. The white-petalled daisy-type flowers are on longish stalks. The aromatic leaves grow alternately on the stem and are finely fragmented. The plant is downy. It grows on gravelly pastures, roadsides and heaths, and is often seen in the south and west of Ireland, more rarely in the rest of the country. The cultivated non-flowering variety "Treneague" is sometimes planted in gardens to make scented chamomile lawns. The flowers bloom from June to August.

Chamomile tea, made out of the dried flower heads, is still used as a cure for indigestion in many countries. In Ireland it was considered a remedy for pleurisy, whooping cough and consumption, and was given as a tonic; even inhaling the aroma was said to be health-giving.

Chamomile is native to western Europe from the Netherlands southwards, to North Africa and to the Azores.

Common Mallow • *Malva sylvestris* • *Hocas*

Common Mallow, or Rags and Tatters, is a medium-sized perennial. The flowers have five heart-shaped petals; they are a purple colour with darker veins. The kidney-shaped leaves are large, toothed, lobed and have long stalks. The plant is slightly hairy. This good-looking plant grows on roadsides and waste places, often near houses or ruins. It is fairly common in coastal regions of the south, less common inland and rare in the north. Flowering time is from June to October.

Common Mallow grows in Britain and throughout Europe.

Foxglove • *Digitalis purpurea* • *Méaracán dearg*

Foxglove is a tall biennial, occasionally a perennial. The flowers grow in a spike and are a pinkish purple, or occasionally white; they are tubular, and spotted inside. The leaves are oval, soft and downy. This rich-looking plant grows, and looks magnificent, on shady banks and at the edge of woods where the soil is acid. It is an effective garden plant for the shade and is cultivated in many forms. The name *Digitalis* comes from the Latin for thimble, from the shape of the flowers. The plant is poisonous. The drug Digitalin is made from the leaves and used to treat heart disease. In Ireland Foxglove was sometimes used as a remedy for weak hearts; this must have killed many. The flowers are out in late June, July and August.

Grass of Parnassus • *Parnassia palustris*

Grass of Parnassus is a small perennial. The flowers grow singly on long stalks; they have five white petals with darker veins. The leaves are smooth-edged and heart-shaped. The plant grows in damp pastures, sometimes high up on mountains, and equally often lower down by river or lakesides. It is found in the west and centre of Ireland, but is not native to parts of the south-west and north-east. The flowers bloom in July and August.

This exquisite plant may have been referred to in the 1st century AD by Dioscorides. He wrote, "The grass which grows on Parnassus … bears leaves like to Ivy, a white flower and of a sweet scent." (John Goodyear's translation.)

Grass of Parnassus grows in some districts of Britain, in Europe and in temperate parts of Asia.

Greater Spearwort • *Ranunculus lingua*

Greater Spearwort is a tall perennial of the Buttercup family. The flowers are yellow, shiny and twice the size of a Field Buttercup. The bluish green leaves, unlike deeply cut buttercup leaves, are long, pointed and toothed, just slightly; they seem to grip the stem. The stem creeps and roots in the mud, and then grows upwards. This striking plant is found in ditches and fens in the Irish midlands, and has travelled up to Dublin via the canals, but is less seen in the rest of the country. The cultivated variety "Grandiflora" makes a decorative marginal plant for garden ponds and lakes. The flowers bloom from June to August.

Greater Spearwort is becoming rare in Britain. It grows throughout Europe and in Siberia.

Harebell • *Campanula rotundifolia* • *Méaracán gorm*

Harebell, in Scotland called Bluebell, is a small, well-known perennial. The flowers are pale blue and bell-like. The lower leaves are round and on long stalks, the upper ones narrow. The stems are fragile. This exquisite plant grows in dry grassy places, sandhills and poor soil generally. It is common near the north and west coasts but not often seen in the rest of the country. The name *Campanula* comes from the Latin word meaning a bell. There are several cultivated varieties; one, "Alba", has white flowers. The flowers come out in July and August.

Harebell grows in Britain and in the temperate regions of Europe.

Herb Bennet • *Geum urbanum* • *Machall coille*

Herb Bennet (once called Herb Benedict), or Wood Avens, is a small- to medium-sized perennial. The flowers are small and pale yellow with five wide-open petals; they are solitary on long stalks. The leaves are deeply toothed and lobed. The seedheads are bristly and long-lasting. Herb Bennet sometimes hybridises with Water Avens. It grows at the edge of woods, in shady damp places and is common all over the country. The roots smell of cloves; in some countries they were hung by the door to repel evil spirits. The flowers bloom from June to September.

Herb Bennet is found in Britain, in most parts of Europe, in western Asia and in North Africa.

Lax-flowered Sea Lavender • *Limonium humile*

Lax-flowered Sea Lavender is a small perennial. The flowers are lilac-coloured, close together and grow in flat-topped clusters. The leaves are narrow and stalked. Stems form branches low down with flowers growing on them. In this the plant differs from the similar Common Sea Lavender (*Limonium vulgare*) as flowering branches of the latter form high up on the stem. In any case there is no Common Sea Lavender in Ireland. Lax-flowered Sea Lavender forms attractive clumps on salt marshes and on muddy shores round the east, south and west coasts of Ireland. Flowering time is July to September.

Lax-flowered Sea Lavender is a northern plant. It grows on the north coast of Britain and on the European coast from Sweden and Norway to Brittany.

Lesser Stitchwort • *Stellaria graminea*

Lesser Stitchwort is a small perennial. The flowers have five deeply cleft white petals, no longer than the sepals; the anthers are red and the flowers grow in a loose cluster. Seedheads hang down at first, then rise to become horizontal. The leaves are narrow, pointed and stalkless. This, like the larger Greater Stitchwort (*Stellaria holostea*), is a common plant in Ireland and grows on light grassy soils, usually not on lime. The plant was given the name *Stellaria* because of its star-like flowers. Flowers appear from June to August.

Lesser Stitchwort grows throughout Britain, Europe and Asia.

Meadow Cranesbill • *Geranium pratense*

Meadow Cranesbill is a medium-sized perennial. The flowers are large and violet-blue. The leaves are deeply cut, the stems slightly hairy. The fruit droop at first and then become erect. The plant grows on banks and waste places and is one of the loveliest wild Geraniums. In Ireland it is only native in a small area near the Giant's

Causeway in Antrim, where it is prolific. It is seen occasionally elsewhere but is almost certainly a garden escape. It is grown in gardens in many varieties, among them the double blue "Flore pleno", and the white, dark-veined "Kashmir White". The flowers open from June to September.

Meadow Cranesbill is widespread in Europe and parts of Asia, including the Himalayas and Japan.

Meadow Vetchling • *Lathyrus pratensis* • *Pis bhuidhe*

Meadow Vetchling, or Yellow Pea, is a clambering perennial of the Pea family. The bright yellow flowers grow in a loose cluster, or spike. The leaflets are narrow and grow with a branched tendril between them. It is common in damp meadows and ditches all over Ireland. The plant must not be confused with Bird's-foot Trefoil (*Lotus corniculatus*); the leaflets of Meadow Vetchling are much narrower. It has slight similarities with the Everlasting Pea of gardens. The flowers bloom from June to September.

Meadow Vetchling is found in much of Northern Europe, Siberia, the Himalayas and Ethiopia.

Pink Butterwort • *Pinguicula lusitanica*

Pink Butterwort, or Pale Butterwort, is the smallest of the three Irish Butterworts; it is also the last to flower. The flowers are a pale lilac and yellow colour. The leaves are a drab green; they form a basal rosette which stays visible through the winter. Like its fellows it grows in damp conditions, in bogs and by mountain streams. It is often found in the extreme west but is more rare in the rest of the country. Like the others it is insectivorous, oozing sticky fluids which, with leaf edges that roll inward, trap and digest insects. It is as elegant-looking as its fellow Butterworts. Flowering time is from late June to September.

Pink Butterwort is a western European plant. It grows in some western parts of England and Scotland, in western France, western Spain and Portugal.

Pipewort • *Eriocaulon aquaticum*

Pipewort is an interesting perennial water plant. The flowers are whitish and button-like; they are held well above the water and are often damp and glistening. The narrow and translucent leaves grow in a totally submerged rosette. The plant is found in shallow, still water on peaty soil. It is native to the west of Ireland in shallow lakes from Donegal southward to Kerry, but is only really prolific in Connemara. The enthusiastic and meticulous botanist, Dr Walter Wade, Professor of Botany to the Dublin Society, discovered the plant there in 1801; he was delighted to find such numbers of this unusual species which, he claimed, had only been seen before on the Isle of Skye. The flowers appear in July and August.

Pipewort is unknown on the continent of Europe and in Britain except in a small part of the West Highlands of Scotland. There is an identical, or closely related, plant in North America.

Restharrow • *Ononis repens* • *Sreang bogha*

Restharrow (known as Cammock in parts of Britain) is a small shrub of the Pea family, partly creeping and partly erect. The flowers are pink and grow from the leaf axils. The leaflets are oval and slightly toothed. The stem and the young shoots are hairy; sometimes there are soft spines. Restharrow is meant to indicate poor or neglected land. It grows in dry waste places and on sandhills and is often found in the south-east of the country, more rarely in the south, west and north. It is absent from many midland counties.

The rootstock of Restharrow often creeps under ground, and is so strong that it will "wrest the harrow" from its proper direction. Hence the name of the plant. This is the only type of Restharrow native to Ireland; Spiny Restharrow (*Ononis spinosa*) is not found here. Flowering time is July to September.

Restharrow grows in Britain and much of Europe, east to Estonia and south to Bulgaria, often on calcareous soils.

Rosebay Willowherb ● *Epilobium angustifolium*

Rosebay Willowherb (sometimes called Fireweed) is very tall perennial. The flowers grow up in a spike, but loosely; there are four purple sepals and four irregular rosy petals. The leaves are pointed and willow-like; they grow alternately up the main stem. It has long been a rare and colourful plant found on mountain ledges. Recently it has taken to growing in hedges and on the margin of woods and bogs, but not nearly as wildly as in Britain, where it has spread in the last fifty years through disturbed land, wood clearings and roadsides. The name "Fireweed" was given it because it thrives on ground where fire has been. The flowers appear from July to September.

Rosebay is found in Europe, Asia and North America.

St Dabeoc's Heath ● *Daboecia cantabrica* ● *Fraoch gallda*

St Dabeoc's Heath is a small straggly shrub, a form of heather that grows up well through other plants. The drooping flowers are large and rosy purple; they are more spaced out than those of other heathers. The leaves are dark above and white beneath. The stems are straggly and weak. It grows among rocks, by the sides of acid lakes and on heaths. It is prolific in Connemara, in some places growing to the edge of the Atlantic, and is found in Mayo, but more rarely. It is cultivated as a garden plant in many varieties, among them the deep purple-flowered "Atropurpurea" and "Alba Globosa" with broad white flowers. Flowering time is from June to October.

This heath was first discovered in Ireland by Edward Lhuyd on his journey round Ireland in 1700. He learnt that women wore the plant to protect their chastity.

St Dabeoc's Heath is not native to Britain. It grows in western France, north-west and central Spain and north-west Portugal.

Sea Holly ● *Eryngium maritimum* ● *Cuileann trá*

Sea Holly, once called Sea Eryngo or Sea Holm, is a small to medium-sized perennial. The flowers have pale blue dense heads surrounded by spiky, mauve bracts. The shiny bluish leaves grow in threes up the stems, and have stiff spines. The stems are stiff also and, because they come from a creeping rootstock, many of them quickly form a little bush. The plant grows on sand, and is found in many places round the coast. This is the only *Eryngium* to be found in Ireland. The Field Eryngo or Watling Street Thistle (*Eryngium campestre*) is very scarce in Britain and unknown in Ireland. Sea Holly is cultivated by gardeners as a border plant with strong effects, as are related *Eryngiums* of African and Asian origin. The flowers are in bloom in July and August.

Sea Holly grows on sand all round the coasts of Europe.

Self-heal ● *Prunella vulgaris* ● *Ceannbhán beag*

Self-heal is a small creeping perennial. The flowers are violet-coloured and occasionally pink or white. The leaves are oval, pointed and slightly toothed; the lower ones are stalked. The stems are hairy. The plant grows on damp pastures, roadsides and heaths and is abundant in these places.

Self-heal, as its name implies, was once considered to have important medicinal qualities. In Ireland it was used as a remedy for sudden strokes. In other countries the plant was used for dressing wounds. The name *Prunella* is said to come from the German *Bräune*, a word for quinsy or croup, which the plant was reputed to cure. Other names for Self-heal were Hook-heal and Sicklewort. Culpeper wrote that doctors were unnecessary if one had Self-heal. This view is now discredited. The flowers bloom from late June to September, occasionally until October.

Self-heal grows throughout Britain, southern Europe, temperate Asia, North Africa, North America and Australia.

Traveller's Joy • *Clematis vitalba*

Traveller's Joy (sometimes called Old Man's Beard or Virgin's Bower) is a strongly climbing perennial. The flowers consist of four greenish white sepals, usually bending back; the stamens are prominent. The leaflets are grouped in fives, the groups growing opposite each other. The fruit are like balls of down all through the autumn and winter, and give the plant its name Old Man's Beard. The plant grows by its twisting leafstalks to dramatic heights, sometimes up trees and telegraph poles, making vast festoons. It is a scrub, hedge and woodland plant and likes growing on limestone. It is not native to Ireland, always a garden escape, and is scattered in the south and north of Ireland but absent from Donegal, Galway and some midland counties. The flowers appear in July and August.

Traveller's Joy grows in the south of England, in Europe from the Netherlands southwards and in North Africa.

Tormentil • *Potentilla erecta* • *Néalfhartach*

Tormentil is a perennial, sometimes erect, sometimes forming a mat. The flowers have four bright yellow petals and four sepals. The leaflets grow in groups of three or five; they are unstalked and deeply cut. The plant grows in acid or slightly acid soil on many banks, heaths and hills and likes drier root conditions than other *Potentillas*. It differs from others also in having four petals instead of five. Tormentil has tannin in the roots; in the past country people in Ireland used it to treat burns. The flowers are in bloom from June to September.

Tormentil grows throughout Britain, Europe, north-west Asia and North Africa.

Water Germander • *Teucrium scordium*

Water Germander is a sprawling perennial. The flowers are a pale purple and grow in whorls up leafy stems. The leaves are oval, stalkless and slightly toothed. The stems and leaves are soft and hairy. The plant grows by fresh water at lakesides. It is very rare, but can be found along the banks of the River Shannon, mainly beside Lough Ree and Lough Derg, and in turloughs in Clare and Tipperary. It is pollinated by bees. Flowering time is in July and August.

Water Germander is rare in Britain. It is more widespread in Europe south of Scandinavia.

Water Lobelia • *Lobelia dortmanna*

Water Lobelia is an aquatic perennial of the Campanula family. The flowers are a pale mauve and hang elegantly on a slender stalk, well above water level. The leaves are in a completely submerged basal rosette. The plant roots in acid shallow water. It is frequently found in turf-margined lakes from Kerry northwards, through Clare, Galway and Mayo to Donegal, and is common in most of Achill Island's lower-level lakes. It is rare in the rest of the country. Lobelias are named after Mathias de l'Obel, the distinguished Flemish botanist who studied in the 16th century. The flowers appear in July and August.

Water Lobelia is found in lakes in north-west Britain and in north-west Europe.

Water Mint • *Mentha aquatica* • *Mismín dearg*

Water Mint is a short- to medium-sized perennial. The flowers are dense and lilac-coloured; they grow at intervals high up on the stem finishing with a group of flowers at the top. The stamens protrude; the calyx is long and hairy. The leaves are stalked, toothed and grow opposite each other. The stems are stiff. Like many mints, Water Mint likes wet ground, so that it is found in marshes and lake shores throughout Ireland. The leaves give off a strong minty scent when crushed. Water Mint sometimes hybridises with the ordinary garden mint, Spear Mint (*Mentha spicata*) to give peppermint, as well as with Corn Mint (*Mentha arvensis*). The flowers appear in July, August and September.

Water Mint grows in Europe, south-west Asia, North and South Africa and Madeira.

Wood Sage • *Teucrium scorodonia* • *Úr sléibhe*

Wood Sage, or Germander, is a small to medium perennial. The paired flowers are a greenish yellow and grow on branched spikes. The anthers are maroon-coloured and prominent. The leaves are heart-shaped, toothed, wrinkled and downy. The stem is reddish and square. The plant usually grows in acid soil and is found on dry heathy places and open woods. It is fairly common in the mountains but scarcer in the lowlands and hard to find in the centre of the country. Flowering time is July and August.

Wood Sage is widespread in western Europe and in Croatia.

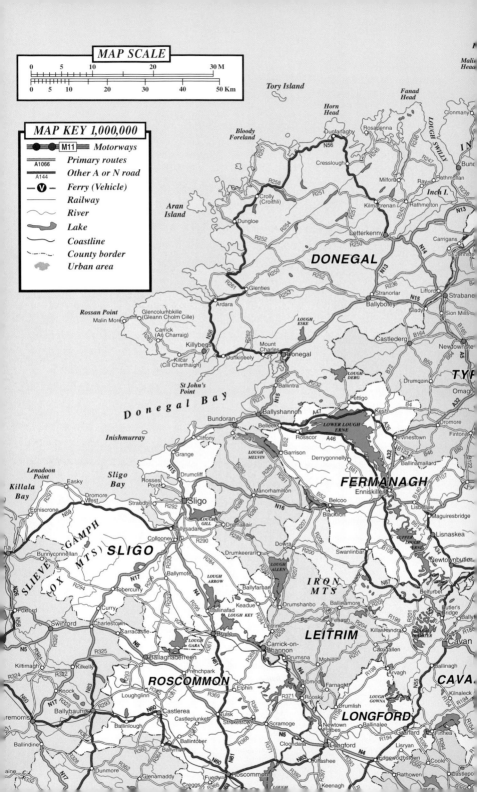

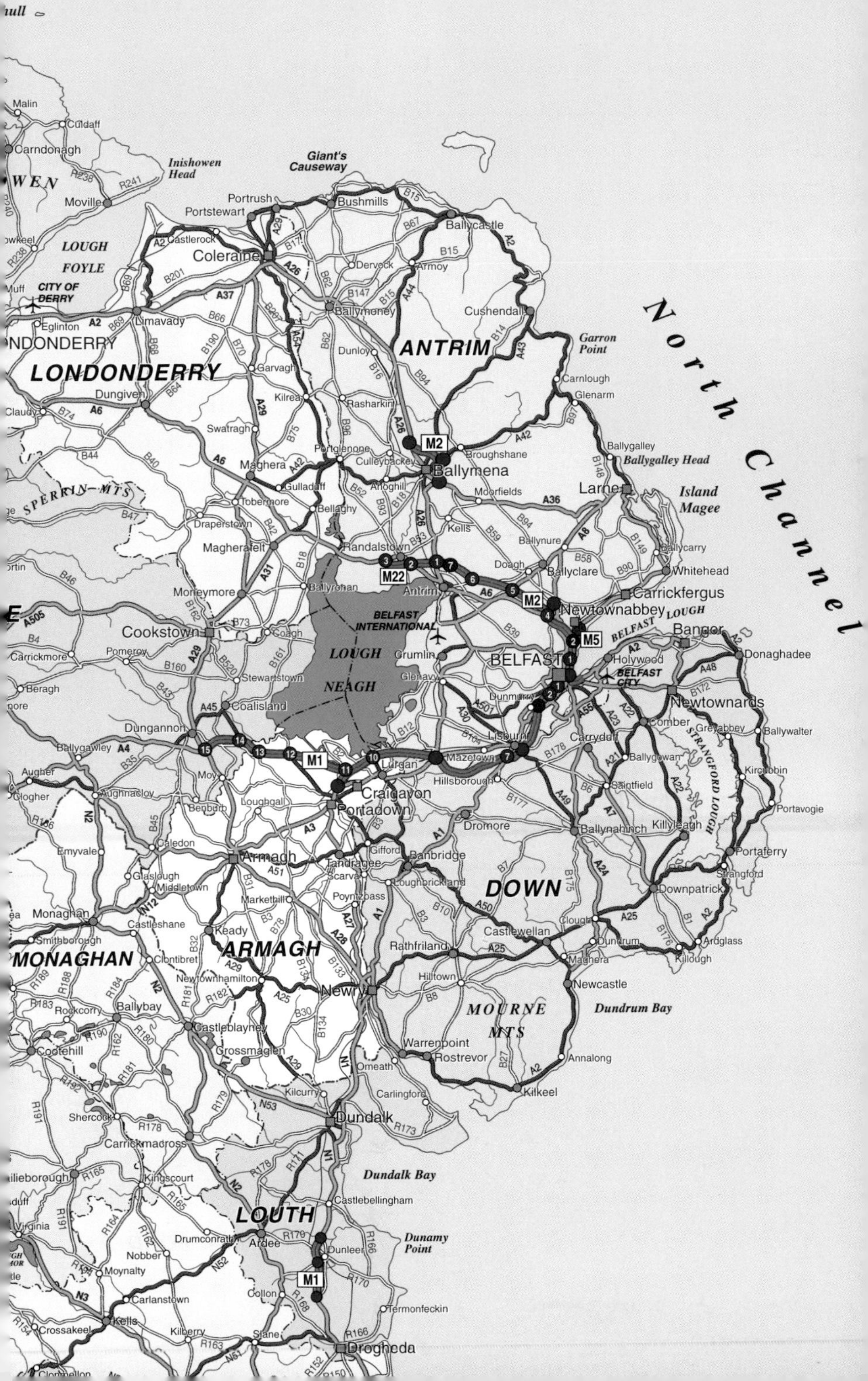

North Channel
Giant's Causeway
Inishowen Head
LOUGH FOYLE
CITY OF DERRY
Malin
Culdaff
Carndonagh
Moville
Portrush
Portstewart
Bushmills
Ballycastle
Castlerock
Coleraine
Dervock
Armoy
Ballymoney
Cushendall
Garron Point
Eglinton
Limavady
LONDONDERRY
ANTRIM
Dunloy
Garvagh
Kilrea
Rasharkin
Carnlough
Glenarm
Dungiven
Claudy
Swatragh
M2
Broughshane
Ballygalley
Ballygalley Head
Portglenone
Culleybackey
Ballymena
Maghera
Gulladuff
Ahoghill
Moorfields
Larne
Island Magee
SPERRIN MTS
Tobermore
Bellaghy
Kells
Draperstown
Magherafelt
Randalstown
Ballynure
Ballycarry
Doagh
Ballyclare
Whitehead
M22
Antrim
Carrickfergus
Moneymore
Ballyronan
Newtownabbey
BELFAST LOUGH
BELFAST INTERNATIONAL
Cookstown
Coagh
M5
Bangor
Pomeroy
Carrickmore
LOUGH NEAGH
Crumlin
BELFAST
Holywood
Donaghadee
BELFAST CITY
Glenavy
Stewartstown
Beragh
Dunmurry
Newtownards
Coalisland
Lisburn
Comber
Greyabbey
Ballywalter
Dungannon
Carryduff
STRANGFORD LOUGH
Ballygawley
M1
Mazetown
Lurgan
Ballygowan
Kircubbin
Augher
Moy
Hillsborough
Saintfield
Clogher
Aughnacloy
Craigavon
Portavogie
Benburb
Loughgall
Portadown
Dromore
Ballynahinch
Killyleagh
Caledon
Emyvale
Gifford
Banbridge
Armagh
Tandragee
Portaferry
Scarva
Strangford
Glaslough
Middletown
Loughbrickland
DOWN
Downpatrick
Markethill
Poyntzpass
Monaghan
Castleshane
Castlewellan
Clough
Keady
Smithborough
Rathfriland
Dundrum
Ardglass
MONAGHAN
Clontibret
ARMAGH
Maghera
Killough
Hilltown
Newtownhamilton
Newry
Newcastle
Dundrum Bay
Rockcorry
Ballybay
MOURNE MTS
Castleblayney
Cootehill
Warrenpoint
Rostrevor
Crossmaglen
Annalong
Omeath
Kilkeel
Carlingford
Kilcurry
Shercock
Dundalk
Carrickmacross
Dundalk Bay
Kingscourt
Castlebellingham
LOUTH
Virginia
Drumconrath
Ardee
Dunany Point
Dunleer
Nobber
Moynalty
Collon
Carlanstown
Termonfeckin
Kells
Crossakeel
Kilberry
Slane
Drogheda

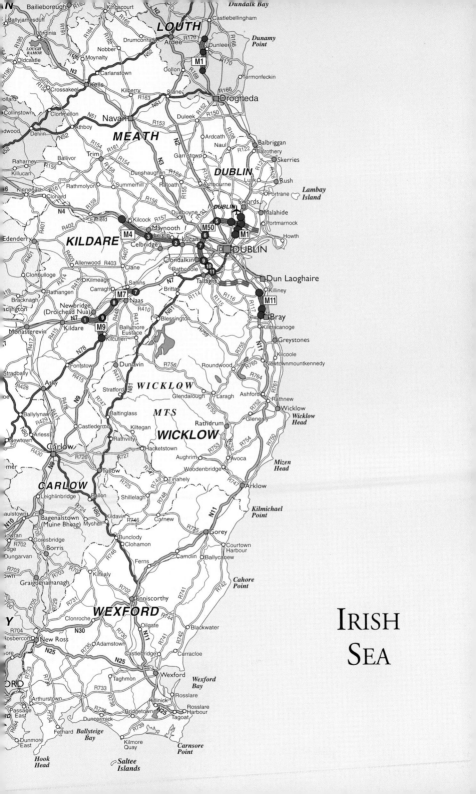